Blacks in the Jewish Mind

Blacks in the Jewish Mind

A Crisis of Liberalism

Seth Forman

NEW YORK UNIVERSITY PRESS

New York and London

NEW YORK UNIVERSITY PRESS
New York and London

© 1998 by New York University

Library of Congress Cataloging-in-Publication Data
Forman, Seth.
Blacks in the Jewish mind : a crisis of liberalism / Seth Forman.
p.   cm.
Includes index.
ISBN 0-8147-2680-1 (acid-free paper)
1. Afro-American—Relations with Jews.   2. Liberalism—United
States—History—20th century.   I. Title.
E185.61.F7216   1998
305.896'073—dc21   97-45457
                          CIP

New York University Press books are printed on acid-free paper,
and their binding materials are chosen for strength and durability

Manufactured in the United States of America
10 9 8 7 6 5 4 3 2 1

For Danielle, who made of our home a sanctuary.

Contents

Acknowledgments

Most scholarly research is performed in relative isolation, but the development of a manuscript inevitably draws into its orbit a number of individuals without whose assistance its completion would not be possible. First, there are all those people who have offered the moral and spiritual support without which the author would long ago have abandoned the project. In this respect I owe a tremendous debt to my wife, Danielle, and to my mother, Edith Forman. Neither of these two women ever countenanced for a minute the inevitable self-doubt involved in writing a book or the recurring feeling that my time might he better spent at some other pursuit. The personal sacrifices Danielle has made to see this project through is testimony to her unwavering commitment to my happiness.

I would also like to thank, in memory, my beloved father, Gerald Forman, who managed, against terrific odds, to leave me with an important fragment of the enormous Jewish past.

In a similar vein, I would like to thank all of my friends and relatives who have ever furtively asked the hated question "How is the book going?" only to receive a caustic and surly reproof. Many thanks to Pat and Marie Vecchio, Andrea Forman-Morris, and Greg Morris, as well as to Larry Alper, Joe Willen, Marge Glueck, Stuart Besen, Rob Ciccotto, Billy Ferro, Scott "Scotch" Janicola, Marty "Marts" Paulker, and Gary "Gazzo" Rosenthal, who never failed to support my endeavor, however different from their own. Arriving at a crucial moment in the development of the manuscript, Joshua B. Morris never let me lose sight of life's larger purpose. Special thanks to Chip and Diane Burman, who, at crucial intervals, consistently indulged me in the illusion that my work might be of interest to someone other than myself.

This book began as a doctoral dissertation, which cannot be completed without the selfless help of an academic mentor and adviser. I am convinced that I found the best there is in Dr. Matthew Jacobson, currently of Yale University, whose tireless and painstaking efforts on my behalf are beyond reciprocation. Dr. Jacobson is a scholar and teacher of such immense skill and patience that if I can do for my future graduate students only half of what he has done for me, my career goal will be largely fulfilled. In this regard I must also mention Dr. David Burner of SUNY at Stony Brook, a "second reader" who has been more generous with his time and erudition than anyone bearing such an appellation need be. Thanks also to Dr. Carole Kessner and Dr. Nikhil Singh for their thorough reading of the manuscript and helpful comments.

Special thanks to Dr. Lee E. Koppelman of the Center for Regional Policy Studies at SUNY at Stony Brook and the Long Island Regional Planning Board, a mentor and role model for so many students and staff over the years. While Dr. Koppelman is involved in policymaking at all levels of government and planning, his students and employees always come first. His support and encouragement of my educational pursuits, along with his personal guidance and friendship, have been an indispensable part of the past five years of my life.

Regarding the actual details of my research, I would like to thank a number of individuals. Ms. Syma Horowitz and Ms. Michelle Anisch, of the Blaustein Library of the American Jewish Committee in Manhattan, and the interlibrary loan librarians at the Frank Melville Jr. Memorial Library at SUNY at Stony Brook, notably Ms. Donna Sammis and Ms. Victoria Grasso, were extremely helpful in providing access to an enormous amount of obscure material.

My editors at New York University Press, Jennifer Hammer and Despina Papazoglou Gimbel, helped me turn a sloppy doctoral thesis into a presentable scholarly book, a seemingly impossible task. For their competence and professionalism I give them my most heartfelt thanks.

Finally, thanks to Samara Eve Forman, whose imminent arrival proved to be my greatest inspiration.

Introduction

Race Relations and the Invisible Jew

There are cases where success is a tragedy.
—Abraham Cahan, *The Rise of David Levinsky*

[T]here is nothing so indigenous, so 'made in America' as we.
—W. E. B. Du Bois, *Dusk of Dawn*

Since the early 1970s, the relationship between Blacks and Jews has been the subject of a substantial amount of scholarly attention, not least because of the conflicts between the two groups that came to the surface in the 1960s. During this period, long-standing differences over such issues as community control of school districts, racial preferences, the role of Israel in world politics, open admissions at universities, and the anti-Semitism of some controversial Black leaders began to outweigh the mutually perceived common interests that had for decades worked to cement cooperation between significant segments of both groups.[1]

In light of these developments, it is not hard to see why scholars in search of a better understanding of the relationship between Blacks and Jews continue to see this history in the framework of alliance and conflict. Jonathan Kaufman epitomizes this predisposition in his 1988 book *Broken Alliance: The Turbulent Times between Blacks and Jews in America,* in which he laments that throughout his volume "runs a remembrance of a time when great changes seemed possible and people embraced alliances and coalitions—and puzzlement and sadness that politics and personal relationships have today become polarized and fragmented."[2] Even Murray Friedman, a writer who views the prospects for a future Black-Jewish alliance with an unusual degree of ambivalence, confesses in his 1995 book *What Went Wrong: The Creation and Collapse of the Black-Jewish Alliance,* "I do not

2 | BLACKS IN THE JEWISH MIND

pretend to be neutral on the subject of the Black-Jewish alliance; it has meant so much to me for so long."[3]

The framework of alliance and conflict has, at times, been a useful way of thinking about the past and has resulted in perhaps the most extensive body of knowledge on the interaction of two American ethnic groups that we now possess. But this approach has carried with it a number of limitations traceable to the highly contested and extremely volatile nature of race relations. In writing about Blacks and Jews, many historians have been unwilling to relinquish some standard and highly valued presumptions about white racism and its impact on Blacks and have therefore approached the subject of Blacks and Jews as merely an extension of the study of relations between Blacks and whites. Needless to say, this historiographical dynamic has resulted in an interesting and disturbing irony. The inclination has been to interpret the behavior of both Blacks and Jews as typical of the broader patterns that have characterized race relations in the United States, lacking any of the extraordinary character that, one would presume, had originally drawn so many writers to the subject in the first place. Specifically, there has been an apparent unwillingness on the part of historians to explore the reasons for and the meaning of what, considering the legacy of white racism in the United States, appears to have been an unusually high degree of sympathy toward Blacks within Jewish circles and, on the other hand, considering the general decline of anti-Semitic attitudes, a surprising and persistently high level of anti-Semitism among Black Americans. Historians straining under the pressure of contemporary racial politics have sought to smooth over a history characterized by the peculiar unevenness and unpredictability of human interaction and have engaged in a considerable amount of scholarly acrobatics in order to do so. The result has been a series of interpretations that redefine benevolent Jewish attitudes toward Blacks as primarily motivated by self-interest and, to that extent, not markedly distinct from the racist attitudes of the larger white society. Black anti-Semitism, within this scholarly paradigm, has become only the most vocal manifestation of a largely justified animosity toward whites. Robert Weisbord and Arthur Stein's *Bittersweet Encounter* was the first attempt to survey the history of Blacks and Jews in the wake of the tumult of the late 1960s and is typical of this approach. The central purpose of this book, as stated by its authors, is to prove that "the racism of many Jews is inseparable—and indistinguishable from—white American racism." The authors claim that Black anti-Semitism has been wildly exaggerated and conclude their volume by asserting that American Jews have been equal partners with white gentiles in America's racist past. "The Jewish community is faced with the challenging task of marshaling its considerable resources and energies to assist the Black man's quest for freedom and equality," the authors write. "For it has been true of American Jewry . . . that when all is said and done, more has been said than done."[4]

The difficulties that stem from squeezing the history of Blacks and Jews into the familiar pattern of white racism and Black victimization are two-fold. First, the impropriety involves forcing Black history into a paradigm that denies the fullness of Black humanity and the rich texture of Black life—the failure, in the words of Ralph Ellison, to recognize that "Negroes have made a life upon the horns of the white man's dilemma." Second, and more to the point for the purposes of this book, consigning Jews to the role of white oppressor obscures their unique approach to race relations and, by extension, American life in general. It is the absence of any sustained or consistent analysis about what the distinctive Jewish posture toward Blacks tells us about American Jews that this book attempts to address. American Jews of all backgrounds seemed singularly drawn to the enormity of the race question throughout the postwar period. By exploring the attitudes of Jews while they were engaged in a number of specific racial episodes—desegregation in the South, integration efforts in the North, the ascendance of certain Black writers, and the advent of Black Power—it is possible to construct a foundation for understanding American Jewish life. This analysis attempts to uncover the reasons why Jews got involved in Black affairs in such a large way, what the implications of their particular involvement has been in terms of Jewish culture, and what all of this can tell us about American Jews and their lives today. In this sense, the study is an exercise in self-reflection, using Jewish thinking about Black Americans to illuminate the often complex amalgam of emotions, memories, presumptions, and beliefs that constitute Jewish identity.

The necessity of rescuing Jewish history from the mantra of white racism becomes manifest when one considers the intensity of the effort to submerge Jewish particularity. Since the late 1960s a generation of scholars has carved out careers documenting the nature of America's "color line," a social phenomenon even those possessing only the most rudimentary knowledge of America's racist past should be generally familiar with. It is no wonder that this scholarly endeavor has borne enormous fruit, with radical historians and activists such as Vine DeLoria, Robert Blauner, Stephen Steinberg, Ron Takaki, Michael Omi, and Howard Winant generally succeeding over the past three decades in establishing the separation of Blacks and whites as the key to understanding American pluralism. With the work of these authors, the idea that the experience of European immigrant groups in the United States has been categorically different from the experience of Blacks, insofar as access to power and economic opportunities are concerned, has become thoroughly ensconced.[5] The catchphrase of this scholarly perspective is "white skin privilege," an allusion to what these critics believe has been a permanent advantage enjoyed by European ethnic groups over dark-skinned Americans in making their way to middle-class respectability.

Such scholarly revisionism was originally a reaction to the movement of liberal social scientists in the early 1960s toward a cultural explanation for the inferior socioeconomic status of Blacks and other similarly deprived minority groups. While the "culture of poverty" explanation for the failure of the underclass to improve their lot can be traced to Oscar Lewis, the scholarly debate has been focused rather myopically on the work of Nathan Glazer and Daniel Patrick Moynihan in their seminal tract, *Beyond the Melting Pot,* and other writings.[6] Glazer and Moynihan argued that continuing Black deprivation was a function largely of Black cultural deficiencies resulting from centuries of slavery and racial discrimination. In the optimistic light of the postwar civil rights legislation, Glazer and Moynihan interpreted the ongoing Black migration to Northern cities as similar to the earlier migration of European immigrant groups. For these theorists, when Black Americans could find their footing in the urban milieu, developing strong institutions of self-help, a more stable family life, and political unity, they would eventually take their place as equal partners in a culturally diverse urban system.

By contrast, rather than seeing Black Americans as having shared an urban experience similar to, if somewhat more difficult than, that experienced by the wide variety of European immigrants, the radical scholars see Blacks, and in some instances other racially distinct groups such as American Indians, as having been the victims of internal "colonialism." Race prejudice thoroughly shut these communities out of the most important opportunities and deprived them—through legal, cultural, and economic discrimination—of their ability to compete for opportunities on an equal basis against whites. For these scholars, ethnic whites may have participated in competition with each other, but the boundaries that separated them with regard to residential communities, marriage, political power, and employment were far more permeable than the racial boundary that excluded Blacks. From this perspective, it is the "color line," the disenfranchisement of Black Americans, that is the most fundamental and enduring fact of America's group life in the twentieth century, not the marginally significant cultural distinctions among white ethnic groups.

The disastrous implications of radical scholarship in terms of American Jewish history can be seen in the work of the prominent sociologist Stephen Steinberg. Professor Steinberg has devoted the better part of his twenty-five-year career to proving that the importance given to culture and ethnicity in explaining social stratification among American ethnic groups is all part of an elaborate racist myth. In his highly regarded 1989 book *The Ethnic Myth,* Steinberg set out to prove that the success of white ethnic groups in such areas as politics, industry, labor, and education has been far more attributable to favorable social and economic circumstances than to anything having to do with cultural habits, customs, or beliefs. For example, Steinberg insists that "Jewish success in America was a matter of historical timing. . . . [T]here was a fortuitous match between the experience and skills of Jewish immigrants, on the one hand, and the manpower needs and opportunity structures on the other."[7] For Steinberg, not only were distinctive ethnic cultures relatively insignificant for the advancement of white ethnic groups, but the variations in economic and social mobility between white ethnic groups owed almost nothing to cultural attitudes. In an earlier book, *The Academic Melting Pot,* Steinberg argued that the differences in the levels of success achieved by Italian Catholics and Jews in higher education through the 1970s were due primarily to the highly disparate social and economic experiences of both immigrant groups, rather than to distinctive group attitudes toward education. Accordingly, while Russian Jews had "rich intellectual traditions, it is also true that . . . they were heavily concentrated in middle-class occupations," which fostered an absorption of the middle-class respect for education. By contrast, Southern Italians were antagonistic toward education because they came to America as peasants tied to the soil, with limited expectations for advancement. In other words, American Jews "did not become middle-class and produce a class of scholars because they placed a special value on learning, but because they were middle-class first, and then adopted education as a component of middle-class values."[8]

Scholars like Steinberg make no secret of the motivation behind their efforts to virtually extinguish ethnic culture as a significant factor in explaining America's ethnoracial hierarchy. These efforts stem from the conviction that white racism is an enduring and immutable feature of American

life that can be combated only by the permanent institution of racial preferences. Whereas earlier in the century social scientists had used the presumed biological inferiority of Blacks as a way to excuse white racism,
many radical scholars feel that today the explanation of cultural deficiency
is used by some social scientists, and others in the sphere of public policy,
to excuse persistent white racism.

That Steinberg has had the expansion of affirmative action on his mind
all along is evinced in a later volume in which he finally reveals the ultimate
goal behind denying the importance of cultural differences in American
life. Steinberg's attempt to prove that Blacks continue to face a unique and
debilitating level of discrimination in *Turning Back: The Retreat from Racial
Justice in American Thought and Politics* is apparently motivated by his perception that the system of race preferences is under attack.[9] Reflecting the
extreme cultural relativism that informs so much of the literature on race
today, Steinberg admits that he is deeply offended by suggestions that certain groups possess cultural traits that result in greater economic success
than certain other groups. There is something wrong with presupposing
that "we have qualities that they are lacking," Steinberg insists, and his
logic for doing so is simple. If it can be shown that all white European
immigrant groups had more or less equal access to economic opportunities
from which Blacks were excluded, then the present system of compensatory
treatment based on race is made, not only more palatable, but necessary
and just. It is not an accident, then, that this effort to erase the cultural
distinctiveness of white ethnic groups has occasionally emphasized American Jews. It is the Jews, after all, who stand out in the public conscience
as having the strongest claim to historical victimization and whose affluence
appears to have defied what structural determinists like Steinberg predict
should happen when people are deprived of opportunities for advancement.
If it is possible to prove not only that Jews received certain advantages not
available to Blacks but that the privileges accruing to those with white skin
were the primary catalyst for Jewish advancement, it would go a long way
toward justifying racial preferences.

Central to the effort to "whiten" the American Jewish experience has
been the denial of Jewish exceptionalism, the idea that the Jewish experience in America has been unique. The remarkable economic advance of
Jews into the middle and upper classes has inspired a number of observers
over the years to conclude that Jewish culture seems to have been exceptionally well disposed to the American ideals of universalism, equality, individualism, and free markets.[10] Almost half a century ago, the sociologist

Robert Park, speaking of the industry, enterprise, and individual drive of America's Jews, recommended that Jewish culture and history be taught in public schools so that there would be a more complete understanding of American values.[11] More recently, the renowned historian of race and slavery David Brion Davis has suggested that American Jewish history provides a test case for the values of a meritocracy, a society in which the distribution of rewards and penalties takes place according to the character and capabilities of individuals.[12] In his landmark study *Assimilation in American Life,* Milton Gordon wrote "The rise in socio-economic status of the Eastern European Jews and their descendants . . . [is] the greatest collective Horatio Alger story in American immigration history."[13] At least on the surface, then, as Robert Park suggested, American Jews are unique in that they are the group that has most fully realized the "American Dream" and that has absorbed the values of individualism, equality, freedom, and enterprise to the point where it could be said of them that they are like all other Americans—only more so.[14]

But the radical attack on culture as an explanation for ethnic mobility now demands a frontal assault on the idea of Jewish exceptionalism. Karen Brodkin Sacks has attempted to show that the theorists of American Jewish exceptionalism are gravely mistaken in their belief that Jewish success in America has been the result of such cultural traits as strong family ties, a high value placed on education, and hard work. Taking her cue from Steinberg, Sacks argues in her article "How the Jews Became White Folks" that Jewish immigrants at the turn of the century had timed their move to the United States to meet rising labor needs. Even the remarkable Jewish success in higher education beginning in the 1920s, Sacks insists, was a result not of cultural values but of the combination of revised college curriculums and the Jews' good fortune in having to compete academically almost exclusively against homework-shirking white Protestants. "In a setting where disparagement of intellectual pursuits and the gentleman's 'C' were badges of distinction, it was not hard for Jews to excel," writes Sacks.[15]

The postwar economic boom, which was accompanied by massive government programs like the G.I. Bill of Rights and Federal Housing Administration mortgage insurance, were largely responsible for the mobility of Jews and other "Euro-ethnics" in the postwar period, according to Sacks. Because of changing racial attitudes precipitated by the war against fascism, Jews and other ethnic groups became newly accepted entrants into the category of "white Americans," fully eligible to enjoy the rights and privileges accruing thereto. While racial attitudes were changing, Blacks were still prevented from taking part in many of the opportunities of the postwar economy, which were effectively "Jim Crowed." While Sacks does not bother to determine if Jews benefited from racially exclusionary government programs any more or any less than other groups of whites, this oversight does not prevent her from labeling these programs "affirmative action" for all white males or from lumping Jews together with other whites as equal partners in a white opportunity pool. "Jews' and other white ethnics' upward mobility was the result of programs that allowed us to float on a rising economic tide," writes Sacks.[16] So, the story goes, the miraculous timing that characterized the Jewish migration to the United States at the turn of the century sustained itself virtually throughout the postwar period, as Jews were fortuitously well situated to take advantage of postwar prosperity and changing racial attitudes. Jews, like all other white ethnic groups, were essentially passive players and furtive beneficiaries of a century of increasing economic wealth and government good cheer.

There is obviously a lot to be said for the view that Blacks, at least until very recently, have been deprived of numerous rights and privileges available to Americans of European descent. It is also no secret that many immigrants from Europe not only discovered the social, economic, and political value of having white skin upon their arrival in the United States but in fact became contaminated by native racist bigotry as well. Yet, a number of important and troubling questions come to mind when considering the radical critique of race relations and of Jewish mobility in particular, mostly having to do with the extent to which cultural values shape external conditions and the extent to which they are a product of those conditions. For example, while the prior possession of industrial skills may explain some of the unusually rapid economic success of immigrant Jews, is this sufficient in itself to explain the remarkably broad range of Jewish achievement in such diverse fields as retail trade, the film industry, high finance, physics, journalism, fiction writing, medicine, law, theater, the composition of popular music, and even organized crime? Moreover, do the skills possessed by Jews, which were allegedly so helpful to their advance in the industrializing United States of the late nineteenth century, also account for the rapid advance of Jewish migrants to other, less well developed economies like those of South America?[17] Other pertinent questions come to mind as well. If Blacks were so completely shut out of postwar affluence, how does one explain that the greatest economic gains for Blacks relative to whites occurred in the 1940s and 1960s and that by 1966 the gap between Blacks and whites on a whole range of socioeconomic measures, including home ownership, had been substantially narrowed?[18] To what extent did the vast expansion, in the 1960s, of government antipoverty programs aimed at Blacks compensate for discrimination in older postwar government programs? Finally, if whiteness alone explains the more rapid advance of European ethnics, how does this square with the rapid mobility of certain other nonwhite groups, including Caribbean Blacks?[19]

For our purposes, however, the most troublesome aspect of the radical view of race and culture is its failure to recognize anything distinct about the Jewish experience in America, and this handicap operates in at least one area that is perhaps even more consequential than Jewish mobility. Just as the imperative of the color line has necessitated the historical reconstruction of Jewish economic mobility to fit the categories of white skin privilege, so, too, has there been a need to "normalize," or "whiten," what seems to be unusual Jewish political behavior. Quite simply, at least as much as their unusual economic mobility, American Jews appear to have been exceptional in their historical adherence to the traditions of modern liberalism, a liberalism that includes such values as individual freedom, equality of opportunity, universal education, and the belief that government should soften the rough edges of private markets. Obviously, it would be a mistake to attribute a monolithic liberalism to American Jews. Highly pluralistic throughout modern history, Jews have been "Tories, Confederates, and Know-Nothings as well as Socialists, Progressives and liberal Democrats."[20] But the persistence of a widespread liberalism among American Jews has resulted in political behavior, particularly on social welfare issues, that seems nothing short of, well, *exceptional*. The rise of modern Jewish liberalism during the New Deal years of the 1930s seemed, at the time, to coincide with Jewish working class interests, and so therefore not particularly "exceptional." But, after World War II, as Jews rapidly moved out of the working class and left the immigrant ghettos behind, they maintained their liberalism.[21] As two prominent sociologists recently concluded, "while Jews earn more than any ethnoreligious group for whom data exist (including Episcopalians), they are more liberal to left in their opinions than other white groups, and they vote like hispanics."[22] While the nature of Jewish liberalism may now be evolving, recent polls indicate that, more than any other group of comparable socioeconomic status, Jews continue to cling to the values of equality and the welfare state.[23] Jews continue to show a preference for higher government spending on the poor, gun control, freer immigration, a woman's right to abortion, and tax increases as a way of reducing the government deficit, and they oppose government spending cuts.[24] Essentially, as one sociologist recently wrote, "political allegiance in the United States is affected most strongly by economic status—but Jews break the pattern."[25]

There has been considerable speculation as to the causes of the Jewish attraction to liberalism. Some have seen the wellspring of American Jewish liberalism in the values of the Torah, in which the high regard for *Zedakah* (literally "righteousness"), learning, and nonasceticism appear to be reflected in Jewish respect for welfare, education spending, and government interventionism in general.[26] Others have interpreted Jewish liberalism as the twentieth-century extension of the response to European emancipation, which originated with the left and was opposed by the predominantly anti-Semitic right.[27] Another interpretation has it that the liberalism of most second- and third-generation American Jews stems from lingering feelings of marginality.[28] But, whatever the emphasis, central to any explanation of American Jewish liberalism is the Jewish experience of vulnerability in the lands of the diaspora, which has served to foster the belief among contemporary Jews that wealth and income are perhaps not the most important elements to consider when pondering Jewish well-being.[29] That is, being a religious minority with a unique history of persecution and vulnerability has imbued Jews with a more conscious recognition that the values of individual freedom, merit-based advance, political and religious liberty, and civic equality are matters of paramount importance, even more so than marginal economic gain.

These attitudes have been reflected in Jewish attitudes toward Blacks. There remains little doubt that Jewish interest in Black affairs was strengthened after 1915, the year a Jew named Leo Frank was lynched by a Georgia mob after being falsely convicted of raping and murdering a fourteen-year-old employee of his family's pencil factory.[30] The uncommon sympathy American Jews seemed to take on for Black Americans in the wake of the Frank lynching reflected the concerns of the recently arrived Eastern European Jews, who had suffered similar kinds of mob violence. There were, to be sure, a number of instances in which certain other ethnic groups before World War II, still victimized by various levels of discrimination, saw parallels between themselves and Black Americans and rejected an identity based on "whiteness."[31] Thus, Poles in Chicago generally saw the post-World War I race riots there as an affair between whites and Blacks that did not involve them. Italian immigrants in Louisiana mixed socially and culturally with Blacks at the turn of the century and were clearly distinguished from Southern whites. Similar examples of immigrant group–Black amity exist for Greek immigrants in Gary, Indiana, the Chinese in Mississippi, and the Irish of the early 1820 and 1830 migrations.[32] But these instances of immigrant group–Black solidarity were subplots against the more common theme in which immigrants and native Blacks generally saw each other, for a host of complicated and unfortunate reasons, as rivals for the common goal of full citizenship.[33] After 1915 it appeared that American Jews were alone among American ethnic groups in seeking out similarities between themselves and Black Americans and, at least in elite circles, in mobilizing politically around an alliance with Black Americans. As one scholar recently put it, the Frank lynching "ultimately eclipsed all of the frantic distancing strategies intended to mark off the boundaries between the two groups."[34] Jews and Jewish organizations during this period contributed heavily to organizations such as the National Association for the Advancement of Colored People (NAACP) and to dozens of other philanthropic projects designed to help Blacks, including the funding of Black education in the South. Major Jewish figures like Julius Rosenwald, Jacob Schiff, and Felix Warburg contributed to dozens of Black elementary and vocational schools and institutions of higher and professional education, hospitals, orphanages, libraries, settlement houses, and social clubs. Of all Black school children in the South, it is estimated that at one time 25 to 40 percent were educated in schools constructed with funds from Julius Rosenwald, the Jewish magnate of Sears Roebuck fame.[35]

But the need to extinguish cultural deficiencies as an explanation for Black poverty and to augment the explanatory power of white racism has necessitated the reconfiguration of the Jewish posture toward Black Americans as typical white exploitation and self-promotion. This revisionism has by now a long tradition, beginning with some prominent figures associated with the Black Power movement of the late 1960s. Black Power sought to remove whites from the civil rights struggle and to consolidate Black leadership within the movement. As Jews made up a disproportionately large segment of the liberal civil rights leadership, the struggle to achieve the destruction of the integrated civil rights movement necessarily included an effort to vilify Jewish activism. Harold Cruse spearheaded this attack in his 1967 volume, *The Crisis of the Negro Intellectual,* in which he argued that Jews, be they in the Communist party of the 1930s, the interracial civil rights coalition of the postwar decades, or the social sciences, had become a huge problem for Blacks precisely because they had so identified with the Black struggle. While Cruse did not concern himself with the question of why Jews tended to identify so strongly with Black causes, he insisted that Jewish involvement in interracial politics "has further complicated this emergence of Afro-American ethnic consciousness."[36] For Cruse, as well as for other Black power theorists and activists, the role of American Jews as "political mediator" between Blacks and whites was "fraught with serious dangers to all concerned" and must be "terminated by Negroes themselves."[37]

While Cruse's rhetoric may have put off some moderates, his thesis, essentially that Jewish support for Black equality has been deleterious to Black Americans, has exhibited an impressive amount of staying power. Most recently, the political scientist Andrew Hacker has argued that Jewish involvement in racial matters amounted to an "ego trip" in which Blacks were reduced to junior partners and that this "raises the question of whether the well-meant motives underlying Jewish racism put it on a different level from biases that are obviously less sympathetic."[38] Thus, in the view of some, has the historic Jewish contribution to civil rights become no more noble than a lynching bee.

Other prominent scholars have traveled a far more circuitous route to arrive at similar conclusions. Speaking of the civil rights alliance of Blacks and Jews between the years 1910 and the early 1930s, the Pulitzer prize-winning historian David Levering Lewis argues that both Jewish and Black leadership were dominated by assimilationists, joined together in the common cause of maintaining their dominance within their respective groups. The migrating hordes of East European Jews and poor Southern Blacks to Northern cities concerned elite German Jewish and "talented-tenth" Black leaders, who feared that the less refined newcomers would exacerbate white nativism and racism and botch their program of assimilation. For Lewis, it was not a common history of oppression that resulted in good will on the part of Jews but merely self-interest. "It seems evident that what Jewish and Afro-American elites principally shared was not a similar history but an identical adversary—a species of white gentile. Theirs was a politically determined kinship, a defensive alliance, cemented more from the outside than from within."[39] Like Harold Cruse before him, Lewis insists that this opportunistic alliance served Jewish purposes far better than Black purposes, as it allowed Jews to fight against discrimination by using Blacks as surrogates. Ultimately, the alliance pigeonholed Blacks into an "unworkable paradigm of success," an acceptance of a set of social and political rules by which Jews would be permitted to advance but by which Blacks would not.[40]

By interpreting the Jewish concern for equal rights during the interwar years as the narrow, self-serving project of assimilating Jewish elites, Lewis ignores what appears to have been an almost universal preoccupation with the condition of Blacks on the part of Jews, a fixation that included the overt friendliness toward Blacks of predominantly Jewish labor unions and the virtual outpouring of sympathy from most large-circulation Anglo-Jewish and Yiddish periodicals and newspapers.[41] These are inconvenient items for revisionist historians like Lewis, who would apparently rather surrender the complexities of American ethnic history to the more pressing need to prove the uniformity of white racism. For these writers, American Jews are problematic because their unique empathy with Black Americans, stemming from the historically ambiguous relationship of Jews to power, appears to threaten the integrity of the all-important color line.

Unfortunately, it is not at all difficult to see that maintaining the purity of the color line bears an unmistakable resemblance to the aims of certain Black extremists. Race agitators like Louis Farrakhan, Leonard Jeffries, Tony Martin, and others are most interested in proving the moral inferiority of white people and therefore share with radical scholars a "Jewish problem" relating to the ambiguity of Jewish racial identity. Having simultaneously benefited from democracy and enlightenment, yet having suffered, in some instances unspeakably, at the hands of the Western world—of being, in the parlance of contemporary race discourse, neither "Black" or "white"—Jews represent a threat to the crude dichotomy of white "sin" and Black "virtue" that informs the worldview of both radical scholars and Black extremists. It is for this reason that the particular anti-Semitism coming from Black anti-Semites mostly concerns itself with ensuring the "whiteness," or the empowerment, of the Jews—"Jews in Hollywood conspire to degrade Blacks," "Jews ran the slave trade," "Jews have their hands around the throat of the federal government." While one must not confuse the blatant racism of a Farrakhan or a Jeffries with the more nuanced, socially constructed racial hierarchies of Lewis and Steinberg, it is not difficult to see that the objectives of the extremists and the radical scholars have converged at the point of totalizing Black oppression.

One need only look at the extent to which some of the most dubious claims about Jews have been used to chart the direction of recent historical research to confirm the common objectives of the extremists and the academy. Despite substantial scholarship indicating that Jews were largely closed out of the Atlantic slave system and that individual Jews probably owned fewer slaves in the American South than did free Blacks, two prominent American historians identify as one of the most important areas for future study the role of Jews in the slave trade of Holland, France, England, and Newport, Rhode Island, as well as their role in the plantation system of the South.[42] In the realm of popular culture, the celebrated Berkeley scholar Michael Paul Rogin identifies Jews as the leading culprits in the enslavement of Blacks through popular images. According to Rogin, Jewish performers like Al Jolson donned the blackface mask not merely to share in the power of Black expressiveness or to hide their Jewishness, as other scholars have suggested, but to accentuate their whiteness, demonstrate their superiority to Blacks, and gain acceptance in the Hollywood melting pot when Blacks could not. Disregarding the risk that socially marginal Jewish performers took in "blacking up," Rogin sets out in *Black Face, White Noise* to "untie the knot" that hides the Jewish dominance of a racist mass culture behind Jewish liberalism and to reveal "their own stain of shame."[43] Rogin is joined in his efforts by the historian Jeffrey Melnick, who suggests that the involvement of both Jews and Blacks in the development of popular music was anything but a harmonious, cross-cultural enterprise. Attacking the claim that Jewish suffering gave Jews an affinity for the tonalities of Black music, Melnick argues that Jews like Irving Berlin and George Gershwin skillfully created the myth that they were the proper interpreters of Black culture, elbowing out "real" Black Americans in the process. Despite evidence from Black musicians and critics that Jews in the music business played an important role in paving the way for mainstream acceptance of Black culture, Melnick concludes that "while both Jews and African Americans contributed to the rhetoric of musical affinity, the fruits of this labor belonged primarily to the former."[44] Even the work of certain Jewish scientists concerning racial groups is not safe from the academic onslaught. One scholar has set out to show that the Jewish anthropologist Franz Boas, widely credited with the largest role in eviscerating the scientific racism of the nineteenth century, subscribed in substantial degree to white racist views on Black capabilities.[45]

The extent to which some historians are willing to go to portray Jews as progenitors of the white racist tradition is exhibited in an essay by the acclaimed historian of civil rights Taylor Branch. In his 1992 essay "Blacks and Jews: The Uncivil War," Branch strains credulity in trying to document that American Jews have been "perpetrators of racial hate" but is forced to look outside the American context to the state of Israel for his evidence. In the mid-1980s, Branch claims, three thousand members of a sect of Black Jews from Chicago under the leadership of Ben-Ami Carter were denied citizenship under the Israeli Law of Return because of anti-Black sentiment among Israelis. But the authenticity of Carter's claim that he and his followers were indeed Jewish is open to investigation, as are the claims of all those seeking Israeli citizenship under that country's Law of Return, particularly Jewish converts. It is true that the question of "who is a Jew" is a heated topic in the Jewish world, but Branch's imputation that Carter and his followers were not given immediate citizenship because they were Black seems baseless, particularly in light of Israel's successful airlift of thousands of Ethiopian Jews in the early 1990s.[46] More important, like the issues of Jews involved in the slave trade, of Hollywood's "Jewish" racism, and of Franz Boas's views on race capabilities, it is difficult to ascertain the usefulness of these approaches, except as they serve to erase the Jewish fog that obscures the color line in American race history.

The trouble with revisionist race history is not that all of its claims are false. Jewish involvement in Black affairs, to be sure, has never been devoid of self-interest. Liberal Jewish civil rights activists have often been the most vocal in claiming that helping Blacks was good for the Jews. Nor is the attempt to "whiten" Jewish history purely a matter of historical impropriety, particularly in the American context, where oppression has not been at the center of the Jewish experience. Aside from erasing the truly admirable record Jews have amassed on racial matters, the fundamental problem with the revisionist history is that it denies American Jewish exceptionalism and therefore leads to the assumption that Jewish "whiteness" vis-à-vis Black Americans has always been advantageous from the standpoint of American Jews. By denying the reality of a unique Jewish past, and, therefore, its impact on Jewish identity in the United States, the revisionist history fails to recognize the incongruence between the liberal accommodation Jews made with America and the reality of American Jewish life. While prior histories by authors like Lewis and Cruse speak to what they believe has been the negative impact of the relationship on Blacks, no one has ever explored the possibility that the Jewish involvement with the Black struggle for equality may, in certain instances, not have been beneficial for *Jews*. What, the unanswered question now seems to be, does the Jewish posture toward race and Black Americans, as an integral component of American Jewish liberalism, tell us about the Jews as a distinct cultural group? Specifically, it needs to be determined whether the persistence of a widespread liberalism among American Jews has resulted in attitudes toward Blacks and issues of racial equality that are consonant with the interests of all the various and sundry communities that constitute American Jewry.

What needs to be observed more carefully in this respect is the tenuous place Jews occupy in American history relative to the centrality of Blacks in that history. Black Americans are, after all, the "omni-Americans," a people whose experience is at once defined by and defining of the American experience. Black group consciousness and identity begins (and, many would argue, ends) in America. On the master-occupied slave plantations of the South, most of which kept small numbers of slaves, African cultural idioms such as voodoo and witchcraft gave way to distinctively Black American cultural expressions, fashioned over time by creative responses to slavery and oppression. This is not to say that some of these cultural adjustments, such as in song and dance, cannot be traced to Africa but only to assert that the "Africanness" of these traits was transformed by the peculiarly American context of the slave experience. Over time, Blacks eventually adopted even the Christian faith of the relatively homogenous Protestant culture into which they were brought.[47] Thus, Blacks were able to devise a distinctive Black American culture, based on common African origins but drawing almost exclusively from American sources.[48] Perhaps this is why the transnational quest for a Black identity, even as embodied by the largest Black Nationalist movement, led by Marcus Garvey in the 1920s, has failed to move beyond America's borders in any tangible way.[49]

Perhaps it is also why American culture draws from the Black experience almost as much as Black culture draws on the American experience. The two are intertwined and inseparable. As the Black writer Albert Murray has written, "American culture . . . is . . . incontestably mulatto. Indeed, for all their traditional antagonisms and obvious differences, the so-called Black and so-called white people of the United States resemble nobody else in the world so much as they resemble each other."[50] The Black American, therefore, despite the long history of segregation and exclusion, is always and forever present in the American drama, reminding white America of its imperfect past and pressing the formidable weight of Black history upon the American conscience as a reminder that there has always been an "other" in its midst, different yet somehow remarkably familiar.

What, then, can be made of the claim for American Jewish exceptionalism, for the assumption that Jewish values are "quintessentially" American, that American Jews are like all other Americans, only more so? Jewish history, after all, is transnational, beginning long before the advent of the United States and far beyond its borders. The modern Jews' search for identity began in Europe, and the awful transgressions that bear so formidably on Jewish consciousness owe almost nothing to the American experience. The key to understanding the exceptional nature of American Jews, and the manifestations of this exceptionalism in the realms of economic mobility and political liberalism, lies in the extent to which the integration-survival dilemma pervades the Jews' collective conscience.[51] For the majority of American Jews, most of whose descendants came from premodern Eastern Europe, it was the United States that offered to them the Enlightenment's "brutal bargain" of acceptance into civil society at the price of a submerged cultural distinctiveness.[52] The promise for American Jews in the twentieth century was that Jews, on condition of conformity to American cultural and political norms, would be treated as individuals like everyone else. The temptation was intense. Since Jews were strangers in Europe before they came to the United States, and inevitably the opportunities for emancipation were greeted by them with considerably more enthusiasm than they were by other immigrant groups that had never been completely excluded from the social and political life of their lands of origin.[53]

On the other hand, in coming to the United States, other ethnic groups had made a conscious break with their pasts, while the Jews, whose ethnic and religious identity were bound together and not limited by geography, made no such conscious break.[54] The act of leaving one's country of origin for Jews did not necessarily constitute stepping out of one's history. While a number of American immigrant groups retained strong nationalistic feelings for their mother country, the Jews were unique in that they came to the United States with an internalized national culture of the spirit, not necessarily threatened or weakened by the act of moving from one country to another.[55] This dynamic resulted in what one sociologist has labeled the "ambivalent American Jew," a figure consumed by a conflicting desire for both acceptance and difference. Knowing that the United States bore no responsibility for Jewish history and so offered the Jews no special quarter, Jews set about adjusting their Jewishness to American life, and the connecting link for Americanization was liberalism.[56]

It is through this connecting link that the historian Hasia Diner locates Jewish involvement in the Black American struggle for equality. As Diner has explained, the unique history of Jewish persecution bound Jews to the American ideals of equality and freedom far more intensely than even the "real Americans" and thus made it possible for Jews to carve out a place for themselves in American life by helping Blacks.[57] Liberalism and involvement in Black affairs was, in large measure, an accommodation of Judaism and the Jewish past to American life.

But an important question arises as to how effective this accommodation has been for Jews, who now find themselves living in a nation that, due to the enormity of the Black experience, has become defined by the racial division between white and Black, or perhaps between white and "non-white." In one historian's estimate, "Liberalism has served Jews well in their quest for a secure American identity, but that has less to do with Judaism than with the imperatives of Americanization . . . liberalism has been the preeminent ideology of acculturation."[58]

Blacks in America had never seriously been offered the "brutal bargain" offered to the Jews, having been disenfranchised for most of their history. Even when Black Americans were legally enfranchised in the early 1960s, it was never fully expected that their distinctiveness would disappear or that Americans would be able to erase the memories and scars resulting from the nation's sordid past. This situation has provided Black Americans with certain cultural and political advantages. As Gerald David Jaynes and Robin Williams write in their book *A Common Destiny,* "the long history of discrimination and segregation produced among Blacks a heightened sense of group consciousness and a stronger orientation toward collective values and behavior than exists generally among Americans."[59] Despite vast and growing differences between the Black middle and lower classes in recent decades, Blacks continue to show a remarkable degree of solidarity based on what is perceived to be a shared experience of oppression. The psychologist Ellis Cose has used the term "Black rage" to describe the sense of outrage that many in the Black middle class share with their poorer brethren.[60] Despite the large number of Black leaders and intellectuals who have tried to articulate a unifying theme for a Black identity free from the spirit of radical racial protest, the iron cage of historical white racism and its institutional "correction" in the system of race preferences today, has served as the central organizing principle for the Black community, even as white racism itself has receded.[61]

American Jews, by contrast, are a "people divided."[62] As early as the 1920s, the religious divisions among American Jews had became permanent, with second-generation Jews adopting various modes of secularization in their efforts to obtain acceptance. The Orthodox, Reform, Conservative, and Reconstructionist branches of Judaism, by the 1930s all distinctly separate groupings, in the 1990s vie amid dissipated resources for the loyalty of the shrinking second, third, and fourth generations of Jews.[63] Today, the attenuation of Jewish culture in the United States, despite isolated signs of vitality, seems to continue unabated. The 1990 National Jewish Population Survey (NJPS) found that 52 percent of Jews who married after 1985 married non-Jewish partners. Sixty to 70 percent, or 3.5 million of America's 5.5 million Jews, are unaffiliated, belong to no synagogue, and, in most cases, do not hold membership in any Jewish organization or institution. While 4.4 million people claim to practice some form of Judaism, as many as 1.1 million identify themselves as Jews by birth only but not by religion. Recent polls show that the connection of young American Jews to Israel, which for a short time acted as the glue that held American Jewry together, is rapidly eroding.[64]

To some degree, the cultural problems of the Jewish community must be seen within the context of societal divisions that have afflicted the totality of American life since the 1960s, problems that are invariably related to the "culture wars": the triumphalism of the religious right, the declining appeal of liberal religion, and the continued assimilation of white ethnic groups.[65] Yet the very reaction of American Jewish organizations to Judaism's cultural dilemma indicates that Jews in America face some unique difficulties. While a 52 percent rate of exogamous marriage would not so much as raise an eyebrow among other white ethnic groups, groups that have experienced out-marriage rates upward of 70 and 80 percent for two decades or more, the NJPS has been a clarion call for America's Jews. The *Long Island Jewish World* stated recently that "virtually every organization and academic program on the communal map has announced new studies or programs involving their particular search for the alchemy of continuity."[66] As one Jewish sociologist commented on the cultural crisis within American Judaism, "the despair and confusion of American Jewry in the face of this crisis has no parallel in other religious communities."[67]

The kind of cultural dissolution that currently afflicts American Jews has not generally been a factor in Black life. Blacks have achieved a certain amount of success in institutionalizing the idea of Black marginalization and in extending to themselves certain advantages accruing to a contemporary racialized American scene. Whatever else the ubiquitous reminders of Black victimization might mean for Black economic mobility, social integration, and race relations, winning official confirmation of collective status through race-based governmental programs, open college admissions, Black electoral districts, "Afro-centric" school curricula, corporate hiring preferences, government set-asides, and private and not-for-profit foundation support has assured Blacks a powerful form of racial identity. Black Americans have utilized, with impressive effectiveness, the special place they occupy in United States history in order to develop a cultural unity that has, for the most part, escaped American Jews.

Knowing that their claims to special treatment in the United States are not strong, American Jews have not generally sought this kind of official support for their own group solidarity and have failed on their own to define new cultural forms capable of securing Jewish communal sustenance.[68] The identification with the Black struggle for equality, rooted in the memory of Jewish suffering but not in the reality of contemporary Jewish life, has prevented Jews from seeing that they are not integral to American life and culture, as Black Americans and Black culture appear to be, and that their own collective needs may, at various historical junctures, be more pressing than the Black need for social redress. For whatever else the Black fight for racial equality has meant, it has never been, and is not now, a struggle principally about the continued corporate existence of Black Americans. Conversely, the struggle for corporate existence appears to be one in which American Jews are now intimately engaged. For all the freedom and opportunity the United States has offered citizens of Jewish background, it may ultimately prove to be a place far more conducive to the development and maintenance of a strong Black identity than of a strong Jewish one. Many commentators, attempting to explain the cause of Black anti-Semitism, continue to believe that Jews have made it socially and economically in the United States and that this success evokes envy in Blacks.[69] But this long-held assumption needs rethinking in light of recent developments. Is it not the Jews who, as the twentieth century winds down, have a great deal to envy about Blacks? Has not the American Jew replaced the Black American as this nation's true "invisible man?"

This Book and a Word about "Who Is a Jew"

Chapter 1 of this book discusses the geographic division between Jews living in the South and Jewish organizations and leaders in the North over the issue of racial desegregation in the wake of the Supreme Court's 1954 decision striking down the doctrine of "separate but equal" facilities in the nation's public schools. The revulsion of American Jews against racial bigotry and the belief that Jewish well-being is tied to the cause of Black equality made it impossible for many Jewish leaders to empathize with the very real threats to Jewish communities in the South stemming from overt support of radical desegregation. The inability of Northern Jewish leaders to see that Jews, before the battle for desegregation, were not generally victims in the South and that the racial caste system in the South situated Jews favorably in the Southern mind, or "whitened" them, was an early warning that American Jewish leaders and intellectuals, when it came to the race issue, would continue to respond to memory and self-image more than to the reality of Jewish life in modern America.

Chapter 2 looks at the response of Jewish leaders and intellectuals in the North to the shift in the civil rights struggle from the South to the North in the late 1950s and early 1960s. By this time, increasing affluence and suburbanization made residential community and proximity, along with participation in secular Jewish organizations, the strongest forms of identity for many Jews living in the urban metropolis. Yet most Jewish critics intensified their calls for racial integration in residential communities, schools, and communal institutions, despite the potential danger to these vital forms of Jewish communal sustenance.

The issue of Black writers and critics in the New York Intellectual community in the late 1950s and early 1960s is explored in chapter 3. Perhaps no other identifiable group of American Jews has so exemplified the Jewish push to succeed and to gain recognition, and to do so without the debilitating attachment to Jewish tradition, as the coterie of mostly Jewish intellectuals that coalesced around *Partisan Review* in the 1930s. Sons and daughters of immigrants, the New York Intellectuals held up individual freedom and urban cosmopolitanism as the highest ideals and set about building a modernist and staunchly anti-Communist high culture in the United States. While the issue of race was not paramount for most New York Intellectuals, there were several New York writers whose work on race became emblematic of their general approach to art, culture, society, and, of course, Jewishness.

By most historical accounts, the rise of Black Power, the attack on liberal integrationism, and the 1967 Six-Day War in the Middle East changed the dynamics of the relationship between Blacks and Jews in the United States. A number of well-publicized confrontations between these two groups, symbolized most dramatically by the New York City teacher's strike of 1968, resulted in the widespread impression that the stated Jewish interest in strengthening the system of individual advance by merit was incompat-

ible with growing Black demands for a redistribution of power and resources. But an analysis of the statements of Jewish leaders and intellectuals
who became actively engaged in the race issue between 1967 and 1972
indicates that a large number found a great deal to sympathize with in the
Black Power movement. Many Jewish leaders and intellectuals sided with
the new radicalism, urged understanding of Black demands for such policies
as community control and racial preferences, and insisted, against the view
of Black Power leaders, that Jews were still victims who belonged on the
side of the Black oppressed. Central to this more radical position among
Jewish leaders and intellectuals was the frequent comparison between Zionism and Black Power. It is in this period that the truly integral nature
of the attachment of many Jewish leaders and intellectuals to the Black
struggle for equality is revealed in its most blatant forms.

At this time, some Jewish leaders and intellectuals articulated a more
conservative approach to Black Power. Chapter 5 of this book looks at the
position of some conservative elements in the orthodox Jewish community;
conservative segments of poorer, more religiously observant working-class
Jews and the Jewish Defense League; and the former Jewish radicals, many
associated with the New York Intellectual milieu, who helped pioneer the
neoconservative movement in the United States. Neoconservatism was the
largest and most influential politically conservative movement among secular Jews in the postwar era, and this book ends with its arrival in 1972.
With the Jewish neoconservatives, the full range of contemporary Jewish
positions on race, all of which in one way or another remained mired in
the discourse of liberalism, had been fully articulated.

An intellectual history that concerns itself with how American Jews
think on any topic inevitably becomes bogged down in the questions of
"who is a Jew" and what is and what is not "Jewish" about their views.
Since American Jews are involved in almost every walk of modern life,
they are often possessed of multiple identities. In the postwar period, for
instance, throngs of social scientists of Jewish birth have written on the
issue of race relations. It seems axiomatic to declare the work of the majority of these authors inappropriate for inclusion in this book, as the authors themselves would no doubt insist that their work is a product of the
commitment to the evaluative standards of modern social science and not
to their "Jewishness." Certainly, an argument could be made that the commitment of so many Jewish scholars to "objective" social science speaks
volumes about the "Jewishness" of these authors, and indeed an argument
about the nature of the "Jewish" attraction to objective social science is

advanced in chapter 2. But, in general, it has not been my purpose to deconstruct texts or to speculate as to the underlying psychological motives of writers of Jewish birth. In order to avoid an undue amount of projection and reliance on innuendo, the most liberal definition of who is an American Jew and whose thought, therefore, constitutes a valid primary source for inclusion in this analysis has been employed. For the most part, anybody who claims to be Jewish, has lived in the United States for most of his or her professional life, and is writing about Blacks or any issue pertaining to Black Americans, is considered a valid primary source for the purposes of this book. The claim to Jewishness can take many forms in addition to a statement to such effect within a particular text or speech. If an author is of Jewish birth and is writing for a specifically Jewish publication or for the sake of a Jewish audience, his or her work is considered fair game for analysis.

There is no doubt that, in a study of this magnitude, there will be important omissions. No single volume can capture the entire universe of Jewish thought on any issue. All that an author can hope for is that the dominant strains, trends, and characteristics of a particular historical topic can be illuminated and interpreted in an honest and open manner. The reader, of course, will be the judge of whether this objective has been achieved.

1

The Liberal Jew, the Southern Jew, and Desegregation in the South, 1945–1964

To an astonishing degree they [the Jews] have made the fight of the American Negro their fight.
　　—James Farmer, Chairman, Congress of Racial Equality, 1964

Though both types [of prejudice] have sharply declined in recent years, anti-Negro prejudice is still far more prevalent in modern America than anti-Semitism.
　　—Thomas F. Pettigrew, *Jews in the Mind of America,* 1965

Of all the changes in American life that resulted from World War II, perhaps none was as profound as the reformulation of American ideology in the sphere of intergroup relations. The victory over the axis powers and European fascism compelled the United States to rectify the disparity between the reality of its group life and the ideals of equality and freedom. The Swedish sociologist Gunnar Myrdal thought that the war had made the contradiction between the system of values to which Americans were in theory committed and the nation's actual racial practices particularly glaring and that circumstances provided the United States with its greatest opportunity for ameliorating group problems. "The American creed," as Myrdal called it, consisting of the values of liberty, equality, justice, and fair opportunity for all, created a "moral dilemma" for Americans confronted by the nation's highly imperfect adherence to these values.[1]

The war revived the idea that what united Americans was a great deal more important than what divided them, and the new attitude was expressed through popular music, radio shows, and the consensus history being written by some of the country's most respected historians.[2] The new ideological formulation was embodied in the statement of purposes of the Common Council for American Unity, a group long interested in ethnic affairs: "To help create among the American people the unity and mutual understanding resulting from a common citizenship, a common belief in democracy and the ideals of liberty . . . and the acceptance, in fact as well as in law, of all citizens, whatever their national or racial origins, as equal partners in American society."[3]

Perhaps no group imbibed of the new dispensation as enthusiastically as American Jews. The late historian Lucy Dawidowicz called the period after 1945 the "Golden Age" of American Jewry and wrote that the "experience of the war years had had a transfiguring effect on American Jews and on their ideas of themselves as Jews."[4] Having made important contributions to the war effort, many Jews felt the tension between their identity as Jews and as Americans dissipate. The Nazis were the enemies of both the Jews and the United States, thus rendering anti-Semitism the attitude of a defeated enemy rather than of the ideal American. Indications that anti-Semitism was on the decline were overwhelming. Public opinion polls taken between 1940 and 1962 reveal that anti-Semitism, as measured by the number of non-Jews who thought Jews were radicals, had too much power, were "unscrupulous," or lacked culture and good breeding was at historically low levels.[5] The barriers that had prohibited Jews from getting into prestigious colleges and universities declined in the 1950s, as these institutions focused on academic achievement as the primary factor for admission. The increasing tolerance of America's social life was accompanied by an expanding economy that saw new opportunities open up for Jews and other minorities. While pockets of exclusion remained, Jews exhibited high economic mobility, high per capita income, and disproportionate representation in professional, managerial, executive, and proprietary positions in the economy.[6] Polls also revealed a greater acceptance of Jews in politics, as political campaigns became increasingly void of overt anti-Semitism. By 1962, three-fourths of Americans claimed they would vote against a candidate solely because he was anti-Semitic.[7] The decline of political anti-Semitism was symbolized by the demise of the notorious Jew-baiting congressman from Mississippi John Rankin. By 1947 Rankin had been turned out by Mississippi voters in a runoff election to fill the seat of the deceased Senator Theodore Bilbo, if not because of his Jew hatred, then at least in spite of it. Five years later Rankin lost his own congressional seat in a runoff election with another incumbent congressman. "The demise of Rankin," writes historian Edward Shapiro, perhaps over optimistically, "meant the virtual end of anti-Semitism in Congress."[8]

Other evidence of the decline of anti-Semitism in the immediate postwar period abounded. No larger anti-Semitic activity was ignited when Julius and Ethel Rosenberg were convicted of espionage and executed in the 1950s, nor did the populist anti-Communist crusade of the Wisconsin Senator Joseph McCarthy descend into Jew-hatred.[9] The new willingness to accept American Jews as full citizens also became apparent in popular culture. In 1945 Bess Meyerson became the first Jew to win a Miss America contest, and fans cheered Hank Greenberg as he led the Detroit Tigers to victory over the Chicago Cubs in the World Series. But the most dramatic change in America's perception of the Jew showed up on the big screen. Hollywood saw the reversal of the "de-Semitizing" of movies in the thirties that had anglicized the names of Jewish characters or removed them entirely from movies. Films like *The Sands of Iwo Jima* (1949), *Action in the North Atlantic* (1943), *A Walk in the Sun* (1945), *Objective Burma* (1945), *Pride of the Marines* (1945), and *The Purple Heart* (1944) prominently featured Jewish characters in war-time situations, often unabashedly proclaiming their Jewishness and the belief in the equality of all men. In 1947, *Crossfire* and *Gentlemen's Agreement,* Hollywood's two preeminent films on anti-Semitism up to that time, vied for the Academy Award for best picture.[10]

"Like All Other Americans . . ."

But if Jews were pleased with the decline of anti-Semitism in postwar America, there was still a sense of uneasiness. For one thing, the Holocaust weighed heavily on American Jews, whose feelings of vulnerability were accentuated by the knowledge that the fate of their European brethren had not mattered very much to the Allied powers. For another, the American celebration of diversity had been something less absolute than it appeared to be. For the most part, the message of diversity and group pluralism was almost always assimilationist in that the objective was to achieve ideological consensus and unity as the foundation for domestic tranquility. As the historian Philip Gleason wrote of the new order, "Ostensibly, it repudiated assimilation; in fact it embodied assimilation because it assumed that everyone agreed about basic matters that were actually distinctive to the United States."[11] Allegiance to the liberal values of democracy, freedom, equality, and respect for individual rights constituted the new "American identity," but the precise role of ethnic loyalties in American life was left undefined.

This ambiguity exacerbated what for American Jews had been a decades-long debate over what would constitute Jewish identity in America and the proper degree of assimilation. The reaction of some of the Jewish critics at *Commentary* magazine to Laura Hobson's *Gentlemen's Agreement,* and to the 1947 Hollywood movie based on that novel, provides some insight into the difficulties Jews faced.[12] The American Jewish Committee had founded *Commentary* in 1945 as "an act of faith in our [the Jews'] possi-bilities in America" and in the belief "that out of the opportunities of our experience here, there will evolve new patterns of living, new modes of thought, which will harmonize heritage and country into a true sense of at-homeness in the modern world."[13] But *Gentlemen's Agreement* revealed that the synthesis between heritage and country that *Commentary* hoped for remained elusive.

Hobson's story features a gentile journalist named Phil who, in an at-tempt to get a fresh angle for a series of articles for a mass-circulation magazine, decides to disguise himself as a Jew so that he can discover firsthand the nature of anti-Semitism. Through Phil's relationship with his gentile fiancée, and her unwillingness to sell a family home in Connecticut to Phil's Jewish friend, the subtle, genteel anti-Semitism of the middle and upper classes is revealed. For this achievement, the film drew accolades from Elliot Cohen, the editor of *Commentary,* who raved that the "plain fact is that *Gentlemen's Agreement* is a moving, thought-provoking film, which dramatically brings home the question of anti-Semitism to precisely those people whose insight is most needed—decent, average Americans."[14] What Cohen liked best about the film was Phil's masquerading as a Jew, because it underscored the notion that anti-Semitism was always a matter of "false identity, the hallucinatory identification of flesh-and-blood Jews with that centuries-old myth of the Western world: the somehow-sinister Yid."[15] The belief that Jews possessed no distinctive Jewish traits or cultural behavior patterns that could elicit discriminatory behavior from non-Jews was expressed through Phil's experiences with restrictive covenants, gen-tile-only job ads, arbitrary insults, the schoolyard fights of his child, and the gamut of institutional exclusion.

But there was a flip side to all of this. Cohen noted that the message of the film seemed to be that tolerance is necessary because we are all the same: "The converse seems to be that if we weren't, one would not need to be tolerant."[16] In reference to Phil's ability to slip unimpeded in and

out of his Jewish disguise, another *Commentary* critic wrote in her review
of the novel that "Mrs. Hobson recognizes no valid differences between
them [Jews and gentiles] except the differences created, on the Gentile side,
by a state of mind ignorantly . . . and, on the Jewish side, by the awareness
of being discriminated against."[17] Cohen himself warned that making tolerance conditional on uniformity is risky business and insisted that, to most
Jews, being Jewish is more than "being religious in the creedal sense" and
joining the fight against anti-Semitism: "There is a richness, variety, and
value in group life that the 'no difference' formula overlooks." The literary
critic Leslie Fiedler put the question of Jewishness in Hobson's novel succinctly: "What, after all, *is* a Jew in this world where men are identified
as Jews only by mistake, where the very word becomes merely an epithet
arbitrarily applied?"[18] But *Gentlemen's Agreement* was an attempt to close
the gap between liberalism in practice and liberal ideals, and anti-Semitism
for the postwar American liberal was clearly a case of mistaken identity in
which the world thinks that Jews are different when in fact they are like
everyone else.

". . . Only More So"

While most white ethnic groups in the postwar period experienced some
difficulty negotiating this "no difference" formula, the dilemma for American Jews was more acute.[19] Before the war American Jews had wrestled
with issues of Judaism and Jewishness, or whether Jews constituted an ethnic nationality, a religious group, or both. During the war, high levels of
anti-Semitism and discrimination had continued as an issue around which
all Jews could unite. In addition, the cause of Jews in Europe and Palestine
drew many of those on the margin into Jewish circles. After the war, the
decline of anti-Semitism, the establishment of a Jewish state in 1948, and
the increasing affluence and suburbanization of Jews and other Americans
made it far less obvious how American Jews differed from other Americans
in their social and political interests. It was in this atmosphere of acceptance
and openness that the Marxist-turned-Jewish theologian Will Herberg espoused his belief that American pluralism was rapidly becoming a pluralism
of the major religious faiths, each representing an equally valid expression
of a common American faith, rather than a pluralism of ethnic groups that
lent itself to competing loyalties.[20]

The question of religious meaning itself was a troubling matter for

American Jews. If Judaism had gained equal legal and social status with Christianity, then discrimination and exclusion could no longer be the focal point for the concept of "chosenness" that had been at Judaism's spiritual core throughout the ages and that had long blurred the line in Jewish thought that separated the Jewish religion from Jewish peoplehood. This sparked a debate in which some Jewish scholars, like Herberg and Arthur A. Cohen, called for a revitalization of Jewish life through ritual and others, like the conservative rabbi Robert Gordis, who urged Jews to revitalize their religious life through a commitment to social justice. Nevertheless, the Holocaust, the failure of the Allies to do enough about it, and lingering pockets of discrimination made it likely that many Jews would continue to identify with the one aspect of being Jewish most accessible to them: the experience of anti-Semitism and the fight against it. As the historian William Toll has written, "the great majority of influential rabbis and lay-men set about reconciling the Jewish sense of chosenness with the moral mission of America as exemplar of democracy and self-determination."[21]

Increasingly, many Jews found their religious identity in the work of national defense organizations like the American Jewish Committee, the American Jewish Congress, and the B'nai B'rith's Anti-Defamation League (ADL). These organizations continued with their original mission to act politically on behalf of Jews as an ethnic group with distinct interests, while simultaneously becoming more important in defining the religious dimension of Jewish life in terms of democracy, equality, civil rights, and racial brotherhood.[22] After World War II, many young Jews took jobs as civil servants in Jewish communal agencies and helped shape Jewish identity as they did so.

For many Jews, the fight against anti-Semitism in America through the liberal formula of equality, individuality, and rationality, along with the issue of support for a Jewish state in Palestine, took precedence over the formulation of a specific religious identity and in a sense substituted for such an identity. Liberalism and the fight for equality also represented one way by which Jews could sustain a distinctive group purpose in the democratic project. In his 1945 essay "Full Equality in a Free Society," Alexander Pekelis, the legal counsel for the American Jewish Congress, declared that "the philosophy and practice of cultural pluralism offer the opportunity for a new form of Jewish autonomy." It was Pekelis's belief that Jewish identity could be catalyzed by providing a Jewish platform for general political action and by reconciling the need for communal purpose with the need for faith. "American Jews will find more reasons for taking an affirmative attitude toward being Jews . . . if they are part and parcel of a great American and human force working for a better world . . . whether or not the individual issues touch directly upon so-called Jewish interests," Pekelis wrote.[23] Pekelis was typical of most Jewish communal leaders who viewed their efforts as part of a larger struggle against the problem of prejudice and discrimination toward any group of people. As the famed attorney for the American Jewish Congress Will Maslow would say of the Jewish motivation to join the civil rights movement, "you can't fight discrimination against one minority group without fighting it against others. It was logical for Jews and Negroes to cooperate."[24]

This approach to identity found the Jews at the core of the fast-developing postwar civil rights coalition. The recent comments of Jack Greenberg, the illustrious civil rights lawyer, about Jewish attraction to civil rights reveals how overwhelmingly this impulse was related to Jewish identity. Like Will Maslow and Alexander Pekelis, both of whom immigrated to the United States as children, Greenberg came from an "Eastern European, Socialist-Zionist culture," which his father had brought with him from Poland. This "culture," rather than Judaism per se, instilled in Greenberg the "belief that discrimination and persecution were evils and that Blacks, like Jews, suffered from a deep, economically based, racially motivated hatred that had to be opposed." But Greenberg confesses that it "might be facile to attribute too much to the Socialist-Zionist milieu" in which he grew up. Socialist Zionism could not account for those German Jews who came out of a very different background, yet still supported civil rights, people like Herbert Lehman, his niece Helen Buttenweiser, Arthur Springarn, and Lessing Rosenwald, all associated with either the American Jewish Committee or the NAACP. As Greenberg explains it, "that pro-civil rights sentiment spanned German and Eastern European Jews suggests the power of the shared experience of anti-Semitism and its resemblance to the Black experience."[25]

The incongruity of the Jewish emphasis on anti-Semitism as the central mode of group identity and the simultaneous leveling of anti-Semitism in the United States was conspicuous enough for the Columbia University economist Eli Ginzburg to take note of in his 1949 volume, *Agenda for American Jews*. Ginzburg warned that a Jewish identity based on fighting anti-Semitism would not provide a sufficient basis for the sustenance of the Jewish community. "Today at least among large numbers of American Jews," he wrote, "the 'defense activities' have usurped a position of priority. This was more or less inevitable since many of these Jews have lost all interest in positive Jewish values[;] their entire adjustment is externally oriented."[26] But Ginzburg's warning went unheeded and, according to one historian, "Working for a society in which economic disadvantage and intolerance would have no place became for Jews an almost religio-cultural obsession."[27]

As the national Jewish organizations and other liberal groups began to win major legal and legislative victories at the state and federal levels, local and national Jewish "defense" agencies, which were originally formed to combat anti-Semitism, became "community relations" agencies and shifted their focus to the broader battle for civil rights. In 1945 the American Jewish Congress began working with the NAACP to form the central axis around which other groups—including the American Civil Liberties Union, the Jehovah's Witnesses, the Japanese-American Citizen's League, the Anti-Defamation League, the National Lawyers Guild and the AFL-CIO—gathered to campaign for antidiscrimination statutes and fair employment practices legislation. In 1947, in response to a request from the NAACP to support an antilynching bill in Congress, the more politically reserved American Jewish Committee formally made the commitment to minority causes not specifically Jewish with the statement that "it is a proper exercise of the powers of our charter that the AJC join with other groups in the protection of the civil rights of the members of all groups irrespective of race, religion, color or national origin; and that it is our general policy so to do."[28] At the 1956 Conference of the National Community Relations Advisory Council, the coordinating body of six national Jewish organizations and thirty-five local community relations councils, the chairman, Bernard Trager, pointed out that "the entire substantive program of Jewish Community Relations rests upon the thesis that Jewish equality is only as secure in a democratic society as the equality of other groups."[29]

The alliance that linked Black and Jewish civil rights groups between the years 1945 and 1964 has been called the "Golden Years" of the Black/Jewish alliance.[30] Ostensibly, the goals of both groups were similar—the end of legal segregation and the destruction of legal barriers to full inclusion. But the places from which American Jews and Black Americans arrived in this civil rights coalition were demonstrably different. For whatever else motivated the Jewish involvement in the cause of equal rights for Blacks, and there can be no doubt that this included commitments derived from Jewish theology as well as the shared experience of oppression, participation in the civil rights struggle also represented one of the ways by which Jews could continue to identify as a distinct cultural group within a pluralistic democracy, rather than being seen merely as individuals who adhere to a separate but increasingly homogenous religious faith.

That this was a radical approach to Jewish identity in America can be seen by what the postwar civil rights movement revealed about Black identity. Since the end of the slave system in the American South, Black American political discourse has embodied the competing impulses of separatism and integration. One strain espouses the view that Black Americans constitute a permanently excluded race whose full participation in American democracy will never be realized and the other the belief that Blacks are an ethnic group capable of winning legal equality and full integration in American life. During World War II, Black leaders of the NAACP, the National Urban League, and other organizations were strengthened in their arguments against racial separatism by the reaction against the racial theories of the Nazis, and they won partial victories in integrating work places and the armed forces.[31] After the war, most Black leaders continued to commit themselves to ethnic group politics, using the legal system and, later, political agitation to promote their interests. The fight for full integration and the battle for desegregation in the South meant that Blacks had accepted, for a time, a more conservative definition of Black identity, one that saw Blacks not as a separate civilization charged with forming the vanguard of a race-based international coalition against Western domination, as some Black nationalists had wanted, but as a group of Americans eager to take their place in America's ethnic flux.[32]

The Jews in America were facing a far different situation. At the very moment they became aware that it was possible for them to "melt" away as an ethnic group, they were refusing to do so, in part, through their involvement in the march for equal rights. The decision of the major Jewish organizations to pursue civil rights for all constituted a commitment to Jewish "otherness" through liberalism, while the same decision on the part of Black organizations and leaders constituted a commitment to Black "sameness" (or at least Black "similarity"). As William Toll has written, Black Americans "have approached ethnic pluralism as the more conservative option, while Jewish leaders see it as the more radical, because each group has come to politics from a very different social status."[33] The irony was that many Jews viewed the broader struggle to tear down the legal barriers to full integration as one way by which Jews could stave off complete assimilation.

"Like All Other (White) Southerners . . ."

Perhaps the most rewarding effort of the Black-Jewish alliance came in 1950, when the American Jewish Committee hired the Black psychologist Kenneth B. Clark to conduct a study on the impact of segregation on Black children. Professor Clark found that segregation had a profound impact on the psychology and self-esteem of Black children. After Clark presented his findings to a White House Conference on Children, NAACP lawyers asked him to assist them as an expert witness in three of the four cases they were bringing before the Supreme Court. In its famous *Brown v. Board of Education* decision of May 1954, which found that racial segregation in America's public schools was unconstitutional, the court cited the original Clark manuscript in its famous footnote eleven, as well as two other investigations conducted by the American Jewish Congress.[34]

It was immediately clear that this court decision would cause a serious division among America's Jews. The Jews who lived in the Southern states most impacted by the Brown decision had long acclimated themselves to a social and political milieu very different from that familiar to Jews in the North, and they had long dropped any pretensions to being an ethnic group with a distinct political outlook. The Jews of the South did not share the psychological attachment to the Black cause that so many Northern Jews did, and the matter of civil rights was not integral to their identity as Jews, as it had become for so many Jews in the North.

The predominance of peddlers and small merchants among the Jews who had migrated to the Southern region of the United States inspired the historian Stephen Whitfield to describe the position of Jews in the South in the following way: "Few in number and unobtrusive in manner, most Southern Jews have seemed to want nothing more than to make a living; their history can perhaps most fully be categorized as a branch of business history."[35] Living in a region characterized largely by an overpowering caste system and fierce racial bigotry, Southern Jews trod lightly and made their way in a place that was largely ambivalent about their presence. Since their arrival in the South in 1733, Jews had faced periods of significant discrimination and had been subject from time to time to a number of legal proscriptions, as they were throughout most of prerevolutionary America. In colonial times, Jews were permitted to hold public office in none of the thirteen colonies. Other legal restrictions prohibited Jews from voting and from worshiping in public. But these restrictions were very loosely applied and were aimed at disabling Catholics far more than Jews.[36] Perhaps the most significant strain of Southern anti-Semitism came in the form of the agrarian populism of the 1890s, whose obsession with money, credit, and conspiracy led writers like Ignatius Donnelly to identify the Jew with the usurer and the "international gold ring."[37] While populist denunciations of Jews were primarily rhetorical and rarely resulted in riots, pogroms, or even exclusionary laws, the former populist rabble-rouser Thomas E. Watson was able to incite the mob that lynched Leo Frank using anti-Semitic imagery.[38] For the most part, however, these kinds of actions were tempered by countervailing Southern ideas concerning the equality of all white men, the overriding concern with the subordination of Blacks, and the usefulness of the Jewish presence as merchants and artisans. In general, anti-Jewish attitudes peaked in times of crisis but subsided when crises ended, much as they did elsewhere in the nation.[39]

Spread thinly throughout the vast region, Jews in the South tended to avoid taking public stands on controversial issues. When the issue of slavery tore the country in two during the Civil War, for example, Southern Jews largely accepted slavery and supported the South. "The behavior of Jews towards slaves seems to have been indistinguishable from that of their non-Jewish friends," wrote Bertram Korn.[40] "It is true, however," he noted, "that their small number militated against the creation of a distinctively Jewish approach to any political or social question other than anti-Semitism."[41] The Southern Jewish approach, then, to any political or social question was not necessarily to avoid anti-Semitism, though that concern was always present; the Jew's position as peddler or merchant—and, therefore, as alien in a region so characterized by a commitment to agrarian ways—made it likely that he would adopt the attitude of his customers or keep silent about his differences, not only because he feared physical reprisal but because his livelihood depended on not rocking the political boat.

Given all of this, the Southern Jew, whose social position remained precarious, was quite shaken by the desegregation movement in the South, which came to a head in May 1954 with the Supreme Court's decision striking down the constitutionality of "separate but equal" public schools. Albert Vorspan, the Reform Jewish leader and civil rights activist, wrote that "the segregation crisis has shaken Southern Jews more severely than any national event since the civil war."[42] As during the Civil War, the Jewish community of the 1950s constituted less than one-half of 1 percent of the Southern population and was largely composed of merchants dependent on the goodwill of the community. This time, however, the situation had become even more perilous, because Jews in the South had gained a modicum of respect among white Southern gentiles. As one Jewish businessman from the South explained it, "The small town Jew in the South 'arrived', perhaps to a greater degree than that of his co-religionists in other sections of America. That is what makes so painful his current dilemma involving the Negro problem. He has something precious to lose—his acceptance as 'one of us.' "[43]

For some Jews in the South, the situation was more complicated because of the willingness of the Jewish merchant, beginning after the Civil War, to cater to Black clients as well as white. The "success of the Jewish merchants is believed to be due to winning the negro trade," wrote John Dollard in his study *Caste and Class in a Southern Town.*[44] Dollard went on to explain the reasons for the success of the Jewish merchants among Black customers. Whereas the gentile white store owners would say to a Black customer, "Well, boy, what do you want?" even if the Black customer was eighty years old, the Jewish merchant would manage to skirt the issue by saying, "What can I do for you?" Jews were also more willing to let Blacks try on merchandise without being obligated to make a purchase. The need to appeal to both Blacks and whites necessitated that the Jewish merchant strive to avoid alienating either party.[45] It was a position that Black Americans themselves seemed to be aware of. Dr. Kenneth Clark believed that Southern Jews were vulnerable to the propaganda, subtle pressure, and threats from the more aggressive segregationist groups and that the more sensitive Southern Blacks were aware of the Jews' delicate situation. Clark quoted a Black American couple he was visiting in South Carolina in 1957 after listening to a Jewish political candidate on the desegregation issue. "He hasn't taken a stand on it and we don't think it would be fair to ask him to take a public stand. He owns a business and if he said that he was for desegregation he might hurt his business. He is no worst. He must be better."[46] After talking with several hundred Black residents of the South, Clark concluded that "this sensitivity seems to dominate the general attitude and feelings of Negroes toward Jews in the South."[47]

". . . Only Less So"

On balance, Southern Jews remained cautious on the issue of desegregation, often pressuring national Jewish agencies through local community councils to soft-pedal the issue so as not to associate Jews with the cause.

In one instance, the Jewish Federation of Montgomery, Alabama, threatened to silence the national Jewish agencies by withholding its yearly allocation to them.[48] The general strategy of laying low on the part of many Jews in the South is reflected in the finding of a 1959 survey that showed that two-thirds of Southern gentiles did not know where their Jewish neighbors stood on the issue of desegregation. Only 1 percent of white gentiles surveyed felt that Jews were the group that had "done the most to stir up trouble over the [race] issue in those Southern communities where a serious dispute exists over the Supreme Court decision."[49]

Nevertheless, while Jews in the South did not embrace the cause of desegregation with as much enthusiasm as Northern Jews or the national Jewish organizations did, polls and surveys from the period indicate overwhelmingly that Jews were, on the whole, more accepting of desegregation than other Southern whites. In 1960, a survey indicated that Jews were more than twice as likely as Southern Protestant whites to feel that desegregation was both inevitable and, in general, desirable in the long run, and only about one-third as inclined as the latter to believe that Blacks were constitutionally inferior to whites. Moreover, only a handful of Jews were actively racist beyond the conformity apparently required for maintaining their businesses or professional careers in strongly segregationist communities.[50] One researcher, Joshua Fishman, found that many Southern Jews who objected to the public statements of national Jewish organizations often privately agreed with them.[51] In a survey administered between 1959 and 1962, Alfred Hero found that Southern Jews were "distinctly less inclined than white Southern gentiles to express segregationist, and particularly racist, ideology." Hero explained that even when educational, occupational, and social differences were held constant, "significant differences [between Southern Jews and Southern gentiles] were evident in their views on race relations." The survey found that the majority of Jewish informants ranged from "mild segregationists to integrationists" and that "white gentiles of similar occupation and income were almost twice as likely as the local Jews to be relatively strong white supremacists."[52]

In another study of a Southern Jewish community, the political scientist Theodore Lowi found that Jews who had lived in the South longer tended to be more conservative politically than Jews who had recently moved to the South but that "the old Jews will make the inevitable adjustment to integration more easily and more quickly than their white Christian brethren. . . ."[53] Another poll, this one conducted by a private testing agency at the request of the *Catholic Digest,* showed that, while 65 percent of white

Protestants and 63 percent of white Catholics living in the South opposed racial integration, only 46 percent of Jews opposed it, and this number reflected the likelihood that Jews in the South, as the most insecure group, were less likely to give interviewers honest answers on controversial issues.[54] According to a study of Jews in Roanoke, Virginia, in the mid-1950s, 70 percent of the Jews surveyed supported the Supreme Court's decision to integrate the public schools.[55] These survey findings were backed up by the testimony of at least one major Black leader. The Reverend Fred Shuttlesworth, a close aide to Dr. Martin Luther King Jr., claimed that "the response of Southern Jews to the [civil rights] movement certainly compares favorably with that of numerous other white groups."[56]

Nevertheless, the response of Southern Jews was considered entirely inadequate by many liberal Jews in the North and by the national Jewish organizations, for whom the fight for racial integration had become a particularly Jewish concern. For many Northern Jews and for the national Jewish organizations, the situation of the Jews in the South as a relatively privileged people challenged their fundamental beliefs about what it meant to be a Jew and about the sacred connection between race prejudice and anti-Semitism. The conflict consisted in the belief of Southern Jews that desegregation in the South had a more direct impact on them than on other Jews and that their immediate safety and social standing were at stake. The national Jewish agencies, on the other hand, believed that the civil rights crisis extended equally to all Jews across the land.

The roots of this crisis appeared to be in the incompatibility of the liberal view of anti-Semitism with the actual experience of Jews living in the South. The approach that the national Jewish organizations took toward anti-Semitism and group prejudice was embodied in the findings of the series of studies produced under the auspice of the American Jewish Committee and the Anti-Defamation League.[57] Essentially, these studies reinforced the liberal belief that the causes of bigotry and discrimination were the same no matter whom the object of hatred was and that, therefore, wherever prejudice against one group was found, prejudice against other minority groups was almost always just off the horizon. The lead study in this series was *The Authoritarian Personality,* conducted under the leadership of the Marxist émigré scholar Theodore Adorno and published in 1950. This study found "a syndrome of unenlightenment" that linked intolerance to personality structure and reported that people who manifested intolerance toward one group had a high degree of intolerance toward all groups because certain human needs had been repressed during their childhoods.

In accordance with these findings, liberals believed that prejudice and discrimination were indivisible and that, as long as one minority group was being persecuted, no minority group was safe.[58]

Adorno's study has been severely criticized for its reliance on abstract theories of personality at the expense of historical data and trend analysis, for its lack of a true understanding of American culture, and for its implication that authoritarian traits are the exclusive domain of those on the political right.[59] But the national Jewish organizations were galvanized by its findings, which confirmed the belief that Jewish self-interest was at stake in the struggle for Black equal rights and that Jewish involvement was therefore more than justified. Shad Polier, the vice president of the American Jewish Congress, writing on behalf of the Congress's Commission on Law and Social Action, explained that "with respect to the community as a whole, we view the fight for equality as indivisible and as part of the general struggle to protect democracy against racism. Hence, any manifestation of racism, whether against Jews, Negroes, Japanese, Puerto Ricans or others, affects all Americans, majority and minority alike."[60] Another communal leader, David Danzig, stated in an address to the Southwest Regional Conference of the American Jewish Committee in 1959 that "some Southern Jews believe that because the Negro is the traditional target of hostility, they can ward off trouble by staying out of the desegregation battle. History has shown the fallacy of this position time and again. . . . Quite aside from the moral obligations of citizenship, Jews cannot expect to be permitted to remain on the side-lines."[61]

But, in fact, this appeal to self-interest did not resonate with Jews in the South. Their experience was not consistent with the liberal image of the South as a violent and savage place for all minorities. As the historian John Higham has written about attitudes toward Jews throughout the United States, "diverse and conflicting attitudes have always existed side by side in American minds," and this ambiguity evinced itself in the South.[62] For almost every instance of observable anti-Semitism, a countervailing philo-Semitism could be discerned. Louis Galambos found that Southern farmers were far more likely to attack big business than Jews at the turn of the century, indicating that rural Southerners' animosity over their rapidly changing environment was not completely unfocused. John Higham maintains that the Ku Klux Klansmen of the late nineteenth and early twentieth centuries centered their anger on the distant Jew of the Northern urban centers and felt "guilty and ashamed at picking on the Jews whom they had known as good neighbors all their lives."[63] As far back as the Civil War when General Ulysses S. Grant issued his infamous order number eleven, which expelled Jews from the department of the Tennessee, public opinion so heavily favored the Jews that the order was completely ignored in certain communities.[64] It has also been pointed out that even before the Civil War, and especially after it, the political climate in the South was such that Jews were able to hold a number of powerful elective and appointive political offices.[65] Between 1945 and 1970, Southerners elected at least twenty-seven Jewish mayors, thirty-eight Jewish state legislators, and sixty-six other Jewish city councilmen and miscellaneous officials.[66]

The historic lack of a consistent and systematic anti-Semitism in the South can be attributed to two phenomena, one being the dominance of Protestantism in the region and the South's reverence for the Old Testament. The editor of the *Carolina Israelite,* the author and humorist Harry Golden, has argued that from this Anglo-Calvinist devotion to the Old Testament and the Hebrew prophets came a solid tradition of philo-Semitism. "The rural peoples of the South hark back to the agrarian civilization of the original thirteen colonies, and they are living heirs of the old American tradition of philo-Semitism," wrote Golden. It is for this reason that in the South, the Jew is a Jew by religion and not by secular ethnic culture, for to the Southern white Christian he represents the "unbroken tie with sacred history and the prophets of the bible, he is the 'living witness' to the 'Second coming of Christ,' the link between the beginning and the end of things."[67]

The racial divide was, of course, a more substantial reason that anti-Semitism in the South remained tempered. "Negroes acted as an escape-valve in Southern society," wrote Bertram Korn. "The Jews gained in status and security from the very presence of this large mass of defenseless victims who were compelled to absorb all of the prejudices which might otherwise have been expressed more frequently in anti-Jewish sentiment."[68]

While there were a variety of caste and class distinctions among whites in the South, the presence of Blacks and the primacy of the color line fostered the acceptance of Jews in high places. As I. J. Benjamin wrote, "The white inhabitants felt themselves united with, and closer to, other whites—as opposed to the Negroes. Since the Israelite there did not do the humbler kinds of work that the Negro did, he was quickly received among the upper-classes, and early rose to high political rank."[69] In this sense then, not only did Black Americans act as a "lightning rod for prejudice"; Southern fears of Black advance also relieved Southern Jews of the animus caused by economic competition with other whites, an animus many Northern Jews felt keenly.

The postwar liberal assumption that ethnic prejudice is unified and all of the same kind is almost certainly mistaken. Scholars have long pointed out that the prejudices held by bigots about different groups vary in source and kind and have a great deal to do with the type and intensity of discrimination that is meted out. It has been argued, for instance, that the anti-Black hatred of the classic racist is motivated by conscious and unconscious anxieties and the projection of these anxieties onto Blacks.[70] However, these projected images differ significantly from those held by the classic Jew hater. Whereas the anti-Black bigot sees Black Americans as mentally inferior sexual predators, the classic anti-Semite is more likely to see Jews as brainy and conspiring. In his study of anti-Semitism, Norman Cohn points out that "the fantasy of an infinitely powerful, world-dominating conspiracy does not, in fact, get projected onto Negroes, and that may well be why not even the most fanatical Negro-haters dream of genocide. It is a different matter with the Jews. . . . Jews are seen above all as 'bad' parents, and this makes them seem so overwhelmingly powerful that the only way to cope with them is to destroy them utterly."[71]

Perhaps the most eloquent refutation of the liberal belief in the "unity of prejudice" comes from George McMillan, an expert on the Ku Klux Klan. McMillan has explained that to "hate Blacks is not to hate everything else equally as well. If blackness can become symbolic enough in a psychological sense, then hatred of Blacks can sufficiently fill your psychological need to hate."[72] An interview with a small-town newspaper editor in the South recorded by Eli Evans for his study of Southern Jews confirms McMillan's contention. The editor associated the fairly decent treatment of the Jews in the South with the Southerner's guilt over race. "Jewish people were white and they were the good and generous people. We felt sufficiently guilty about colored prejudice to make up for it with them."[73] For these reasons, it is not surprising that Charles Stember found, in his study *Jews in the Mind of America,* that between 1939 and 1962 the South (excluding Blacks) was the least anti-Semitic of all the regions in the United States.[74] There were, in fact, indications that the "disunity" of prejudice, or the existence of intolerance toward one minority group and not necessarily another, was not restricted to the South. In 1958, roughly two-thirds of whites in a nationwide Gallup poll said they would vote for a well-qualified man nominated by the political party of their preference if he were Jewish; only two-fifths said they would if he were Black. The percentages of white Christians in the early 1950s who said it would be "a little distasteful to eat at the same table" with a Black ranged from 50 in Elmira, New York, to 92 in Savannah, Georgia. The percentages who said that it would be distasteful to eat with a Jew varied from only 8 percent in Steubenville, Ohio, to 13 in Savannah.[75]

Ironically, it was a vociferous attack by a national Jewish leader on the issue of desegregation in the South that put the lie to the belief that bigotry was indivisible. In a widely read article entitled "Recklessness or Responsibility," Isaac Toubin, the director of the American Jewish Congress, defended Jewish involvement in the struggle for desegregation by reiterating the position of the national Jewish agencies that civil rights was a national and international problem. To support his argument, Toubin used the example of the Arab League's operations in South America. The Arab League had published attacks on the Jewish community of the United States, accusing it of being responsible for the exploitation of Black Americans. Toubin argued that this propaganda jeopardized the security of Argentinean Jewry and that it was incumbent upon American Jewish defense agencies to furnish proof that they had done much on behalf of Blacks in the United States. Toubin exclaimed that "if the Jews had done nothing, what would we have been able to reply?"[76] Clearly, Toubin failed to see that the use of Black suffering by Arab anti-Semites to attack Jews proved that bigotry against one group did not, necessarily, imply bigotry against the other.

Jewish leaders associated with the civil rights cause and national Jewish organizations continued to press their belief that Jews were directly threatened by discrimination against Blacks and that race prejudice and anti-Semitism went hand-in-hand. Toubin himself wrote that the national Jewish agencies know "the real security of the Jew can be achieved only in a society which advocates full equality for all . . . they know that anti-Negroism is a prelude to anti-Semitism."[77] A number of Jewish academics promulgated this line of thought, as well. Charles Glicksberg, a professor of English at Brooklyn College and a frequent contributor to Jewish periodicals, wrote that "if prejudice, whatever the particular form it takes, is indivisible, then so long as one minority group is persecuted on account of color or creed, religion or ancestry, the Jew is not and cannot be free."[78] Louis Ruchames, the acclaimed historian of the American left and the director of Hillel Foundations of Western Massachusetts, speaking to a crowd during Negro History Week in 1955, observed that, because of the Nazi Holocaust, Jews had a particular attraction to the idea of the unity of persecution. Ruchames wrote that the idea that "no minority group is safe while others are victims of persecution, has been seared into our minds and hearts through the burning flesh of six million of our brethren in Europe." Ruchames also demonstrated that many Jews felt that their own well-being was peculiarly tied to the well-being of Black Americans: "I know of no more appropriate and meaningful act then to join our observance with that of the Negro people, whose history touches ours at so many points and whose welfare is so directly related to ours."[79] Dr. Sanford Goldner, who wrote a publication for the Committee for Negro-Jewish Relations on the West Coast, believed that the segregationists of the South and America's anti-Semites were, "in almost complete detail, one and the same." Therefore, Goldner believed, Jews had a special concern with the plight of Black Americans. "The massive struggle of the Negro people is therefore our struggle. The main and most powerful blow against anti-Semitism in America is the blow against the enemies of the Negro people. The self-interest of the overwhelming masses of the Jewish people therefore demands that they identify themselves with this fight."[80]

The strength with which liberal Jews felt this unity with Blacks resulted in many instances in an alarming insensitivity to the circumstances of Jews in the South. Carl Alpert, writing in the respected journal of opinion *The Reconstructionist* in 1946, identified a "Jewish Problem in the South," in which he accused the Jews of the South of being accessories to the crime of injustice to Blacks. "The law makes provisions, we must remember, for accessories before and after a crime. Southern Jews, alas, go beyond passivity—they are accessories."[81]

Some Jewish leaders believed so strongly that the Jewish fate was tied to that of the Blacks that they described the Jews' stake in desegregation as equal to their stake in the defeat of Nazi Germany during World War II. At the 1956 National Jewish Community Relations Council meeting, Professor Arnold Rose, a coauthor with Gunnar Myrdal of the classic *An American Dilemma,* compared the reluctance of Jews in the South to speak out in favor of desegregation, and what he perceived to be its muzzling impact on national Jewish organizations, with the actions of Nazi collaborationists: "If [Jewish leaders] do not take a long run and courageous view of the current crisis [on segregation], they are playing the same role as the collaborationist Jews played in Europe during the Nazi period."[82]

Referring to Senator James Eastland, a segregationist from Mississippi, another Jewish writer also drew an analogy between Southern Jews and Nazi collaborationists: "Shouldn't the Anti-Defamation League's educational effort include a comparison between fascism in Germany and its counterpart, Eastlandism in the South? Surely the Jewish collaborators of Hitler are despised by the masses of Southern Jews. Everyone knows that silence and appeasement only brought destruction to the appeasers and to those who thought they could save themselves by silence and non-resistance."[83]

It became virtually impossible for many Jews to disentangle Blacks and Southern Jews after the emergence of the white citizen's councils. The white citizen's councils were a collection of loosely connected grass-roots groups that sprang up in Indianola, Mississippi, in opposition to the Supreme Court's 1954 desegregation decision. The councils varied in strength and size across the South, but their common purpose was to stop or at least slow down integration in public schools. The councils concerned many Jews in both the North and the South, mostly because of their resemblance to the Ku Klux Klan, especially the original Klan of the Reconstruction period. But there were crucial differences between the two organizations. The councils strove hard to achieve respectability, drew their membership from the most respectable citizens in the community, shunned the violence of the Klan, and gave prominence to speakers from the universities and the ministry at their meetings. The white citizen's councils also tried not to become associated with anti-Semitism, though their record on this remains debatable. Asa Carter's North Alabama Citizen's Council was limited to those who believed in the divinity of Jesus, but that was the exception. The Mississippi Council once sent out some anti-Semitic literature, but, when challenged, its leader quickly apologized, claiming that some of his best council members were Jews. The lack of respect afforded anti-Semitism in the South was evinced in the reaction to a Memphis speaker who remarked at a rally that "The NAACP is the worst organization to come along since the one that crucified Christ—and I may as well say it—it's the same organization." The conservative newspaper *Commercial Appeal* attacked the meeting for its anti-Semitic overtones, and the council issued a lengthy apology the following day.[84]

The real problem for Southern Jews came when they had to decide, not whether the councils were anti-Semitic, but whether to join them. Citizen's councils carefully canvassed Jews, and the danger in refusing to join or sign petitions was apparent: many Jewish business owners ran the risk of losing a substantial amount of commerce, and many others simply ran the risk of being labeled an outsider, a "Nigger lover," or a communist. A small minority of Jews joined willingly out of conviction. Others joined so as not to be singled out for attention. But most did not join. The dilemma of the Southern Jew was summed up by one who did not join: "I lost friends, I'm sure of that, and maybe some business, but I felt I just couldn't do this. I tried to explain to them that while we shared much in this community, the Jewish tradition would make it impossible for me to do this. I think some understood. Others, I guess, won't want to."[85]

For the national Jewish organizations, the issue of the citizen's councils was clear cut: through the racism and alleged anti-Semitism of the councils, Jews and Blacks were tied. In 1958, the Anti-Defamation League issued a report stating that the citizen's councils were one of three types of organizations through which the forty organized anti-Semitic groups that were operating in the South at the time worked. While granting that the councils varied widely in their approach toward anti-Semitism, the report said the councils had recently crystallized into essentially a single movement that covered the entire South.[86] A reporter for *Jewish Life* wrote that "the strong anti-Semitic current in the white citizen's councils is a clearly established fact by now."[87] Isaac Toubin of the American Jewish Congress wrote that the fear of reprisal felt by Southern Jews revealed that the white citizen's councils as well as the Ku Klux Klan, at heart, were as opposed to Jews as they were to Blacks. "They understand," Toubin wrote of the Southern Jew, "the mind and the intent of the hate-monger who today suppresses the Negro and tomorrow, with equal venom, may suppress the Jew."[88]

For the most aggressive Jewish civil rights activists, terrorist violence against Jewish institutions in the South confirmed their view that Jews and Blacks shared the same position in the civil rights struggle. Between June 1, 1954, and October 12, 1958, there were eighty-three bombings in the South, including seven bombings and attempted bombings of Jewish institutions. Albert Vorspan, the director of the Committee on Social Action of the Union of American Hebrew Congregations, the national body of the Reform movement, believed that the message of the bombs was that "hatred is indivisible. The Jew is caught up in the storm of the South whether he likes it or not, and there is no place to hide."[89] Apparently, that Jews were caught up in the storm had its positive aspects for Vorspan, who seemed pleased that the bombings had once again established Jews as certifiable victims. "The Jew has often been the barometer of the moral health of a society," wrote Vorspan. "The bombers have again unwittingly rendered to the Jew this tribute. The years ahead will demonstrate whether American Jewry will be worthy of this compliment."[90]

But where the series of synagogue bombings and attempted bombings signaled for Jews like Vorspan the need for more intense Jewish involvement in the desegregation battle, many Jews, Northern and Southern, were convinced by the bombings that the leadership role of liberal Jews and national Jewish organizations in the movement for desegregation rendered Southern Jews a vulnerable target for extremists. Responding to surveys that found a higher incidence of anti-Semitic attitudes among white segregationists in Southern communities under pressure to desegregate than in the region generally, Alfred Hero concluded in his study that "the discomfort among many Southern Jews over support of desegregation and racial equality by national Jewish organizations . . . is understandable, as is their sensitivity to any Jewish prominence in liberal movements, especially racially oriented ones."[91]

Some national Jewish organizations made attempts to reconcile their commitment to civil rights with the safety concerns of Southern Jews as they became sensitized to the dangers Jews faced in the South. In the past, the ADL had been excoriated by Southern rabbis for being insensitive to the position of Southern Jews. In a memorandum, a well-known leader of the ADL wrote, "[W]hy be too intimidated by the fear and anxiety of some Southern Jews and some Southern non-Jews? We have a responsibility to moral principle, to the Negro community, and to fellow Christians who join with us on this issue."[92] But during a controversy sparked by a July 7, 1958, editorial in the Virginia newspaper *The Richmond News Leader,* which blamed the ADL's distribution of pro-integration materials for the rise in anti-Semitism in the South, the national office of the ADL demonstrated a willingness to compromise with Southern Jews. The editorial suggested that Southern Jews reevaluate their relationship with "a Jewish organization that foments hostility to Jews."[93] The national office of the ADL in New York saw the editorial as a poorly disguised attempt by the *News Leader* to drive Jews out of the desegregation effort. Many Jews in the South, however, agreed with the editorial that the national organization had "plunged the Jewish community into unnecessary confrontations with their neighbors."[94]

In response to this immediate crisis, the local Virginia ADL office and the national office worked out an agreement in which the local office would temporarily refrain from the use of literature, films, and activities that could be interpreted as dealing with the issue of racial desegregation, and the national organization agreed on a resolution that any action taken by the national ADL that would affect a regional constituency would be undertaken only after consultation with that constituency. In effect, the national organization agreed that while it would not shift away from its pro-integration stance, "it was prepared to move in a cautious manner in the super-heated atmosphere of Virginia."[95]

The change in attitude of those Jewish organizations that became more sensitive to the concerns of Southern Jews resulted in some animosity among the major defense organizations. At a 1956 symposium in Miami, representatives of the American Jewish Committee and the B'nai B'rith indicated that quiet, behind-the-scenes methods might be more appropriate for Jews who wanted to exert their influence without jeopardizing the safety of the Southern Jewish community. The representatives of these groups advocated "education"; one of them claimed that "while we are in favor of the Supreme Court decision, we do not believe the Jews of the South are expendable."[96] The representatives of the Jewish Labor Committee (JLC), an organization formed in 1934 to defend the rights of Jewish workers, also expressed sympathy with a more subtle approach. Emanuel Muravchik of the JLC offered the solution "to do sometimes publicly, always privately, that which will advance desegregation." He cautioned Jews not to be first, not to act alone, but to join with other groups that were moving in the desired direction. A representative from the American Jewish Congress, however, made a straightforward demand that there be no doubletalk, that Jewish leaders and organizations speak up and say publicly what they were saying behind closed doors. The Jews of the South, he thought, should not hang back one step behind other groups that were advancing on the issue.[97]

The American Jewish Congress seemed to be the most militantly desegregationist of national Jewish communal organizations; it had apparently not retreated in response to local protests.[98] Isaac Toubin of the American Jewish Congress charged in May 1956 that two national Jewish organizations had been conspicuously silent on the desegregation issue. Apparently alluding to the American Jewish Committee and the Anti-Defamation League, Toubin claimed that "the white citizen's councils of the South have not only blackmailed their Southern Jewish neighbors, but effectively silenced two national Jewish organizations which pride themselves on their defense of civil rights of all."[99]

In part, this organizational conflict had its roots in the history of the organizations involved. The American Jewish Congress, as the representative agency of the Eastern European Jews, had always been more politically aggressive than the staid German-Jewish-led American Jewish Committee and B'nai B'rith's Anti-Defamation League, both of which preferred to emphasize educational efforts to combat discrimination. But the charge by Toubin that the American Jewish Committee and the Anti-Defamation League had submitted to the pressure of the citizen's councils 'was not true. The American Jewish Committee had always committed itself to a pragmatic rather than to a doctrinaire approach to civil rights and had from the beginning agreed to consult with Southerners on policy.[100] In recognition of Southern Jews' legitimate concerns, the Committee adopted new guidelines in 1959 on the issue of desegregation in the South. The guidelines reflected the notion, promulgated by Southern Jews, that race relations in the South were the problem of the nation as a whole, not the special problem of the Jews or other minority groups. It warned Jews to guard against making themselves a target by entering into "public debate with anti-Semites; answering charges or otherwise assuming defensive positions" and recommended that Jewish participation in programs aimed at prescribing law and order be taken in "conjunction with other community groups representing a cross-section of the community."[101] The Committee did continue to pursue its commitment to desegregation by distributing fact sheets and pamphlets identifying hate groups, sharing data with law enforcement officials, conducting investigations into synagogue bombings, preparing studies on more than five hundred instances of racial violence, and lobbying Washington for stronger action.[102]

The terrorist bombings and the willingness of some national Jewish organizations to shift policy in response to the safety concerns of Southern Jews demonstrated an admirable regard on the part of some agencies for the safety of local Jewish communities. But the differences between the Jews of the North and those of the South over what methods to use to oppose segregation should not be minimized, particularly as they relate to Jewish identity. Jewish identity was perhaps more attenuated in the South, but it relied more heavily on religious forms than the ethnic/political identity of the majority of Jews in the Northern-based civil rights movement.[103] The conflict between the Jews of the North and the Jews of the South over racial desegregation reflected the difference between liberal Jews for whom, on balance, the Black struggle for equality came to take precedence over any perceived threats to the welfare of fellow Jews and a group of Jews who were perhaps the first in the United States to discover that their collective well-being was not directly linked to the fate of Black Americans. The point here is not to enter a debate concerning the ethical precepts of Judaism as they relate to civil rights or to posit a specific Jewish tradition, but rather to demonstrate that the Southern Jewish community was loath to link its religious identity with strong political imperatives, as had so many liberal Jews.[104]

Specifically, Southern Jews were uncomfortable with approaching desegregation as a distinctively "Jewish concern." Morton Gaba, the executive director of the Jewish Community Council of Norfolk, Virginia, explained that it was of primary concern to the Southern Jew that the battle for desegregation be fought by Jews on an individual basis, as Americans, rather than as Jews. As Gaba wrote, "we feel that those of us who are strongly moved by the issue should act solely as individuals and not as representatives of another minority group. I feel certain that point of view represents majority thinking."[105]

Rabbi Gerald Wolpe, the spiritual leader of Synagogue Emmanuel in Charleston, South Carolina, recommended that "Jewish 'self-protection organizations' do not rush into print with opinions which are not based on personal investigation in the South" and that Jewish professionals "refrain from arriving armed with programs of action which were outlined in the insulated security of a New York office."[106]

Perhaps no one expressed the exasperation of some Southern Jews better than Rabbi Perry Nussbaum of Jackson, Mississippi. Nussbaum had an admirable record on speaking out on civil rights but explained that he was not inclined to ask the same of his congregants: "In the Delta area of our state, where the Jewish merchant is pressured into taking sides, I would be the last to ask that he make a martyr of himself and his family and prepare to move when he is compelled to join the citizen's council."[107] In 1963, after the death of the Black civil rights leader Medgar Evers in Mississippi, Nussbaum bitterly reported that all the clergymen in his state who had been outspoken in the cause of civil rights had been removed or forced from their pulpits—all except him. Nussbaum concluded his article with this lament: "Support for civil rights? Who argues? A solution to the problem of the last survivor, who has it?"[108]

It is no accident that the bulk of the criticism of the national Jewish organizations came from Southern rabbis, communal leaders who often found themselves in the most precarious of circumstances. The clergy generally held a status in the South that was rarely afforded them in the North, and Southern rabbis were considered the spokesmen for the Jewish community, thus helping to create a natural friction between them and the national Jewish agencies, led in many instances by secular Jewish leaders. Writing in *Conservative Judaism,* Rabbi William Malev of Houston, the spiritual leader of one of the South's largest Conservative congregations, explained that, in the South, Jews were seen by non-Jews as a religious and not as an ethnic group, in which capacity they were not a minority but one-third of the community of the "three great faiths." The defense organizations, on the other hand, were an anomaly to the non-Jew in the South and served to confuse outsiders as to who in fact was a legitimate representative of the Jews. Because the ADL is a secular organization like the NAACP, Malev argued, it is despised in the South and therefore is a liability to Southern Jewish communities. Malev recommended that the national defense organizations stop "their unfortunate habit of beating the drum on every possible occasion" and "let religious leaders of the Jewish communities be the spokesmen for them." Malev clearly articulated the Southern belief that it was Jewish leadership on the matter of desegregation that had linked Jews and Blacks in the minds of Southern racists, but that in fact this linkage was false. "It is because the demagogue and the agitator equate the Jew and the Negro, and thereby separates the Jew from the rest of the community, that much of the difficulty has come."[109]

While there were a number of outspoken integrationist rabbis in the South, including Charles Mantinband of Mississippi, Emmet Frank of Virginia, and Jacob Rothschild of Georgia, in general the Southern rabbinate varied in its approach to desegregation according to the size of the Jewish population in the general community, the openness of the community, the number of "Old South" Jews in the congregation, and the proportion of congregants who were businessmen.[110] But even Jacob Rothschild, one of the most outspoken integrationist rabbis, expressed his doubt that "the rabbi in today's South will serve any good purpose in leading crusades. Where there are forces at work in the community—human relations councils and the like—he should become a part of them by all means. But let him labor alongside others of like mind and dedicated purpose."[111]

The testimony of these Southerners indicates that the heart of the problem between Northern and Southern Jewry involved the question of Jewish identity. Many Southerners had long accepted the definition of Jewishness as strictly a religious designation, one that many Northern Jewish liberals were uncomfortable with and were trying to mitigate through political activism. It is not surprising, therefore, that much of the criticism of Southern Jewry that came from the North on the desegregation issue centered around the identity of Southern Jews and their alleged willingness to assimilate. For liberal Jews who had so fully based their own identity on the crusade for desegregation, the identity of Southern Jews who appeared lukewarm or apprehensive about desegregation became highly suspect. A tepid approach by any Jew toward desegregation, in the mind of the liberal Jew, was the ultimate sacrilege.

One Jewish civil rights lawyer compared the anxious Jews of the South to the Marrano Jews of Spain who publicly denied their Judaism during the inquisition.[112] Writing in *The Reconstructionist,* Carl Alpert explained that the problem with the Southern Jew was not that he was more anti-Negro than his gentile neighbor: "his only crime is that he is like his neighbor. The sort of Jews who fear to be distinctively Jewish might gain some comfort from that thought, and use it to prove again and again that Jews are no different from anybody else, as if that fact itself were a virtue."[113] Joel Dobin, a rabbi from Pennsylvania who visited a community in the South for six months, complained that it was an "incorrect" Jewish orientation that was at the heart of this small Southern Jewish community's lack of enthusiasm for the desegregation campaign. While acknowledging the peculiar economic and social pressures on Southern Jews, Dobin wrote that "there is a need for constructive action. There is a need for reviving in these Jews a sense of positive Jewish identification."[114]

Albert Vorspan conducted one of the most vitriolic attacks on the Jewishness of Southern Jews for what he considered its lack of aggressiveness in the area of civil rights. Making reference to an Episcopal priest who had excommunicated a congregant who objected to attending church with Blacks, Vorspan asked, "[C]an this be said of Jews?" Coming from a leader of Reform Judaism, a movement whose very existence is predicated upon Judaism's lack of a central authoritative body with powers of excommunication (*cherem*), this is startling.[115] More than the other Northern liberals, Vorspan defined Judaism in terms of radical racial protest and then questioned the Judaism of anyone who did not adhere to this criterion. In a tirade that reads as if it had been written by a member of the Orthodox leadership at the turn of the century, when Reform Judaism was in its ascendancy, Vorspan decried the excessive tolerance of American Judaism: "There are no standards for synagogue membership. . . . He [the Jew] has only to pay his dues in the temple and he has as much right there as anybody else. . . . Are there no lines to be drawn? No standards to be met? No demands to be made upon ourselves?"[116]

It is not necessary to endorse the lack of resolve demonstrated by many Southern Jews on the issue of desegregation, or to deny that the relationship of many Jews in the South to the idea of Jewish peoplehood had become severely attenuated, to see that a pattern among liberal Jewish leaders had emerged. In this pattern, the needs of sizable Jewish communities are relegated to second-tier status behind liberal objectives, in this case racial integration. The opposition of the local Jewish community to the presence of nineteen Conservative rabbis at a protest march in Montgomery, Alabama, in May 1963 dramatized the differences between Southern Jews and liberal Northern Jews. Andre Ungar, perhaps the most prominent member of the rabbinical delegation, reported that the local community seemed to be saying, "Boychiks, we know you are right, but still, how could you do this to us, your brothers?" and the rabbis were saying, "Jews, dear scared little Yidden, how can you side with racism, with Hitler's heritage; and yet, you are our brothers, and we love you, we love you, forgive us, please."[117] One cannot help noticing the irony in a group of Southern Jews, most of whom had long deemphasized Jewish solidarity, asking the rabbis for special consideration in the name of Jewish brotherhood. But this episode also demonstrates that, in the battle over desegregation, the needs of Southern Jewish communities in conflict with liberal ideals were sacrificed to the increasingly dubious need of Jewish liberals to be counted among the persecuted. As the remaining chapters show, this pattern continued in the 1960s, when the Black struggle for equality moved North and again posed serious challenges to Jewish communities throughout the nation, most of which, like many Jewish communities in the South before them, were entering the advanced stages of assimilation.

It is perhaps appropriate, then, to conclude this episode in the history of Blacks in Jewish thought with Harry Golden, the editor of the *Carolina Israelite,* a figure whose life in many ways embodied the fissures between Southern and Northern Jews and whose keen insight helps to illuminate the misconceptions of both groups of Jews. Golden was born on New York's Lower East Side. He moved to the South in 1941, when he was in his late thirties, to begin publishing the *Carolina Israelite* from his North Carolina home. A prolific humorist, Golden used his famous wit to mercilessly lampoon racial segregation in the South. In response to a series of laws passed by the North Carolina Legislature in 1956 to prevent the integration of that state's public schools, Golden introduced what he called his "Vertical Negro Plan." Golden had noticed that the tremendous industrial growth and economic prosperity experienced by the South in the decade after World War II had been accomplished by the elimination of "vertical segregation." That is, the tremendous buying power of the South's twelve million Black Americans had been harnessed by the admittance of Blacks into white supermarkets, grocery stores, banks, telephone booths, department stores, and drug stores. In all of these purchasing situations, Golden noted, the Black is required to stand up. By contrast, "It is only when the Negro 'sets' that the fur begins to fly." So Golden proposed that the South could comply with the Supreme Court's ruling on segregation by passing an amendment "which would provide only desks in all the public schools of our state—no seats." Golden explained that since "no one in the South pays the slightest attention to a Vertical Negro . . . this will completely solve our problem."[118]

Golden also offered his "White Baby Plan to End Racial Segregation" after he noticed that several Black school teachers were admitted to a segregated movie house when they were accompanied by the children of their white friends. Golden suggested that whites could solve their baby-sitting problems and Blacks could go to the movies wherever they wanted if whites would "pool their children at a central point in each neighborhood" so that Blacks could pick one up every time they wanted to go to the movies. "Eventually," wrote Golden, "the Negro community can set up a factory and manufacture white babies out of plastic, and when they want to go to the opera or to a concert, all they need to do is carry that plastic doll in their arms."[119]

Golden's own favorite was his "out of order plan." Golden had once prevailed on the manager of a department store to shut the water off in his "white" water fountain and put up an "out of order" sign. Over time, whites began to drink out of the water fountain designated for the "coloreds," and by the end of the third week everybody was drinking the "segregated" water. Golden proposed that a special government committee be set up to investigate his "out of order" plan. "It is possible," he wrote, "that the whites may accept desegregation if they are assured that the facilities are still 'separate,' albeit 'out-of-order.' "[120]

In his more serious moments, Golden had much to say about the relationship between Black Americans and Jews and about the subject of desegregation. Golden's viewpoint was clearly that of the Northern liberal, and his friend Eli Evans would later comment that since Golden's audience was in the North, "he wrote from the perspective of the peddler's pushcart, relevant for the immigrant generation but less valid for Jews in the South."[121] So it was typical of Golden to suggest that, in the deep South of 1956, "the white man fears the Negro; the Jew fears the white man; and the Negro, the focal point of this entire embroglio, fears no one."[122] Anyone even vaguely aware of the region's sensibilities could see that the Black in the South had quite a bit to fear from white men. Like many

Northern liberals, Golden looked with awe at the new willingness of Blacks to risk personal safety for their rights and with disdain at the fear of Southern Jews. But from his North Carolina perch, Golden was able to see insightfully, and to express more eloquently than many other liberal Jews, precisely why the Jews of the South were not benefiting from the system of segregation.

Golden shrewdly distinguished between what Southern Jews had come to accept as equality and what full equality really meant, pointing out that the Southern Jew "prides himself on being well-integrated in the gentile society of his community, yet he will argue for hours against the publication of a resolution passed by some organization far away in New York. And he does not see any inconsistency in this."

Most important, Golden was sensitive enough to see that in some ways the situation of the Jews in the South was more tenuous than that of the Blacks. The Jew in some ways envies the Black, Golden thought, because, despite never having been entirely excluded from the white gentile world, the Jew still asks, "What will happen to us here?" The Black, in contrast, "never thinks of himself in terms of actual survival. All the Negro wants is to ride the buses, go to better schools and get better jobs. No one has yet heard him say 'What will happen to us here?' "[123]

Perhaps, then, to a degree rarely noted, Northern and Southern Jews were responding the best way they knew how to similar historical pressures. Perhaps liberal Jews in the North were also asking themselves, "What will happen to us here?"—but in reference to the increasingly open and democratic United States. While Southern Jews faced issues of physical safety and economic viability, the issues facing Jews outside the South were freedom and assimilation, and their answer to the challenge of Jewish survival was reflected in the adoption of the cause of racial justice as their own. At the very moment Jews outside the South became aware that it was possible for them to "melt" away as an ethnic group, they were refusing to do so, in part through their involvement in the march toward desegregation.[124] If the Jews of the South had internalized the attitudes of Southern whites, only less so, they believed this was the best way to ensure their survival. If the Jews in the North had absorbed the postwar commitment to freedom and equality, only more so than other Americans, they believed that was one way of ensuring communal purpose and survival. Just as Golden suggested that Jews in the South envied the Blacks, the involvement of Northern Jews in the civil rights movement, and their insistence that desegregation was every bit as much a Jewish fight as it was a Black fight, indicates that in the deepest recesses of their consciousness, liberal Jews may have coveted the special status of Black Americans, the weight of whose historical presence on the American scene precluded any foreboding about group survival.

2

Jews and Racial Integration in the North, 1945–1966

Jewish life is social, rather than spiritual. . . . One half of Jewish identity is the product of Gentile exclusiveness and the other half is the product of Jewish association. —Mordecai Kaplan

All too often, the legitimate association of Jews with each other for relevant group purposes is used as a rationale for irrelevant exclusion of others. —Manheim Shapiro

From the time that the Supreme Court declared race segregation in public schools unconstitutional on May 17, 1954, until around 1960, the story of racial segregation and the battle to end it was primarily a story of the South and the border region, where segregation was enforced as a matter of law. But by 1960 the number of Black Americans living in Northern cities had swelled considerably, moving the focus of the fight for equality to the North. Between 1950 and 1960 the twelve largest cities gained nearly two million Black residents. Whereas in 1950 the resident population of only one of these cities contained a Black component approaching 20 percent, by 1960 Blacks made up a fifth of the population in seven and a majority of the population in Washington, D.C.[1] The problem of Black inequality was no longer a problem primarily associated with the Mississippi Delta or the newly emerging cities of the South but rather affected the big cities of the North (and the West) such as New York, Philadelphia, Washington, Chicago, Detroit, Milwaukee, San Francisco, and Los Angeles, as well as a host of smaller cities.[2] While segregation by race or ethnicity was outlawed in the North, residential patterns tended to reflect the voluntary decisions of individuals who preferred to live close to others of the same cultural background, giving rise to a spatial arrangement that included substantial ethnic and racial segregation. The existence of these subcommunities became more important for many white ethnics, whose ties to an ethnic subculture had become more tenuous in cities where public interactions between individuals were increasingly fluid.[3]

In an environment in which racial consciousness had been raised to new heights by the civil rights movement, the comparatively depressed condition of Black neighborhoods became increasingly obvious. The continued migration from the South of Blacks with poor job skills and low levels of education had combined with a changing economy, increased suburbanization, and continuing racial prejudice to intensify the physical deprivation and isolation experienced by Black communities. The pattern of segregation by ethnic subcommunity gave many the impression that discrimination and prejudice in the North were at the heart of the problem of racial inequality, just as it had been in the South, and suggested that the existing patterns of informal group interaction would have to be substantially modified.

Inevitably, American Jews found themselves at a peculiar impasse with regard to the demands for racial integration. As Jews gained wider acceptance and continued to assimilate, living lives that in their most important aspects were increasingly similar to the lives of other Americans, a concrete and distinct Jewish culture continued to recede. American Jews still identified as Jews, but that identification was based far less on the religio-cultural structure that earlier generations of American Jews had than on a sense of Jewish belonging and community. The sociologist Milton Gordon's distinction between the cultural behavior patterns and the social structure of ethnic groups was perhaps nowhere more relevant than in the case of the Jews.[4] Gordon identified a pattern whereby ethnic groups in America subordinate their ethnic viewpoints in the sphere of public life but privately rely heavily on ethnic-based social institutions. American Jews, in large measure, expressed their identity as Jews by associating with and living among other Jews, which put the very essence of Jewish identity on a collision course with the growing civil rights demand for racial integration. The two dominant modes of postwar Jewish identity, Jewish support for civil rights and the maintenance of autonomous Jewish communities, came into direct conflict.

The Jewish Problem with Integration

The question of equality for Black Americans in the Northern cities was far more complicated than it had been in the rigidly segregated Jim Crow South. The most prominent Black spokespersons and their white allies adhered to a program of full and equal citizenship for Black Americans, but as it became less clear what true equality really meant in the North, confusion set in over the best way to go about achieving it. "Equality under the new conditions of urban life," wrote the historian of race and nationality Oscar Handlin, "is far more complex than under the rigidly defined relationships of the Jim Crow system. . . . [In the North] the law does not single the Negro out for special liabilities. . . . Yet the Black man remains unequal."[5] The Black American in the North suffered from a different kind of separateness, termed de facto segregation, "the result of his concentration in distinct residential districts and the product of a cycle in which lack of skill condemns him to inferior jobs, poor income, poor ghetto housing and slum schools."[6] In this sense, the obstacles to social and economic mobility that Blacks faced were similar to those faced by other groups that migrated in large numbers to America's cities. There were, however, a number of substantial differences that made the problems of Black Americans more difficult to overcome. First, the lines that separated white ethnic groups were clearly nowhere as strong as the residential and occupational color line that served to exclude Blacks.[7] In general, Black adjustment was made more difficult by dark skin and the low status conferred upon those who possessed it. The second difference was the changed spatial and political arrangement of the large metropolitan areas in the years after World War II. Thanks to a combination of postwar affluence, new technology in home building, and federal government subsidies, large numbers of white Americans in the late 1940s and 1950s realized their dream of home ownership and left the cities for newly built suburban communities. The infiltration of Blacks into the large cities of the North after the war was accompanied by a commensurate departure of a newly expanded white middle class.[8] White suburbanization was accompanied by the relocation of businesses and jobs to the suburbs and the wider use of automobiles, both of which served to magnify the social differentiation among income groups separated not only by geography but by access to jobs and services. In short, while Blacks possessed significant political power in the cities by the late 1950s, the problem they encountered, according to one analyst of the race crisis, "is that this new political power is being exercised in a governmental unit, the suburb-constricted city, which is totally inadequate to meet the Negro's many problems."[9]

All of these developments pointed to the fact that the disabilities that afflicted Black Americans as a result of generations of deprivation would not immediately disappear once legal obstacles were abrogated. Nevertheless, the successes of the legal battle against segregation in the South proved powerful enough so that the one-dimensional nature of the race problem there was superimposed on the multidimensional nature of the problem in the North. Most civil rights leaders came to regard racial segregation as the root cause of Black inequality, and racial balance as the only solution. In arriving at the conclusions they did and in sticking with their Southern strategies, one historian wrote of the civil rights activists, "they have paradoxically accepted the contention of the white supremacist that there is really no difference between the North and the South, that the one region does directly by law what the other does indirectly by practice."[10]

The Black demand for a new order in the North came almost inevitably on the heels of the decolonization of Africa and the emergence of independent African states. In less than twenty years after the end of World War II, thirty-one independent Black African nations had been formed. In identifying with the new countries of Africa, Black Americans were not really rekindling their identities as long-lost Africans as much as they were reshaping their identities as Americans and assuming a more bold and assertive posture. This assertiveness manifested itself not only in student sit-ins in the South beginning in 1960, in the fight of young Blacks like James Meredith for desegregated public schools and universities, or in the efforts of ordinary Black Southerners who marched past hostile crowds in Montgomery and elsewhere but also in the general commitment of the major civil rights organizations to "direct action" demonstrations in the North. The mood was captured in the phrase "New Negro" and differed from all similar phases in Black history in that this time a significant number of whites, bolstered by rising incomes and a deepened appreciation for the injustices suffered by Blacks, were sympathetic toward Black efforts to gain full legal equality.[11] As one magazine editorial put it, "the Negro revolution may be blocked here and diverted there, but it cannot be stopped. . . . Now, with a high and marvelous anger, [Blacks] take to the picket lines, the streets and the jails, brimming with the assurance that they sacrifice in behalf of their children's freedom."[12]

One of the more significant developments in the civil rights movement of the early 1960s was a growing hostility on the part of militants of all races toward white liberals and Black moderates, who were accused of being committed to "gradualism," "legalism," and compromise. "The liberal's anguish stems from one of those tenacious liberal illusions," wrote one militant, "that, contrary evidence notwithstanding, they could achieve integration at no cost or inconvenience to themselves."[13] Civil rights militants downplayed the fact that the climate for significant racial change had been largely achieved by white liberals and that some of the demands being made by Blacks regarding the end of de facto segregation, such as bussing white children into predominantly Black schools to achieve racial balance, appeared antithetical to certain liberal ideals.[14] Nevertheless, Jews were implicated in the militant attacks if for no other reason than their preponderance among postwar liberals. The white liberal who is attacked as a hypocrite "is generally (even if this is not spelled out) the white *Jewish* liberal," wrote the sociologist Nathan Glazer, "and it could hardly be otherwise, in view of the predominance of Jews among liberals."[15] Even after the legal victories that culminated in the 1954 *Brown* decision, Jewish liberalism continued to manifest itself in support for liberal political candidates and in Jews' disproportionate involvement in civil rights groups like the NAACP, the Congress of Racial Equality (CORE), and the Student Non-violent Coordinating Committee (SNCC). Also noteworthy was the work of Jewish activists like Arnold Aronson of the Leadership Conference on Civil Rights, Isaiah Minkoff of the National Jewish Community Relations Council, Rabbi Joachim Prinz of the American Jewish Congress, Kivie Kaplan of the NAACP, and Joseph Rauh of Americans for Democratic Action, all of whom played outstanding roles in organizing the historic March on Washington in the summer of 1963 and the passage of the 1964 and 1965 civil rights acts, the crowning achievements of the civil rights revolution.[16]

But Jews were implicated in the militant demands for integration in another, more problematic way. In a widely read article, Nathan Glazer explained that mandatory racial integration challenged group life in the North as no other ethnic group demands ever had before it and that for many white ethnics this constituted an unfair burden. Social networks that run along ethnic, religious, and racial lines largely determined an individual's fate, wrote Glazer, but the "new Negro demands challenge the right to maintain these sub-communities far more radically than the demands of any other group in history . . . the force of present-day Negro demands is that the sub-community, because it either protects privileges or creates inequality, has no right to exist."[17] Put another way, the pressure for integration brought to bear by civil rights activists differed qualitatively from that of earlier immigrant groups in that it rejected the maintenance and improvement of the ghetto in favor of its dissolution.[18]

But as American Jews moved away from the earlier forms of religious and cultural expression, Jewish identity came to rely even more intensely on Jewish fraternization. The sociologist Charles Liebman has suggested with regard to Jewish identity in the postwar period that "the essence of American Jewish identity, the core meaning of American Judaism for many American Jews, may very well be their social ties to one another."[19] It was not only that Jews in the postwar United States felt more comfortable among other Jews but that, as the historian Edward Shapiro points out, "associational Jewishness was the best way, and for some the only way, they knew of assuring Jewish continuity."[20] Other important critics have lent this development the gloss of their own sociological acumen. Addressing his colleagues in the Rabbinical Assembly in 1959, the founder of Reconstructionism, Mordecai Kaplan, wrote that "Jewish life is social, rather than spiritual. . . . One half of Jewish identity is the product of Gentile exclusiveness and the other half is the product of Jewish association."[21] The Jewish critic Leonard Fein has similarly described American Judaism as communal, rather than theological. "Ours is not a personal testament, but a collective and public commitment. . . . What defines the Jews *as Jews* is community: not values, not ideology."[22]

The most popular forms of Jewish expression in the postwar decades continued to be contributing widely to Jewish organizations, philanthropies, and synagogues, living in close proximity to other Jews, and sending offspring to Jewish summer camps—actions that brought Jews into social proximity.[23] This characteristic of American Jewish life has sometimes been called the "civil religion" of American Jewry, a reference to the specific way in which American Jews have, despite an enormous amount of ideological disunity, managed to build an identity as one component of *K'lal Yisrael,* or the "people of Israel."[24] Faced with the familiar modern dilemma of balancing full integration with maintaining group distinctiveness, American Jews managed through their secular organizations to "achieve unity, purpose, and identity as a moral community which transcends (without excluding) the overtly religious ideology and practice of the denominational movements of American Judaism."[25] Without fully recognizing that they were doing so, American Jews created an American Jewish polity, a "matrix of voluntary organizations and associations which carry out functions of community wide concern."[26] Beyond the federation, an organizational structure designed to reduce the costs and burdens on potential contributors of multiple charitable campaigns, other secular organizations, such as the American Jewish Committee, the American Jewish Congress, Hadassah, B'nai B'rith, and synagogue-based social clubs, provided a framework for identification and social contact within the context of a respectable communal rationale.[27] The concerns of the major Jewish organizations may have shifted significantly during the postwar era, from, say, an emphasis on immigration settlement to Jewish defense and support for Israel, but there is little doubt that the Jewish polity had become the principal focus of Jewish religious faith and unity in America.

Nothing, however, seemed to bring Jews closer together than the neighborhoods in which they lived. The historian Deborah Dash Moore has shown that in the 1950s second- and third-generation Jews continued to cluster in predominantly Jewish communities at almost the same rate as the Jews of the immigrant generation, even though new residential opportunities were opening up. In these ethnic enclaves, Jews were able to express their Jewishness unselfconsciously. "They turned to their neighborhoods to translate what Jewishness meant into a livable reality and to their public institutions to give expression to the varied content of Jewish ethnicity," Moore explains. The associational patterns of the Jewish neighborhood were strengthened with networks of occupational ties. "Through residential concentration, New York Jews often acquired a psychological attitude of a majority, in a country where they were a small minority. The clustering of thousands of Jews into city neighborhoods made Jewish living comfortable and natural."[28] In New York and other large cities, temples and synagogues as institutions espousing particular religious doctrines had become peripheral to the interests of most Jews. Philanthropic, mutual-aid, and fraternal organizations had emerged as the principle outlet for Jewish extracurricular activities.[29] Even during what Nathan Glazer termed the "Jewish Revival" of the 1950s, American Jews did not really demonstrate any strong religious drive but rather looked to the flourishing new synagogues and community centers to meet the social needs of individual Jews. In his search to find a basis for Jewish continuity in the postwar decades, Glazer focused on the attraction of the "holy community," the idea that Jews are bound together, rather than on the acceptance of a specific set of beliefs.[30] For this reason, Glazer wrote, "since the Second World War, Jews have moved from one concentrated Jewish area only to create new ones— and largely out of their own desires."[31]

That Jewish self-segregation had become more important with the thinning of Jewish identity in the postwar decades can be seen in a *Commentary* article from 1958, in which a Jewish writer tells of the difficulties he faced when he considered selling his North Shore Long Island home to a non-Jewish family. The author writes that the Jews were "herding" themselves back into ghettos, not out of a fear of anti-Semitism, but out of a fear of their own Jewishness. "They have so few positive reasons why they're Jews they're afraid to live in a mixed area where they might have to stand up and be identified. So they flock to these all-Jewish communities where they can be anonymous and the problem doesn't exist." The tone of the article is one of exasperation at these parochial attitudes, but the author finally relented and sold his home to Jews. "So North Shore Community Homes can relax now," the article concluded.[32]

That Black demands for racial integration would be particularly troublesome for Jewish communities did not escape the notice of some Black activists. While the Black image of the Jew as a nonwhite would go through a significant transition in the late 1960s, inspiring a whole new dynamic in race relations, a number of Black writers acknowledged that Blacks traditionally viewed Jews as something other than just another white ethnic group.[33] In the late 1940s James Baldwin wrote that Blacks believe the Jew "has suffered enough himself to know what suffering means" and that an "understanding is expected of the Jew such as none but the most naive and visionary Negro has ever expected of the American gentile."[34] But in terms of racial integration, at least one well-known Black journalist suggested that Jewish racial otherness in some cities was the single greatest obstacle to achieving racial balance. In his book *The Negro Revolt,* Louis Lomax wrote that while Jews were more than just another group of whites, "they are a people with a tradition, which, as both a theoretical and practical matter, offends Negroes."[35] Lomax accused the Jews of being more opposed to integration than other whites not because they hated or discriminated against Blacks but because they strove to realize that element of their Jewishness that called for "togetherness." Lomax believed that Blacks in cities with large Jewish populations were discriminated against, not primarily because they were Black but because they were gentiles. Following this logic, Lomax asked a series of pertinent questions: "How do you satisfy a Jew's right to live among other Jews without abrogating my right to rent or buy the house next to his? What modern Solomon can mediate the conflict that arises when I try to rent a store on Harlem's 125th Street from a Jewish landlord who wants another Jew to have the space?" While the Black American was inspired by the ambition "to get the hell out of the Negro ghetto" as soon as he could, Lomax wrote, the Jew was "motivated in precisely the opposite direction."[36]

Other civil rights activists were less understanding of Jewish "togetherness" than Lomax, and this led to virulent attacks on the predominantly Jewish leadership of the garment trade unions.[37] The largest Jewish-led unions, the International Ladies Garment Workers Union (ILGWU), the Amalgamated Clothing Workers, and the United Hebrew Trades, had been historically friendlier toward Blacks than most other trade unions, but it was precisely this friendliness that made them, rather than the more exclusionary Irish and Italian building trades unions, the target of civil rights activists.[38] Despite the unions' historical willingness to reach out to Blacks, by the 1960s garment union old-timers were engaging in strategies designed to keep recently hired Black and Puerto Rican employees out of the increasingly scarce better-paying jobs.[39] But the ILGWU's efforts to respond to the shrinking of the white ethnic labor pool by hiring Blacks and Puerto Ricans in the first place reveals that the attack on the Jewish-led labor unions as an enclave of Jewish solidarity was anachronistic. While the unions had been in the past perhaps the most important ethnic-based organizations for Jews, by the time of the civil rights attacks they had become increasingly less Jewish, and young Jews were not looking to them as a source of future economic mobility or Jewish communal sustenance. While Jewish leaders continued to dominate the unions, by the late 1950s they were dealing increasingly with non-Jewish workers.[40]

Nevertheless, in pointing out the importance to Jews of voluntary association, Black critics like Lomax exhibited keen insight. The decline of the Jewish-dominated unions was just one element of the broader disappearance of the immigrant stamp on Jewish life, and many Jews sought to associate closely with Jews in other venues precisely because the institutions of the immigrant generation were dying. The evolution of civil rights liberalism from desegregation in the South to racial integration in the North had, in a sense, forced Jews to decide the mode of identity to which they were most committed: liberalism or community. As the walls of exclusion began to fall, the need for Jews to prove that they were like everyone else began to give way to a need to prove that they were still somehow different. Jewish commitment to liberalism and the cause of equal rights for all had been, for more than a decade, the predominant mode of expressing that difference. By clinging to the liberal ideal of full equality for individuals and aligning themselves with Blacks, American Jews were assured that they were performing a very particular Jewish moral function. But the advent of the integration movement in the North forced Jews to ask themselves the meaning of this stance. Black demands for integration and racial balance posed serious questions for Jews dependent for a living Jewish identity on neighborhood uniformity, Jewish community centers, day schools, summer camps, and other communal arrangements.

Aware of this conflict, a small number of Jewish writers began to question the assumptions upon which many Jews predicated their unconditional alliance with the civil rights movement. C. Bezalel Sherman, a sociologist and writer associated with the Labor Zionist monthly *Jewish Frontier,* agreed that Jews had a responsibility to support Black rights but argued that the headlong stride for complete racial balance would only intensify de facto segregation and that it would be particularly deleterious for the Jewish community, for whom the loss of neighborhood schools would severely impact attendance at afternoon schools. "Jewish education, the most important instrument of Jewish group survival, would thus be destroyed to the benefit of no one."[41] Abraham Duker, the Yeshiva University historian and librarian, shared Sherman's concern. Duker believed that proposals to bus children out of neighborhood schools to achieve greater racial balance posed a serious threat. "[W]e . . . are struggling for cultural and religious survival, and as a group we have rights to both. Negro spokesmen have shown little understanding of this aspect of Jewish life."[42]

For the most part, though, the identification with the struggle of Blacks proved too powerful for liberal Jewish communal leaders to realistically assess the condition of the Jewish community and its interests relating to racial integration. Rather than deal openly with the major cultural problems associated with growing freedom and assimilation, liberal Jewish leaders defined the well-being of the Jewish community as one with the success of an increasingly militant fight for racial integration. Many believed that Jewish ambivalence over any aspect of the militant civil rights program itself posed the greatest threat to American Jews as Jews, and identified integration as a moral imperative on which the future of the Jews in the United States was staked. Obviously aware of the problems of Jewish communal erosion, many of these leaders argued that, by providing the Jewish community with an opportunity to renew its commitment to the Jewish ethical tradition, the new militance of the civil rights movement would work to strengthen Jewish identity. In this sense, Jewish continuity and survival had become so linked in the mind of liberal Jewish leaders with active participation in the fight for racial integration that the possibility of a clash between Jewish communal survival and the civil rights movement was rarely entertained.

Jewish Civil Rights Militants and Integration

The idea that the integrity of the American Jewish community was inextricably linked to the growing militance of civil rights protest was perhaps most memorably stated at the historic March on Washington in August 1963 by Rabbi Joachim Prinz of the American Jewish Congress, a refugee from Nazi Germany. Rabbi Prinz declared that the Jewish historic experience of three and a half thousand years commanded that Jews speak out. "[I]t is not merely sympathy and compassion for the Black people of America that motivates us," Prinz declared. "It is above all and beyond all such sympathies and emotions a sense of complete identification and solidarity born of our own painful historical experience." Without making explicit his support for a program of full integration, Rabbi Prinz made it known that there were no Jewish concerns about integration that superseded the importance of support for the militant civil rights program. "Even those who believe that we have our own problems and should have little time to meddle in this understand that we would forfeit our place in America as a spiritual and religious force if we were to stay out."[43]

Abraham Joshua Heschel, perhaps the most influential Jewish theologian of the postwar period, also maintained that the march toward full racial integration could result in a spiritual renewal for American Jews. A professor of ethics and Jewish mysticism at the Jewish Theological Seminary and a refugee from Nazi Germany, Heschel became the chief spiritual spokesman for American Judaism during the 1950s and 60s. Heschel was extremely active in the civil rights movement and marched alongside Martin Luther King and Ralph Bunche at the head of the famous 1965 civil rights march from Selma to Montgomery. But he made his biggest splash two years before the march, at the 1963 National Conference on Religion and Race in Chicago. At this centennial commemoration for Lincoln's Emancipation Proclamation, Heschel noted that the first racial dialogue took place between Moses and Pharaoh, and he described racism as the world's greatest threat to mankind.[44] Heschel believed strongly that nobody was free of the obligation to be a civil rights activist, proclaiming at one point that "There is an evil which most of us condone and are even guilty of: *indifference to evil"* and excoriating all Americans for their complicity in the evil of racial injustice. "Some are guilty, but all are responsible." [45] A genuinely powerful and original theologian, Heschel went so far as to define the Jewish community in relationship to the struggle for civil rights. Speaking directly to his coreligionists, Heschel articulated what became perhaps the most characteristic impulse of liberal Jewish expression. "The plight of the Negro must become our most important concern. Seen in the light of our religious tradition, the Negro problem is God's gift to America, the test of our integrity, a magnificent spiritual opportunity." [46]

By the early 1960s, large numbers of American Jewish leaders and intellectuals had identified so strongly with Heschel's belief that they neglected to address the specific complications for Jews that stemmed from the prospect of unimpeded racial integration. As race militants, these Jewish spokespersons joined in the attack on the white middle class in general and on the Jewish middle class in particular, identifying Jewish purpose with civil rights militance and often substituting civil rights activism for the more difficult task of developing a sustainable, functional mode of Jewish living in the United States. These Jewish critics showed little sympathy for middle-class Jews caught between their belief in racial justice and their desire to maintain distinctive Jewish communities and institutions in both the cities and the suburbs of postwar America.

One of the more outspoken critics was Charles Silberman, a journalist and editor at *Fortune* magazine, whose widely read and highly regarded 1964 volume, *Crisis in Black and White,* was one of the first efforts to attack the theory that the problems of Blacks in Northern cities were similar to those of other immigrants and to emphasize the special difficulties caused by color and race discrimination. [47] Silberman believed that American Jews had not adequately understood the shift in the civil rights struggle from the early legal battles to the more militant techniques of the early 1960s. "The fight for racial justice has radically changed character and direction in the past several years, but we Jews—and by 'we Jews' I mean the leadership of the major Jewish religious and lay organizations, not just our benighted rank and file—have not changed with it," Silberman wrote. [48] Silberman insisted that as a "committed Jew," he was sure that "our own survival is at stake, for our inaction undermines that passion for freedom and that commitment to justice which always have been a justification of our survival as a people." [49] Attacking the Jewish middle class for being bound to material gain and for failing to support serious social change, Silberman described their mind-set: "We'd like to participate in the fight for racial justice, all right, but not if it means that we must soil the middle-class garments of respectability all of us—rabbis and laymen—have learned to wear."[50] Ironically, at the same time that he excoriated the middle class for its lack of involvement in the civil rights struggle, Silberman castigated white liberals for their support of Black causes, which had kept Blacks in a state of dependency. "White philanthropy, white liberalism, white sympathy and support . . . have had a similar effect of preventing African-Americans from standing on their feet."[51] The result, according to Silberman, "has been a serious strain between African-Americans and white liberals; including . . . Jewish white liberals."[52]

Perhaps the most radical attack by a Jewish leader on middle-class Jews with regard to civil rights was that of the well-known rabbi and activist Arnold Jacob Wolf. In his essay "The Negro Revolution and Jewish Theology," Wolf accused the entire Jewish community of being incurably racist and "bourgeois." For Wolf, the Jews were the people who kept the racist and evil capitalist system going. Wolf explained that Jews, like the people in his own congregation, were largely entrepreneurs, advertising executives, promoters, small manufacturers, salespeople, and tax experts whose function in American society it was "to grease the wheels of capitalism—that very capitalism which first fires and last hires Negro workers, that very capitalism whose profits are squeezed from machines destined to displace the Negro as America's muscle."[53] Wolf argued that the "American Jew lives by his superiority to and distance from the American Negro and the American poor" and that the Jewish community made showy gestures that looked supportive of Black rights but nevertheless did not put at risk the Jews' own position in America. The Jew "will approve of integration, but oppose every possible step toward it. He will support non-violence . . . but never participate in direct action. . . . The bourgeois Jew will hold art fairs for civil rights organizations and not demand to know where the money goes, because he does not really care."[54] After upbraiding American Jews for their alignment with ineffectual Democratic policies, Wolf issued a political litmus test of his own, surmising that Jews must serve God politically by becoming a "pressure group for higher taxation . . . for mental health . . . [and] for civil rights."[55]

The Jewish race militants were so convinced of the moral primacy of civil rights and that the fate of the Jews was tied to a program of militant activism that at least one of them drew an analogy between Jewish hesitance on racial integration and the indifference of average Germans to the Holocaust. Rabbi Henry Cohen of Philadelphia insisted that "some Jews are as indifferent to the fate of the Negro as were so many Germans to the fate of the Jew!"[56] But while Cohen chose the citizens of Nazi Germany as a mode of comparison, two prominent Jewish sociologists, B. Z. Sobel and May L. Sobel, were convinced that middle-class Jews were more analogous to the antebellum Quakers. The Sobels worried about Jewish continuity, but they identified the threat to continuity in the possible Jewish withdrawal from civil rights activism, not in the challenge posed by racial integration to Jewish association. It was their opinion that the pressure from rank-and-file Jews on Jewish organizations to withdraw from the civil rights movement was leading the Jewish community the way of the Quakers. The Quaker church, the Sobels explained, had been opposed to slavery before the Civil War and had cleansed its own house of slaveholders but had refused to take up cause with the abolitionists or to risk a North/South split in the church. They consequently lost support and membership, becoming a quaint but insignificant religious group because of their inability to "move beyond the level of liberalism which had become institutionalized by the 18th century."[57] The alleged Jewish withdrawal from civil rights was a similar case, and Jews were losing sight of their "central binding mission," putting the Jewish community's survival into serious doubt. The "Jews of the past saw in their lives a mission to live the Torah, to speak to the world of the one true God, and of a latter age to bear the message of prophetic justice and social melioration. There is no comparable central idea for them as a group in the 20th century," the Sobels wrote.[58] For the Sobels, the commitment to civil rights could now form the basis for solidarity and a "guiding idea" for the Jewish community. The Sobels urged community leaders to act as a "goad and a rod" to push the Jewish community into action, even in the face of open hostility. "Large-scale work in and with the Negro community must be undertaken, even in the face of a rebuff from the revolutionary Negro leadership, and work in the Jewish community should be intensified even in the face of violent reaction."[59]

That Jewish race militants saw the struggle for racial integration as the primary vehicle for a strong Jewish identity could be seen in the way some of them viewed the alienated Jewish youth from the North who made up such a large contingent of the civil rights volunteers in the South throughout the early 1960s. Charles Silberman believed that many of these youth had drifted away from Judaism because the Jewish community lacked a commitment to social action. "Can we find no way by which young Jews can participate in the civil rights movement as Jews?" he asked.[60] Silberman was not alone in his belief that the way to stronger Jewish identity among

Jewish youth was through greater civil rights activism. Albert Chernin, the director of community consultation for the National Jewish Community Advisory Council, noted that many of the young Jewish students who took part in Freedom Summer in Mississippi in 1964 and did not identify as Jews were in fact acting as Jews but simply did not know it. According to Chernin, it was the job of Jewish community relations agencies to make them know it.[61] A former Anti-Defamation League official, Murray Friedman, ventured to argue that the youngsters who participated in direct action protests in the South were acting as Jews in the sense that Judaism contains large doses of egalitarianism. "It is as if these boys were wearing their Yarmulkes without knowing it," said Friedman.[62] Marvin Schick, an orthodox Jewish writer and a New York City mayoral aid, even urged the orthodox community to meet alienated youth on their own turf. While he ruled out making religious compromises with this alienated youth, Schick felt that advocacy of civil rights by the orthodox community "can help to prepare the way for a relationship with alienated young Jews."[63]

But, by all indications, it was unlikely that the adoption of more militant civil rights activities by the Jewish rank-and-file could have inspired a closer connection with young Jews who had identified more strongly with left-leaning social movements. Many of these activists consciously rejected any Jewish motive for their actions. One young Jewish "freedom fighter" who participated in a symposium in 1965 insisted that "it would be more accurate to call my background progressive, rather than Jewish."[64] Another participant explained that he decided to participate in Mississippi in the summer of 1964 because he identified more with being an American than with being a Jew. "I got involved in this great conflict with myself as to my role as a Jewish American," he explained. "Was I to be the one to be pushing for the development of the State of Israel? Was I a Jew in that sense, or was I an American? I concluded that I was an American and that this [civil rights] was the struggle that was being fought."[65] Another participant explained his problem with defining Jewishness as his motivation for participating in "Freedom Summer." "The trouble with this question is that when we say, what is there about being a Jew that brought you down [South], well, all kinds of people are down, Christians are down, and agnostics and atheists." The young man explained that he thought it was "destructive" to bring "one's Jewish tradition and background into this."[66]

Similarly, the two most famous young Jews to participate in, and ultimately to give their lives to, the civil rights struggle in the South, Andrew

Goodman and Michael Schwerner, were quite ambivalent about their Jewish identity. These two idealists and civil rights martyrs were killed by white racists along with their Black companion, James Earl Chaney, in the summer of 1964 in Mississippi. It is reasonable to assume that Goodman was influenced more by his Communist background than by his Jewish background. Goodman's parents were sympathizers who often held fundraisers in the 1950s in their Manhattan apartment for professors accused of Communist ties. The convicted Communist spy Alger Hiss was a visitor to the Goodman home. Schwerner identified himself as an atheist who believed in the infinite perfectibility of men. Deciding at age thirteen not to become a bar mitzvah, he later declared that he was not Jewish but rather "only" a man.[67] There seems to have been an interesting generational dynamic going on among the Jews of the left which would become far more pronounced with the radicalization of the youth movement in the late 1960s. Whereas the promise of universal equality had made leftism in all its varieties appealing to earlier generations of young Jews marked with the indelible etchings of the Jewish ghetto, later generations of young Jews seemed to have absorbed much of the older generation's universalism but little of the Jewish ghetto. It seems more accurate to say that those Jewish youth who found meaning only in civil rights activism had not been running away from a static or "irrelevant" Judaism but in fact had never really been affected by any meaningful Jewish experience. As the journalist Jack Newfield put it, the young alienated Jews were "the children of economic surplus and spiritual starvation who sought to give meaning to their lives by identifying them with a cause greater than their own personal needs."[68]

The reaction of Jewish race militants to the issue of rising Black anti-Semitism revealed that, in some cases, their commitment to radical racial change transcended even the most rudimentary concerns about basic communal defense and safety. The most conspicuous instance of Black anti-Semitism was the growing popularity of the Black nationalist Nation of Islam. The seething poverty of most Black slums made the nationalist philosophy of the Black Muslims appealing. The Nation of Islam, which derived much of its philosophy from Marcus Garvey and the Moorish Temple Movement of Noble Drew Ali of the 1920s and 1930s, preached Black supremacy, racial segregation, social uplift, and economic self-reliance. The philosophy of the group, led by "Messenger of Allah" Elijah Muhammad and his second-in-command, Malcolm X, taught that Blacks were God's original creation and that "out of the weak of the Black Nation, the present Caucasian race was created." The central myth of the Black Muslims involves a Black scientist named Yakub who created the evil white race in a cave laboratory as an experiment to spite God and his favorite tribe, the Black tribe of Shabazz. The first group of white people to emerge from Yakub's cave were the Jews, who went on to inhabit Europe and become civilized. It is ironic that in attempting to explain the historical subjugation of Blacks, the Nation of Islam adopted Western, Christian, and even Jewish motifs in their mythology. Apparently, Elijah Muhammad himself was pegged for the biblical figure of Moses, charged with leading his people out of the United States, the Black man's Egypt.[69] While Jews were thought to be devils just like all other whites, they were singled out as especially malicious. "Jews are the Negro's worst enemies among whites," wrote the Black Muslim Minister Jeremiah X. "Unlike other whites, Jews make it a practice to study Negros; thus they are able to get next to him [*sic*] better than other whites. He uses the knowledge thus obtained to get close to the Negro, thereby being in a position to stab him with a knife."[70] It is noteworthy that despite the Black Muslim rejection of Christianity, the image of the Jew in Nation of Islam rhetoric remained pretty much the standard fare of Christian anti-Semitism—namely, that of the Jewish conspiratorial usurer, exploiter, and thief. In a standard speech at Temple Number Seven in Harlem, Malcolm X explained that the Jews "know how to rob you, they know how to be your landlord, they know how to be your grocer, they know how to be your lawyer, they know how to join the NAACP and become the president. . . . They know how to control everything you got." Malcolm continued "Goldberg always catches ya'. If Goldberg can't catch ya', Goldstein'll catch ya'. And if Goldstein don't catch ya', Greenberg will catch ya'."[71] Like so many others during this era of growing militance, Malcolm took aim at Jews for their liberalism. On a nationwide broadcast Malcolm said about sheriff Jim Clark of Selma, Alabama, the man who used cattle prods on civil rights demonstrators, "Clark is a wolf but the Jewish liberal is a fox, and the wolf is better because with him you know where you are."[72] Some of Malcolm's fulminations were aimed at displacing Jews from their historic role as victims. "Everybody talks about the six million Jews," he complained, "but I was reading a book the other day that showed that one hundred million of us [Black Americans] were kidnapped and brought to this country—*one hundred million.* Now everybody's wet-eyed over a handful of Jews who brought it on themselves. What about our one hundred million?"[73]

Black anti-Semitism did not spring forth only from the Black Muslims. By the early 1960s, angry and more militant young Black leaders like Cecil

Moore of Philadelphia, who thought every Jew in the civil rights movement was "a goddam phoney," gained sizable followings.[74] By 1966, even leaders of civil rights agencies that had received huge financial support from Jews demonstrated significant anti-Semitism. The most notorious case was the February 3, 1966, meeting of the board of education in Mount Vernon, New York, called to discuss desegregation of the local schools. When no progress was made toward integration, Clifford A. Brown, the educational chairman of the Mount Vernon chapter of the Congress for Racial Equality, shouted: "Hitler made one mistake when he didn't kill enough of you Jews." James Farmer, the national director of CORE, ordered an investigation to determine the "context" in which Mr. Brown made his remark but went on to say that "also intolerable" were the school board's delaying tactics in ending de facto segregation in the city's schools. Farmer's unwillingness to unconditionally denounce Brown for his comments prompted Will Maslow, the executive director of the American Jewish Congress and a long-time civil rights lawyer, to resign from the national advisory board of CORE.[75]

Jews also had reason to believe that many Blacks shared the anti-Semitism of some of their leaders. A 1964 study by the University of California Survey Research Center found that Blacks were significantly more likely than whites to accept economic stereotypes about Jews, with 54 percent of Black Americans ranking "high" on a scale of economic anti-Semitism.[76] Malcolm X's declaration in January 1964 that "the streets are going to run with blood" and that "Black people are going to explode" was followed that summer by a riot in Harlem, the first of a string of 329 riots to take place in 257 cities across the country between 1964 and 1968. While factors other than anti-Semitism were clearly at the heart of these disturbances, in the summer riots of 1964 cries of "Let's get the Jews" were reported in the press. One report had it that Jews owned as many as 80 percent of the furniture stores, 60 percent of the food markets, and 54 percent of the liquor stores burned and looted in the 1965 riot in the Watts section of Los Angeles.[77]

While many Black leaders, including Martin Luther King Jr. and Roy Wilkins, were quick and thorough in condemning manifestations of Black anti-Semitism, even friendly Black leaders were inclined to soft-pedal the issue. At a convention of the American Jewish Congress in 1966, the civil rights leader and staunch alliance builder Bayard Rustin said that he wanted "to point out that the term anti-Semitism as applied to Negroes and white

Christians in this country is not the same thing, and cannot be the same thing. . . . There is no feeling among black people in this country that they are superior to Jews, nor is there among black people in the country a belief that, somehow, Judaism is in a fix."[78]

While this kind of response is to have been expected from Black leaders eager to keep attention focused on racial injustice against Black Americans, a much stronger response would have been expected from American Jewish leaders and intellectuals who had, since the Holocaust, become extremely sensitive to even the most superficial manifestations of anti-Semitism. But for many Jewish race militants, the importance of racial integration was so essential to their definition of Jewishness that they tolerated a level of anti-Semitism from various segments of the Black community that they would probably never have tolerated from white anti-Semites. The commitment of these Jewish race militants to civil rights and racial integration was so complete that any Jewish impulse toward self-defense and recoil was subordinated in defining the religious imperatives of the Jew. Thus, at the same 1966 American Jewish Congress convention addressed by Bayard Rustin, Charles Silberman delivered an address in which he claimed "anti-Semitism is irrelevant to a consideration of Jewish responsibility because, in the most fundamental sense, that responsibility stems from *us* and not from Negroes." This statement came as a particular surprise since Silberman claimed to have been not three feet away from CORE official Clifford A. Brown in Mount Vernon when he made his statement about Hitler and the Jews. Nevertheless, it was what Silberman called the "mirror image" of Black anti-Semitism—"Jewish anti-Negroism"—that concerned him most. Jewish "anti-Negroism" referred to the "race prejudice . . . very deeply rooted in the American Jewish community" and "the Jewish opposition to school integration, to housing integration, etc."[79] Jews, in short, were against integration, and this was tantamount to racism. "Unfortunately, the leaders of the Jewish community have not addressed themselves to . . . the . . . emergence of full-fledged, as well as rhetorically camouflaged, Jewish anti-Negroism."[80]

At the same conference, Rabbi Arthur J. Lelyveld, the president of the American Jewish Congress, made a similar point. "I do not serve the cause of Negro emancipation because I expect the Negro to love me in return," he stated. Lelyveld criticized Jews who wanted to focus Jewish energies and resources on Jewish education and Jewish culture, rather than on integration and civil rights, arguing that the Jewish community had the resources to do both. "This is a professional intellectual rationalization of that disinclination to be 'involved' which is so widespread in our time. It is so much more comfortable to divert one's gaze."[81]

Albert Vorspan, an official of the Reform movement's Union of American Hebrew Congregations, attacked those he believed were considering withdrawing from the civil rights movement because of Black anti-Semitism. Vorspan wrote, "We are not in the fight for human rights because we want Negroes to like us . . . but because it is our task as Americans, our religious imperative as Jews, and our duty as human beings."[82]

Some Jewish race militants argued that the anti-Semitism of the Black Muslims was not as bad as white anti-Semitism and did not hold Blacks responsible for the kinds of attitudes they held. Often, it was explained, Black anti-Semitism was merely a reaction to white racism or economic circumstances. Along these lines, Rabbi Kurt Flascher differentiated the Black Muslim anti-Semitism from that of white right-wing anti-Semites like George Lincoln Rockwell. "We differentiate between an out-and-out anti-Semite like Rockwell, whose entire program is to preach the extermination of the Jews, period, and the Black Muslims, which is essentially a reaction to the racism and the terror and the brutalities to which the Negro people are exposed."[83]

Morris Schappes, the long-time radical and editor of the Marxist-oriented *Jewish Currents,* also expressed understanding for the racism and anti-Semitism of the Muslims, saying that it was similar to Jewish prejudice against non-Jews arising from the history of anti-Semitism. "I can understand the Black Muslims' attitude and feeling, because I think it arises from the same frustration and fear," wrote Schappes.[84]

At the 1964 convention of the American Jewish Congress, Shad Polier, an AJC official, reiterated his belief that Black anti-Semitism was essentially the result of a search for scapegoats, but he added that he did not believe that it or Black nationalism was "pervasive or enduring." What concerned Polier most was that Jews might respond by leaving the struggle for civil rights. "What concerns me, as a Jew," Polier said, "is not so much the phenomenon of Negro anti-Semitism but the response of the Jew to that phenomenon. It is all too easy and natural for the response to be one of resentment, fear, and hostility. . . . I am concerned lest these things happen to the Jew." Polier said he had faith that this would not happen because "the Jew will not betray his heritage."[85] At the same meeting, Stanley Lowell, chairman of the New York City Commission on Human Rights, also reproached Jews who would shirk their responsibilities in the struggle for equality because the "latent anti-Semitism of a fraction of the Negro community is now more open and apparent."[86]

While some Jewish race militants blamed Jews for Black anti-Semitism, which they believed was primarily a reaction to Jewish and white opposition to integration, others took a more indirect attack, arguing that Black anti-Semitism was essentially economic in nature, and blamed Jews for exploiting Blacks. Paradoxically, some of the race militants who took this approach found themselves admonishing Jews for their opposition to integration while demanding that they remove themselves as business owners from Black communities. The fear that Jews might be disproportionately responsible for Black economic exploitation was based on the old socialist belief that economic relations between sellers and buyers must always be hostile and on the mistaken notion that the objects of irrational prejudice could somehow reduce the amount of prejudice aimed at them by simply changing their behavior. Many Jewish race militants were bolstered in these beliefs by a selective reading of the work of the sociologist David Caplovitz, who found that the residents of poor neighborhoods were not only more likely to pay more for inferior goods and services but were also more likely to be taken in by dishonest and semidishonest marketing and financing schemes.[87] Interestingly, while Caplovitz made no attempt to quantify the Jewish element in ghetto business enterprise, he concluded that merchant-consumer relationships may take a variety of forms. While admitting that the outcome of these relationships may be hostile, Caplovitz stated that "It is of some interest that the [Jewish] salesmen are sometimes viewed as friends. I suspect that a more thorough study might show that the poor often turn to the merchants with whom they deal for a variety of services apart from merchandise . . . the poor may consider the merchants as their allies."[88] Anecdotal evidence from Black Americans like the comedian Dick Gregory and the economist Walter Williams, both of whom credit Jewish storekeepers in their predominantly Black neighborhoods with extending themselves to residents personally and financially, has tended to corroborate this view.[89]

While the nature of the economy of slum areas and the roles of the participants in it remains complex, many Jewish leaders chose to emphasize Caplovitz's negative findings regarding the sinister role of ghetto merchants and salespeople and used this to explain Black anti-Semitism. The well-known rabbi and author Harold Schulweis of Temple Beth Abraham in Oakland, California wrote of his experience in which a Black friend had told a joke implying that Jews exploit Blacks economically and insisted that, because of the truthful essence of this joke, Blacks had a right to be anti-Semitic. After this experience, Rabbi Schulweis did his own research and diligently read not only Caplovitz's work but writings by such militant Blacks as Jeremiah X, James Baldwin, and Louis Lomax, and he concluded that his Black friend was right—Blacks have a right to hate Jews. "I will not deny it," wrote Schulweis, "I do not relish the thought of meeting up with my Black friend again." The solution for Jews in Schulweis's determination was to remove themselves from the Black ghetto altogether. "There is always an alternative to complicity with evil. The alternative for the Jew is to get out. GET OUT. This is no way for Jews to make a living." [90]

The line of reasoning that asked Jews to integrate more fully with Black Americans while simultaneously demanding that Jews dismantle any remaining neighborhood contact with Blacks by closing or selling Jewish-owned shops and buildings in Black neighborhoods found adherents on the editorial board of the *Reconstructionist*. The editors of this prominent Jewish journal of opinion claimed that "anti-Semitism" tended to escalate with the rise in retail prices "because Jewish retailers are held most responsible." It was recommended that a large fund be established to settle Jewish storekeepers in other neighborhoods. Strangely, just as they had recommended the separation of certain Blacks and American Jews, they simultaneously called for a cooperative effort to increase personal contacts between Jews and Blacks. "So long as Jews know only maids, porters and other menial workers, and so long as Negroes know only landlords and storekeepers, a wholesome and constructive dialogue between the two groups will never be achieved." [91] Apparently, the *Reconstructionist* editors were beset by a peculiar class chauvinism that held that respectful relationships between Blacks and Jews could be achieved only by individuals who shared the same professional rank.

Many of the Jewish race militants did not consider that the emergence of populist and anti-Semitic elements from the civil rights movement might constitute a reasonable pretext for Jews to reevaluate their support for the more militant aspects of the civil rights movement and preferred to quell the complaints of the Jewish rank-and-file rather than address rising anti-Semitism among Blacks. In their effort to maintain their links to the Black cause, it seems some of the most liberal of the Jewish leaders forgot to stand up for the most important liberal ideals. The militance of some Jews on the issue of racial integration prevented them from making the cultural decay of American Jewry and the question of how the civil rights struggle in the North affected Jews the first priority. In their one-dimensional use of the concepts of social justice and Jewish commitment, the race militants never acknowledged that hesitation among Jews on the issue of integration could have been, in some instances, an honest disagreement over the specific applications designed to achieve justice and equality for Blacks, rather than a disagreement over the general principles. While racism undoubtedly existed among American Jews, it seems probable that consideration of Black demands for integration involved an array of concerns that went to the heart of Jewish identity and communal survival.[92]

Jewish Social Theorists and Integration

Given the importance to American Jews of maintaining formal and informal group ties, it is not surprising that a few Jewish social theorists emerged as the most important champions of the view that Blacks constitute an ethnic group similar in kind to other ethnic groups, rather than a unique social category. While these theorists were likely to acknowledge the unique problems faced by Blacks, they generally sought, through the interpretation of race relations and the solutions to racial inequality that they advocated, to steer Black activism between the generally accepted parameters of urban group interaction. This view largely reflected ambivalence with respect to Jewish culture and ethnic attachment. Specifically, the liberal universalism that so many Jewish intellectuals shared, and the value it placed on the primacy of individual choice in human relations, prevented them from seeing the ethnic group as anything more than a conduit for values that may provide the individual with useful economic tools but that could not be a dynamic and structurally central force in a person's life. Accordingly, they acknowledged that slavery and racism had taken a huge toll on the Black sense of identity and unity and that Blacks had first to become a united ethnic group with a strong sense of history and culture if they were to better compete in the urban environment. But they generally insisted that this unity be based not on race militance or on a strict color consciousness, which might inhibit or restrain individual Blacks from participating in a common culture or from attaining cherished personal aspirations. As a result, these theorists often found themselves in the awkward position of espousing Black solidarity and self-help, while rejecting Black nationalist solutions that appeared to threaten individual autonomy. To put it another way, through their interpretation of race relations in the United

States, some Jewish social theorists hoped to encourage the making of a Black ethnic group along the lines of the liberal Jewish one into which they themselves had been born. Whether this liberal pluralistic model of group relations, in which the primacy of individual choice is preserved along with the existence of ethnic subcommunities, was an appropriate one for Black Americans has become a topic of heated debate among scholars and activists over the past couple of decades.[93] But few have acknowledged that this model of liberal pluralism may not have been the social arrangement most conducive to Jewish communal sustenance.

While the reasons for the attachment of Jewish academics and intellectuals to liberal universalism are complex, a number of explanations have been proffered, including such psychological manifestations as "alienation," "marginality," and "self-hate."[94] But the idea that Jewish intellectuals felt "alienated" or "marginalized" in a postwar America characterized by increasing levels of tolerance seems less robust than it might have before the war.[95] While it is true that Jewish academics have been found to be relatively uncommitted to Jewish religion, they have also not been totally detached from ethnic group concerns.[96] Rather, at least among those in the social sciences and the humanities, Jewish attraction to liberal universalism can probably best be explained in terms of an unapologetic urban cosmopolitanism. Jewish intellectuals were generally beneficiaries and advocates of the "cosmopolitan" ideal that was ascendant among American intellectuals through the mid-1960s and that promoted the view that the ability to apply reason to experience united all people and was more important than the inherited characteristics that divided them.[97] The assumption upon which the ethos of cosmopolitanism was predicated, that the individual worth of human beings came not from the race or ethnic group into which they were born but from the ability to contribute to areas of knowledge in which all can equally share, carried tremendous appeal for second-generation Jewish intellectuals, many of whom still felt stigmatized by the immigrant ghettos of their youth. For these Jews, creating a society in which the inherited differences between people were tolerated but in which all men were considered the same under the skin was perhaps the most worthy objective.[98]

This liberal cosmopolitanism impacted the view of a number of prominent Jewish sociologists and critics of ethnic groups in the United States, including such renowned figures as the sociologist Nathan Glazer and the influential social theorist Irving Kristol. Nobody did more than Glazer in the early 1960s to promote the idea that Blacks would soon constitute an ethnic group in America's Northern cities, an equal among the family of American ethnic groups. In a number of well-known articles, and in his seminal sociological tract of 1963, *Beyond the Melting Pot,* written with Daniel P. Moynihan, Glazer set forth the ideas that would become for the next decade the guiding philosophy on American ethnic groups.[99] Confronting directly the idea put forth by Will Herberg and others that American white ethnic groups had "melted" away in the decades immediately following World War II, Glazer argued that in fact the ethnic identities of most Americans, particularly in large urban areas, remained intact and meaningful for political, sociological, economic, and psychological purposes. By the third generation, Glazer believed, the descendants of immigrants had become "Americans" in dress, language, and most vital concerns, but he found that they still voted differently, had different ideas about sex and education, "and were still, in many essential ways, as different from one another as their grandfathers had been."[100] While many interpreted Glazer's thesis as a celebration of ethnicity, in fact the key to the success of this plural system was the primacy of individual choice. "Individual choice, not law or rigid custom, determines the degree to which any individual participates, if at all, in the life of an ethnic group, and assimilation and acculturation proceed at a rate determined in large measure by individuals."[101]

Glazer treated Blacks in New York City as one group in a society made up of a number of ethnic and interest groups, which, as such, would fight to improve the lives of individuals through existing economic and political channels and, in some instances, through alliance with other ethnic groups. While the situation of Blacks was different in degree and intensity, their movement up the economic and social scale would closely resemble the upward movement of other ethnic groups. Unlike those in the South, Glazer argued that racial attitudes in the North were, at least in the legal and political realms, of the "American creed" and that, particularly in New York City, "the larger American experience of the Negro, based on slavery and repression in the South, would be overcome, as the Negro joined the rest of society, in conflict and accommodation, as an ethnic group."[102]

Irving Kristol was also disturbed by the idea of treating Blacks as a special "pathological" case because of their history of discrimination. In a provocative analysis, Kristol argued that the situation of Black Americans in Northern cities differed from that of previous ethnic groups in obvious ways but that the widespread similarities with other immigrant groups in Northern cities far outweighed these differences. Kristol believed not only that increasing numbers of Blacks were joining the middle class but that there were in fact historical antecedents for the Black condition, particularly in the case of Irish immigrants in the mid-nineteenth century. If anti-Black prejudice in the mid-1960s was worse than anti-Irish prejudice ever was, Kristol argued, public policy was far more powerfully antidiscriminatory than it had been previously, and Blacks were securing much more assistance from government than any other group had before. "It is impossible to strike any kind of precise equation out of the opposed elements," wrote Kristol, "but my own feeling is that they are not too far from balancing each other." [103]

It seems that for Glazer and Kristol, the problem for Blacks was not that they fell outside the ethnic pattern but that they had been so badly off within it and that this had a lot to do with the perceived lack of a definable and distinct culture that could unite Blacks in a community based on self-help. In this belief, they were undoubtedly influenced by the example of the American Jewish community, which itself had benefited from a long tradition of communal service and self-help, including the establishment of settlement houses, Young Men's and Young Women's Hebrew Associations, family desertion bureaus, educational alliances, and job training agencies.[104] While it is difficult to determine how important these communal self-help efforts were for individual Jews, the stress that some Jewish ethnic theorists put on self-help as the central characteristic of successful ethnic groups reflected the secular and utilitarian standard by which they measured the value of ethnic-group belonging. This utilitarian view of ethnic groups can be seen in the thin and narrow lines along which the Jewish social theorists tried to walk with respect to Black solidarity under the program of "Black Power" and what this revealed about their attitudes toward the Jewish community. The qualifications with which they laced their calls for Black self-help, the virulence with which they criticized the movement toward Black solidarity on the basis of essentialist notions of race, reflected not only the liberal cosmopolitan approach to ethnic cultures but also the deep personal ambivalence with which they viewed Jewish ethnicity.

There is no doubt that the impulse for social organization and mutual self-help among Black Americans was stifled from the earliest days of enslavement. Slave codes brought to the United States from the Caribbean, and later adopted into American colonial and state laws, prevented the gathering of more than four or five slaves without a white person present. Along with the Black Codes, which prevented commiseration between slaves, these devices effectively muted the development of unity and the sense of a shared fate. To be sure, free Blacks in both the North and South did organize themselves into a number of successful societies dedicated to self-improvement and uplift, but these were generally decimated by restrictive legislation in the South, and by immigrant agitation in the North. More important historically was the emergence of the self-help philosophy of Booker T. Washington at the turn of the century, which favored the development of usable job skills, and, of Marcus Garvey in the 1920s, who championed Black entrepreneurship and helped institute "Buy Black" campaigns. But, in the postwar era, the need to institutionalize Black self-help took a back seat to the fight for full legal rights associated with such organizations as the NAACP. By the late 1950s, the goal of legal equality had come to dominate Black life at the expense of the goals of communal self-improvement.[105] This was one reason for the growing appeal of the Black Muslims in the 1960s. The Black Muslims had reached deep inside the Black community to activate the latent impulse for self-help that had been nurtured so effectively by Booker T. Washington and Marcus Garvey. While the Muslims did not relinquish the belief that whites were ultimately responsible for the degradation of Blacks, they did preach that the worst crime committed by whites was inculcating in Blacks the idea of their own inferiority. Accordingly, in what is widely considered to be one of the greatest ironies in American radicalism, the Muslims preached the virtues of chaste middle-class behavior and Black enterprise and became staunch advocates of values very similar to those associated with the white Protestant ethic.[106]

While the Black Muslims remained a small minority in the Black community, attracting no more than one hundred thousand members and experiencing only marginal growth between 1960 and 1964, their call for Black self-help was a major impetus for the emergence of Black Power and Black separatism in the middle and late 1960s. The Black Power movement was the general description of that portion of the civil rights movement that became dissatisfied with integration and the principle of nonviolence.[107] In the Northern cities, Black Power's meaning became more vague, with some Black leaders using the slogan as a means for communal separation and other militants using it as a political tool to obtain such controversial demands as preferential hiring and communal control of school districts.[108] Be that as it may, the one thing most Black Power activists agreed on was the need to sustain a more intense Black consciousness, the foundation for which was the sanctification of the historical legacy of white racism.

While the emphasis on race as a unifying theme may have been necessary and inevitable in a nation that had for so long justified its subjugation of Blacks on the basis of skin color, it caused some Jewish social theorists to sour on Black Power as a solution to Black problems. The difficulty emerged primarily because the Jewish theorists tended to view the ethnic group as a voluntary social construct that could assist individuals in making their way in the world but not as something that required complete separation and absolute loyalty. It seems likely that the centrality of individual choice in this view of pluralism had much to do with the attempt on the part of these theorists to balance the needs of the individual against the exigencies of group self-help by finding a Black nationalist alternative to the Black Muslims, one in which individual choice would be preserved and a narrow racial essentialism rejected.

Irving Kristol, for example, attempted to revive the self-help ideal of Booker T. Washington, claiming that militance was not "everything" and that no people could regain its dignity by forgetting its forefathers. Kristol drew an analogy between the Black separatist impulse to repudiate the Black "Uncle Tom" image and the similar impulse that had characterized Jewish nationalism in the nineteenth century. At that time Jews revised their own history by substituting fighting Jews like Bar-Kochba for the saintly self-effacing Jews like Rabbi Akiba, who negotiated with the Romans to preserve a "saving remnant" of Judaism. Just as Bar-Kochba was the Jewish equivalent of the Black slave rebel Nat Turner, and Rabbi Akiba the Jewish Uncle Tom, there was even a movement to replace surnames given the Jews by "gentile" authorities with Hebrew names, just as Blacks were looking to replace their "slave" names in the 1960s. Eventually, when Jews established the state of Israel and anti-Semitism declined, this tendency diminished, and Jews realized that the interpretation of their history as one long series of heroic rebellions omitted much that defined the character of the Jewish people. Now, too, Kristol felt, Blacks were in jeopardy of losing important parts of their history, including the dignity with which "Uncle Tom" and Booker T. Washington comported themselves, particularly Uncle Tom's demonstration that even when Blacks were physically enslaved, they were never spiritually enslaved. "The Negro," wrote Kristol, "having achieved equality, will still have to establish a satisfactory sense of his own identity. And on this question, there appears to be at present more confusion than is desirable."[109] In order to take their place as a group among equals, Kristol argued, Blacks would have to be more of a community than they currently were, but those Black separatists who attacked the Black middle class as submissive "Uncle Toms" were doing a terrible disservice. It was the economic success of the Black middle class, after all, that would have to form the basis for the success of Blacks in the future. For Kristol, with each step toward equality it was becoming more urgent for Black Americans to achieve a "proud and meaningful collective definition of their past," but he wondered if it was necessary for "the American Negro [to] deny his past and debase his present to seize his future?"[110]

The most serious attempt to find a more moderate Black nationalism and to repudiate the racial extremism of the Black Muslims came from the sociologist Howard Brotz, whose landmark study *The Black Jews of Harlem* delved deeply into the question of cultural unity in the Black community.[111] Like Glazer, Brotz believed that the goal of the Black American should be "nothing less than the transformation into a normal American ethnic community, with its pride and community loyalty which are based not on resentment or hatred of whites but on an inward self-respect resulting from achievement."[112] But more clearly than the others, Brotz revealed his liberal faith in the ultimate goals of "normal American ethnic" communities: specifically, that they should be supportive and helpful to individuals, and that above all the primacy of individual choice as to the level of participation in ethnic life and belonging should be preserved.[113] Brotz argued that the struggle for civil rights had been harmful to the development of the Black community in that the fight against segregation tended to draw attention away from building self-help mechanisms. But, for Brotz, both the accommodationism of Booker T. Washington and the "protest" leadership associated with the civil rights militance of W. E. B. Du Bois left little room for the building of a viable Black nationalism. One relegated Blacks to a separate but unequal existence, and the other enjoined dependence on white society.[114] The key for achieving further success toward Black equality was the maintaining of ethnic choice for both Black and white communities. By this criterion, the doctrinaire Black nationalism of the Black Muslims failed as completely as the accommodationist and civil rights protest models, with its view that the only way for Blacks to gain respect was to leave the white community altogether or to dominate it. The problem with twentieth-century Black nationalist ideology as manifested by the Black Muslims and Marcus Garvey is that it responded not with the idea of a moral community but rather with the idea of a "sect" whose standards of Blackness an individual was not free to accept or reject. "Yet, is a Negro inwardly free if he feels less free to straighten his hair than a white person does to blacken himself in the sun?" asked Brotz.[115]

The challenge facing Black leadership, as Brotz laid it out was to create a voluntary community with such pride so that white society would feel free to woo Blacks. It was in this vein that Brotz looked to the example of the Black Jews of Harlem.

Like Black Muslims, with whom they shared many views and with whom they may in fact share a founder, a man named W. Fard who had studied Judaism and influenced Marcus Garvey before converting to Islam, the Black Jews began to appear in the 1920s.[116] They contended that Black Americans were really Ethiopian Hebrews, or Falashas, who were robbed of their religion and culture by slavery. Like the Muslims, they rejected the name "Negro," insisted that they must recover their religion again to become a viable community, emphasized entrepreneurship and sober living, and rejected pork and other foods, sexual promiscuity, and conspicuous consumption. But the Black Jews were not enamored of the absolute racial withdrawal from the white world or the unconditional race loyalty that the Muslims practiced, and this made them attractive to Brotz as the basis for a Black nationalist alternative. The emphasis for the Black Jews was on achievement, and their own educational institutions were considered a supplement to the public schools rather than a replacement. Brotz felt that this positioned the Black Jews well to influence individual Black success while fostering a certain amount of integration and acceptance, the hallmarks of the liberal approach to American ethnic groups.

It was not surprising that Nathan Glazer responded enthusiastically to Brotz's work, hailing his book as "the single most important intellectual contribution to the understanding of the Negro revolution that has yet been written."[117] The value that Glazer saw in Brotz's contribution was that it underscored the idea that assimilation in the United States had always been partial—that at some point the dominant groups expected that the assimilating group would want to hold back and maintain its cohesiveness.[118] But unwittingly, in championing the moderate nationalism of the Black Jews, Brotz and Glazer neglected to consider the important potential implications for the Jewish community. Characteristically, both writers dismissed the religious impulse toward Judaism of the Black Jews as secondary to the social advantages such a religious identification might offer for Blacks. As a culture, Judaism was useful for Blacks only insofar as it provided a tool by which they could gain communal autonomy and solidarity and thereby enhance the social and economic status of Black individuals. "From my sociological point of view," wrote Brotz, "it is this rather than the purely religious considerations which are the crucial aspect of this sect."[119] Neither Glazer nor Brotz considered that the religious impulse of Blacks toward Judaism, despite its mixture of mythology and theological distortion, could have provided renewed vigor and purpose to a Jewish community that had lost its ideological consensus. For these theorists, the cultural autonomy exhibited by the Black Jews, and the widening of the opportunities for assimilation this autonomy might bring, was of paramount importance. On the Jewish side of the issue, Brotz and Glazer simply never considered that the lack of a religious consensus among Jews presented a problem that might be addressed by the introduction of new and enthusiastic adherents to Judaic religious doctrines. The sociologist Milton Himmelfarb ventured to explain the lack of missionary fervor on the part of liberal Jews in general. "Diffident about our religion and tradition among ourselves," he wrote, "we can scarcely be expected to commend them to others. . . . In the United States, we could probably welcome a fair number of Negroes into our midst, if we wanted to. That would be good for them—so a Jew ought to assume—and especially good for us."[120] Rabbi Stephen Schwarzchild, the editor of the quarterly *Judaism,* took Brotz to task for his hands-off approach toward the Black Jews. The "only cogent question is whether these Negroes are now or are becoming Jews . . . perhaps Judaism will do for them, and they for us, exactly what the diagnosis of our common disease requires," Schwarzchild wrote.[121]

In the case of Nathan Glazer, it is particularly noteworthy that he did not see the Black Jews as an important spiritual opportunity for American Jewry, for he had by this time written extensively of the spiritual crisis plaguing American Judaism. In *Beyond the Melting Pot,* Glazer accurately described a Jewish community in New York that seemed to be losing its purpose. The failure of American Jews to develop a "satisfying pattern of Jewish middle-class life," Glazer wrote, "reflects the general unease of American middle-class life, as well as the specific Jewish dilemma of finding, in this amorphous society, a balance between separation and the loss of identity."[122] Nevertheless, Glazer believed that the solution to the crisis of American Jewry lay, not in looking inward, in reevaluating religious commitments and practices, or in reaching out to Black Jews, but rather in maintaining the historical commitment to liberal and radical causes. It was not, after all, the Jewish religion that had constituted the primary Jewish contribution to American life, according to Glazer, but rather the achievements of "gifted young Jews" in the arts, radical politics, and the labor movement. Glazer wondered where, with the disappearing of these "de facto" Jewish environments, these energetic young Jews would continue to come from. "One wonders about the supply of such young people in the future," wrote Glazer, "will they emerge from the comfortable middle-class group? One also wonders where they will go."[123]

Like so many other Jewish leaders, Glazer turned to the battle for racial integration as a way by which American Jews could revitalize themselves as a group and maintain their commitment to liberal and radical (i.e., Jewish) causes. Glazer's recommendation, astounding in light of the central role played by secular communal agencies in American Jewish life and identity, was the wholesale turnover of Jewish agencies to Blacks.[124] Entering a major debate within communal circles regarding the purpose of Jewish agencies in the United States, Glazer categorically sided with those leaders who felt Jewish energies and resources should be shifted toward a focus on the needy non-Jewish and nonwhite groups of the inner cities, and he used his considerable scholarly erudition to defend this position.

Despite the severe crisis of purpose American Jews were experiencing, Glazer argued that, among the three dominant ethnic minorities in the cities at the beginning of the 1960s—Catholics, Jews, and Blacks—Jewish needs were the least and their communal resources the greatest. Although Jews had not had many civic or political dealings with Protestants in the big cities, it was the WASPS whom they most resembled in their reform-mindedness, abhorrence of machine politics, and support for civil service laws. Moreover, to the extent that Jews wanted to maintain a separate subculture, Glazer pointed out that rarely did they demand help from the government in doing so. Compared to Catholics, who were concerned with the imposition of strict moral codes in the public sphere and public support of parochial schools, and Blacks, who looked to the public realm to right the wrongs of discrimination, "the Jewish group is the one that is capable of the greatest objectivity."[125] If American Judaism was to survive, Glazer believed, it would have to develop a tradition of "non-self-interested action for others." Jews must no longer "take it for granted . . . that their educational enterprises and welfare agencies should exist only to serve Jews, that in effect their responsibility in providing services for those damaged by life remains restricted to their own group," Glazer wrote.[126] But simply providing services for needy non-Jewish groups was not enough. Glazer suggested that Jewish agencies become public agencies rather than just "Jewish" agencies. This included the wholesale turning over of Jewish community centers and synagogue centers and intergroup relations agencies—"if one could think of any way of doing it"—to the Black community. "It would help us all in the end, if we could."[127] For Glazer, the turning over of Jewish communal agencies to Blacks was one way Jews could continue to be Jews.

The question of the destiny of Black Americans and American Jews in Glazer's early work brings us to the heart of a major interpretive debate in the field of ethnic group sociology. Glazer's liberal version of urban group dynamics as expressed in *Beyond the Melting Pot* and other works has in recent decades become the prototype for contemporary neoconservative ethnic analysis, having been redefined as such by radical scholars who reject the "ethnic" view of Black Americans and who caution against pounding "the square peg of race into the round whole of ethnicity."[128] But Glazer himself did not see his work from the early 1960s in a conservative light, and when we look at that work more closely it becomes apparent that he held views about the special needs of the Black community that only a short time later he himself would forcefully repudiate.[129]

Far from being someone who denied the unique difficulties faced by Blacks in the urban environment, Glazer was in fact quite sensitive to the special needs of Blacks and willing to consider substantial changes to the established pattern of group relations if it meant racial progress. For example, despite what he had written about preserving the integrity of ethnic group social networks, Glazer favored a militant approach to public school integration and empathized with Black parents who did not want to send their children to all-Black schools. "Negro parents cannot take the position that Irish or Jewish or Italian parents took before them—all this will change. . . . Their history is different, their situation is different, their sense of self-confidence and self-worth is different."[130] In light of this, Glazer supported the policy of "permissive zoning" championed by many integrationists and opposed by many white groups, not on the grounds that it would achieve the racial balance for which it was designed but rather on the grounds that it would provide greater freedom for the parents of Black children in poor neighborhoods.[131]

Perhaps the most surprising element of Glazer's early work concerned the issue of race preferences. By 1965 Glazer noticed that the substantial increases in funding for Black school districts had resulted in so little educational progress that the efficacy of continued increases in public spending had been thrown into doubt. In a move that seems ironic for the scholar who would later become the most articulate opponent of affirmative action, Glazer supported hiring professionals in social welfare, including teachers, on a racial group basis, a policy he felt might improve chances for the success of Black and Puerto Rican students.[132] It was within the Black and

Puerto Rican communities, Glazer felt, that the pressure for achievement, change, and improvement of the lower classes would most likely be found. "I think we can draw degrees of understanding and commitment from Negroes to help Negroes, Puerto Ricans to help Puerto Ricans, that we cannot in general expect to draw from professionals of other groups." This recommendation for preferential hiring would be "a special American way to the welfare state," in Glazer's view.[133]

Years later, Glazer would appropriately describe the kinds of positions he took in the early 1960s as "mildly radical," and this "mild" radicalism was as evident in the solutions he recommended for Black problems as they were in the solutions he recommended for Jewish problems.[134] If Glazer's recommendation that young Jews pursue "non-self-interested action for others" came to fruition in the involvement of Jewish youngsters in the radical political movements of the late 1960s, if race preferences in hiring would eventually become institutionalized, and if the consequences of both these developments were enough to make Glazer himself their most important and persuasive critic, one can only conclude that it might have been better never to have suggested what it would only later become necessary to repudiate.[135]

Jewish Communal Services and Racial Integration

Glazer's suggestion that Jewish agencies be turned over or dedicated to the cause of Blacks placed him in the middle of a major debate within the world of Jewish communal services. After World War II, differences arose in the ranks of Jewish communal service organizations over the division of resources between the concerns of society at large and those that were specifically Jewish. The vast institutional network of Jewish communal agencies found fewer and fewer Jews among its social service clientele, and Jewish communal leadership struggled over redefining those agencies' mission.

Some Jewish commentators felt that Glazer's suggestion of turning over Jewish agencies to Blacks was an invitation to greater Black anti-Semitism. C. Bezalel Sherman thought that the wholesale conversion of Jewish facilities into facilities for serving Blacks would go far toward creating expectations of Jews that were impossible to meet. "In essence, this is another way of attributing to the Jews greater responsibility for poverty among Negros. . . . Noble on the surface, such suggestions are in reality a disservice to the Negro community, whose crying need is self-improvement as part of its fight for equality."[136] Lloyd Gartner, a professor at the Jewish Theological Seminary, also thought it would probably not make sense for decaying Jewish agencies to convert into vibrant Black agencies because it would be most beneficial for Blacks to get the experience of establishing these institutions themselves.[137] William Avrunin of the Detroit Jewish Welfare Federation argued that, while Jews as individuals had a responsibility to take action to improve community services in communities where there were no Jews, this should not be done by Jewish agencies on a sectarian basis. "[T]he problems of the inner cities are far too vast for Jewish agencies to shoulder the burden alone," Avrunin concluded.[138]

On balance, however, Glazer's suggestion was popular among Jewish communal service leaders, most of whom believed that Jewish agencies had a part to play in the care of non-Jewish populations, that this role was indeed obligatory rather than optional, and that the Jewishness of the agency pointed to that obligation rather than called it into question.[139] Rabbi Seymour Cohen of Chicago, the vice president of the Synagogue Council of America, exclaimed that the Jewish community "has an abundance of resources—the experience and basic know-how in the field of family life" and asked if it would "be too much to ask that some of our skill be used to help the Negro family?" Cohen reported with pride that a number of Jewish community agencies had turned over their facilities to the Black community, pointing specifically to the establishment of the Anna B. Waldman center, the successor to the famed Irene Kaufman Settlement House in Pittsburgh.[140]

Many Jewish communal service leaders emphasized the idea that Judaism and Jewish institutions must maintain their "relevance" to the modern world in order to ensure Jewish continuity and that serving Black and other needy communities was an essential part of doing this. Once again, the attack on the Jewish middle class was integral to this argument. One participant at the 1963 annual meeting of the National Conference of Jewish Communal Service in Cleveland, Ohio, believed that it was the Jewish "skill of voluntary community involvement" that was the true Jewish contribution to American life and that that skill was indeed threatened by the move of the middle class to the suburbs.[141] Manheim Shapiro, an official of the American Jewish Committee and the editor of *The Jewish Digest,* attempted to redefine just what constituted a "Jewish purpose" regarding the obligations of Jewish agencies. Shapiro raised the question of whether it would not be a worthy "Jewish purpose" to provide services as Jews for

Blacks who needed them and could not otherwise obtain them. While there were circumstances in which "Jewish purposes" were served by having agencies be exclusively Jewish in composition, Shapiro attacked Jewish associationalism as a form of identity and maintained that it often served no sound Jewish purpose. "All too often, the legitimate association of Jews with each other for relevant group purposes is used as a rationale for irrelevant exclusion of others."[142] Shapiro took the opportunity to express his hostility toward the suburban Jewish "ghettos" by lambasting the Jewish tendency toward social exclusion. "Not only do they [the Jews] fail to meet Negroes, they also fail to meet white Christians on a friendly basis, and they even fail to meet other Jews of a background or commitment other than their own. In lives which are narrow and confined, in which comfort, convenience and sameness are the goals, we will have little opportunity to live out our belief in equality."[143]

One of the more thoughtful responses regarding the role of Jewish communal agencies in the civil rights struggle came from Rabbi Arthur Hertzberg, a noted historian of Zionism and a longtime leader in Jewish organizational life. At the annual convention of Jewish Communal Service in 1964, Hertzberg said that "segregation is immoral and abhorrent to Judaism," but he was ambivalent regarding the role of Jewish agencies in achieving integration. Hertzberg believed that, along with anti-Semitism, philanthropy was the only issue around which modern Jews have been able to unify themselves. "During the last two centuries," Hertzberg said, "Jews who have been able to agree on nothing else have found it possible to construct a community in which all share equally, and as Jews, on the basis of overarching responsibility for less fortunate Jews."[144] The problem for Hertzberg with using anti-Semitism and philanthropy as unifying forces was that they shared the unfortunate characteristic of eventually working against Jewish particularism by expanding their focus to populations other than Jews. Just as many Enlightenment Jews left the folds of Judaism to join radical forces and fight anti-Semitism by changing society under the rubric that "bigotry is indivisible," so too does Jewish charity respond to the "classic Jewish warrant" that "we must take care of the poor who present themselves to us without regard to race, creed, or color."[145] The more successful Jews are in providing charity to other populations, the less of a solidifying agent Jewish charity becomes. "Like anti-Semitism, charity, which was imagined as a last bastion of Jewish particularism, is the shading off into an activity which inevitably acts to dissolve the specific Jewish community."[146]

Hertzberg took issue with the arguments that Jews could not close off their charities to human suffering of any kind or refrain from contributing as Jews to the wider democratic society and argued that safeguarding a particular identity was not in itself an affront to other people. Jews "owe an obligation to say to ourselves and the Negro community that, from the Negro perspective, civil rights is indeed the problem, for Jews . . . it is one of several problems. It certainly does not outrank for them the question of their own spiritual and cultural survival in America, or their concern for the rest of world Jewry," Hertzberg wrote.[147]

Not surprisingly, most of the discussants at the National Conference of Jewish Communal service did not agree with Rabbi Hertzberg that the civil rights struggle and Jewish communal services run at cross purposes. Participants on the whole shared Nathan Glazer's view that Jewish agencies had a part to play in the civil rights struggle and that this was not only obligatory but would in fact work to restore Jewish purpose. The thrust of this position was that the aims and purposes of Jewish agencies and the need to remain "relevant" to contemporary problems pointed to that role rather than away from it.[148] The view of Albert Chernin, the director of community consultation for the National Jewish Community Relations Advisory Council, was representative. Chernin expressed concern that Rabbi Hertzberg's vision of a clash between Jewish survival and the civil rights revolution might shift the focus from what he saw as the fundamental threat to Jewish survival—"indifferentism and irrelevance." Chernin wrote that the universal nature of the Black struggle was not a threat to Jewish particularism because the essence of the Jewish experience was that it fostered a humanistic attitude and that the whole purpose of Jewish existence was to perpetuate the universal truths to which it was committed. "[T]he urgent business of Jewish community relations agencies, for that matter all Jewish agencies, is civil rights *and* Jewish survival," Chernin wrote. "They do not collide; on the contrary, they may be mutually reinforcing."[149]

The predominant view of some of the most distinguished Jewish social scientists and leaders of Jewish communal service was that the Jewish community could find meaning and purpose by participating in the Black fight for equality. The preoccupation of some Jewish social theorists with the development of a positive Black subculture reflected the positive social and economic experience American Jews had enjoyed as an ethnic subculture in the United States and the particular affection they felt for the new freedom and opportunities that had opened for them as individuals. But it also embodied the belief that the motive force underlying group unity should be voluntary and nonideological, a reflection of the liberal Jewish commitment to individualism and choice. For these Jewish figures, the test of group effectiveness was not the structure that the group provided to an individual's life, or the meaning one found in its core beliefs, values, and rituals, or the loyalty and obligations it demanded of its members, but rather how well it defended the social and economic interests of individuals. Most of these Jews held fast to this belief in analyzing the conditions of both the Black and the Jewish communities. For the Jewish social theorists Nathan Glazer, Howard Brotz, and Irving Kristol, as long as the ethnic group in question fostered the development of its individual members, it was viewed positively. Internal development and strengthening of group ties were acceptable so long as the long-range focus was on moving members up and out into the larger general culture. While Jewish social scientists and Jewish communal service leaders in general seemed aware of the growing cultural malaise of the Jewish community, few bothered to set a new direction for American Jews beyond attempting to revive, and in some cases radicalize, a civil rights liberalism that was quickly coming to the end of its life as a viable mode of Jewish identity.

Labor Zionism and De Facto Segregation

One group of Jewish thinkers that was consistently engaged with issues concerning Blacks were the Labor Zionists who wrote for the journal *Jewish Frontier*. The Labor Zionist movement in the United States is of particular interest in that its premises became, during the 1930s and 1940s, the basis upon which mainstream American Jewry would throw its support behind the creation of a Jewish state. Through its various youth groups, its intellectual leadership (which included such luminaries as Hayim Greenberg, Mordecai Kaplan, and Horace Kallen), and its influence at the pivotal Biltmore Conference of 1942 and the American Jewish Conference in 1943, the Labor Zionists were able to define a Jewish nationalism in accord with the predominantly liberal religious and political character of American Jews.[150] To a large extent, it was the Labor Zionist doctrine, a mixture of socialism and Zionism, that guided the activities of the *Yishuv*, the Jewish community in Palestine before the State of Israel was founded, as well as the first socialist government of the state of Israel under David Ben Gurion.

More interesting for the purposes of this book, the writers at *Jewish Frontier,* an English-language monthly that began publication in 1934, were, in the words of the sociologist Marshall Sklare, the "Jewy Jews." These writers were distinguished from most liberal Jewish intellectuals, including the famed "New York Intellectuals," in that they were boldly committed to a combination of Jewish nationalism, socialism, anti-Communism, and democracy. They aspired to be "nationalist without being chauvinist" and in this way separated themselves from Jews associated with liberal intellectual forums such as the *Menorah Journal, Commentary,* and *Reconstructionist,* all of which were generally less committed to a strong Jewish nationalism.[151]

The Labor Zionists were never of one mind on any political issue, but they expressed a uniform ambivalence about the compatibility of American liberalism and a strong and unified Jewish community. For example, the 1966 Labor Zionist Organization of America convention broke out in a huge debate over the issue of compensatory race preferences in employment. While the final convention statement contained an endorsement of compensatory race preferences in educational opportunity, it stopped short of endorsing them in the field of employment, where it asked for only the "expansion of opportunities." Those on both sides of the issue used the principles of Labor Zionism to arrive at their conclusions. The side that favored preferential treatment for Blacks in employment argued that, just as the Jewish people needed to gain access to its own land in order to achieve equality with other nations and utilized a form of international preference to obtain such access, so, too, did Blacks need preferred access to jobs to achieve equality with other groups in America. The delegates who opposed preferential treatment argued that the lesson of Labor Zionism, which emphasized the settlement and farming of the land in Palestine, was that a group of people can achieve equality and dignity only through its own labor, and not through the device of aid distributed on the basis of something other than merit.[152]

An even more provocative debate ensued over a proposal to counteract Black anti-Semitism by removing the Jewish presence in Black ghettos. The convention never did resolve this debate, and the proposal was never added to the final statement of the convention on the Zionist grounds that Jews should maintain their place and conduct themselves with dignity wherever they were. "Particularly resented," wrote Daniel Mann, "is any suggestion that the Jew as a Jew is responsible for anti-Semitism; this is precisely the 'defense mentality' which has been bitterly opposed by Zionists for years."[153] The convention also rejected the proposition that Jewish agencies should be maintained by Jewish funds for the primary purpose of funding programs for Black neighborhoods and clientele, a position favored, as previously discussed, by many Jewish communal service leaders.

Nevertheless, after World War II, and especially after the founding of the State of Israel in 1948, the Labor Zionists experienced an identity crisis not dissimilar to that of other American Jews.[154] As fighters and advocates for the Jews in America, Labor Zionists were quite sensitive to the nature of group life in the United States, but they were haunted and confused by their commitment to two sometimes conflicting goals: the Zionist commitment to Jewish peoplehood and the socialist commitment to universal equality. Equality was perhaps the one word most expressive of the Labor Zionist ideology: equality for Israel in the family of nations, equality for the Jews as an ethnic group in the United States, and equality as a social principle. In the end, despite the sincere commitment to the principle of Jewish communal strength, the commitment to social equality seemed to win out, leaving many of the Labor Zionists only a stone's throw away from the civil rights positions advocated by the majority of liberal Jewish leaders.

The ambivalence of the Labor Zionists toward racial integration was demonstrated in the debate tripped off by an article published in 1964 by Marie Syrkin, "Can Minorities Oppose 'De Facto' Segregation?"[155] In this controversial essay, Syrkin, the strong-minded daughter of the socialist Zionist theoretician Nachman Syrkin, argued that, except for avowed assimilationists, Jews had never made complete integration a goal and that the insistence of large segments of the Black community for complete integration posed a huge problem for American Jews.

Specifically, Syrkin explained that she had grown up in New York City in neighborhoods that were predominantly Jewish and had therefore attended predominantly Jewish public schools. While it was difficult to determine how much of this segregation was voluntary and how much forced, Jews never believed that the relative lack of gentiles in their presence was evidence of discrimination. Syrkin believed that in the Jews' struggle to achieve greater economic, social, and educational mobility, the emphasis was almost always on better housing and better education, "not on the enforced presence of non-Jews on the premises."[156] Syrkin wrote extensively on American education systems for such liberal journals as *Common Ground,* the official journal of the Common Council for American Unity, but broke with many of her liberal colleagues by insisting that, if the schools reflected the population of the surrounding area and its residential distribution and the school board had not been found guilty of excluding particular students, this could not reasonably be called segregation, for segregation implied a willful process of exclusion.[157] Syrkin concluded that "a minority may justly oppose the quality of housing, schooling or job opportunities available to it, but with what grace can it object to a preponderance of its own people?"[158]

What disturbed Labor Zionist writers about Syrkin's article was that it took the problem of their movement's clashing ideals head on. The suggestion of American Labor Zionists that vibrant Jewish communities could obtain in places other than Israel had never been put to a real test. While most of the Labor Zionists agreed that the traditional cohesion supplied by the Jewish religion had been shattered, few had been willing to offer a viable program for regaining it. Syrkin did just that when she argued that if Labor Zionist philosophy were to bear any fruit, it would require the "flesh and bones of a culture and a society—the Jewish neighborhood, the Jewish language, Jewish creative arts, Jewish cuisine—a sense of community."[159] Like other Jewish leaders and intellectuals, many Labor Zionists balked at this difficult proposal because of its open opposition to what they viewed as the legitimate struggle for Black integration. A symposium in *Jewish Frontier* held shortly after Syrkin's article appeared indicates that while Labor Zionists believed in the right of Jews and other minorities to self-segregate, their sensitivity to Black demands and their commitment to equality seemed to override this important Labor Zionist principle.

Many writers in the symposium agreed that Jews, as a persecuted minority, had much of interest to say about the race problem, but they maintained that Blacks faced special problems that Syrkin had ignored in her essay. "Let us at least afford to the Negro the same uniqueness that we have claimed in the past as Jews. When we discuss problems of education, let us do so with reference to the very special problem of the Negro as regards education," wrote Aaron Kohn, a member of the Central Committee of the Labor Zionist Organization of America. "When we discuss the problems of racial imbalance, let us realize the very special conditions for the Negro created by racial imbalance . . . and in considering these unique racial problems let us be prepared to arrive at solutions equal to the proportions of the problem."[160]

Daniel Mann, the executive director of the Labor Zionist Organization of America, insisted that the differences between Blacks and Jews were not only enormous but crucial, primarily because, with minor exceptions, Blacks did not have their own unique culture to live by in their own segregated communities. "Not only did you tear my ancestors away from their origins," wrote Mann of the Black American viewpoint, "but now you bar my access to your identity which should also be mine."[161]

Perhaps, though, the most reasonable and articulate response of the Labor Zionists to Syrkin's article was the answer supplied by the Zionist scholar Ben Halpern. Halpern criticized Syrkin's article for being too general and rejected some of its specific implications. How, Halpern asked, can we compare segregated trains, buses, or restaurants to schools? Certainly, Halpern insisted, the use of buses or trains carried nowhere near the same consequences as the type of school one attended. Schools were indeed compulsory, Halpern argued, because they were vital to success in achieving liberty, equality, and fraternity and should therefore be subject to de facto desegregation before buses and cafeterias.[162] Syrkin, Halpern felt, was repulsed by demands for enforced de facto desegregation because of the Jewish situation, not necessarily because of the situation of Blacks. Halpern, in turn, was repulsed by Syrkin's unabashedness in thinking only of the impact on the Jewish community. Halpern noted that very few Black leaders feared the assimilation of their people but that assimilation was seen as a very real threat among Jews. "To oppose de facto segregation," wrote Halpern, "is in the eyes of the Jewish survivalist, to support assimilation. . . . But cannot Jewish leaders have enough sympathy with the Negro situation to understand if this reaction is not shared by the Negro leadership?"[163]

While Halpern appropriately asked Syrkin to see the Black position, the question he and the other respondents failed to address was the one asked by Syrkin herself in her article: How could a minority "survive without either a sacrifice of its identity or its equality," particularly in a society that was moving toward representative equality and forced integration.[164] In the end, the majority of Jewish thinkers associated with Labor Zionism, sensitized to the Black condition by Jewish history, arrived at a view of Black demands for full integration not so very different from that of the Jewish race militants and liberal social theorists. Like the other Jewish leaders and intellectuals, in negotiating the questions concerning group life in America that had been brought to the surface by the Black demand for integration, the Labor Zionists became consumed by the very real needs and demands of Blacks and neglected to address the pressing needs of the Jewish community for unity, direction, and inner purpose.

3

The New York Intellectuals and Their "Negro Problem," 1945–1966

You can't turn Black experience into literature just by writing it down.   —Harry Lesser in Bernard Malamud's *The Tenants*

Lesser, you tryin to fuck up my mind and confuse me. I read all about that formalism jazz in the library and it's bullshit. You tryin to kill off my natural writin by pretending you are interested in the fuckin form of it.
          —Willie Spearmint in Bernard Malamud's *The Tenants*

Comparisons of contemporary Black intellectuals with the famed "New York Intellectuals" of the 1940s, 1950s, and 1960s provide a convenient backdrop for the discussion of the approach to art, politics, and race of that mostly Jewish group of intellectuals Norman Podhoretz once referred to as the "family."[1] The New York Intellectuals constituted a loosely knit group of writers and critics who came of age during the 1930s to challenge the Communist influence in American intellectual life.[2] Over the next fifty years, and through roughly three generations of writers, these intellectuals used a small coterie of low-circulation, high-brow journals like *Partisan Review* and *Commentary* to heavily influence the direction of politics, literature, art, and culture in the United States.[3] Specifically, the New York Intellectuals attempted to foster a unique combination of anti-Communist, left-wing politics, and high modernism in literature and the arts. While their legacy is a hotly debated topic among academicians today, it is probably fair to say that the New York Intellectuals succeeded in delegitimizing the Stalinist influence in American cultural life and played a large role in the transfer of the modern art scene from Paris to New York in the 1950s.[4] But by the 1960s, the reappropriation of revolutionary Marxism by the New Left, the ascendancy of Black radicalism, and the romanticization of the Third World required that the New York Intellectuals reposition themselves in relation to the new radicalism. This resulted in the shattering of long-time friendships among the New York crowd and the splintering of the group. Combined with the subsequent deaths of a few key writers and the general dispersion of the American intellectual scene, this rupture has inspired some critics to lament the demise of the public intellectual. Most notably, Russell Jacoby in his 1987 book *The Last Intellectuals* writes disparagingly of university domination over American intellectual life and declares the New York Intellectuals the greatest and last group of critics to reach a large, educated public.[5] In the late 1990s, some critics suggest, a number of Black intellectuals, most of them associated with universities, have stepped into this void to take a public role in a United States consumed with issues of race, ethnicity, gender, and popular culture. Black academics like Cornel West, bell hooks, Gerald Early, and Henry Louis Gates Jr. are said to have revived the role of the public intellectual, "bringing moral imagination and critical intelligence to bear on the definingly American matter of race—and reaching beyond race" to voice what one critic calls "the commonality of American concern."[6] The extent to which the writing of these Black academics has bridged the gap between their highly specialized fields and often radical opinions and an educated general public has been the topic of at least one devastating critique.[7] But the comparison of the Black intellectuals with the New York Intellectuals of the past is instructive as much for the differences between the two groups as it is for the characteristics they share.

Some of the points at which the two groups diverge have much to do with the changing intellectual climate over the past few decades. The Black intellectuals are far more at home delving into the various forms of popular culture and deriving meaning and significance from them. In this they have participated in the general blurring of the lines between "high" culture and "low" culture that has occurred since the 1960s and which for all practical purposes has erased a distinction that was central to the modernist concerns of the New York Intellectuals. It is also the case that most of the Black intellectuals have risen to prominence within the academic fortresses of American universities, usually in Black studies departments, whereas most of the New York writers began their careers as free-lance critics and essayists, a distinction that is vital to understanding the role of Jewish intellectuals in American life and one that will be discussed more fully in the conclusion to this chapter. But most important, the New York Intellectuals and the Black intellectuals arrived at their feelings about their own identities as Americans from highly divergent starting points. "Although the New Yorkers are perhaps best known for their Jewishness," writes Robert Boynton, "it wasn't until relatively late in their careers that they made their ethnic heritage a conscious component of their intellectual lives. By contrast," Boynton continues, "most Black public intellectuals have had the concept of Blackness at the very center of their thinking from the start."[8] The New York Intellectuals were primarily second-generation immigrants who spent most of their early years trying to convince themselves and anyone else who would listen that their Jewishness did not matter on the most important questions in life. By contrast, the Black intellectuals, having been born into the firmament of the civil rights revolution of the postwar decades, were indoctrinated with the belief that politics and race are intricately and intimately connected. "What Marxism was to Lionel Trilling, Clement Greenberg, Philip Rahv, and company, Black nationalism is to West, Gates, Hooks, et al.: the inspiration, the springboard, the template, but also the antagonist and the goad," writes professor Martin Berube.[9] In other words, the Black intellectuals were born Black; the Jewish intellectuals had to discover their Jewishness.[10] While one must appreciate the increasingly dominant role of universities in American intellectual life, an understanding, at some level, that the Black intellectuals have come to prominence with a surfeit of institutional support, whereas the New York Intellectuals had to prove to the world that they were "Americans" before gaining widespread recognition, suggests that the Black past weighs far more formidably on the formation of American institutions than the Jewish past ever has. This point is central to an understanding of the historic role played by Blacks and Jews in the United States and, by extension, to the roles of Black intellectuals and Jewish intellectuals in American culture. That Black intellectuals have gained national prominence writing primarily about being Black, while the New York Intellectuals gained prominence, at least initially, by putting as much distance between themselves and their Jewishness as possible speaks volumes about this social dynamic. That the New York Intellectuals understood implicitly the rather inconsequential nature of the cultural relationship of Jews to the United States is evinced in their attempts to balance the requirements of Jewish culture and American culture, of modernism and politics, and of race and art. Looking back, the efforts of the New York Intellectuals to create a truly cosmopolitan high culture based on the standards of Western modernism may have been an impossible dream, given the ferocity of the current opposition to such a goal. But it was also probably more successful than any other attempt before or since to create a common high culture in the United States in which all can share equally. Perhaps more interesting is the way in which the New York Intellectuals struggled with their own place as Jews in creating such a shared culture, and the intellectual acrobatics some of them engaged in when they discovered that the Black experience in the United States did not lend itself to the ideals of ethnic choice and the aesthetic autonomy of art upon which so many of them had staked their careers.

Jewishness and the New York Intellectuals

In a well-known essay, Irving Howe wrote that the New York Intellectuals represented perhaps America's only claim to an intelligentsia and ascribed to them the following characteristics: they were anti-Communist, radical, and had a fondness for ideological speculation; they wrote literary criticism with a strong social emphasis; they "revel[ed] in polemic"; they strove self-consciously to be "brilliant"; they played a role in the internationalization of American culture, "serving as a liaison between American readers and Russian politics, French ideas, and European writing"; and they were "by birth or osmosis" Jews.[11] Howe's inference that all of the intellectuals associated with this group were Jews is, of course, not true. Non-Jewish associates of the group included such notables as Elizabeth Hardwick, Dwight MacDonald, Edmund Wilson, Mary McCarthy, F. W. Dupee, William Barrett, James Baldwin, and Richard Chase, as well as such "kissing cousins" as Robert Lowell, Ralph Ellison, John Berryman, Murray Kempton, Michael Harrington, and James Agee. Nevertheless, Norman Podhoretz, a member of the third and last generation of New York Intellectuals, justified the term "Jewish" to describe this milieu on the basis of "clear majority rule and by various peculiarities of temper."[12] The overwhelming majority of New York Intellectuals were of Jewish background, and the concerns and preoccupations of the group over the decades reflected its Jewish composition.

Given the Jewish makeup of this intellectual family, it is interesting to note how completely the New York Intellectuals reflected the crisis of Jewish ambivalence in America. Largely the children of immigrant Jews who wanted to break free of their parent's tradition-bound world, the New York Intellectuals originally viewed themselves as "marginal men" caught between a Jewish culture they no longer wanted and an America that did not fully accept them. The sociologist Daniel Bell has written that for the bulk of Jewish intellectuals, the anxiety was translated into the struggle between fathers and sons: "Few generational conflicts have had such exposed nakedness, such depths of strain as these."[13] A poignant depiction of this strain takes place in Isaac Rosenfeld's novel *Passage From Home.*[14] The protagonist, Bernard, describes a scene in which his father enters his bedroom, walks around, and stops in front of the bookcase, staring at the books. "He always seemed to regard them as strange and remote objects, symbols of myself, and they related to him—it was with his money that I had bought them—and yet as alien and hostile as I had myself become."[15] "Nobody," Irving Howe wrote, "who has been brought up in a Jewish family . . . can read this passage without feeling that there is true and accurate perception."[16]

This feeling of marginality among the New York Intellectuals explained a great deal about their attraction to radicalism in the 1930s. They sought not to hide their Jewishness or to pass for non-Jews but to "overcome" their Jewishness by putting it behind them.[17] In fact, being of Jewish background seemed to endow them with a special gift for radicalism. As Jews, most of the intellectuals had been restricted from careers in universities and other avenues of employment and had witnessed the frightening rise of anti-Semitism in the United States between the world wars. This only compounded their feelings of alienation derived from the history of persecution their parents brought with them to America and fastened them on the side of the persecuted. Unlike the non-Jewish radicals of the period, therefore, the New York Intellectuals were also attracted to radicalism because it allowed for a degree of continuity with their Jewish past and served as part of their transition from the ghetto to the larger society. In the end, wrote one historian, they "joined because the radical movement provided specific outlets for . . . [their] talents . . . and because it allowed them to apply their heritage in a new and appropriate manner, rather than requiring to cast it off. . . . They planned to be emissaries from their parents' world, not exiles."[18]

The Jewish intellectuals did not convert or renounce their Jewishness, then, but neither did they strongly affirm it. In a February 1944 symposium entitled "Under Forty: American Literature and the Younger Generation of American Jews," conducted by the *Contemporary Jewish Record,* the pre-

cursor to *Commentary* magazine, many of the core players in the first generation of this New York Intellectual milieu expressed their ambivalent
feelings toward being Jewish.[19] The most prominent literary critic of the
group, Lionel Trilling, maintained that "as the Jewish community now
exists, it can give no sustenance to the American artist or intellectual who
is born a Jew."[20] The art critic Clement Greenberg voiced similar feelings,
writing that "Jewish life in America has become, for reasons of security, so
solidly, so rigidly, restrictedly, and suffocatingly middle class. . . . No people
on earth are more correct, more staid, more provincial, more common-
place, more inexperienced."[21] The writer and critic Alfred Kazin asked
what was Jewish about the American Jew—"What does he believe, especially in these terrible years, that separates him at all from our national
habits of acquisitiveness, showiness, and ignorant brag?"[22]

To the extent that Jewishness offered the New York Intellectuals the
psychological posture of "alienation" and put them in an advantageous
position to lead the political or cultural avant-garde, they flaunted it. The
poet Delmore Schwartz, for example, declared that, through anti-Semitism,
"the fact of being a Jew became available to me as a central symbol of
alienation, bias, point of view, and certain other characteristics which are
the peculiar marks of modern life, and I think now, the essential ones."
But for the most part, Jewishness was allowed no broader claims.[23]

Nevertheless, a number of postwar developments seriously challenged
alienation as a common mode of identity for the New York Intellectuals.
During the 1940s and 1950s, the decline of anti-Semitism resulted in the
widespread recognition of the work of some New York Intellectuals, and
the broad audience of mass-circulation magazines began to open up for
many of them. The novels and criticism of such writers as Saul Bellow,
Isaac Rosenfeld, Delmore Schwartz, Lionel Trilling, Alfred Kazin, Bernard
Malamud, and Philip Roth began to attract widespread attention, as did
the art criticism of Clement Greenberg, Harold Rosenberg, and Meyer
Shapiro. Other New York Intellectuals found jobs in universities that had
previously been closed to them, all of which made further declarations of
alienation seem unbecoming. Another factor in the postwar changes was
the experience of the New York Intellectuals with the Communists during
the war. Disturbed by the willingness of the Communist groups on American soil to countenance Stalin's dictatorship, as well as by the barbarity
visited by fascism on Europe, the New York Intellectuals began to regard
the middle class as an important bulwark against totalitarianism.[24] Eventually, the impact of the Holocaust occasioned a reevaluation of what being

Jewish meant to the New York Intellectuals. The Holocaust weighed heavily on the psyche of the New Yorkers in a way they did not realize until
much after the war, a delayed response that Irving Howe called a kind of
"culture lag," a "recognition behind reality."[25] The Holocaust obviously
caused Alfred Kazin to rethink his disdain for the common Jews about
whom he had written with such derision during the war. In his autobiographical *New York Jew*, Kazin wrote, "[I]n my private history of the world
I took down every morsel of fact and rumor relating to the murder of my
people. . . . I could imagine my father and mother, my sister and myself,
our original tenement family of 'small Jews,' all too clearly—fuel for the
flames, dying by a single flame that burned us all up at once."[26]

Before the war, Irving Howe confessed that the sense of Jewishness in
intellectuals like himself tended to be overshadowed by a commitment to
cosmopolitan culture and socialist politics. "We did not think well or
deeply on the matter of Jewishness—you might say we avoided thinking
about it," Howe wrote.[27] But after the war, many Jewish intellectuals found
it difficult and unnecessary to continue subordinating their Jewishness to
other commitments and he came to regard himself as a "Jewish intellectual
with cosmopolitan tastes," as efforts "to grapple with the Holocaust, all
doomed to one or another degree of failure, soon led to timid reconsid-
erations of what it meant to be Jewish."[28]

The impact of the Holocaust on the New York Intellectuals was demonstrated by the torrid response evoked by Hannah Arendt's essay *Eichmann
in Jerusalem: A Report on the Banality of Evil*, which appeared originally in
the *New Yorker* magazine.[29] Reporting from Israel on the trial of the Nazi
war criminal Adolph Eichmann, Arendt tried to fit the Nazi slaughter of
the Jews into her highly regarded theory of modern totalitarianism.[30] Essentially, Arendt saw Eichmann and the other Nazi officers who oversaw
the destruction of European Jewry as "banal" rather than personally evil,
mere cogs in the wheel of a highly technical system that defied conventional political categories. Arendt also implicated the Jews in their own
destruction, charging that the Jewish councils, some of which had coop-
erated with the Nazi authorities, were a part of the totalitarian system. The
response to Arendt's reportage was fierce. Both Howe and his colleague
Lionel Abel, not satisfied with writing critical reviews, held a symposium
and protest meeting about the book at the Hotel Diplomat in midtown
Manhattan at which a throng of New York Intellectuals and others
pounded tables and shouted their views on the Arendt thesis. Norman
Podhoretz not only wrote a critical review of Arendt's essay in *Commentary*

but debated Arendt in the spring of 1965 in a University of Maryland gymnasium packed with supporters for both sides.[31] Podhoretz had written his critical review despite personal fears that doing so would end his close relationship with Arendt. The relationship did in fact cool considerably.[32] Howe later said of Arendt's book that it was one of the most troubling intellectual events of the 1960s for him and that this was so probably because of the guilt he experienced over his initial tepid response to the Holocaust.[33]

But if the greater acceptance of Jews in America and the Nazi Holocaust forced some of the New York Intellectuals to reconsider their Americanness and their Jewishness, these reevaluations were not consistent or uniform within the group. Some New York Intellectuals became enthusiasts of the existentialist Jewish philosopher Martin Buber or of Hasidism. Irving Howe began a long career of translating and publishing Yiddish literature. Alfred Kazin discussed his Jewish immigrant upbringing in *A Walker in the City* (1951), and Lionel Trilling even wrote about "Wordsworth and the Rabbis."[34] But of the efforts by some writers like Harold Rosenberg, Clement Greenberg, and Paul Goodman to redefine their Jewishness in the late 1940s and early 1950s, Irving Howe explained that they "wrote with some wariness, as if determined not to surrender the stance of marginality; they were fearful of even appearing to return to the parochialism of middle-class Jewish life."[35] In general, the tolerance expressed by some New York Intellectuals for the American middle class was not shared by all and certainly did not extend to the American Jewish community or to religious observance. As Norman Podhoretz noted, "If most of the contributors to the 1944 [*Contemporary Jewish Record*] symposium later came to discover great fascination and virtue in traditional Jewish culture, very few of them ever acknowledged the unfairness of the charge that Jewish life in America bore no trace of the admirable characteristics of the Jewish past."[36]

By and large, after World War II the New York Intellectuals faced a question similar to the one faced by the American Jewish community as a whole: what should constitute Jewish identity and distinctiveness when the walls of exclusion and prejudice come tumbling down? The Holocaust and the expanding opportunities of the postwar decades rendered "alienation" obsolete as a mode of Jewish identity, a fact evinced by the reaction of the New Yorkers to the Beat writers of the 1950s; but their relationship to Jewish life and thought remained ambiguous.

Alienation and the Black Hipster

Black culture has often constituted something of a counterculture in the United States, and Black men have long been associated with the national "id." Lively debates have racked the social sciences over the origins of Black culture in the New World, but there is no doubt that a distinctive Black cultural style dating back to the days of slavery had emerged in the United States, based on resistance to white oppression and, in many instances, the repudiation of white norms.[37] In the twentieth century the confluence of large-scale Black migration to Northern cities, Black ghettoization, and the hope arising from new opportunities saw the maturation of this Black "counterculture." By the 1920s, Black culture took the forms of the hot jazz music of Louis Armstrong and the new Black urban style. Jazz music was both dangerous and liberating in that it provided an expressive outlet for the idea that the human body might be the most important source of freedom and happiness in a world marked by oppression and sadness.[38] The "hipster" was the name given to the new Black man of the streets who developed a cultural style that would, in succeeding decades, become the dominant motif in American popular culture. The hipster was heir to a Black cultural legacy that, along with music, dance, and dialect, was perhaps its most persistent idiom: the archetypical Black male renegade who refuses to abide by the law, practices intimidation, and often garners the stamp of the "bad nigger." The "bad nigger" has long been a source of pride among Blacks, dating back to a time when runaway slaves were called "ba-ad nigger" by other slaves.[39] In the 1920s and the decades that followed, the "hipster" was in many ways a manifestation of the "bad nigger," a miscreant who experimented with new variations on the theme of Black deviance.

By the late 1940s, a number of white radicals had become attracted to the "hip" culture of "bebop," a technical innovation in jazz music developed by Black musicians, which also served as a protest against the failure of the commercialized "swing" movement.[40] As LeRoi Jones (later Amiri Baraka) explains in his book *Blues People,* bebop functioned as a reaction against white swing and placed Black music once again "outside the mainstream of American culture."[41] To the hedonistic sensibility already prevalent in the jazz world, the hipsters added an unmistakable note of social and political revolt. For some white radicals, bebop offered the authenticity and cool cynicism they found impossible to retrieve from Cold War-obsessed mass culture and the complacent political liberalism that accompanied it.[42] A number of white intellectuals, in particular the "beat" writers

Herbert Huncke, William Burroughs, and Jack Kerouac, paid homage to this Black underworld, but a few intellectuals associated with the New York crowd did as well.[43]

No one even marginally associated with the New York Intellectuals went as far as the novelist Norman Mailer in championing the liberating image of the "bad nigger." In his famous essay "The White Negro," Mailer insisted that the Black male was the quintessential modern man, alienated from all things but his most basic needs and the antidote to mind-numbing suburban conformity. The Black man in America, Mailer wrote, had two alternatives—to live a life of complete subjugation or to live a life of constant danger—and this condition allowed him to break the dull monotony of middle-class life to become America's only true existentialist, "the man who knows that if our collective condition is to live with instant death by atomic war, relatively quick death by the State . . . or with a slow death by conformity . . . then the only life-giving answer is to accept the terms of death . . . to divorce oneself from society, to exist without roots, to set out on that uncharted journey into the rebellious imperatives of the self."[44]

There had been after World War II, according to Mailer, a ménage à trois of the Black male, the Bohemian, and the white juvenile to form the white hipster, and Mailer enlisted the Black hipster's white counterpart in the cause of undermining the values and myths of the 1950s. "The hipster cuts through and exploits the hypocrisy of the period," wrote the critic Morris Dickstein, and "transcended the sham of suburban religiosity and churchgoing."[45] The hipster, both Black and white, was an American "countermyth" that served for radicals like Mailer to replace revolutionary Marxism as a way to shake America out of what they believed was an insidious postwar serenity. "In his search for a sexual life which will suit his orgiastic needs," Mailer wrote in defense of his controversial essay, "the hipster willy-nilly attacks conventional sexual morality. . . . If capitalist society is grounded upon property relations, these relations are wed to monogamy, family, and the sexual strictures which maintain them."[46]

Mailer received some support from a few of the New York critics who themselves were not content with the level of America's discontent. While many of these critics conceded that Mailer was prone to indulge in bouts of hyperbole and public posturing, they believed that the image of the white hipster was a compelling one whose defiance of American norms was worthy of serious attention. "In a queer but real sense, the hipster is the monk of the present Dark Ages," wrote the critic George Steiner. "The

Hipster is a living indictment of the American dream—of the belief in material success and 'well-adjustments.' " For Norman Podhoretz, Mailer alone among the writers of the 1950s approached the issue of sex on its own terms and brought to the subject a readiness to find the meaning of these terms. The literary critic Diana Trilling also believed in the efficacy of Mailer's project. His willingness to ask the ultimate question we are all faced with in our time—from which, the ego or the id, shall we derive our moral sanctions—and his success in facing the enormity of that question convinced Trilling that Mailer's talent was more than trivial.[47]

But, for the most part, the New York critics agreed that the Black hipster remained as much a myth as Mailer's imaginary white hipster. According to these critics, the white hipster and the Black hipster were not representative character types. One writer observed that, just as white hipsters disparaged Black hipsters when they weren't around for being narrowly interested in white women, the Black hipsters were prone to saying among themselves "man, those *fay* cats are pretty cool and don't want us to be Uncle Toms, but they still want us to be spooks. They don't really dig us as a people; they just dig us for our music and our pot."[48] For this reason, Ned Polsky remarked, the idealization of the Black male by many of the radical intellectuals and beatnik writers of the 1950s was "an inverted form of keeping the Nigger in his place."[49]

Ironically, Norman Mailer, who seemed to model his own personality on the white hipster, could not himself make the connection with the Black hipster he so strongly believed in.[50] The Black writer James Baldwin, a homosexual who had called Mailer's essay "downright impenetrable," wrote that his relationship with Mailer suffered in the 1950s from the white writer's refusal to give up the myth of Black sexuality. "The sexual battle-ground . . . is really the same for everyone, and I . . . was just about to be carried off the battleground on my shield . . . so how could I play, in any way whatever, the noble savage."[51] Baldwin explained that matters between the two were not helped much by the fact that the Black jazz musicians in Paris among whom they found themselves did not consider Mailer in any way "hip." Mailer did not know this, according to Baldwin, and Baldwin could not bring himself to tell him. "He never broke through to them . . . ," wrote Baldwin, "and they were far too 'hip' . . . even to consider breaking through to him. They thought he was a real sweet *ofay* cat, but a little frantic."[52]

For the most part, those New York Intellectuals who thought more often and more seriously about their own Jewish identities and about the relationship of Black Americans to society and culture did not subscribe to Mailer's idealized view of Black existence and preferred more specific treatises on the condition of Black Americans. Irving Howe, the editor of *Dissent* when that magazine published Mailer's article, wrote that he was "overwhelmed, delighted to have the piece" after Mailer had sent it to him but that he later experienced guilt over having printed the article in full, including parts that explicitly endorsed violence. "I should have fought with him about that one passage," wrote Howe, "the existential analysis of those hoodlums beating up the storekeeper—which I now think is pretty much nonsense."[53] Mailer himself later admitted to having second thoughts about the article, saying that he was afflicted by self-doubt at the time and was using drugs and that had written the piece primarily for the satisfaction of his own ego rather than to influence public opinion.[54] Norman Podhoretz may have been one of the first critics to hold up Mailer as a serious high-brow talent, but to the romanticization of Black men he gave no quarter. "I doubt if a more idyllic picture of Negro life has been painted since certain Southern ideologues tried to convince them things were just as fine as fine could be for the slaves on the old plantation."[55]

Nat Hentoff, a young New York journalist and jazz critic, agreed that Black Americans "do use their senses more than the 'squares,' and that in this respect theirs is a more intense way of life."[56] But Hentoff felt strongly that the life of the typical Black American was anything but the "enormous" one Mailer had made it out to be. Aside from the sexual confusion and impotence experienced by Black men due to their economic dependence on women, Hentoff felt that "fundamentally Mailer appears to be unaware of the depth of anxiety, desperation, and sheer physical discomfort which ghetto living imposes on all the poor, hip and square."[57] Hentoff, in effect, joined many social scientists in excoriating those who lionized the Black male because they had ignored the likelihood that many generations of ghetto pathology had seriously discredited the myth of Black sexual potency. James Baldwin put the point most succinctly when he asked of his friend Mailer, "Why malign the sorely menaced sexuality of Negroes in order to justify the white man's sexual panic?"[58]

This underside of the Black ghetto was seen keenly by another Jewish intellectual associated with the New York crowd, Seymour Krim. Krim, a marginal figure in New York Intellectual circles, wrote about the excitement he found in the Black community in Harlem, but he was notably more realistic about the condition of Blacks than Mailer was and about how his Jewishness influenced his view of Black Americans. Krim admitted

that more "than most white or non-Negro men I have haunted colored
society, loved it . . . sucked it through my marrow."[59] Coming from a
comfortable, Jewish, middle-class family, Krim explained that it was a
"sense of identification stemming in part from my being the unreligious
modern American Jew who feels only the self-pitying sting of his identity
without the faith" that gave him his "girlish, milky notions about the
natural greatness of Negroes."[60]

When Krim became a teenager, his love for jazz and his "raging enslavement to sex" came together for him in the Black woman, the "jazz
queen, someone who loved to ball, could never get enough, was supreme
physically, rhythmically, ecstatically—'oh, baby, give it to me!' "[61] Krim
found himself frequenting jazz joints and prostitutes in Harlem, and he
learned to appreciate Harlem's life and bounce—"the entire place was a
jolt to anybody with a literary or even a human imagination."

Interestingly, the Harlem bars were more alluring to Krim than the
downtown white ones because, he admitted, society had judged him to
be superior to the rest of the patrons. This made Krim, for the first time
in his life, comfortable associating with both sexes. In this, Krim felt very
much like a Southern "white cracker," whose psyche was impregnable
because he always had an inferior class of people below him. "It was
an astonishing revelation," wrote Krim, "to realize that you could be a
better person—more attentive, calmer, happier . . . for the *wrong reasons.*"[62]

Nevertheless, by his third month of Harlem cruising he had become
aware of the "low, cruel, ignorant, selfish, small-minded side of uptown
life." Krim's senses were "humbled time and again by the sight of men
beating women, hustlers drunkenly cursing and clawing each other . . . or
how some date I was out with was afraid to go home to her old man (the
pimp she lived with)."[63] The human good Krim appreciated so much in
Harlem, the good that "lay just an inch away from its flip into unarguable
nastiness," often took that "flip" into nastiness. "I could never immunize
myself . . . to the garbage in the streets . . . the pawnshops five to a block,
the rat-infested tenements . . . the feverish traffic in drugs, the hordes of
sullen-faced, corner-haunting hustlers, the waste of money on adolescent
trinkets, the wild red rage on the broken-beer bottle 5 A.M. streets and
the ceaseless stealing."[64]

Jewish Cosmopolitanism and the Black Writer

Linked almost congenitally to rationalism and modernism, the New York Intellectuals in the postwar period rejected alienation and nihilism as cultural ideals. As Norman Podhoretz explained it, the proclivity of the 1950s bohemians for "bop" language and jazz was a way of demonstrating their contempt for "coherent, rational discourse which, being a product of the mind, is in their view a form of death."[65] That the New York Intellectuals did not share the alienation of the beats or the Black hipster reveals the primacy of the "cosmopolitan" ideal in their criticism. Implicit in their rejection of the idealization of the Black man was the belief that nothing about an individual should be inferred from his past. The modern culture of the West, they felt, provided the foundation for the emergence of a sophisticated modern culture that would transcend the artificial borders that divided regions, races, nations, and sexes. The task as the Jewish intellectuals first saw it, according to the historian Terry Cooney, "was to extend the reach of secular rationality; to escape the bounds of provincialism; to raise American culture to the level of the most advanced European literature; and to construct in the process a society that would welcome members of all groups as full participants."[66] For the most part, the New York Intellectuals seemed to be enthusiastic adherents of an ideal that proclaimed that an ethnic heritage or philosophical tradition should be preserved to the extent that it could expand the horizons of knowledge but that to the extent that it cut one off from other experiences it should be discarded. This cosmopolitan ideal, according to the historian David Hollinger, is "decidedly counter to the eradication of cultural differences, but counter also to their preservation in parochial form."[67]

Underlying the cosmopolitan ideal was a belief in the "polyvocality" of the individual, the belief that individuals could speak with many voices and should be free to pledge their allegiance to a variety of social categories. Harold Rosenberg gave the most succinct description of the cosmopolitan approach to the modern condition when he explained that "being born a Jew does not save us from . . . the modern condition of freedom to make ourselves according to an image we choose."[68] There was "room in the contemporary human being to be many things and nothing," and what Rosenberg valued most about America was that "being an American means being free precisely in that the American possesses that room, and can keep multiplying and transforming himself without regarding . . . his nationality."[69] The New York Intellectuals valued modern literature precisely because of its complexity and multiple meanings. In literature, as in life, they avoided any commitments that would limit the scope of their experience.

While a number of recent scholars have shown that the constant effort to recreate ethnic orientations, to tear down old boundaries that separate people and build new ones, gives the ethnic perspective in literature an increasingly modernist slant, the New York Intellectuals, on the whole, did not see this modernist potential in ethnic particularism.[70] If the New York Intellectuals had entered the war between consent and descent over which would rule the relationship of ethnicity to American culture, they had landed decidedly on the side of consent. The New York Intellectuals did not see ethnicity, particularly as it pertained to their Jewish background, as a dynamic or enervating force, but rather perceived it as a static and confining vessel of the past. Perhaps this is why it was not until the late 1950s that the New York Intellectuals identified Henry Roth's 1934 *Call It Sleep* as a great modernist novel. As one writer has pointed out, Roth's novel was at least as Jewish and certainly more modernist than the work of Delmore Schwartz, and yet the New York Intellectuals picked up Schwartz as a group hero and not Roth.[71] If one could argue that the New York Intellectuals were turned off by the proletarian tone of Roth's novel, rather than its Jewishness, more indicting evidence of their negative view of ethnicity in literature comes from the response of some New York Intellectuals to the rising interest in Yiddish literature in the 1950s. When Irving Howe and Eliezer Greenberg, a well-known Yiddish writer, published *A Treasury of Yiddish Stories* in 1955, the editors themselves commented that Yiddish literature had been largely second rate and that none of the Yiddish writers could rightfully be placed with the long list of Western literary immortals.[72] Howe later said of his own work with Yiddish literature that he approached it "with the detachment of an anthropologist" and that he had considered it a kind of a side job—"one day a week away from the Viet Nam war and the polemics with leftist ideologies into which I had locked myself."[73] Norman Podhoretz commented after reading the book that he found "the pleasure I derived was quite unlike the pleasure I get from good fiction. It was the pleasure of old world charm and quaintness, titillating but not challenging, and therefore not to be taken too seriously."[74] "For better or worst," Podhoretz wrote on a separate occasion, the New York Intellectual "made a moral decision not to be . . . confined by his Jewishness; he wanted to be a man of broad cultivation and wide sympathies."[75]

The power of modern art for the New York Intellectuals derived from its ability to uphold its independence from ideology. Clement Greenberg summarized the position on art and politics of the New Yorkers when he wrote, "True, I may be a socialist, but a work of art has its own ends, which it includes in itself and which have nothing to do with the fate of society."[76] The idea of the aesthetic autonomy of art, a concept long associated with modernism, was central to Greenberg and the other New York Intellectuals. As Norman Podhoretz explains, art for the New Yorkers was not a means to an end, of liberating the masses or bringing about revolution. "For better or for worse . . . I do not regard literature as an end in itself. . . . I do not go to literature for the salvation of my soul . . . and I do not expect it to redeem the age, but only to help the age become less chaotic and confused."[77] The New York Intellectuals understood that art, particularly the modern novel, was infused with political meaning, but they believed it was the singularly tough task of the critic to determine when the political "interruption" of a piece of literature was welcome and when it was not. "We had meant, I think," wrote Irving Howe, "that a work of literature has distinctive properties and must be perceived and judged according to categories distinctive to its kind."[78]

These strongly held views about the relationship of ethnicity and politics to a work of art brought the issue of Black literature to the serious attention of certain New York Intellectuals. The race revolution of the middle to late 1960s had as one component a breakthrough in Black writing and publishing that the *New York Times* called nothing less than a "Black Revolution in Books."[79] At the helm of the "Black Arts movement" were Black writers like James Baldwin, Lorraine Hansberry, LeRoi Jones, Eldridge Cleaver, and Julius Lester, among others, who wrote works of fiction saturated with political and racial self-consciousness. "The Black Arts Movement is radically opposed to any concept of the artist that alienates him from his community," wrote Larry Neal, the spokesperson for the new Black Aesthetic, who insisted on the wedding of art and politics.[80] Black writers found themselves at the center of the political ferment of the 1960s, leaving a number of New York Intellectuals in a position vis-à-vis the infiltration of politics into Black writing strikingly similar to their position in the 1930s, when a renascent *Partisan Review* broke away from the Communist-inspired, socially conscious proletarian literature of that decade. Initially, the New York Intellectuals believed that, like Jews, Black Americans would be able to share in the cosmopolitan culture of the New York writers, but some began to doubt this possibility after the promise of full racial integration had failed to bear fruit by the early 1960s.

The challenge of the Black Arts movement to the cosmopolitan outlook of the New York Intellectuals must be seen in the context of the nation's changing intellectual life, particularly the rise of Black Power and the New Left. In the 1960s, disillusionment with the use and misuse of Western economic and military power in the Third World drew many intellectuals toward an extreme cultural relativism. In the hands of radicals, the idea that there was value in the study of all civilizations was transformed into the idea that "people of color" and women, those groups that had historically occupied subservient roles in the West, perceive the world differently from white men and that there is no received "canon" or agreed-upon body of great imaginative works. From this viewpoint, universal standards of truth and beauty do not exist, and texts and ideas are no longer acts of individual self-expression but merely ways of exercising power. Hence, texts are "authorless," reflecting the political perspectives of social groups, not of individuals. Writers become important, or "great," to the extent that they communicate the experience of the group they are presumed to represent.[81] One of the key notions embodied in the new critical thinking involved the idea that members of minority groups and women possessed a racial or gender consciousness that not only governed their artistic interpretations but rendered such work inaccessible to "outsiders." In other words, the idea that all humans were, through the use of reason, capable of entering the experience of others, or that any human could step outside of his or her own experience to communicate ideas to others, was repudiated. Accordingly, the theories of critics like Richard Gilman, who suggested that white critics engage in a moratorium on judging Black writing, and the Black poet LeRoi Jones, who argued that white listeners could never understand the music of Black jazz musicians, gained widespread acceptance.[82]

The idea that there existed unbridgeable gulfs between people of different racial or ethnic backgrounds, or between any human beings, was anathema to the cosmopolitan ideal cherished by the New York Intellectuals. The assumption that race, ethnicity, or gender is first and foremost in a person's experience negated the view that humans were capable of a variety of identities and psychic connections. The New York Intellectuals took the view that if the canon of Western literature was deficient in any area, it was in the failure of Western intellectual elites to seek out important creative works by minority writers and women; but by no means should literature be judged by the extent to which it relates the experiences of these groups.[83]

Interestingly, the response of the New York Intellectuals to the new critical thinking unfolded closely around the life and work of the Black writer James Baldwin. As the former *Commentary* staffer Nathan Glazer recalled, Baldwin began his career by writing for the journals controlled by the New York Intellectuals such as *Partisan Review* and *Commentary*, journals with editors and contributors who had hope for American pluralism and race relations. Glazer wrote of Baldwin, "[H]ow he came to us I don't recall, but I do recall our pleasure that a remarkable young Black writer—how remarkable we didn't yet know—had come to us."[84] Glazer explained that Baldwin wrote poignantly about the Black condition in America and that his position on Black leadership was not very different from the way the Jewish intellectuals writing in *Commentary* felt toward the "official" Jewish community. "The Negro press supports any man, providing he is sufficiently dark and well-known—with the exception of certain Negro novelists accused of drawing portraits unflattering to the Negro race," Baldwin had written. This was "exactly what a Jewish writer, thinking of the difficulties of Isaac Rosenfeld and Philip Roth, might have written," Glazer explained.[85]

In two of his earliest essays—"Everybody's Protest Novel" and "Many Thousands Gone"—Baldwin had criticized the treatment given to the Black experience in the genre of protest novels, from Harriet Beecher Stowe's abolitionist *Uncle Tom's Cabin* (1852) through Richard Wright's *Native Son* (1940) and *Black Boy* (1945), for their "rejection of life, the human being, the denial of his beauty, dread, power, in its insistence that it is his categorization alone which is real and which cannot be transcended."[86] Baldwin saw Stowe's figure of Uncle Tom, the Black slave who is "Jet-black, wooly haired, illiterate" and "phenomenally forbearing," and Wright's Bigger Thomas, the snarling, menacing, Black murderer and sexual predator, as symbols used by both writers to protest the condition and the history of Black Americans. While Stowe used the Uncle Tom character to express the virtuous rage of a white abolitionist and Wright created Bigger Thomas to destroy the myth of Uncle Tom, Baldwin saw that both images of the Black male failed to contend with the possibility of his humanity. The whole idea of Bigger Thomas, Baldwin wrote, "carries, implicitly, the most remarkable confession: that is, that Negro life is in fact as debased and impoverished as our theology claims."[87]

Many in the New York Intellectual world were deeply taken by Baldwin's attacks on Black protest literature. Nevertheless, by 1963 Baldwin had become disillusioned with the idea of integration and more sympathetic to Black nationalism. Baldwin's historic 1963 essay, *The Fire Next Time*, about the Black Muslims, reflected a sense of the simmering rage that existed in the Black community and that would, after the urban riots of the mid-1960s, become a prominent feature of Black political discourse.[88] Baldwin did not agree with the entire program of the Black Muslims, which included the effort to establish a separate Black nation on United States soil, or with their belief that the dignity of Black Americans could be salvaged only by the use of violence. But Baldwin did agree with the Muslims' assertion that the "white man's heaven is the Black man's hell"; that what the Muslims said about the evils of white America were essentially correct; and that if something was not done about it soon, Blacks might understandably turn to violence. Baldwin also retained a high degree of ambivalence toward the efficacy of racial integration by asking, "Do I really *want* to be integrated into a burning house?"[89]

Baldwin's essay hit home with the New York Intellectuals because it marked a shift in the Black writer they believed most closely shared their commitment to the cosmopolitan ideal. Some New York Intellectuals were convinced by Baldwin's shift that perhaps the Black experience weighed so heavily on Black writers that here, too, something other than aesthetic judgments must be employed in evaluating the work of art. In other words, perhaps for the time being, the Black writer in America, due to the verities of his historical experience, could not take his place as an equal in the culture of high modernism. What is perhaps most interesting about the reactions of certain New York critics to these developments is the way in which their reflections about Blacks were so thoroughly commingled with their Jewish identities.

Norman Podhoretz, Leslie Fiedler, and the Fantasy of Miscegenation

Norman Podhoretz was one intellectual whose disillusionment with Baldwin inspired a brisk response that, when combined with the history of his early tenure as editor of *Commentary* magazine, reveals much about the Jewish identity of the New York Intellectuals. Until this stocky and combative intellectual took over the editorship of *Commentary* in 1960 at the precocious age of thirty, the magazine had been liberal under the editorship of Elliott Cohen but generally restrained by a staunch anti-Communist line. When Podhoretz took over, he brought the magazine to the left, interspersing articles by young radicals like Staughton Lynde, H. Stuart Hughes, and Paul Goodman with the usual *Commentary* articles. More important, Podhoretz believed strongly that the Jewish community in the United States was neither monolithic in its desires nor fully aware of its needs, and he was determined to make *Commentary* a forum for this ambivalence. The "new *Commentary*," according to Podhoretz, "bespoke, and reflected, a more advanced stage of acculturation than the old, and was accordingly more general than Jewish in emphasis."[90] Between 1960, when Podhoretz took over, and 1966, the circulation of the magazine grew from roughly twenty thousand to sixty thousand by appealing to a readership that was "neither especially religious nor much Zionist" but that "keenly awaited *Commentary* every month as if it were a public realm in which Jews were permitted to live on the questions."[91] Perhaps the changes Podhoretz effected were best summed up by a letter to the editor in April 1961 in which the author wrote "though I read many periodicals regularly, *Commentary* became one of them only a few months ago, for the magazine interests me precisely to the extent that the new editorial regime has de-Judaized its contents."[92]

It was probably no coincidence that the most radical thing Podhoretz would do with *Commentary* in his early years there was prompted by James Baldwin's *The Fire Next Time.* Baldwin's essay had confirmed for Podhoretz the already strong sense of skepticism with which he viewed liberal integrationism, and in his controversial article "My Negro Problem—and Ours" it is possible to see precisely how Podhoretz's vague "cosmopolitan" sense of Jewishness was reflected in his assessment of the role of Black culture and of Jewish culture in American life.[93]

Podhoretz was less disturbed by what Baldwin had to say in his essay than by what he felt was the poor treatment he had received from Baldwin throughout the writing of it. As he tells the story in his autobiographical *Making It,* in keeping with the new radicalism of the magazine Podhoretz had asked Baldwin, a friend of the "old" *Commentary,* to write a piece on the Black Muslim movement. Baldwin agreed to do it, and the two met regularly and communicated by mail throughout the composition of the work. Following a period of a few weeks in which there had been no communication, Podhoretz phoned Baldwin about the progress of the piece, only to be told by Baldwin that he had sold it to the *New Yorker* magazine for twelve thousand dollars, roughly twenty times the amount *Commentary* was able to offer. "I was thunderstruck," wrote Podhoretz; no "greater violation of the ethics of the trade could be imagined."[94] Not knowing what to do and believing that legal action against Baldwin would be "unseemly," Podhoretz told almost everyone he knew about what had happened and found that the responses people gave to his story were, in his judgment, far more understanding and forgiving than they would have been if a white writer had done what Baldwin allegedly had done. At a meeting with the Black writer over drinks, Podhoretz told Baldwin that he had dared to do what no white writer would have done because he knew white guilt would exonerate him. After Podhoretz explained to Baldwin that he suffered from no such guilt, Baldwin urged him to get his feelings down on paper. Just as Podhoretz had played a role in encouraging Baldwin's essay, Baldwin encouraged Podhoretz to write his.

The result was "My Negro Problem," a mea culpa in which Podhoretz described his lifelong difficulty trying to reconcile the liberal belief that all Black Americans were persecuted with his own experience of being victimized by Blacks. The concept that Blacks were always oppressed was almost as difficult for Podhoretz to grasp as a young Jewish boy growing up in Depression-era Brownsville as was the idea that all Jews were rich. The only Jews Podhoretz knew were poor, and the only Blacks he knew were the ones who were doing the persecuting—"and doing it, moreover, to me."

Podhoretz went on to describe a number of boyhood incidents in which he was bullied by Black boys from his neighborhood, the most formative one being the time Podhoretz was waylaid by two Black classmates with a baseball bat while he was standing alone in front of the brownstone walkup in which he lived. As an intellectual writing about this incident, Podhoretz tried to understand why the interethnic battles, which were common among white ethnic groups, seemed to have a special intensity when the opposing groups were Black and white. "Why, *why* should it have been so different as between the Negroes and us?" he pleaded. Podhoretz argued that the usual explanation—that Black Americans hated whites because of the "entrapment that poisons the soul of the Negro" and that whites hated Blacks because of an unacknowledged guilt—contained some truth, but that this was not the whole issue. The answer came from the idea propounded by both James Baldwin in his essay "Nobody Knows My Name" and Ralph Ellison in *Invisible Man* (1952)—that white people refused to *see* Black Americans and that this perceptual deficiency worked in both directions. Black Americans knew that what whites saw in them was the color of their skin and that in white eyes they were all alike, and therefore something less than human. Similarly, despite having lived a life that would appear to exonerate him from the white world's sins, Podhoretz found that his own white skin was enough to mark him in Black eyes as the enemy, even though he was not, "and in a war it is only the uniform that counts and not the person."[95]

Podhoretz admitted that this psychological projection operated on him, for he looked at Black boys in his neighborhood as symbols, "the very embodiment of the values of the street—free, independent, reckless, brave, masculine, erotic." Conversely, Podhoretz believed the noontime lunches of spinach and potatoes his mother prepared for him, his prudent behavior in the face of authority, and the hat and mittens his mother forced him to wear in the winter were secretly envied by the Black boys. The upshot of all the psychological dueling was that just as—"we have it on the authority of James Baldwin"—all Black Americans hate whites—all whites "are sick in their feelings about Negroes."[96] Podhoretz did not deny that all whites, including immigrant Jews, might have received certain benefits just by virtue of having white skin, but he insisted that in his own case, and in the case of most of the Jews he had grown up with, having white skin had not been noticeably beneficial. Just as Podhoretz believed himself to be only marginally better off than the Black street toughs who beat him up as a youngster, so he saw no particular advantages accruing to a white writer like himself that had been denied to a Black writer like James Baldwin. In fact, both the Black street toughs and Baldwin appeared to share significant advantages vis-à-vis white liberals in their respective realms. What disturbed Podhoretz most was that, in seeing all whites as similarly situated, Blacks and white liberals were not only blurring important differences in the social status of whites but encouraging bigotry in Blacks that would never be tolerated in whites. "There are the writers and intellectuals and artists who romanticize Negroes and pander to them, assuming a guilt that is not properly theirs. And there are all the white liberals who permit Negroes to blackmail them into adopting a double standard of moral judgement, and who lend themselves . . . to cunning and contemptuous exploitation by Negroes they employ or try to befriend."[97]

Most of the New York writers considered Baldwin, on the basis of his early essays, to be a Black intellectual in almost exactly the same sense as most of them were Jewish intellectuals. "As they [Jewish intellectuals] had moved out of the milieu into the broader world of Western culture, he [Baldwin] had too, taking his bearings as a writer not from ancestral ethnic sources but from the traditions of the literary mainstream," Podhoretz once wrote.[98] But *The Fire Next Time,* along with the soft response of white liberals to Baldwin's alleged professional duplicity, had caused Podhoretz to doubt the efficacy of integration. The only possible solution to America's racial problem that Podhoretz could imagine was a wholesale fusion of the races through miscegenation. Podhoretz believed that there should be little cause for distress in the Black community if this were to happen, for there was little in the Black past that Blacks should want to preserve: "His past is a stigma, his color is a stigma, and his vision of the future is the hope of erasing the stigma by making color irrelevant, by making it disappear as a fact of consciousness." [99] Podhoretz later admitted that his solution of miscegenation was rather naive since, as Ralph Ellison subsequently pointed out to him, the children of mixed racial sex would be considered Black. [100] But Podhoretz was not proposing miscegenation as a viable solution so much as he was promoting the idea that the result of racial fusion would be the most desirable outcome to America's racial dilemma. It is perhaps most revealing that Podhoretz had come to this conclusion about Black culture and the Black past by way of his own ambivalence as a Jew. "In thinking about the Jews I have often wondered whether their survival as a distinct group was worth one hair on the head of a single infant. Did the Jews have to survive so that six million innocent people should one day be burned in the ovens of Auschwitz?" [101] Podhoretz had earlier recorded similar feelings about the Jewish faith. Proclaiming the likelihood of the emergence of a new religion that would gradually take over the world and displace those currently in existence, Podhoretz reassured the Jewish readers of *Commentary* in his first year at the helm "that one ought to feel a sense of 'historical reverence' to Jewish tradition, even, or perhaps especially, if one is convinced that the curtain is about to drop on the last act of a very long play." [102] It is no wonder, then, that as a Jew Podhoretz had few qualms about his idea of intermarriage with Black Americans, who are predominantly Christian. When he asked himself if he would want his daughter "to marry one," Podhoretz answered, "No, I wouldn't like it at all. I would rail and rave and rant and tear my hair. And then I hope I would have the courage to curse myself for raving and ranting, and to give her my blessing." [103]

It should be noted that such a positive view of racial mixing appears to be a distinguishing characteristic of the New York critics. Miscegenation has appeared in the literary mind of non-Jewish whites, but it has mostly been regarded with prurient disdain. This has been as true of such American literary giants as William Dean Howells, George Washington Cable, Mark Twain, William Faulkner, Thomas Wolfe, and Allan Tate as it has for out-and-out racists like Thomas Dixon. Essentially, these writers reflected in their work the commonly held notion that miscegenation amounted to racial pollution and often used the dangers of racial mixing to justify continued racial segregation.[104] But for at least a few of the ambivalent Jewish intellectuals, miscegenation was seen in a positive light, holding forth the promise of a universally accessible modern culture that historical Black stigmatization appeared to have rendered impossible. Whereas the opposition to miscegenation on the part of white gentile writers stemmed from the belief in the purity of the white race, the cosmopolitan New York Intellectuals who wrote positively of the idea of racial mixing are notable, at least on some level, for their lack of concern for the sustenance and continuity of Jewish culture. As one writer recently put it, "Jewish intellectuals often saw themselves as prophets of cultural misogyny, standing above all parties and peoples, transcending rather than imitating the divisions among others."[105]

Podhoretz's attraction to the idea of sexual fusion as a solution to the American race problem was shared by Leslie Fiedler, the brilliant iconoclast who had been the first critic to identify interracial, homosexual love as a central motif in American literature. Fiedler insisted that within some of the most highly regarded American classics "are disturbing sexual overtones, which combine with and are reinforced by an uneasy ambivalence toward the problem of race relations."[106] Where homosexuality contradicted the national myth of masculine love, Fiedler believed, the white man's relationship with the Black and the American Indian contradicted the myth of equality, and in American literature these two hypocrisies often come together in the fantasy of boyhood love between two males of different color. The most famous examples Fiedler pointed to included Richard Henry Dana's *Two Years Before the Mast* (1840), the Leatherstocking tales of James Fenimore Cooper (1826–1841), Herman Melville's *Moby Dick* (1851), and Mark Twain's *Huckleberry Finn* (1892). "In Dana, it is the narrator's melancholy love for *Kanaka,* Hope; in Cooper, the lifelong affection of Natty Bumppo and Chingachgook; in Melville, Ishmael's love for Queequeg; in Twain, Huck's feeling for Nigger Jim."[107] Just at the moment when the world's great novels would give us heterosexual passion in all its varieties, Fiedler argued, in American literature "we come instead on the fugitive slave and the no-account boy lying side by side on a raft borne by the endless river toward an impossible escape, or the pariah sailor waking in the tattooed arms of the brown harpooner on the verge of their impossible quest."[108] The white renegade male, then, joins himself to the colored male who has always been a renegade. "Behind the white American nightmare that someday, no longer tourist, inheritor, or liberator, he will be rejected, refused, he dreams of his acceptance at the heart he has most utterly offended."[109]

By the early 1960s, Fiedler commented that the task of mythologizing the relations between Black Americans and whites had passed to the Black writer, "to the descendants of Jim rather than those of Huck," and he took a position on much of this literature that was typical of that of other New York Intellectuals. Richard Wright's *Native Son* was too much of a reaction against the image of Uncle Tom to enable it to outlive the cause that occasioned Wright's wrath. "Uncle Tom and Bigger Thomas, Tom and anti-Tom, are not very different in the end: wooly-haired sniveler and Black bully both sacrificing the possibility of authenticity and full humanity in order to provide 'satisfaction and security' for those bound to them by ties of mutual terror."[110] On Ralph Ellison's attempt to escape the protest genre in his *Invisible Man,* on the other hand, Fiedler wrote that the book lacked authenticity. "Ellison's invisible protagonist . . . seems a secondhand version of the Black man in America, based on a European intellectual's version of the alienated Jew."[111] Fiedler believed the Black American was unable to escape his historical condition. "As long as the Negro remains a Negro . . . a part of his self consciousness must be the consciousness of our offenses against him . . . without a hatred equal to our guilt, he would not know himself for what he is, that is, what we made him."[112]

By the mid-1960s Fiedler was beginning to suspect that the ultimate assimilation of Black Americans through male love and friendship that he had identified in the American literary tradition was beginning to take place, and he also suspected that both colored and white were becoming a *"tertium quid"* that more closely resembled the white myths about the Black American than it did the actual lives of either. In the achievement of the "tertium quo," Fiedler believed, the Jew, the middle-man, could play a special role.[113]

In Fiedler's view, such books as Norman Mailer's *An American Dream* (1965), Nat Hentoff's *Call the Keeper* (1966), and Jay Neugeboren's *Big Man* (1966), as well as his own *The Last Jew in America* (1966), indicated that the job of recreating the Black image away from the old WASP clichés had now fallen to Jewish writers.[114] Ironically, though, Fiedler believed the interests of the Jew and the Black American were irreconcilable. It had become abundantly clear to Fiedler that equality of opportunity would not grant everyone, particularly those who had been brutalized as thoroughly as Black Americans had, a decent life or the possibility of prosperity. This realization, Fiedler thought, would bring nothing but despair for Jews, whose enlightened liberalism would now be the third religion they would have to give up, having already lost orthodoxy and Stalinism/Trotskyism, all within the same century. But there was hope. On a plane to Jerusalem, a man who worked for a Jewish adoption agency told Fiedler that the number of Jewish girls giving birth to illegitimate Black babies was mounting spectacularly. Fiedler had personally spoken with mixed-race couples and found that most of them consisted of "pretty blond Jewish girls and Negro men." From this Fiedler surmised that the Jewish girls were breaking the old sexual taboos against the Black American and that this could very well mean the "beginning of the end" of America's racial nightmare. A new mythology was being invented "though like all new myths this one, too, contains within it one very old, indeed, the myth of the Jewish daughter, Hadassah . . . dancing naked for our salvation before the gentile king."[115] The only problem Fiedler could foresee arising from marriage between Jewish girls and Black men was an increase in Black anti-Semitism, since some Black radicals had accused Jewish women of emasculating Black men. But he preferred to live in the hope of intermarriage between Jews and Blacks, "convinced of its superiority to all the weary mythologies of mere politics."[116]

The radicalism of miscegenation as a solution to the race problem is testimony to the agony Jewish intellectuals experienced in trying to reconcile the situation of the Black American with the exalted idea of a shared culture, and the ease with which a few of them espoused Jewish intermarriage indicates that their commitment to Jewish distinctiveness was perhaps no more intense than their commitment to Black distinctiveness.

Irving Howe and the Black Writer

The belief that the Black experience represented an insurmountable obstacle to achieving a truly integrated high culture perhaps weighed heaviest on Irving Howe. The weaknesses Howe found in the work of Baldwin in *The Fire Next Time* and *Another Country* (1962), and of Ralph Ellison in *Invisible Man*, convinced him that Black American writers could not stay true to themselves without letting some measure of social protest seep into their work, and he addressed the attempts of both writers to declare themselves liberated from the necessity of social protest. In his widely read and controversial 1963 essay, "Black Boys and Native Sons," Howe gave powerful expression to the view that the severity of the Black experience necessarily proscribed the Black writer.[117]

If it was true, as Baldwin had written, that "literature and sociology were not one and the same," then Howe felt it was also true that one "writes out of one thing only—one's own experience." Accordingly, Howe wrote in "Black Boys," "What, then, was the experience of a man with a black skin, what *could* it be in this country? How could a Negro put pen to paper, how could he so much as think or breathe, without some impulsion to protest."[118] The Black writer must confront his own experience in America, Howe thought, and only through this confrontation could he achieve true authenticity. For Howe, Richard Wright's *Native Son* was the greatest achievement in Black writing. "What is more, the very act of writing a novel, the effort to confront what Bigger Thomas means to him, is for such a writer a way of dredging up and then perhaps shedding the violence that society has pounded into him."[119]

Howe believed that it was necessary for Wright, as it was for all Black novelists, to face the terror and violence of the Black past because of one "primary and inescapable truth . . . that violence is central in the life of the American Negro, defining and crippling him with a harshness few other Americans need suffer." It was the necessity to confront the violence in his life that saddled the Black writer with a handicap Howe felt might ultimately keep Black writers from joining the cosmopolitan world of high letters. "Bigger Thomas may be enslaved to a hunger for violence, but anyone reading *Native Son* with mere courtesy must observe the way in which Wright, even while yielding emotionally to Bigger's deprivation, also struggles to transcend it. That he did not fully succeed seems obvious; one may doubt that any Negro writer can."[120] Consistent with his lifelong belief that the social world must sometimes impinge on artistic independence, Howe explained that the special circumstances at hand necessitated a different standard of judgment. "To say this," wrote Howe, "is not to propose the condescension of exempting Negro writers from moral judgement, but to suggest the terms of understanding, and still more, the terms of hesitation for making a judgement."[121]

The discomfort Howe felt with employing special criteria for the judgment of Black literature became apparent by his qualifying hesitance. He agreed that Baldwin had scored a major point when he criticized protest novels for cutting away the positive dimension of Black life; he also acknowledged that the posture of militance exacted a heavy price from the writer, a price that includes the reader's inclination to believe that in Black life "there exists no tradition, no field of manners, no possibility of ritual or intercourse." [122] But in his equivocation, Howe attested to his belief in the primacy of the social world in the affair at hand. "All one can ask, by way of reply, is whether the refusal to struggle may not exact a still greater price." [123]

Ralph Ellison registered on Howe's consciousness because of his alleged attempt to deny or escape his experience as a Black American in his novel *Invisible Man* and in comments he had made after receiving the National Book Award in January of 1953. On this occasion Ellison said of *Invisible Man* that, in order for the novel to fully capture America for its "rich diversity" and "magical fluidity and freedom," he had been forced "to conceive of a novel unburdened by the narrow naturalism which has led, after so many triumphs, to the final and unrelieved despair which marks so much of our current fiction." [124]

In "Black Boys," Howe argued that *Invisible Man* was a "brilliant but flawed achievement," which stood with *Native Son* as the major works composed by Black Americans, and the one novel that came closest to a nonprotest novel. The story of the journey from South to North of the young Black boy, from childhood humiliations at the hands of whites, to a Southern Black college, from job to job in the North, and finally into the hands of the Harlem Communists, avoided "for long stretches" the formula of protest that Baldwin had eloquently described, yet was not so perfectly free from the "ideological and emotional penalties" suffered by Black Americans in the United States. The brilliance of the novel was Ellison's "rich and wild inventiveness" and his ability to capture the "hidden gloom and surface gaiety of Negro life." But Ellison could not avoid getting caught up in the "idea of the Negro." What irked Howe most was the hero's assertion at the end of the novel, as he "finds himself" in some unspecified way, that "my world has become one of infinite possibilities." Howe called this technique of proclaiming self-liberation a favorite strategy of the 1950s but a strategy that "violates the realities of social life, the interplay between external conditions and personal will." It was impossible, Howe felt, to define one's individuality without dealing with social barriers that stood in the way. "Freedom can be fought for, but it cannot always be willed or asserted into existence. And it seems hardly an accident that even as Ellison's hero asserts the 'infinite possibilities' he makes no attempt to specify them." [125]

Howe's contention that Baldwin and Ellison masqueraded as "Native Sons" to hide the fact that they were "Black Boys" evoked a reply of considerable depth and authority from Ellison, which appeared in *The New Leader*.[126] Ellison rebuked Howe sharply, stating that the casual reader would interpret Howe as saying that the Black American is a living embodiment of hell. "He seems never to have considered," wrote Ellison of Howe, that "American Negro life . . . is also a discipline. . . . There is a fullness, even a richness here; and here despite the realities of politics, perhaps, but nevertheless here and real. Because it is a human life."[127] Claiming the right to polyvocality that the Jewish intellectuals claimed for themselves, Ellison wondered why, if Howe believed Wright had an authentic Black American tone, that was the *only* authentic Black tone. "He [Wright] had his memories and I have mine, just as I suppose Irving Howe has his."[128]

As his reply to Howe unfolded, it became obvious that Ellison had attempted to claim for the Black writer the role of the cosmopolitan intellectual that had appealed so much to the Jewish writers and that a succeeding generation of Black critics would try to retrieve after the Black Arts movement of the 1960s.[129] Ellison insisted that his literary ancestors were Tolstoy, Hemingway, Marx, T. S. Eliot, Pound, and André Malraux, more so even than Richard Wright, and he pleaded for his work to be judged by those high standards of modern culture. "I can only ask that my fiction be judged as art; if it fails, it fails aesthetically, not because I did or did not fight some ideological battle," Ellison wrote. It is worth noting that, while Howe never identified himself as a Jew in his essay, Ellison took the liberty of doing so. "Thus I felt uncomfortable," Ellison wrote, "whenever I discover Jewish intellectuals writing as though they were guilty of enslaving my grandparents, or as though the *Jews* were responsible for the system of segregation. Not only do they have enough troubles of their own, as the saying goes, but Negroes know this only too well."[130]

Howe, in the words of the critic Daniel Aaron, did not believe the Black writer could go the route of other ethnic American writers in passing from "hyphenation" to "dehyphenation," in which minority writers pass from the periphery to the center of society, "viewing it no less critically, perhaps, but more knowingly." Speaking of Howe, Aaron wrote that "Even the well-wishers of the Negro, it seemed, were imprisoned by their liberal stereotypes, asserting unequivocally that all Negroes had identical experiences, bore the same psychic wounds, suffered the same slights and irritations." "By the same logic," Aaron continued, "the Jew was somehow betraying himself and Jewry in the act of transcending his Jewishness."[131] Omitted from Aaron's critique, however, was Howe's explicit declaration that the Black experience in America was so different in kind from that of the Jews, or of any other group, that it was impossible for a Black to work outside of that experience, whereas a Jewish writer in America quite possibly could.

It is here that Ellison's statement that Howe had been identifying himself with the white power structure by assuming a guilt for Black misery for which Jews can not properly be blamed takes on real meaning. Ellison had written that this phenomenon was typical of Jewish intellectuals and that it was unfortunate, because he considered "the United States freer politically and richer culturally because there were Jewish Americans to bring to it the benefit of their special forms of dissent."[132] But he did not allow for the possibility that Howe's identification with the suffering of Black Americans itself constituted a special form of Jewish dissent. As Cynthia Ozick has written of the Howe-Ellison exchange, Howe may indeed have been unconsciously identifying, as Ellison had charged, but it was as a Jew and not with the white power structure. "Howe's call for the 'impulsion to protest' was not a matter of burnt cork," wrote Ozick; "he was not coming on as a make-believe Negro (and certainly not as a make-believe member of the 'power structure'), but rather as a Jew responding implicitly and naturally—i.e., vicariously—to an urgent moment in history, applying to that moment the 'benefit of [his] special form of dissent.' "[133]

It is probably appropriate here to read Howe's critique in the context of his lifelong struggle with Jewish identity, for Howe obviously felt that his own experience as a Jew made far less of an impression upon his consciousness as a writer than Ellison's experience as a Black man had made on his. When socialism reached an impasse in the postwar years, Howe said that his "reconquest of Jewishness" had become an important project in his life. But even Howe could not explain what this "reconquest" meant. "I had no aptitude for religion, little taste for nationalism, and rarely a wish to go back to old neighborhoods." Howe explained that Jewish intellectuals like himself in the postwar period "were living through a confused experience of self-acceptance . . . we were now learning to accept the ease that might come from acknowledgment and even taking pleasure in ties with a past that, in any case, had become an integral part of our being." "History," he wrote, "was handing out cruel blows, teaching cruel lessons."[134] When Howe died, in 1993, his friend and critic Leon Wieseltier wrote that he could not count the number of breakfasts over which Howe had lamented the decline of the secular Jewish world. He had lived with the feeling that he was a "man without contemporaries," Wieseltier wrote.[135] Not even his substantial commitment to the translation of Yiddish literature enabled him to "solve . . . the problem of 'Jewishness'."[136] Howe's view of Jewish culture as a relic of the past is revealed by his comments regarding the overwhelming popular reception of his landmark history of the Jewish immigrant world of New York's Lower East Side, *World of Our Fathers* (1976). Many Jews turned to this book, Howe felt, because it provided a fragment of a past no longer available to them, upon which they could sentimentally fasten a fading national or religious identity. "Some of this turning back strikes me as a last hurrah of nostalgia. Each day, necessarily, it keeps getting weaker and sillier."[137] It is instructive to note in this respect that, even for the purposes of his debate with Ellison, Howe remained insistent over the years that he did not approach the discussion from any particular Jewish standpoint, that, in other words, while Ellison could not help writing from his Blackness, he himself was free to choose the lens through which he viewed the world.[138] Given the discomfort Howe experienced with defining his Jewishness, it is not unreasonable to assume that his view of the Black writer and his predicament was informed by his own sense of Jewish loss and that it was not with condescension but with envy that he looked at the Black writer, who, at least for the time being, would not have to engage the cryptic forces of loss and remembrance. Perhaps Howe felt that the anxiousness of Ellison and Baldwin to announce their liberation from the historical pressures of the Black experience was not only a literary impossibility but a personal impropriety as well.

Be that as it may, the only thing that can be said with certainty about the Howe-Ellison exchange is that it reflected the difficulty a "Jewish intellectual with cosmopolitan tastes" had in determining the boundary line between the pressures of the social world and art. Howe himself admitted to having been guilty of waging his own personal battle over the point where ethnicity ends and art begins in his bout with Ellison. By the early 1960s, after the Black Arts movement had rejected Ellison's point of view in favor of a nationalist and separatist style in Black writing, Howe sheepishly acknowledged victory but conceded that his own view had been mired in indecisiveness. "My view that the Negro writer, while trapped in a historical situation that makes protest all but unavoidable, nevertheless seeks to find ways of mediating between the gross historical pressures that surround him" would strike the literary intellectuals "as a token of equivocation, if not worse."[139]

Blacks and Jews in American Intellectual Life

The Black American, both in the literary world and in the social world, posed a major obstacle to the cosmopolitan ideal cherished by the New York Intellectuals. The cosmopolitan ideal was antithetical to the "cultural populism" fostered by the Communists of the 1930s, which had emerged again in the 1960s, giving life to the idea that cultural and social minorities, such as Black Americans, ethnic groups, gays, and women, could achieve cultural enfranchisement through the validation of their group membership. As one scholar described this friction between intellectual viewpoints, cultural "production came to be valued not for its aesthetic or intellectual distinction but for its representative powers. . . . The New York Intellectuals also faced the problem of cultural enfranchisement, but . . . [t]hey looked for enfranchisement . . . through the entry into the already existing universality of European culture."[140]

Unable to countenance the thought of living in a world where a shared culture was not possible, and fully aware of the insurmountable nature of America's race problem, the Jewish cosmopolitans negotiated the race crisis in a variety of ways. Irving Howe believed that, at least for the time being, Black writers would continue to be shackled to the Black past, unable to achieve literary authenticity without first "protesting" against social conditions, and prohibited from reaching the true aesthetic heights of cultural modernism. Norman Podhoretz and Leslie Fiedler dreamed of washing away the Black experience and its scars—benevolently, to be sure, but away nevertheless—through the surreal solution of miscegenation. Whatever else one can say about these attempts to deal with America's race problem, they deeply reflected the Jewish ambivalence of the cosmopolitan intellectuals. That American intellectual life would one day become as disconnected and fractious as some of the Jewish cosmopolitans feared it would is perhaps not as significant as the ease with which some of them approved of marrying off Jewish daughters to preserve that ideal.

Before one rushes to judgment, however, it is necessary to view the Jewish ambivalence of the New York Intellectuals and the approach they took towards race and culture in light of the realities of Jewish life in the United States. The history of the Jews in American literature before the 1940s and 1950s is instructive in forging an understanding of this phenomenon. While there were a few celebrated individuals like Abraham Cahan and Ludwig Lewisohn, American Jews played only a tiny, unimportant role in American letters before the war. Moreover, the role that these isolated individuals did play had little to do with their being Jewish but rather was related to their having learned to "pass." Norman Podhoretz has written that the ability to operate in an unobtrusive manner within accepted literary terms may have been a prerequisite for this kind of passing.[141] In the 1930s, there were a number of talented Jewish writers in the United States, but their work was still confined to the experience of the Jewish ghetto, which served to prohibit its wider appeal. But the decline of anti-Semitism and the greater acculturation of Jews after World War II served to create a tension between the promise of assimilation and the life of the immigrant past that was distinctly American, a tension through which American Jewish writers were able to find their entrance into the literary imagination. The Jewish imagination by itself was not capable of weighing on the American literary conscience in any significant way. It had first to be transformed before it could resonate widely. It is true that the famous Jewish triumvirate of Saul Bellow, Bernard Malamud, and Philip Roth has been given all the highest honors that American letters can bestow upon a writer. But works by these authors have had an appeal that is tied to their transitional nature, the way they have gone about exploring the circumstances surrounding the transformation of the Jews from a foreign immigrant people to a native American one: they therefore do not really qualify as reflections of authentic Jewishness or of a vibrant Jewish culture.[142] Perhaps it is not surprising, then, that the Black American, the socially most marginal yet historically most integral American, finds his way into so many stories and novels by American Jews. Whether it be the little Black boy in Roth's *Goodbye Columbus,* the Black (Jewish) angel in Malamud's "Angel Levine," the young Black feminist in Jo Sinclair's *The Changelings,* the militant writer Willie Spearmint in Malamud's *The Tenants,* the Black pickpocket in Bellow's *Mr. Sammler's Planet,* or the heroic ghetto youth in Edward Louis Wallant's *The Pawnbroker,* the Black character or the theme of race represents an effort by the author to engage a people organically connected to the United States. Given the precariousness of his own cultural foundations, it was incumbent upon the American Jewish novelist to look outside his tradition for literary sustenance, and he often found it, predictably, in the Black American and his mighty epic. In the words of Ralph Ellison, "what the Jewish American writer had to learn before he could find his place was the American-ness of his experience. He had to see himself as American and project his Jewish experience as an experience unfolding within this pluralistic society."[143]

While it is true that the New York Intellectuals may not have played a large role in helping to sustain or to reinvent American Jewish culture, one can only wonder what could have been achieved had they adopted such a project as their own. It is useful in this regard to explore the fate of those "other" twentieth-century New York Jewish intellectuals for whom Jewishness was indeed central and to whom a volume of essays has been dedicated.[144] With the benefit of hindsight, it now appears that the cultural impact, on both American Jewish life and the broader cultural life of the United States, of these "Jewish" Jewish intellectuals has been perhaps no greater, and possibly somewhat less, than the cultural impact of the New York Intellectuals who did not make Jewishness central to their work. These are the "affinatively" Jewish intellectuals who wrote for such journals as the *Jewish Frontier* and the *Menorah Journal* and who, unlike their cosmopolitan counterparts at *Partisan Review* and *Commentary,* were celebrated not by gentiles and "non-Jewish" Jews but by the international Jewish community that had "remained within the perimeter of Zionism, Yiddishism, Judaism, and Jewish culture in its infinite variety."[145] These "Jewish" Jewish intellectuals included the Labor Zionists Hayim Greenberg, Ben Halpern, and Marie Syrkin; the *Menorah Journal* editor Henry Hurwitz; the Yiddishist Maurice Samuel; the militant Zionist Ludwig Lewisohn; and the theologians Mordecai Kaplan, Will Herberg, and Milton Steinberg, all writers who made Judaism or Jewishness the defining mark of their intellectual pursuits. These intellectuals were "nominatively" Jews, and the central theme underlying the volume dedicated to them is that, while the "Jewish" Jewish intellectuals have not garnered the widespread recognition of their cosmopolitan counterparts, their work is perhaps more worthy of preservation because of its peculiarly Jewish nature. "The effort is a very Jewish one," writes the editor Carole Kessner of the purpose for her volume *The "Other" New York Jewish Intellectuals:* "commitment to the preservation of the worthy past and its incorporation into the present for the sake of the future."[146] Kessner acknowledges that in this endeavor she has been influenced by the work of the author and critic Cynthia Ozick. In her famous critique of Jewish cosmopolitans, Ozick defended Jewish writers with a strong Jewish consciousness on the grounds that their achievements are generally longer lasting and serve to strengthen Jewish culture.[147]

But the fate of Jewish culture and Jewish intellectuals in the United States may be more complicated than Ozick presumes, and her assumption that the specifically Jewish work of Jewish writers will survive among Jews, if not among the general public, appears now to be a shaky proposition. Ozick's premise seems to depend on the survival of a thriving Jewish culture, one with strong attachments to the Jewish past. But in a United States where the Yiddish language has all but disappeared and the knowledge of Hebrew is not much greater, in what meaningful way will the work of secular Yiddishists and Hebraists be remembered?[148] With the focus of world Zionism now shifted to the state of Israel, what is the appeal for American Jews in the works of American Zionists like Ben Halpern, Hayim Greenberg, Marie Syrkin, Ludwig Lewisohn, and Maurice Samuel, all of whom preferred to live out their lives in diaspora? What segment of the Jewish community can now look for inspiration to the work of Trude-Weiss Rosmarin, the long-time iconoclastic editor of the *Jewish Spectator,* or to Henry Hurwitz, the editor of the long-disbanded *Menorah Journal,* a periodical whose primary Jewish interest was anti-Semitism at home and in Europe?[149] It is true that Mordecai Kaplan, the founder of Reconstructionism, a religious philosophy that emphasizes community, remains a prominent and provocative figure in American Jewish thought, and there can be no doubt that the Jewish theology of the one-time Communist, Will Herberg constitutes one of the most provocative philosophical approaches to twentieth-century Judaism.[150] Nevertheless, most of the affirmatively Jewish intellectuals featured in Kessner's volume seem to be possessed of concerns from a different time period, issues peculiar to a specific generation of immigrant intellectuals trained in European universities but unable to find an intellectual niche in the United States. Most of these Jewish intellectuals were immersed in the business of creating or sustaining support for a Jewish state, of championing the Yiddish language, of defining an American pluralism in which Jewish expression would be acceptable, or in reaffirming a Jewish relationship with God after the Holocaust, all worthy projects that, except for post-Holocaust theology, are no longer sufficient to inspire a Jewish community languishing in the cultural malaise of the 1990s. As the Jewish historian Henry Feingold has written of these "Jewy" Jews, not only did they pay their price in fame by confining themselves to the Jewish arena, but this arena itself was fast fading. "The 'other' intellectuals lived at the tail end of a dying culture."[151]

It is with this in mind that the work of the cosmopolitan New York Intellectuals must be evaluated. The historical forces of freedom and assimilation that operated on the New York Intellectuals are the same historical forces that continue to operate on the American Jewish psyche, probably to a far greater extent than the cultural forces of Yiddish, Hebrew, or even Zionism. In this sense the New York Intellectuals spoke directly to the primary question facing most American Jews at the end of the twentieth century: how can one be Jewish in a free, secular society? If the New York Intellectuals chose to emphasize their own transition from being Jewish to being Jewish American, it was because the tension caused by that transition was available to them as the most prepossessing component of their Jewishness.

That the New York Intellectuals themselves were unable to resolve the tension between universalism and particularism puts them in the company of just about everyone else who has tried, perhaps because that is the kind of tension that never really dissipates.[152] Perhaps their greatest indiscretion was not recognizing the power of ethnic identity as a dynamic and changing phenomenon that need not have restricted their ideas about modernism and culture. The New York Intellectuals were well aware of the multiple meanings created by the peculiarly modern dilemma of "double consciousness." They knew, perhaps better than anyone else, that in the contemporary world one can have multiple identities and live in a void between two cultures. But few of them ever looked to ethnicity for the creation of new artistic forms or innovations. It is for this reason, perhaps, that the three New York Intellectuals highlighted in this study—Irving Howe, Norman Podhoretz, and Leslie Fiedler—all proffered the belief in later writings that, with the completion of the Jews' transition from being Jewish to being American, American Jewish writing disappeared as a significant genre in American literature.[153]

This is also probably the reason that, when New York Intellectuals have decided to return to their Jewish roots, as in the case of Alfred Kazin's *A Walker in the City* or in Irving Howe's *World of Our Fathers,* it has usually been in the form of nostalgic remembrances of a time long past. As Howe has written of the popularity of *World of Our Fathers,* perhaps it enabled Jews "to cast an affectionate backward glance at the world of their fathers before turning their backs upon it forever and moving on. . . . My book was not a beginning, it was still another step to the end."[154]

But if the New York Intellectuals were not sufficiently visionary to foresee the possibility of a Jewish literature in the United States beyond the ghettos they had left behind, this was because of the compromises they, as Jewish writers in America, were forced to make before broad public recognition could be bestowed upon them, compromises that Black writers in the United States, to return to our opening analogy, were not forced to make to obtain similar recognition. One must indeed compare the fates of the cosmopolitan Jewish intellectuals with that of Black intellectuals in the United States to fully appreciate the terms upon which acceptance of Jewish writers and critics has been predicated. Norman Podhoretz has pointed out that Ludwig Lewisohn ceased being of any importance in the American literary world after he became a militant Zionist and that his decline was in dramatic contrast to the skyrocketing fame and acclaim that James Baldwin experienced when he underwent his conversion to Black nationalism with *The Fire Next Time*.[155] This contrast between the fates of Black and Jewish writers in the United States continues today. The Black intellectuals who are now being compared to the New York Intellectuals have risen to prominence having first distinguished themselves by their analysis of racial subjects. As Henry Louis Gates Jr. has written, "it is the birthright of the Black writer that his experiences, however personal, are automatically historical."[156] Thus, Cornel West becomes a best seller with his book *Race Matters* (1993), and bell hooks rises to prominence with her book on race, feminism, and culture *Outlaw Culture* (1994), as do Derrick Bell with his mordant look on race relations in the United States, *Faces at the Bottom of the Well* (1992), and Michael Eric Dyson with *Making Malcolm: The Myth and Meaning of Malcolm X* (1995). By contrast, the New York Intellectuals had to first gain prominence by writing books on non-Jewish subject matter before they were afforded the prestige commensurate with their talent. Alfred Kazin had first to write his sweeping survey of American literature, *On Native Grounds* (1942), before he could be comfortable writing *New York Jew* (1978). Irving Howe had to write *William Faulkner: A Critical Study* (1962) before *World of Our Fathers* (1976), Norman Podhoretz *Doings and Undoings: American Writing in the Fifties and After* (1963) before *Making It* (1968), and Lionel Trilling *The Liberal Imagination* (1950) before "Wordsworth and the Rabbis" (1955). As the scholar and critic Ruth Wisse has written of the early New York Intellectuals, the "failure of this predominantly Jewish intellectual community to address the plight of the Jews was as pronounced as its successful advancement into the mainstream of American culture."[157]

What, then, is one to make of the New York Intellectuals, these Jewish writers who seemed to know implicitly that there were certain conditions that had to be met before their work could garner widespread public interest? While the record of the cosmopolitans is nowhere near as admirable as that of the "Jewish" Jewish intellectuals in areas of specific Jewish concern, particularly with regard to the Holocaust and support for the state of Israel, they did deal, in a singularly skilled and noble fashion, with the larger question of being both Jewish and American. The New York Intellectuals allowed generations of Jewish intellectuals and educated lay peo-

ple to sustain their sense of Jewishness by creating an independent intellectual community that brought the highest critical standards to bear on
questions of intense importance to American Jews afflicted with the de-
mentia of double consciousness. As one New York Intellectual described
the virtue of *Commentary* magazine, "one could, it seemed, be actively
Jewish just by reading about the Jews' history, debating the place in culture
of Jewish ritual law, or discerning the American 'emancipation' in the
elegance of the magazine's prose."[158] This must be recognized as a novel
contribution not only to Jewish life in the United States but to the entire
idea of ethnic identity and acculturation in a free society. If the New York
Intellectuals left the womb of the Jewish immigrant ghettos to make names
for themselves, only to return to their roots to find them buried in increasingly shallow soil, they should at least be credited with coming closer
than anyone else has before or since to bridging the void that separates the
Jewish from the American.

4

The Unbearable "Whiteness" of Being Jewish

The Jewish Approach toward Black Power, 1967–1972

[The Jew] can comprehend the Black struggle but only in the context of his own . . . it is time that he realize that he, not today's Black, is the invisible man.   —M. Jay Rosenberg

I hesitate to say this because I know it will be misunderstood, it doesn't come easily to my tongue—[Jews should have] just a little self-pride, to feel that it is an honor to be among the victims of our century.   —Irving Howe

For many American Jews, the late 1960s signaled the end of one era and the beginning of another. On the one hand, the passage of the two most comprehensive civil rights laws by the federal government in 1964 and 1965 represented the high-water mark of the postwar liberal coalition within which American Jews had figured so prominently. On the other hand, the year 1967 brought with it a number of troubling developments. For the second time in thirty years, war in the Middle East in May and June of that year brought Jews throughout the world face-to-face with the possibility of annihilation. The outpouring of support by American Jews for the embattled state of Israel was a measure not only of latent feelings for the Jewish homeland but also of the disturbing perception that if they did not act, the world might once again turn its back on a seemingly overpowered Jewish population. Compounding these forebodings were a number of not completely unconnected domestic developments. New Deal liberalism, a commitment to which had become the backbone of Jewish identity, was breaking up. By the late 1960s the youth-inspired New Left, which had been born in the early part of the decade with a strong strain of humanism and hope, had become radicalized and often expressed this radicalism in ways that many liberal Jews found disturbing. But perhaps the most unsettling development for American Jews was the advent of Black Power, a movement that both caused and in some ways was caused by the deterioration of relations between Jewish and Black Americans. While there had been signs of discontent in both groups for a number of years, for the first time since World War II the commonality of interests could no longer hide the fact that American Jews and Black Americans were so obviously at cross-purposes. Many Black Americans believed that it was time to consolidate their own power and close ranks against outsiders, eschewing the goal of integration in favor of an appeal for "Black Power."

The Black Power movement, which, among other things, defined Jews outside the racialized movement for social change, more than any other development hastened an end to the "Golden Age" of American Jewry, an age in which American Jews could enjoy the luxury of increasing tolerance while linking their identity to a commitment to progressive causes. But rather than adjust their identities in accordance with a revised racial status, many Jews determinedly refused to consider themselves part of "white" America. Jewish intellectuals and leaders could not extricate themselves from the discourse of liberalism and marginality, which for them had come to define the Jewish past and to embody the Jewish present. But the reality of race in the United States meant that the memory of Jewish suffering could not register on a public conscience now wrestling with its more intense and more protracted engagement with Black Americans.

The Black Power Revolution

In the February 1965 issue of *Commentary* magazine, the civil rights leader Bayard Rustin recast the civil rights movement from one that emphasized equality before the law to one that emphasized actual social and economic equality. Rustin wrote that "the legal foundation of racism in America [had been] destroyed" and that the civil rights movement "is now concerned not merely with removing the barriers to full opportunity *but with achieving the fact of equality.*"[1] By the mid-1960s, indeed, many Black leaders began to feel that the strategies employed in the early phases of the civil rights revolution were no longer effective. Passive resistance protests and lunch-counter sit-ins were useful for achieving legal integration in the South, it was true, but they did not produce jobs, education, or health care in inner-city slums.

The problems of the inner city seemed to dominate public discourse as more Black youngsters came of age while living in urban slums and as expectations of advancement continued to grow. From 1940 to 1963 more than three million Black Americans moved from the South to other sections of the country, and by 1966 Black and Puerto Rican children made up a majority of the youngsters in New York City's public school system.[2] Many younger Blacks began to feel betrayed by the established civil rights leadership, which they accused of being wedded to an antiquated program of "gradualism," nonviolent demonstrations, and coalition politics. It made no difference to the "New Ghetto Man" that progress against racial discrimination had been made, as any amount of progress would have fallen short of expectations. The urban Black male had developed a new psyche, completely opposed to the docile and submissive Black American of white racist mythology. The new Black male was politically "hip," tolerant of violence, and loud in proclaiming that he would not passively submit to a life of material deprivation and racial discrimination.[3]

The "New Ghetto Man" was discontent, and he showed it by waging a series of urban riots across the country. On August 11, 1965, the archetypical race riot of the late 1960s took place in the Watts section of Southeast Los Angeles. Watts was demographically representative of other big-city ghettos. Poverty figures showed that four out of ten persons were poor, 38 percent of the families were headed by women, and 47 percent of the children under eighteen lived in broken homes.[4] As on many similar occasions in the late 1960s, the violence began over a routine encounter between police officers and a Black resident, in this case a twenty-one-year-old unemployed Black man who had resisted arrest after being pulled over for driving while intoxicated. Shouting the motto of a local Black disk jockey, "Burn, baby, burn," a crowd of a thousand Watts residents gathered in response to the arrival of police reinforcements. That night young Watts residents attacked cars driven by whites, white news reporters, and cops. The rioting, looting, and burning lasted almost four days, resulting in thirty-four deaths, 1,072 injuries, 977 buildings damaged or destroyed, and four thousand arrests. On the fourth day the National Guard was called in to quell the violence. In all, there were forty-three racial disorders in 1966 and 164 during the first nine months of 1967. Thirty-three of the 1967 riots were of an intensity that required state police intervention, while eight required the deployment of the National Guard.

The riots in Newark and Detroit were on a scale similar to that of Watts.[5] The National Advisory Commission on Civil Disorders, known widely as the Kerner Commission, named for Governor Otto Kerner of Illinois, who chaired it, found that the typical rioter was a teenager or young adult, a lifelong resident of the city in which the riot took place, and, although a high-school dropout, somewhat better educated than his nonrioting Black neighbor. This typical rioter was usually underemployed or employed at menial labor, fiercely proud of his race, extremely hostile to both whites and middle-class Blacks, and, "although informed about politics, highly distrustful of the political system."[6] There were also clear nationalist overtones to the riots, as rioters showed extreme discipline in attacking mostly symbols of white authority in the ghetto—primarily police and white-owned stores—for the most part sparing stores with markings that indicated they were owned by Blacks.[7]

Militant Black nationalists viewed the riots as guerilla wars being fought to liberate Black colonies. The idea that Black ghettos were actually colonies that served to enrich whites living outside the ghetto had its first prominent spokesman in Malcolm X. Before his assassination in 1964, Malcolm had exclaimed that "in every Black ghetto . . . every night the owners of those businesses go home with that Black community's money, which helps the ghetto stay poor."[8] Malcolm also warned that Blacks would take a lesson from the other colonized people of the world. "If white America doesn't think that the Afro-American, especially the upcoming generation, is capable of adopting the guerrilla tactics now being used by oppressed people elsewhere on earth, she is making a drastic mistake."[9] By 1967, men like Stokely Carmichael and H. Rap Brown, successively the leaders of the Student Nonviolent Coordinating Committee (SNCC), picked up Malcolm's read on the Black ghetto and became the two leading spokesmen for revolutionary nationalism. At a July 19 rally, while Newark was cooling down from its riot, Brown shouted that "Honkies" owned all the stores in the neighborhood. "You got to own some of them stores. I don't care if you have to burn him down and run him out. The streets are yours. Take 'em."[10]

The idea that Black ghettos constitute an internal colony within the United States continues to be hotly debated among scholars.[11] But even if the Black ghetto of the 1960s did not possess the most frequently cited attributes of a "colony," it did suffer from sufficiently high levels of exploitation and social isolation to lend the idea substantial emotional validity. "Like the peoples of the underdeveloped countries," Harold Cruse wrote

in one of the most eloquent statements on the subject, "the Negro suffers
. . . the psychological reactions to being ruled over by others not of his
kind."[12]

In the late 1960s, the nationalist interpretation of Black status in the
United States came under the rubric of Black Power. Black Power essentially secularized the separatist impulse of Black nationalism, which had
previously manifested itself in religious form, and produced an ideological
convergence of older nationalist groups and newer militant civil rights
groups such as SNCC and the Congress of Racial Equality (CORE).[13]
Black Power meant different things to different people, but Stokely Carmichael, coiner of the term "Black Power," attacked the idea of liberal
integrationism and alliances with whites on the grounds that it implied that
there was nothing worth preserving in the Black community. "Let any
ghetto group contemplating coalition be so tightly organized, so strong that
. . . it is an 'indigestible body' which cannot be absorbed or swallowed
up."[14]

The attempt to consolidate Black political power along racial lines had
a new international appeal to Black Americans responding to the rise of
the decolonized nations of the Third World. The manipulative Cold War
approach of both superpowers to the aspirations of Third World countries
and the recent civil rights victories inspired among Black Americans a feeling that they were part of an international majority of oppressed nonwhite
people, rather than an isolated minority confined to the United States. The
new international identity gave currency to the concept of "Negritude,"
which linked Black Americans emotionally, biologically, and politically
with other dark-skinned people across the globe and which often resulted
in a virulent antiwhite chauvinism.

The development of antiwhite racism among Black Power leaders was
bound to impact American Jews more than other whites, if for no other
reason than the heavy Jewish involvement in civil rights and Black organizations. One of the most conspicuous instances in which a Black organization with heavy Jewish support and membership turned against Jews was
the case of SNCC. Founded in 1960 on the principles of philosophical
pacifism, SNCC had attracted widespread Jewish support. But dissatisfac-
tion with what the civil rights movement had achieved caused SNCC to
take a major turn by the late 1960s. In 1969, SNCC officially deleted
"nonviolent" from its name, and its leader at that time, H. Rap Brown,
declared that the organization would no longer be associated with such a
concept as a solution to the problems of oppressed people.[15] Before this

declaration, in 1967, SNCC published an attack on Israel in its June/July issue of the *SNCC Newsletter* that borrowed from the most extreme Arab propaganda. The newsletter charged the Israelis with atrocities and published cartoons showing a hand marked with a Star of David and a dollar sign tightening a rope around the necks of the Egyptian leader Gamal Abdel Nasser and the heavyweight boxer Muhammad Ali, implying that the same Jewish forces had both men in their deadly grip. Another cartoon depicted Moshe Dayan, the venerable Israeli general, wearing dollar signs instead of a general's shoulder insignia. "Zionists lined up Arab victims and shot them in the back in cold blood. This is the Gaza strip," the text read, referring to a blurred photograph, "not Dachau, Germany." The text of the newsletter sounded anti-Jewish as well as anti-Zionist themes in a list of indictments the editors called "facts." It stated that the famous European Jewish family the Rothschilds, "who have long controlled the wealth of many European nations" control much of Africa's mineral wealth. "Fact 32" of the SNCC newsletter was particularly intriguing. It said that "under the guise of 'foreign aid' the Israeli *Histadrut* (Labor Organization) has gone into African countries, tried to exploit and control their economies, and sabotaged African liberation movements, along with any other African movements or projects opposed by the United States and other Western powers."[16] In attempting to explain that SNCC was not an anti-Semitic organization, Ralph Featherstone, editor of the newsletter, exacerbated the matter, explaining that he was interested in denouncing not all Jews but "only Jewish oppressors"—a term he applied to Israel and "to those Jews in the little Jew shops in the [Black] ghettos." Featherstone also conceded that he had received some of the information for the SNCC newsletter from Arab sources.[17] The Stanford University historian Clayborne Carson, the eminent chronicler of SNCC, has written that the SNCC newsletter was not written as an official policy statement but probably would have been approved by many of SNCC's leaders. For many Blacks in SNCC, the antiwhite, anti-Israel, and sometimes anti-Semitic stand was, according to Carson, "a test of their willingness to demonstrate SNCC's break from its civil rights past and a reconfirmation that ties with whites were inconsistent with their desire to express racial aspirations and frustrations without restraint."[18]

If one idea was universal among the advocates of Black Power, it was the necessity of a realistic approach to politics. Black Power ideologues believed that the self-interest of American ethnic groups always took precedence over the abstract ideals of equality and brotherly love and that

Blacks had to mobilize as a collective if they were to realize their interests. To be sure, there were prominent Black Powerites, perhaps most appropriately categorized as "alienated revolutionaries," who believed in the efficacy of a call for a separate Black nation. But Black Power spokespersons generally sought to maintain group identity while enjoying the full benefits of United States citizenship. Black Power asserted that "the dominant thrust of Black ideologies has been the desire for inclusion in the broader American society."[19]

This was in fact the central theme of Harold Cruse's landmark volume, *The Crisis of the Negro Intellectual* (1967), in which Cruse excoriated the Black intelligentsia not only for embarking on integrationist schemes over the preceding forty years but also for failing to formulate an effective nationalist program designed to address the very specific problems of Black Americans in the United States. According to Cruse, "most of the post-Garvey religio-nationalist creeds have developed an impractical Back-to-Africa, separatist other-worldliness which is romantic escapism; for if the Afro-American does not find his salvation in the United States he will find it nowhere."[20] In this polemic against the Black left, Cruse criticized the Garveyites for relying on "Back-to-Africa" fantasies, the Communists for allowing Black nationalism to be subordinated to the needs of white Communists, the integrationists for ignoring the realities of group politics, and the ideology of guerrilla warfare, which by the late 1960s had superseded the Marxism of some Black Power activists.[21] For Cruse, "the individual in America has few rights that are not backed up by the political, economic, and social power of one group or another. Hence, the individual Negro has, proportionately, very few rights indeed because his ethnic group . . . has very little political, economic or social power . . . to wield."[22]

It is ironic, therefore, that a movement born of the nationalist impulse in Black Americans would utilize the tradition of American pluralism to achieve revolutionary gains in the sphere of domestic politics, but that is indeed what happened. On the domestic political front, there were essentially three areas of concern for Black Power: community control of government agencies and programs; race preferences; and political power through government jobs and the redrawing of electoral districts. The demands made in these areas reflected a desire to dissipate the white influence on the affairs of the Black ghetto and led inevitably to confrontation with American Jews.

The irony of a clash between Jews and Black Power advocates should not go unmentioned. Black Power sought to obtain political and economic privileges through communal solidarity, while Jews, at least to a certain extent, relied less on group solidarity and political power to achieve their place in American life than most other ethnic groups. There can be no doubt that before the emergence of large-scale bureaucracies and professional specialization in the consolidated economy of the 1920s, American Jews relied on ethnic-based institutions to advance themselves, including Jewish trade unions, an extensive network of Jewish communal services, and Jewish loan associations.[23] Nevertheless, after the first world war, Jews enthusiastically utilized education and certification as a major platform by which to join the middle class, and they relied increasingly on the growing use of merit-based criteria to gain admission to higher education and the professions. The increasing use of objective professional and educational criteria in employment saw a massive alteration in the character of the Jewish workforce by the 1920s, which by 1930 and for the remaining decades of the twentieth century would be characterized primarily by white-collar professional employment. By 1935, a survey sponsored by the New York Welfare Council found that only 3 percent of Jewish households contained fathers employed as unskilled laborers. By the late 1920s, the historian Henry Feingold tells us, "it became clear, [Jews] were not the sons of workers nor would they produce sons who were workers."[24] While white-collar professionals form semiexclusive occupational niches through networks and associations much as blue-collar laborers do, in the case of the professions these exclusionary devices are fueled at least as much by the shared values derived from common occupational and educational experiences as by those deriving from any specific ethnic loyalty.[25] It therefore seems likely that only a small fraction of American Jews owed their middle-class status to anything that could be defined as "Jewish" solidarity. Some critics might argue that Jews advanced into the middle class by utilizing those rights and privileges available to them as "whites" but denied to Blacks, including, in many states, the right to vote, greater residential mobility, and greater access to lending institutions.[26] But even from this perspective, the faster rise of Jews up the socioeconomic ladder compared to other white ethnic groups would have to be addressed before the explanatory power of education and merit in the creation of the Jewish middle class can be invalidated.[27] As the sociologist Nathan Glazer has commented about the Jews in the postwar period, "while America in general became more markedly middle class in its occupational structure, Jews became even more so."[28] Needless to say, the expansion of the public sector after World War II, greater access to higher education, and the implementation of merit-based civil service exams for government employees resulted in disproportionate Jewish representation in the very white-collar public sector professional class from whom Black Powerites would try to wrest control.

The Jewish Clash with Black Power

The conflict over community control in central cities, a subset of the more general New Left rebellion against large bureaucracies and the call for grassroots democracy, resulted in the most serious conflict of all—the New York City teacher's strike of 1968. From the perspective of many inner-city Blacks in the late 1960s, the failure of Northern public school systems to integrate since the *Brown* decision of 1954 and the continuing academic difficulties experienced by many Black pupils indicated that the white civil service bureaucracies charged with overseeing the public schools had failed. Having been promised integration by the powers that be, Black parents became increasingly frustrated; this frustration coupled with the increasingly obvious fact that Black children were not learning led them to drop their original demand for integration and to substitute a demand for local control.[29] In many cases, this put these local Black communities on a collision course with the Jews who had come to staff many of the large-scale urban civil service bureaucracies. In the New York City school system, for example, Jews had replaced Irish-Americans as the majority of teachers, principals, and administrators after the widespread institution of civil service examinations in 1940.[30] This situation came to an unfortunate climax in the Ocean Hill-Brownsville section of Brooklyn in the fall of 1968.

Although formerly a solid Jewish section of Brooklyn, Ocean Hill-Brownsville by 1968 had no white presence except for absentee landlords, shopkeepers, welfare workers, and teachers. As agitation for a larger parental voice in school affairs mounted, Ocean-Hill-Brownsville was designated one of three experimental districts set up with financial assistance from the Ford Foundation. The experiment gave a community-elected neighborhood board and its Black administrator, Rhody McCoy, a measure of local control over policies in the area's eight schools. The project was opposed by the predominantly Jewish United Federation of Teachers (UFT), which feared that decentralization on a citywide basis would damage the union's bargaining power. In the spring of 1968 McCoy, in a controversial use of power, transferred nineteen teachers out of the district without formal charges or hearings, setting the groundwork for a walkout of the 350 teachers in the district and for a series of three strikes later in the fall. Teachers and supervisors spent a total of seven weeks on the picket line, which turned out to be the longest school strike in American history up until that point. The strike paralyzed a school system of more than one million children, sixty thousand teachers and supervisors, and nine hundred schools.[31] What began as a dispute between the Ocean Hill Governing Board and the teachers' union soon turned into a struggle between Black spokesmen and the predominantly Jewish teachers' union.

As the teachers' strike dragged on, ugly manifestations of anti-Semitism and racism emerged. Vulgarities were exchanged between Black parents and picketing teachers. The UFT charged the governing board with inciting violence in the schools themselves. One incident involved the distribution of handbills, written by unknown Black militants, that read "it is impossible for the Middle-East murderers of colored people to possibly bring to this important task the insight, the concern, the exposing of the truth that is a must if the years of brainwashing and self-hatred that has been taught to our Black children by those blood-sucking exploiters and murderers is to be overcome."[32] These handbills had appeared earlier in the spring of 1967, when Robert "Sonny" Carson of Brooklyn CORE held demonstrations to enforce his demand that white principals in Ocean Hill be fired. The UFT, under the direction of Albert Shanker, printed and distributed half a million copies of the leaflet. While a highly controversial report by the New York City chapter of the American Civil Liberties Union accused the UFT of exacerbating racial tensions in the school strike, Shanker and others, including the Anti-Defamation League of B'nai B'rith, declared that anti-Semitism in New York City was at a "crisis level."[33]

There had been other incidents of intimidation during the strike. A Black teacher named Leslie Campbell, vice president of the Afro-American Teacher's Association, spoke at an Ocean Hill-Brownsville school assembly following the murder of Martin Luther King, at which he incited his audience of twelve- and fifteen-year-olds with the following remarks: "Don't steal toothpaste and combs. Steal things we can use. You know what I mean brothers. . . . When the enemy taps you on the shoulder, send him to the cemetery. You know who your enemy is."[34] If the youngsters who witnessed Campbell's diatribe were unsure as to exactly who the "enemy" was, Campbell clarified the matter on a subsequent radio show hosted by the Black activist Julius Lester on WBAI-FM. Over the air, Campbell read a poem dedicated to Albert Shanker by one of his fifteen-year-old students that read, in part, "hey, Jew Boy, with that yarmulke on your head/you pale-faced Jew Boy—I wish you were dead."[35]

In the end, the teachers' union held out, the Ocean Hill-Brownsville experiment failed, and the state suspended the governing board, replacing it with a trusteeship in anticipation of systemwide reform. The Ocean Hill-Brownsville controversy involved misinterpretations, misreadings, and insults on both sides. But perhaps what alarmed the New York Jewish community so much about the school strike was the calm and silence that the instances of Black anti-Semitism elicited from white non-Jews like New York City Mayor John Lindsay and the heads of the Ford Foundation who had helped finance and push the experiment along. Many Jews viewed this as the willingness of a non-Jewish, white "establishment" to sacrifice Jewish interests, embodied in this case in civil service rules and merit-based hiring regulations, in order to keep peace and garner support from a resurgent Black underclass.[36] The union ultimately won the right to return the teachers to the district, and the strike established the UFT as a major force in city and state politics. But the price of victory was high and included the union's image as a liberal and socially progressive force. Be that as it may, the relationship between Blacks and Jews in New York was permanently damaged by the strikes, which effectively weakened the city's liberal political coalition.[37]

The impression of many Jews that there were large numbers of whites, including large numbers of Jews, who were willing to acquiesce to Black demands for more political power and control even at the expense of treasured liberal values was reinforced by events that occurred surrounding the school strike. One of these events involved Thomas Hoving, the white, gentile director of the Metropolitan Museum of Art in New York City. In 1968 the Met exhibited a show titled "Harlem on My Mind." While the show was picketed by some Harlem Blacks for giving what they felt was a romanticized portrait of Harlem life as seen through white eyes, the biggest uproar came from some in the Jewish community who were disturbed by the introduction to the catalogue of the show, written by a sixteen-year-old Black girl, which read, in part, "[B]ehind every hurdle that the Afro-American has to jump stands the Jew who has already cleared it." The young girl went on to declare that anti-Semitism helps Blacks to feel more completely American. After a deluge of protests, the museum hastily included a paragraph of disclaimer, which the American Jewish Congress noted, was "half-hearted and did not end the libel against Jews."[38] Once again, the response of the director of the museum seemed to rankle more than the Black teenager's prose. Hoving declared, "[H]er statements are true. If the truth hurts, so be it."[39] Hoving himself later admitted that he could have used more tact in handling the situation.[40]

Another troubling incident was the selection in 1968 of John Hatchett by New York University to direct its new Martin Luther King Afro-American Student Center. Hatchett, a former New York City public school teacher, had authored an article in the *Afro-American Teacher's Forum* titled, "The Phenomenon of the Anti-Black Jews and the Black Anglo-Saxon: A Study in Educational Perfidy," which accused Jewish educators of mentally poisoning Black pupils.[41] President Hester and other officials at New York University were allegedly not aware of the article when they hired Hatchett, but they sought the help of former Supreme Court justice and United Nations Ambassador Arthur Goldberg in investigating the matter. After speaking with Hatchett personally, Goldberg informed President Hester of his belief that Hatchett understood the injustices and dangers contained in his article and recommended the continuation of his appointment. Hester, in his August 9 announcement that the university would retain Hatchett, stated that he did not believe Hatchett was an anti–Semite in the "classic sense" and that "I think it is true that there is a preponderance of Jewish teachers and administrators. . . . I can understand how someone might make references and still not be anti-Semitic."[42] While many Jewish leaders were outraged by Hester's response, they need only have waited two more months for Hatchett to seal his own fate. On October 8, speaking before seven hundred students at NYU's Bronx campus, Hatchett called Albert Shanker and other white political leaders "racist bastards," which led to his prompt dismissal as director of the Center. Nevertheless, an agreement was worked out with Black students by which Hatchett was permitted to stay on as an "adviser" and was provided university office space.[43]

The demand for Afro-American or Black Studies programs in universities across the country came from a growing feeling among Black students and scholars that the treatment of the Black experience in standard college curricula had been woefully inadequate. Since the basic impetus for Black studies programs originated with Black students on mixed-race university campuses, many of whom were influenced by the student revolts against university bureaucracies, the push for a separate Black studies curriculum was also accompanied by efforts of Black students to retain a say in the development of such programs.[44] Only a few months after the New York public school crisis, sixty-five out of 103 Black students at the nonsectarian

Jewish-sponsored Brandeis University in Waltham, Massachusetts, occupied an administration building in protest against the university administration. Led by a Black Jew, the Black militants announced the establishment of Malcolm X University in the center of Brandeis and demanded that a Black Studies program be instituted at the school in which Black students would have a say in the hiring of faculty and in the design of the curriculum. The militants accused the administration of having a "racist attitude," which must have been discouraging to university president Morris Abram, a man who not only served on the United States Civil Rights Commission but who was instrumental in obtaining Martin Luther King Jr.'s release from a DeKalb county prison in 1960 and who spearheaded the legal fight against the white domination of Southern politics.[45] Abram took a laid-back approach to the crisis at Brandeis, refusing to call the police and carrying on the business of the school from other buildings. Eventually, the militants ended their holdout and a Black Studies Department was created, though on a basis that was satisfactory to the Brandeis faculty.[46]

A more academically damaging and psychologically painful experience for many Jews was the crisis at the City University of New York (CUNY) over the demands of Black and Puerto Rican students for "open admissions" and other changes. City College had been a Jewish enclave for almost three-quarters of a century, primarily because Jews had attended college at two to three times the rate of non-Jewish Americans and because an overwhelming proportion of those students were poor and had no choice but to attend a free college like City. Pre-World War II quotas in most of the Ivy League schools also helped to determine Jewish college-going decisions in favor of CUNY.[47] Jews treated City College much as they did the public school system, as an entrance to the emerging meritocracy of the professions. While the faculty at City had only one truly renowned scholar in the philosopher Morris Raphael Cohen, the intellectual atmosphere fostered by the student body of second-generation immigrant Jews created a college experience of the first order. "It was an extraordinary education," said one alumnus. "At the very least, it was the equal of the best schools in terms of the range of subjects and the depth with which they were studied." As a recent author described it, City College at the zenith of its glory was "a den of precocious boys, at once coddled and driven by their parents, pail and frail, fierce and argumentative, pushy, awkward, sensitive, naive, and fearful."[48]

But in the spring of 1969, Black militants and Puerto Rican students occupied university buildings and succeeded in shutting down the campus as they waited for a list of five demands to be satisfied. The demands consisted of a Black and Puerto Rican freshmen orientation program under Black and Puerto Rican control; a degree-granting school of "Black and Puerto Rican Studies," with student control over hiring; an expansion of the school's remedial programs; a demand that the student body represent the ethnic composition of the public high schools in New York City; and a demand that all students preparing to teach in public schools acquire basic proficiency in Spanish and "Black and Puerto Rican heritage."[49]

After the closing of the campus, court orders to open the college resulted in rioting among white and Black students. Black militants took over classrooms, beating students who would not comply with their demands. Eventually, after a long and difficult struggle, the college adopted an open admissions policy that admitted all students who had graduated with an eighty average or higher from city high schools or who had been in the top half of their graduating class into one of CUNY's senior colleges and accepted all other students into one of the system's community colleges. While some critics have commented that in acquiescing to the demands of Black militants, City College created an environment friendly to increasing anti-Semitism, for most interested Jews the policy of open admissions at CUNY was most disturbing. The decline of standards that so many Jews and others had begun to associate with the panoply of Black demands for preferential treatment had hit home in a sacred institution of American Jewish life. The Jewish presence at CUNY quickly dissipated, going from an absolute majority to 37 percent by 1971.[50]

Affirmative Action, the "White" Jew, and Black Anti-Semitism

Open admissions was just one component of extensive Black demands for preferential treatment, commonly referred to as "affirmative action," and represented the most obvious way in which Black Power activism clashed with the principle of equal opportunity long considered to be a hallmark of American liberalism. Affirmative action had its origins in the early 1960s, when the term "affirmative action" was inserted by Kennedy administration staffers into Executive Order 10925, which banned discrimination in hiring by federal contractors. Nobody paid much attention to the phrase until John Kennedy proposed a civil rights bill in 1963 and President Lyndon Johnson continued the effort, which culminated in the passage of the Civil Rights Act of 1964. Congressional opponents like Senator James Eastland of Mississippi opposed the civil rights bill, claiming that it would impose quotas against whites. Consequently, a sentence was added that explicitly rejected quotas. The Equal Employment Opportunity Commission, which was created by the act, was also stripped of enforcement power and so could not impose quotas. But, in 1965, the concept received its greatest push when President Johnson gave a speech at Howard University in which he used a phrase supplied by a young Daniel Patrick Moynihan: "We seek . . . not just equality as a right and a theory but equality as a fact and equality as a result." Shortly after the speech, Johnson signed Executive Order 11246, which made affirmative action programs the responsibility of an obscure division of the Department of Labor that operated outside the pressure of public scrutiny. For this reason this Executive Order has been called an "invisible milestone."[51] The original Executive Order required only that employees search aggressively for qualified minority applicants, who would then be put in the same pool as other applicants for selection. But by the late 1960s, the merit-based, bureaucratic structure of large or-ganizations proved to be a difficult employment obstacle for many Blacks, most of whom had received inferior education and other social preparations for the taking of standardized tests. Many advocates of affirmative action, both white and Black, viewed achievement in school and test-taking to be too narrow a criterion for the selection of job candidates, or even for college admission. As one writer put it, the "history of affirmative action can be seen as a struggle over the fairness of the modern meritocracy, with minorities arguing that educational measures shouldn't be the deciding fac-tor in who gets ahead and opponents of affirmative action saying that to bend the criteria for Blacks is to discriminate unfairly against more deserv-ing whites."[52]

All of this concerned American Jews a great deal, since large segments of American Jewry had benefited so marvelously from the growth of merit-based advancement. More to the point, those professions in which Jews tended to cluster—public school teaching and other civil service work, college teaching, medicine, and law—were all areas in which affirmative action, whether in hiring or training, would be heavily instituted.[53] The Jewish community has always exhibited sharply contrasting views on affir-mative action, but there is no doubt that the system of racial preferences as it came to be implemented presented a dilemma for American Jewish identity.[54]

As implemented, affirmative action represented a public recognition not only that Blacks were a particularly disadvantaged minority, a presumption with which many Jews would have undoubtedly agreed, but also that Jews no longer were, a presumption that necessitated a serious reconsideration of Jewish identity. The affirmative action designation of Jews as privileged whites was later made official in the 1973 Office of Management and Budget Statistical Directive Number Fifteen, the little noticed federal document that carved out the five official racial categories according to which so many institutions of American life now function. The directive presumed that those individuals who fell into the "African American," "Asian American," "Puerto Rican/Latino," and "Native American/Pacific Islander" categories had been oppressed by those who were in the fifth category, "non-Hispanic whites," to which American Jews now belonged. The implications of this directive for Jews were brought to light in the 1977 Supreme Court case *United Jewish Organizations v. Carey,* in which members of the Hasidic community in Williamsburg, Brooklyn, sued New York state, claiming that the redrawing of electoral districts to ensure the election of minority legislators discriminated against them. The Supreme Court concluded that Hasidic Jews, along with persons of Irish, Polish, or Italian descent, were not within the scope of civil rights protections defined by federal law. "Presumably," writes one critic of that case, "the abstract interests of Hasidim as whites (if such interests exist) were more fundamental than their interests as Hasidic Jews. After all, Hasidim and Italian-American Catholics are part of the same racial community, according to Statistical Directive 15."[55]

While the question of when and to what extent Jews became legally and socially "white" remains a matter of substantial scholarly inquiry, there is no question that the widespread implementation of race preferences represented the most complete and formal recognition of the Jews' status as privileged whites. It was this public association of Jews with the rights and privileges of all other white people that presented the most serious challenge of the Black Power movement to Jewish identity.[56] For although affirmative action eventually widened its base of beneficiaries to include women, the original concept was exclusively racial. Jewish identity had been so enmeshed with a history of suffering that Jewish leaders and intellectuals found it immensely difficult to envision themselves as privileged whites, the way most Black Power advocates saw them. The difficulty American Jews had with adjusting to their civic whiteness, and the virulence with which Black Power leaders insisted upon it, provides a window through which the cultural uncertainty of both Black Americans and American Jews can be clearly seen. Not only is an identity dependent on victim status a cultural bane for the Jewish community in the United States, but the animosity fostered in the Black community by Jewish insistence on this status is an indication of the crippled and lopsided development of Black identity as well.[57]

On the surface, Black Power advocates lamented Jewish involvement in Black affairs because it prevented Blacks from developing a program politically and culturally more suitable for themselves. But a closer look at the work of Harold Cruse and others reveals that the Black Power disdain for the involvement of Jews in Black affairs is somewhat more complicated. What seemed to bother Cruse and others sympathetic to Black Power about Jews was their ambivalent racial identity. Black Power advocates found that, among Black Americans, dark skin and the low status imposed on individuals who possessed it was the most salient and powerful unifying force. Lacking any other universally shared cultural values as powerful as the experience of oppression around which to rally, advocates of Black Power found that their most useful tool for consolidating Black opinion was to stake out the ground of racial oppression as theirs alone and to stand toe to toe against a monolithic white majority. Black Power theorists saw that dealing with Jews and other white ethnics as distinct groups with different histories and varying levels of opportunity and acceptance would reduce the strength of Black claims. Moreover, this strategy was in keeping with the history of most Black Americans, who rarely experienced white power and privilege as ethnically differentiated. For them, American pluralism had always been defined in terms of a biracial polity in which Blacks made up theoretically one-half of the racial dichotomy. Since Jews were the white ethnic group with the strongest collective memory of exclusion and oppression, it was essential that Black Power theorists reduce the history of the Jews to only their experience in the United States, which was relatively privileged, and to the color of their skin, which was relatively white. In the view of Black Power, the tortured history of the Jews might cause them to think that their place in the United States remained alongside oppressed Blacks, but this was no longer a tolerable situation for anyone interested in linking race to persecution in order to unite Blacks and to secure privileges. This motivation was laid bare in Cruse's *The Crisis of the Negro Intellectual.*

Ostensibly, Cruse believed that Jews, whether in the Communist party of the 1930s, the interracial coalition of the postwar decades, or the social sciences, had become the biggest problem for Blacks precisely because they had so identified with the Black struggle in the United States. "What has further complicated this emergence of Afro-American ethnic consciousness is the Jewish involvement in this interracial process over the last fifty-odd years. The role of American Jews as political mediator between Negro and Anglo-Saxon must be terminated by Negroes themselves."[58] But Cruse's disdain for Jewish involvement in Black affairs goes way beyond his concerns about its alleged negative impact on Black leadership capability or Black nationalist ideology. Cruse's central concern about Jews as they relate to Black Americans was their ambiguous relationship to power and oppression.

As Cruse explains it, his Jewish problem begins with the predominance of Jews in the Communist party of the 1930s, a period in which scholars like Herbert Aptheker and other assimilated Jewish Communists assumed the mantle of leadership on Black matters, thus burying the Black radical potential in the slough of white intellectual paternalism. It was Cruse's impression that, while the Jewish Communists repeatedly acted to squelch any nationalistic eruptions among the Black Communists, they rigorously pursued every available strategy to preserve Jewish cultural identity. The Communist party under Jewish influence, therefore, not capitalism, had begun the "great brainwashing of Negro radical intellectuals" and established theoretical dominance over Black Americans.[59]

But Cruse's interpretation of the Jews' role in the Communist party is troubling. To be sure, his resentment toward the white paternalism of the Communist party was well founded, as was his belief that the Communist party promoted Black Americans into leadership positions in the party but effectively controlled them from behind the scenes.[60] But Cruse's experience with Jewish Communists who were wildly nationalistic and concerned with specific Jewish issues appears not to have been representative. Jewish Communists were generally individuals who sought to transcend the divisions between people and who no longer thought of themselves as Jewish. Most Jewish radicals were in fact opposed to Zionism, not only because they were opposed to most expressions of nationalism but because they believed it to be an inadequate answer to the "Jewish problem" and a diversion from the true business of revolution.[61] On the matter of the Communist party position on Jewish issues, one sociologist of Jews and Communism has stated that "on occasion, the party took certain positions on Jewish issues which were attractive to Jews, but in general there was no group in the population for which the party showed more contempt and disdain, in its formulations of specific party positions, than the Jews."[62] For most of the period from the 1920s through the 1950s, the party remained staunchly anti-Zionist. For the Communists, the main enemy in Palestine was British imperialism, backed by Zionism. "We must not let up the attack on Zionism, despite the endangering of the United Front with Jewish organizations," read one party directive. For a brief period between 1944 and 1949, when the Soviet Union was allied with Britain, the Communist party was able to adopt a program more supportive of a Jewish homeland, but the party never backed free immigration to Palestine.[63]

Reading Cruse with all of this in mind suggests that his problem with Jews had less to do with the dominance of Jewish Communists over party policy than it did with the ambivalent racial status that Communist party membership implied. The Communist party appealed to certain Jews because it offered the promise of theoretical equality to members of an historically oppressed group. But the work of consolidating a Black polity around race and oppression that the Black Powerites had embarked on required the elimination of any white ethnic claims to cultural oppression or group vulnerability. Accordingly, Cruse argued that Jews had lost their place among the "have-nots" and gained a place among the "haves." "In America, Jews have no real problems, political, economic, or cultural. And they have no honest cause for complaints about anti-Semitism . . . one might just as easily say that having become the most affluent group in America . . . despite anti-Semitism, is too much of a cross for American Jews to bear under 'democratic' capitalism!"[64] Like other Black nationalists, Cruse internationalized this change in Jewish status by relating it to the State of Israel. Today, "American Jews are a power in the land and should act accordingly. Behind this power, of course, is the State of Israel, which immeasurably enhances the new status of American Jewry as a 'have' group."[65] Cruse believed that the suffering Jews had experienced in Europe had very little bearing on the American experience, and it is here that he reveals his real Jewish problem. "One cannot deny the horror of the European Holocaust, but for all practical purposes (political, economic, and cultural) as far as Negroes are concerned, Jews have not suffered in the United States. They have, in fact, done exceptionally well on every level of endeavor, from a nationalist premise or on an assimilated status." In the United States, according to Cruse, it is Black Americans who are history's chosen people, and now they want to "play this game. When that happens, woe be to the side that is short on numbers," Cruse wrote in an ominous warning to American Jews.[66] Ultimately, for Cruse, the problem was not so much that Jewish activists historically had opposed Black nationalism and favored Jewish nationalism but that Jewish activism implied Jewish victimization, which diluted the Black claim to unchallenged victimhood and denied them the political advantages accruing to such a status.

Cruse was not alone in his attempt to eliminate American Jews in the battle for the title of supreme victim. Evidence from the late 1960s shows that other Black intellectuals sympathetic to Black Power were preoccupied with this "Jewish problem" as well. In his attempt to explain Black anti-Semitism, James Baldwin wrote that one "does not wish . . . to be told by an American Jew that his suffering is as great as the American Negro's suffering. It isn't, and one knows that it isn't from the very tone in which he assures you that it is." To Baldwin, the Jew in America was white, and because of this he had the advantages afforded whiteness. "For it is not here, and not now, that the Jew is being slaughtered, and he is never despised, here, as the Negro is, *because* he is an American."[67]

If the relationship of Jews to power continued to be a confusing and troubling question for American Jews, Black Power theorists and activists suffered from no such confusion and wanted to make it known in the clearest terms just how much a part of the white power structure Jews had become. Some Black Power theorists and activists portrayed Jews not just as white oppressors but as perhaps the most oppressive of all whites. This impulse had been present in Black nationalist ideology from the very beginning. The theology of the Black Muslims taught not only that whites were devils but that a "big-headed scientist" named *Yacub,* or Jacob, the Jewish patriarch, had been the mad scientist who created the white race in a cave, out of which they were eventually led, Jews first, by Moses, to wreak havoc on Black people, God's original creation.[68] The rhetorical patterns assumed in the effort to erase the claim of the Jews on the white conscience reverberated in the language used by those sympathetic with the goals of Black Power in the late 1960s. James Baldwin minced no words in explaining why this was so. "In the American context, the most ironical thing about Negro anti-Semitism is that the Negro is really condemning the Jew for having become an American white man—for having become, in effect, a Christian. . . . The Jew does not realize that the credential he offers, the fact that he has been despised and slaughtered, does not increase the Negro's understanding. It increases the Negro's rage."[69]

The attempt of Black Power radicals to minimize the severity and importance of Jewish suffering was most conspicuous in the usurpation of the language of the Holocaust. The use of such terms as "genocide" and "ho-

locaust" to describe the situation of Black Americans seemed pervasive
among even some of the most prominent leaders in the Black community.
In February 1967, Stokely Carmichael told a Black audience in Oakland
that "we are not talking about politics tonight, we're not talking about
economics tonight, we're talking about the survival of a race of people.
. . . Many of us feel . . . that they are getting ready to commit genocide
against us." In 1968, even a leader of Martin Luther King's integrationist
Southern Christian Leadership Conference said that "genocide" is a danger.[70] James Baldwin, who earlier in the decade had forecast the Black
radicalism of the late 1960s in his essay *The Fire Next Time,* also lent himself
toward this kind of extremism. At one point he asserted that "white America appears to be seriously considering the possibilities of mass extermination."[71] Even when Baldwin attempted to be conciliatory, he was tied to
the imagery of the Nazi genocide. In a well-publicized letter of resignation
from the editorial board of the Black magazine *Liberator,* which, ironically,
had published an article Baldwin thought was anti-Semitic, Baldwin stated
that he did not think America would survive the current storm in race
relations. "Nor should she," Baldwin claimed. "She is responsible for this
holocaust in which the living writhe. . . . We are a criminal nation, built
on a lie, and, as the world cannot use us, it will presently find some way
of disposing of us."[72] Baldwin's use of Holocaust iconology eventually
involved him in a heated exchange with the Jewish editor of the Zionist
monthly *Midstream.* In an article that appeared in the *New York Review of
Books* titled "An Open Letter to My Sister, Miss Angela Davis," Baldwin
compared the indicted Communist conspirator to a Jewish woman headed
for a concentration camp in Nazi Germany, writing, "[Y]ou look exceedingly alone, say, as the Jewish housewife in the boxcar headed for Dachau."
In a fiery essay, Shlomo Katz of *Midstream* accused Baldwin of comparing
the American criminal justice system with Nazism.[73]

In a conspicuous effort at historical role reversal, one Black Power
spokesman even compared American Jews to Nazis. Julius Lester wrote
that in America it was Blacks "who are the Jews. . . . There is no need for
Black people to wear yellow stars of David on their sleeves; that star of
David is all over us. And the greatest irony of all is that it is the Jews who
are in the position of being Germans." Demonstrating Black Power's refusal
to recognize gradations in power among whites, Lester argued that Black
Americans were a colonized people who were not in a position to make
fine distinctions among the colonizers. "Everyone else, the nonblacks, are

the colonizers, and Jews are no exception because they hold only a measure of that power. It is power, and the establishment maintains its power partially through Jews."[74]

Cruse, Baldwin, and the others were not wrong in insisting that racism and anti-Semitism in the United States were of a quite different order. They were not wrong to insist that Jews and Blacks were not "in the same boat" as far as the attitude of white gentiles was concerned. American racism had in a very real way helped define and shape American history, whereas American anti-Semitism had not even constituted a small chapter of it. But it was quite another thing to deny the tenacity of Jewish memory, to deny to American Jews the psychological impact of their history and to disparage the tentativeness with which they viewed their own status in the United States. In a sobering observation, one Jewish writer later commented, "True enough, neither memory nor possibility degrades us here and now, as here and now degrade the Black. . . . [But] how shall we react when . . . Baldwin tells us that our evocation of our past is an occasion for Black rage, when, that is, he asks us to deny our past?"[75]

But despite the unrealistic and often offensive approach the Black Power theorists took, there can be no question they had struck the bull's eye in reading the American Jewish psyche. Black radicals were in large measure correct to see Jewish involvement in Black affairs as a reflection of Jewish identity based on the memory of persecution that no longer spoke to the Jewish present. By the late 1960s, it seems that the phenomenon of religious tolerance had begun to filter down into even the most stubbornly resistant areas of American life. Before 1960, for example, appointments of Jews to high-level college administrative posts were almost unheard of. By the end of the 1960s, such appointments had been made at a number of major institutions, including the University of Chicago, the University of Pennsylvania, the Massachusetts Institute of Technology, Yale Law School, and Harvard Law School.[76] Jewish representation on college faculties and in the student body hit record numbers during this period. In 1971 Jews made up 17 percent of all students at private universities.[77] The opening up of new opportunities for Jews took place in just about all occupations and industries. Not only were Jews prominent among the elite literary critics and editors by the 1960s, but they were increasingly influential in the fields of journalism, publishing, and television broadcasting as well.[78] The postwar resistance of large corporations to hiring Jewish graduates of prestigious colleges and business schools virtually collapsed in the 1960s and 1970s, as such traditionally non-Jewish companies as Du Pont, Bell Labs, AT&T,

Chrysler, Colgate-Palmolive, and Ford appointed Jews to the highest management positions.[79] In addition to these corporations, historically gentile law firms, stock trading companies, and real estate brokerages began to hire on the basis of merit, as more sophisticated skills and knowledge replaced "good breeding" as prerequisites for applicants at firms wishing to maintain their position on the fast track.[80] The face of American politics began to change as well. While Jewish political candidates in largely non-Jewish areas historically faced uphill battles getting elected to office, by the 1960s the gentile resistance to Jewish candidates had started to unravel. Between 1937 and 1961 the proportion of Americans surveyed who said they would not vote for a qualified Jew for president dropped from 46 percent to 23 percent (to 7 percent in 1983).[81] In short, by the late 1960s and early 1970s the United States was open to American Jews (as well as to individuals from other historically marginalized groups) in all of its most important facets.

The pressing issue for American Jews at this time was, therefore, not the danger of external threat or the challenge of expanding civil rights but internal dissolution. As early as 1950, the Jewish immigrant world and its Yiddish press, synagogues, theater, and literature were passing from the Jewish scene, as was the Jewish character of the trade unions. The majority of immigrant Jews had been ritually orthodox but possessed only a superficial knowledge of Jewish religious thought, leaving later generations of American Jews without a substantive pool of knowledge from which to draw. The respected conservative rabbi Robert Gordis testified to the seriousness of the cultural crisis in American Judaism when he wrote in 1955 that the "ills of American Jewry, its vast shapelessness, the incredibly low level of Jewish knowledge, its consequently easy surrender to vulgarity and emptiness . . . all these have persisted too long to be discounted as signs of immaturity or as mere growing pains."[82] In the words of the historian Lloyd Gartner, American Jewish religious and cultural life "was dominated by the quest for an American form of religious tradition and by the effort to maintain institutions unaided by government or federations of Jewish philanthropies."[83]

In their attempt to redefine how the world saw Jewish people by relocating them permanently on the white side of an international racial divide, Black Power theorists and activists hit on a Jewish identity problem that has vexed Jews since the age of Enlightenment. The problem of recasting Jewish identity outside the land of Israel, in a society of relative freedom and opportunity, as something other than a response to external attack and a commitment to progressive causes would emerge as the predominant issue for American Jewry at the close of the twentieth century. The problem is one that afflicts all people who have been historically victimized. In the words of one critic, the dilemma for the Jews is that "an honorable life is not possible if they remember too little and a normal life is not possible if they remember too much."[84] The manner in which most Jewish intellectuals and leaders approached the issue of Black Power and the political radicalism of the late 1960s is, almost in its entirety, a reflection of the Jewish struggle with this fundamental question of selfhood.

Black Power, the New Left, and the Jews

As already mentioned, in the last half of the twentieth century Jewish identity developed with two fundamental emphases, liberalism and the idea of Jewish community. By the late 1960s, Israel had emerged as the central focus of Jewish group-mindedness, and, just as liberalism had come under attack, so, too, had Jewish nationalism. The Six-Day War, in 1967, reactivated feelings for the Jewish state in American Jews that had laid dormant since Israel's birth in 1948 and that many American Jews did not themselves know they had. On the eve of the war, Rabbi Morris Kertzer was able to write that American Jews "find difficulty in feeling the peoplehood of Israel, the mystical bond that unites them with their coreligionists outside the United States."[85] But the crisis of 1967 was severe enough to evoke a flood of emotion in the American Jewish community.

There was no question that the central role played by the Holocaust in the minds of American Jews deeply affected their view of the Six-Day War. Many in the Jewish community sustained a lingering guilt over not having done enough to save European Jews, and Israel was considered the only saving grace of that ghastly event, a constant reminder for many that Jews must fend for themselves. When Israel's Arab enemies surrounded the Jewish state in 1967, many American Jews believed that the coming war might very well result in the second genocidal calamity for Jews in a span of twenty-five years, and Arab leaders gave them every reason to think that this might be so. On May 28, President Aref of Iraq told Iraqi soldiers, "This is the day of battle . . . we are determined and united to achieve our clear aim—to remove Israel from the map." Ahmed Shukeiry, head of the Palestine Liberation Organization, declared that hardly a Jew would survive to be repatriated to Europe.[86] With the possibility of another Holocaust on their minds, American Jews responded as they never had previously to any world crisis. Between the day when Egypt's Gamal Abdel Nasser closed the Gulf of Aqaba on May 23 and the end of the war on June 10, well over one hundred million dollars was raised for the Israel Emergency Fund of the United Jewish Appeal. While there had been vocal anti-Zionist minorities within the American Jewish community, pollsters found that 99 percent of all the Jews in America supported the Israeli position in 1967. Even the militant anti-Zionist group the American Council for Judaism refrained from making public statements until the war was over.[87] In June 1967, more than seventy-five hundred American Jews volunteered to take over the civilian jobs of Israelis who were serving in the armed forces. One man arrived at the Jewish Agency in New York on June 5 and offered his two sons for combat in Israel in lieu of the money he could not afford to donate. Purchases of Israeli bonds soared by more than 130 percent.[88]

As sensitivities were raised by the war, it became clear to many Jews that the two most important aspects of American Jewish identity, the commitment to liberalism and the State of Israel, had come under serious attack. Liberalism and Israel always had their enemies, but this time the attacks were disturbing because they came from former allies on the left, rather than from those on the right—that is, by Black Americans in the Black Power movement and by formerly friendly whites, now a part of the radicalized New Left. The radicalization of the New Left is an integral part of the story of the rise of Black Power and how American Jews related to it, not only because young Jews made up a disproportionately large contingent of the New Left but because the history of the New Left in the 1960s so closely paralleled the development of Black Power. As one student leader put it regarding the central body of the New Left, the Students for a Democratic Society (SDS), "SDS has consistently supported the political viewpoints and actions of the most militant segments of the Black movement and has consciously shaped its own analysis and program in response to those elements as they have evolved during the sixties from Malcolm X to SNCC to the Black Panther party."[89] In many crucial respects, the New Left and Black Power must be analyzed as part of the same phenomenon.

The New Left had its origins in the civil rights protests in the South of the early 1960s. In 1962, while still the student wing of the Democratic Socialist League for Industrial Democracy, SDS had issued its famous Port Huron statement, which emphasized the complicity of big government and big corporations in the exploitation of the common man and the involvement of common people in the solutions to their problems. The authors of the statement defined America's problems not so much in terms of class

divisions, as the "old" left had, but rather in terms of the spiritual deprivation experienced by most people as a result of elites that had captured
large institutions, rendering average citizens powerless, apathetic, alienated,
and without community.[90] The New Left concerned itself with essentially
three areas: the Vietnam War and, by extension, the role of the United
States in world affairs; equality for Black Americans and, by extension,
other subjugated peoples throughout the world; and the role of students
in campus administration and curriculum development.[91]

But the humanism of the Port Huron Statement would soon be transformed into violence and nihilism. Lacking a clear method by which to
achieve their goals, the college students who made up the heart of the
movement, radical student leaders like Abbie Hoffman, Jerry Rubin, and
Mark Rudd, social theorists like Herbert Marcuse and Norman O. Brown,
and the violence of the Vietnam War combined to radicalize the New Left.
At various points during 1965 and after, New Left students moved to shut
down army induction centers and campus ROTCs, burned draft cards, and
participated in campus sit-ins. Eventually, New Leftists became enamored
of such radical Third World revolutionaries as Ho Chi Minh, Che Guevara,
and Mao Tse-tung and of the colonial analogy many Black spokespersons
had ascribed to ghetto conditions in the United States. By the late 1960s,
the New Left began to resemble the old left in its factionalism. The mainstream SDS, which adhered to the view of Third World revolutionaries,
struggled for dominance of the movement with the Progressive Labor
Party, the more militant and orthodox Marxists. By 1969, the mainstream
SDS had formed a committee called the Weathermen, which believed that
the monster of capitalism would be slain by Third World uprisings abroad
and Black uprisings at home and that whites, the beneficiaries of "white
skin privilege," would be unable to participate. After 1969, the Weathermen eventually went underground to plan bombings against capitalism and
so fully accepted a program of violence that the cult murderer Charles
Manson became a party hero.[92]

The rise of the New Left contributed to the feeling of many middle-
class Jews that their interests were under attack. Both the violence the New
Left committed and the violence it solicited from police scared Jews, many
of whom feared they would suffer if the regular procedures of government
and the maintenance of law and order were not upheld. The New Left
opposition to bureaucracies of all kinds implied that it was opposed to those
institutions that embodied the concept of merit-based advancement, particularly within governmental and educational institutions, in which Jews

found a great deal of success. By 1969, one observer noted that "teaching in the university may not turn out to be as good a job as nice Jewish boys used to think." Jewish academics and intellectuals have produced a number of studies and memoirs that reflect widespread disillusionment with the eruption of the universities and the changes it wrought.[93]

At the landmark National New Politics Convention of 1967 in Chicago, the radicalism of the New Left and the Black Power movements converged, alienating many Jewish radicals. At the convention, the SNCC leader James Forman marched into the convention surrounded by men with dashikis and declared himself "dictator." The convention then voted to give Black delegates 50 percent of the votes, thus handing the convention over to their control. The young Martin Peretz, a financial benefactor of the convention and a future editor of the *New Republic* magazine, reported that he was sickened when he witnessed a Jewish radical screaming at one of the caucuses, "After four hundred years of slavery, it is right that whites should be castrated!"[94] The conference became a forum for Black militants, who eventually drafted the policy statement on the Middle East that the convention endorsed. The statement put the convention on record as condemning the "Imperialist Zionist war" of 1967. An alternative resolution calling for Arabs to respect pre-1967 borders was rejected out of hand. Increasingly, a movement that had once been dominated by middle-class white, often Jewish, students had become a movement dominated by Black militants and pro-Third World, often Jewish, revolutionaries. In the words of one New Left journalist, "The New Left caucus meeting in Chicago caused the first real crisis of conscience for the Jewish radicals in the left establishment when it condemned Zionism and the basic validity of a Jewish homeland and nation."[95]

Jews on the Left and Black Power

If the violence and anti-Zionist positions of the New Left frightened some Jews, the disproportionate and sometimes very vocal appearance of radical Jews who supported the New Left or were associated with it came as no surprise to those familiar with the legacy of Jewish political radicalism. The history of Jews in radical movements is long and strewn with examples of the flagrant disregard for mainstream Jewish concerns. Jews had been associated with liberal-left politics since the French Revolution, primarily because that revolution was associated throughout Europe with the belief in equal citizenship and the overthrow of reactionary monarchies. But with the liberalism of the revolution, as with all things, there was a price to pay. In the case of the Jews, the price to be paid would be their dissolution as a distinct people, a presumption held by the leaders of the revolution itself. French politician Clermon-Tonnere told the French parliament after the revolution that "one must refuse everything to the Jews as a nation, but one must give them everything as individuals."[96] The implicit assumption of liberal-left ideology was that Jews would become citizens no different from anyone else and that all forms of parochial identity and tribal loyalties would disappear when exposed to the light of reason and freedom. The left's inclination to view Jewish particularism as reactionary, tribal, and unmodern was epitomized by the Marxist revolutionary Rosa Luxemburg, who commented that "I have no separate corner in my heart for the [Jewish] ghetto: I feel at home in the entire world wherever there are clouds and birds and human tears."[97]

There remained, however, another, perhaps more specific Jewish problem for the socialist wings of the liberal left. While many socialist and Communist movements have supported equal citizenship for Jews, the association of Jews with capitalism and their disproportionate representation among businessmen, traders, and merchants often proved a thorn in the side of radical movements. One of the ways that socialists and Marxists of the nineteenth century dealt with this problem was to interpret anti-Semitism among the masses as a first step in the formation of class consciousness. Talk of "Jewish bankers" and "Jewish conspiracy" for many radicals was a necessary step in learning hatred toward all capitalists, irrespective of religious background. The rise of the *Narodnaya Volya* anticzarist movement in the late nineteenth century was hailed by many young Jewish leftists as evidence that the revolution was under way. Three of the twenty-eight members of the executive committee of this organization, which called for a pogrom in 1881 against the czar, the nobility, and the Jews, were themselves Jewish.[98] The betrayal of the Jews by Jews on the left was exemplified by the debate among French socialists over whether to support the cause of the Jewish French army captain Alfred Dreyfus, a victim of French anti-Semitism who had been falsely accused of espionage. For the revolutionary French left, Dreyfus was a professional soldier, a captain in the Army, and they allowed for no distinction among militarists, even those who were being persecuted for being Jewish.[99]

The inclination of Jewish radicals to sympathize with, or at least to tolerate, the grass-roots anti-Semitism of the masses was evident in the

1960s and was perhaps even more obvious than in the past because much of the "grass-roots" anti-Semitism in the United States came from Black radicals, whose leadership position in the revolutionary movement was beyond dispute. For many Jews on the left, Blacks were not accountable for their own human foibles to the same extent as whites because of their oppressed status, and Black anti-Semitism was seen as the fault of whites and/or Jews. Even some old-time Jewish leftists sided with the radical Black Power crowd and defended it from charges of anti-Semitism. The long-time radical journal *Jewish Currents* and its editor, Morris Schappes, continued to throw support behind SNCC after its turn toward anti-Zionism and anti-Semitism, even while revealing the traditional hostility of Communists toward nationalism of any kind. While Schappes wrote that "white liberal progressives can best combat Black nationalism where it exists by multiplying their activity to enforce the laws and achieve integration," Schappes threw his support behind the newly radicalized James Baldwin and the cause of the Black Panthers. Schappes wrote that Black anti-Semitism was not a harmful form of anti-Semitism because it was "a defensive, not an aggressive, *anti,* no matter how shrilly it is sounded." [100]

Another old-left Jew with a good deal of sympathy for much that had been done by the New Left was the world-renowned linguist Noam Chomsky, who defended the "Black Liberation" movement and the Black Panthers against charges of anti-Semitism. The Panthers had supported the terrorism of the Palestine Liberation Organization and were particularly vituperative toward Israel's supporters in the United States. The June 1967 issue of the Black Panther journal *Black Power* published a song parody that included the following lines: "The Jews have stolen all our bread/Their filthy women tricked our men into bed/ . . . We're gonna burn their towns and . . . piss upon the Wailing Wall/ . . . That will be ecstasy/killing every Jew we see." [101] Nevertheless, Chomsky declared "that the widely voiced claims regarding the alleged anti-Semitism of the Panthers and other groups seems to me severely distorted and misleading," and he complained that Jewish fears of widespread anti-Semitism in the Black Panther party were "so ignorant as to deserve no further comment." [102]

Some leftist Jewish intellectuals accepted Black Power's theory that the only thing significant about Jews in the United States was their white skin and that they were not only heirs to the privileges and power of whiteness but were also guilty of the racism and bigotry of white Christian civilization. The journalist Nat Hentoff revealed his belief that the sum total of being Jewish amounted to being oppressed and that therefore American

Jews, who were no longer oppressed, were not really Jews anymore. "Even more astonishing," Hentoff wrote, playing on the Nazi analogy, "we have been supplanted as Jews. . . . We are, all of us who are white, the *goyim* in America. The further question is: which among us are the Germans?"[103]

Some Jews of the old left made cause with the New Left position on Israel. While support for Israel among the old left was never strong, there was a certain sympathy with the Labor government that ruled the young state. But after the Six-Day War, scholars like Jerrold Katz and Noam Chomsky signed anti-Zionist petitions "on behalf of the peoples of the Third World" that affirmed their identification "intimately and respectfully with their traditions and creative goals."[104] The most influential statement by an American Jewish intellectual on the old left was I. F. Stone's article "Holy War," which appeared in the *New York Review of Books* in 1967. In this piece, Stone claimed to feel "honor-bound to report the Arab side, especially since the U.S. press is so overwhelmingly pro-Zionist." Accordingly, Stone bent over backward to implicate the Israelis in creating the Arab refugee crisis. Stone also put down the State of Israel as an expression of "tribalism," equating those Jews who wanted a state of their own with King Ferdinand and Queen Isabella, who wanted Spain to be only for the Spanish.[105] On a separate occasion, Stone took up the cudgels on behalf of Black militants, writing that the Jews have it within themselves to countenance a little Black anti-Semitism. "The Jews owe the underprivileged a duty of patience, charity, and compassion. It will not hurt us Jews to swallow a few insults from overwrought Blacks."[106]

The inclination of Jewish radicals to sympathize with the Black Power movement was perhaps most evident in the large numbers of Jewish New Leftists who refused to reorder their moral and intellectual priorities along the lines suggested by a strong Jewish identification. While Jews never constituted a majority of the New Left rank-and-file, they did account for a disproportionately large number of its leaders. Important founders of Jewish background included Al Haber, Richard Flacks, Steve Marx, Bob Ross, Mike Spiegel, Mike Klonsky, and Mark Rudd. Nearly half of the delegates to the 1966 SDS convention were Jews, and a number of Jews became SDS chapter presidents at major universities, including Columbia, Berkeley, the University of Wisconsin (Madison), Northwestern University, and Michigan University. Jews also made up a significant portion of the movement's intellectual vanguard. Between 30 and 50 percent of the founders and editorial boards of such New Left journals as *Studies on the Left, New University Thought,* and *Ramparts* were of Jewish background. These included such prominent New Lefters as Norman Fruchter, Robert Scheer, Saul Landau, Martin Sklar, James Weinstein, David Horowitz, Otto Feinstein, Ronald Radosh, and Stanley Aronowitz. Philosophers of Jewish birth were also among the most prominent intellectual mentors of the New left and included such figures as Isaac Deutcher, Herbert Marcuse, and Paul Goodman.[107]

Many analysts struggled to explain the lack of Jewish loyalty among young Jews on the New Left. Some argued that those Jews in the New Left who supported Arab claims in the Six-Day War sprang from the tension created when the permissive, child-centered, idea-oriented environment of their home lives clashed with the rigid rules and regulations of the university. Other analysts continued to emphasize the strong historic Jewish commitment to the left since European emancipation. Still others pointed to the historic phenomenon of Jewish self-hatred, the belief that it is the fault of the Jews that they are disliked.[108] The left-wing historian Arthur Liebman has suggested that the young New Left Jews had inherited a tradition of radicalism from their parents and had been emersed in a whole network of socialist-inspired institutions since childhood.[109] The sociologist Nathan Glazer supports Liebman's contention, adding that the radical secular tradition was reinforced by the strong emphasis on intellectual activity.[110] Of these explanations, Jewish self-hatred was probably the least likely, for most New Left Jews had been raised in leftist homes largely devoid of any positive or negative links to a Jewish community or Jewish thought and need not have rebelled against Judaism or Jewishness to arrive at their positions on Jews and the state of Israel.[111]

The Jewish New Left and the Rejection of "Whiteness"

All of this is not to say that the approach of the New Left toward the question of the Middle East did not deeply wound many Jews who identified with the New Left. While some Jewish New Leftists abandoned the movement, or renounced their Jewishness and stayed, others decided to form the Jewish Liberation Movement. The Jewish Liberation Movement lasted from roughly 1968 to 1974, a period in which a number of Jewish radical newspapers flourished on campuses and radical Jewish groups were born. "Overall, the Jewish New Left was a loose confederation of many autonomous groups that more or less shared a variety of ideas and interests," wrote Bill Novak, the editor of the key journal of the Jewish New Left,

Response.[112] The Jewish New Left, or the "New Jews," essentially concerned itself with the issues of Israel, Soviet Jewry, the "Jewish Establishment," and Jewish "oppression" in the United States. On Israel, New Jews adamantly defended Israel against the charge of colonialism but openly opposed the Israeli government and favored recognition of Palestinian rights to a sovereign state.[113] To be a Zionist, wrote one radical, "does not mean to support the Israeli government."[114] As Jack Nusan Porter, an activist and a chronicler of the Jewish New Left, described it, Jewish radicals in the New Left "will take what is good from Blacks and SDSers but will reject what is bad . . . condemn Jewish slumlords, but will support Black Power demands of . . . more jobs, better housing, community control of schools. . . . They will denounce the New Left's biased account of Zionism yet seek a homeland for the Arab Palestinians."[115]

But while the New Jews were no doubt sincere, in practice what many of them did was appropriate the prophetic tradition of Judaism to support their radical political agenda. Ignoring the rich Jewish cultural tradition, which consists of various and competing strains of thought, New Left Jewish groups such as the Jewish Liberation Project pronounced that "true commitment to the Jewish tradition necessitates participation in revolutionary struggles."[116] Perhaps the most notable example of the New Jews' attempt to use Judaism for radical political purposes was the publication of a document entitled *The Freedom Seder,* compiled by Arthur Waskow, a Fellow at the Institute for Policy Studies in Washington, D.C., and one of the leaders of the New Left-inspired National Jewish Organizing Project.[117] In this document, which appeared in the April 1969 issue of *Ramparts,* Waskow diluted Judaism of its particularity by insisting that while the nationalisms of the Third World were righteous, the Jews must always be universalist. Waskow included in this Passover *hagadah* passages from "the *shofet* [judge] Eldridge Cleaver (who went into exile like Moses)," "Prophet Gandhi" and "Prophet Abrahim Johannes Muste," "Ginsberg the *Tzaddik* [teacher]," "the Prophet Dylan," and "Rabbi Hannah Arendt." When Waskow cited the traditional Seder phrase "This year here, next year in the land of Israel," he was quick to add, "[W]here there is liberty, that is my country. That is my Israel," as if to assure the reader, in one critic's words, "that he is not a Zionist white colonizer preparing to move into the territory of a Third World people."[118] Waskow himself explained that "the Freedom Seder" was not really about Judaism per se but rather about "multiparticularism": "Thus [it] is one experimental effort . . . toward what the tradition calls the Passover of the Messianic Age, the Passover of the liberation of all the nations."[119] Waskow lent credence to the Black radical attempt to soften the severity of the Holocaust and to detract from its singular quality by comparing it to other, quite different human tragedies and by relegating it to a relatively safe past, the dangers of which could not compare to the more ominous contemporary situation. It was Waskow's belief that the Jewish tradition impelled Jews to become committed to a radical transformation of the world, because the "modern superstates are preparing a new and much more thorough Holocaust: the destruction of the Jewish people and of the whole human race."[120]

The Jewish New Left was often incisive in its description of contemporary American life and the cultural price Jews had paid in order to enjoy full participation in it. But the ideological dependency on sustained Jewish oppression drained much of the potency from their otherwise robust Jewish message. Rather than attempt to define possible Jewish alternatives to living an assimilated, middle-class life, the New Jews preferred to continue to define themselves as victims whose greatest responsibility was to assert their brotherhood with the poor, the Black, and the dispossessed. As much as they may have insisted on a muscular Jewish pride, the New Jews refused to relinquish a identity based on the centrality of Jewish persecution.

The New Jews understandably lamented the loss of those elements of Jewishness and Judaism that many believed had been rendered "obsolete" but blamed their loss on capitalist oppression, rather than on democratic freedom. They insisted that, because autonomous Jewish communities would have constituted "indigestible" blocks for the American political system, certain aspects of Jewish culture, particularly the Yiddish language and the observance of the Sabbath, had been wiped out by American cultural and economic pressures. But rather than see these developments as the result of choices made by Jews in an open and dynamic society, the New Jews continued to portray the Jew as a victim, attributing his cultural problems to the "oppressiveness" of American capitalism.

The activists in the Jewish Liberation Movement essentially defied the attempts of Black radicals to label Jews "white," insisting instead that Jews were still allied with the dark-skinned oppressed. Ironically, the New Jews were able to continue their links with the oppressed masses of Black Americans by utilizing the Black Power definition of "whiteness." For the Black Power theorists, "whiteness" was a social designation for people who were beneficiaries of European imperialism and its long history of world conquest. In this sense, whiteness became less about skin color than about one's relationship to power. Who got labeled "white" and who got labeled

"Black" or "nonwhite" had less to do with biology than it did with whether one was a member of a group historically victimized by Western colonialism. By this definition, many New Jews found it easy to categorize themselves as "people of color," since they had been the primary victims in white Christian societies throughout the ages and, in their own eyes, remained in a state of subjugation in the United States. The New Jews argued that the only way Jews were permitted to enjoy the benefits of white skin privilege in the United States was to renounce their Jewishness. This was their explanation for Jewish assimilation and the break with tradition. It was not unprecedented freedom and opportunity that convinced so many Jews that traditional religious observance was obsolete but rather the continuing threat of anti-Semitism. In this view, Jewish economic success was a mere palliative for the spiritual decimation Jews had experienced. Jews, according to the Jewish Liberation Movement, were not white but rather an oppressed people, kidnaped into a Western world that has never accepted or respected them.[121] As one Jewish New Left writer put it, "[W]hen we come to consider whether Jews in America are oppressed, we should not be side-tracked by the fact that they happen to be economically well off and not subject at the moment to the kind of physical oppression faced by Blacks, Indians, and Chicanos."[122] The Jewish New Leftist M. Jay Rosenberg called Jews who repudiated their Jewish heritage "Uncle Toms" and claimed that Jewish Uncle Toms did not understand that their "relevance to the Black struggle is as a Jew and a fellow victim of endless white exploitation."[123]

The idea of the Jew as "middleman" and surrogate oppressor allowed the New Jews to downplay the significance of Black anti-Semitism and sometimes even to defend it. Arthur Waskow explained that the "occasional outbursts of explicit anti-Semitism" from some Blacks scared Jews but that the response should be for the "Jewish grocers and teachers to ally themselves with the Black energies against the social system that had oppressed them all." Through a radical commitment to revolutionism, Waskow argued, Jews could break out of their "mini-oppressor" roles, which the real oppressors had "slotted us into."[124]

Michael Lerner, a young Jewish activist on the West Coast and a future editor of *Tikkun* magazine, argued that Black anti-Semitism was not a serious concern because it was rooted in the "concrete fact of oppression by Jews of Blacks in the ghetto." No matter how inappropriate the response from the Black community, Lerner felt that Black anti-Semitism was nevertheless a disgrace not to Blacks but to Jews. "In short, this anti-Semitism is in part an earned anti-Semitism," Lerner wrote as he counseled Jews to join the Black anti-Semites in condemning the Jewish exploiters.[125]

Other New Jews criticized the Jewish community for not being more understanding of the value of violence to Black Americans. For these Jewish New Leftists, an immoral tactic was seen as occasionally necessary in order to achieve goals, and they likened the use of Black violence to the use of arms by Israelis under Arab attack. "No other alternative is open to the Black man," wrote Joel Ziff, a student at Columbia College and director of the Harlem Educational Program. "The Jewish community can judge the civil rights movement in the same way it evaluated the Six-Day War; although violence is not desirable, the Israeli use of defensive aggression is justified as the only way to stop Arab persecution."[126] Arthur Waskow identified with Black rioters in the urban ghettos, comparing the rioters in Washington, D.C., who, in April 1968, had looted stores of appliances and clothes to the children of Israel who had looted gold and jewels upon their escape from Egypt.[127]

Perhaps the most important legacy of the Jewish Liberation Movement was the Jewish feminist movement. Jewish women had been at the forefront of the women's movement in the United States in the 1960s and 1970s, but not until the early 1970s had they begun to participate in the movement consciously as Jews. While the Jewish feminist movement and its confrontation with Black feminists would not peak until the mid-1980s, the movement itself got off the ground during the late 1960s and early 1970s with the appearance of the first group of articles on Jewish feminism in a special issue of *Davka* magazine, the creation of Jewish feminist groups like *Kol Ishah* and *Ezrat Nashim,* and the appearance of Jewish feminists before the Rabbinical Assembly convention.[128] This activity was followed by a special issue on Jewish feminism in the radical feminist periodical *Off Our Backs* and an anthology of writings from the Jewish women's movement that appeared in *Response* magazine in 1973 and that was later published in book form.[129] Like their mostly male counterparts among the New Jews, the women in the Jewish feminist movement included talented scholars and writers who were working toward a reconstruction of the role of Jewish women within Jewish theology and Jewish organizational life. Writers like Blu Greenberg, Aviva Cantor Zuckoff, Rachel Adler, Judith Plaskow, Arlene Agus, Susan Dworkin, and Paula Hyman wrote incisively about Jewish law, history, and politics in an effort to bring the position of women in Judaism and in the Jewish community in line with modern ideas about gender equality.[130] Nevertheless, like the bulk of the writers in the

Jewish Liberation Movement, the most vocal elements of the Jewish feminist movement had been prodded into thinking more deeply about their Jewishness by Black radicalism, this time in the form of the identity politics of Black feminists, which, in attempting to strengthen linkages with feminists of the Third World, tended to define Jewish women outside the circle of the oppressed. The Jewish lesbian feminist Elly Bulkin has testified that much "as the women's movement of the late sixties and early seventies had its roots in the earlier civil rights struggle and the New Left . . . the increasing number of women who define ourselves as *Jewish* feminists . . . owe a significant debt as well to the emergence . . . of a broad-based Third World feminist movement in this country."[131] As a result, the Jewishness of many Jewish feminists amounted to a fierce defense of their oppressed status both as Jews and as women, deferring, as most Jewish New Leftists did, to the idea that Jews in general and Jewish women in particular continue to be the targets of widespread discrimination and bigotry. Elly Bulkin has written that "Jewishness is not, as many assume, equivalent to whiteness. Racism is a significant problem among [*sic*] Jews." Accordingly, Bulkin attributed the growth of "Jewish feminist consciousness in the past few years . . . to a significant upsurge in anti-Jewish acts in the United States and in other parts of the world."[132]

Like the New Jews, many Jewish feminists were ambivalent about Zionism and the State of Israel, the majority of them supporting a homeland for Jews but having tremendous misgivings about Israeli policies toward Palestinian Arabs.[133] Even the most pro-Zionist feminists often justified their support for Israel in terms of recompense for Jewish suffering and in this way linked their Zionism to the Black struggle for equality. The prominent Jewish feminist Letty Cotton Pogrebin has written in this regard that, to her, "Zionism is simply an affirmative action plan on a national scale" justified by the "intransigence of worldwide anti-Semitism."[134]

After much struggle, many Jewish feminists finally came to rest on an identity defined almost solely by the Jewish relationship to oppression. "White Jews in this society are oppressed as Jews, yet privileged as people with white skin," writes Elly Bulkin.[135] For radical Jewish feminists like Evelyn Torton Beck, Jewish "success" in the United States and elsewhere has always been tenuous and tainted by the larger purpose of Jewish exploitation. "The great American dream, 'from rags to riches,' " writes Beck, "is simply not acceptable to Jews . . . it is only because some groups have 'allowed' it: often . . . with the purpose of using Jews as a buffer and/or as an easy scapegoat when one is needed."[136]

The Jewish New Leftists set the standard for the mainstream Jewish response to Black Power, arguing vehemently that American Jews were still among the oppressed and that their place was still alongside Black Americans. In this, Jewish New Leftists had taken Jewish suffering, the most readily available and usable form of Jewish identity, and made it the defining element in their program. In the mind of Jewish New Leftists, Jews were nonwhite; Black anti-Semitism was antiwhite and therefore not anti-Jewish; the expression of Black Power was identical to the expression of Jewishness and Judaism in its various forms, including Zionism; and Jews were not only playing the role of white oppressors but in fact were abandoning their links to Jewish tradition by not aligning themselves with Black Power. But while Jewish New Leftists prided themselves on a radical approach to Jewish identity, their lead was in fact being followed closely by mainstream liberal Jewish leaders and intellectuals who often shared the New Jews' basic assumptions about Jewish identity and its link to Black Americans.

Liberal Jews and Black Power

Despite the New Left's critique of the Jewish establishment, many establishment figures adhered largely to the New Left's radical interpretation of events as they pertained to race relations and the place of Jews in the United States. That is, a vast majority of Jewish leaders and spokespersons, struggling to deal with the shock of persistent anti-Semitic and anti-Zionist rhetoric coming from the precincts of their historic Black allies, continued to cling, sometimes desperately, to a Jewish identity based on active involvement in Black causes and civil rights. Most of these leaders subscribed to the notion that Black anti-Semitism was negligible or "understandable" given the "uneven" relationship in which the members of both groups were engaged and that Jews themselves continued to be the natural allies of Black Americans because they were, in some ways, still the victims of white Christian discrimination and not fully of the privileged "white" majority. Evidence of these attitudes abounds from the late 1960s.

Major national Jewish organizations and prominent Jewish leaders contributed to a virtual cascade of voices seeking to strengthen Jewish commitment to the Black revolution. The National Jewish Community Relations Advisory Council issued a statement in 1967 on race relations, saying that "for the Jewish community to be deflected from its support and advocacy of equality for Negroes on the ground that Negroes are anti-Semitic would not only be self-defeating, exacerbating precisely what we mean to combat; but would be to repudiate a fundamental tenet of Jewish tradition—equal justice for all."[137] Arthur J. Goldberg, a former Supreme Court Justice and the newly elected president of the American Jewish Committee, at the annual meeting of the Executive Board in 1968 urged that Jews continue to aid Blacks to achieve full equality. "The great body of Negroes," Goldberg said, "do not share the opinion of the few extremists within our own community, and Jews should not be deterred from their obligation to combat bigotry against any minority." Rabbi Walter Wurzberger, the editor of the modern orthodox quarterly *Tradition,* concurred: "Irrespective of all short-term considerations of expediency or enlightened self-interest, we must be guided by our religious tradition which regards involvement with social and economic concerns of all men as a religious imperative."[138] Martin Jelin, the president of the New Jersey area American Jewish Committee, told the New Jersey State Conference that "no matter how trying Jews find Black extremist reaction, we must not forget our relations to Blacks, our feeling of brotherhood and our common destiny." The conference itself adopted a resolution stating that "we must reject the temptation to get out of the struggle for social justice because some elements have resorted to intolerable tactics."[139] Paul Davidoff, chairman of the American Jewish Congress Special Task Force on Negro-Jewish Relations, declared in a speech in 1969 that "Negro anti-Semitism poses little, if any, threat to Jewish institutions or to the survival of the Jewish people. Jews must temper their reaction to the rhetoric of Black Power with this knowledge."[140] Rabbi Harry Halpern, the chairman of the Joint Commission on Social Action of the Conservative movement's United Synagogues of America, wrote that "anti-Jewishness is not an integral part of the Black man's struggle for freedom, identity, and self-determination" and that "Jews must not withhold the support which they have given, in the past, to help the Negro in his desperate battle for real, as opposed to alleged, emancipation." To do so would be "to betray our heritage and the basic principles of our faith."[141] Henry Schwarzchild, a refugee from Nazi Germany, a fellow at the Metropolitan Applied Research Center, and a member of the Commission on Religion and Race of the Conservative movement's Synagogue Council of America, claimed to be appalled by the anti-Semitism he saw in such events as the New Politics Convention in Chicago in 1967. Nevertheless, in his "Jewish judgement," this kind of anti-Semitism should not deter Jews from helping Blacks because the suffering of Black Americans had given them an inexhaustible reservoir of moral credit upon which to draw.[142] During the New York City school strike in 1968, Schwarzchild criticized the Anti-Defamation League report that declared that anti-Semitism was at a "crisis level" because it only diverted energies from the more important civil rights struggle.[143]

In general, Jewish leaders who were concerned that the Jewish community and Judaism remain "involved" in the race revolution and "relevant" to the problems of the inner city excoriated those Jews and Jewish congregations that they believed had abandoned the inner-city ghettos by retreating to the sanctuary of the suburbs. Rabbi Balfour Brickner of the Union of American Hebrew Congregations minced no words: "Too many Jews have removed themselves and their organizations from the inner city even while talking about the need to respond to the urban crisis. This makes us irrelevant to the struggle to rebuild the cities."[144] Harry Fleischman, race relations coordinator for the American Jewish Committee, turned the attack against American Jews, denying that there was a higher level of anti-Semitism in the Black community than among white Christians and insisting that almost every instance of Black anti-Semitism had been repudiated by responsible Black leaders.[145]

With the specter of growing Black anti-Semitism all but undeniable, it took considerable effort on the part of Jewish leaders to continue to downplay its significance. One document that Jewish leaders and intellectuals found helpful was the Anti-Defamation League-sponsored study by Gary T. Marx titled *Protest and Prejudice: A Study of Belief in the Black Community,* published in 1967.[146] The study was prompted by the inner-city riots that took place in New York and in other cities in 1964 and focused on measuring the climate of opinion in the Black community regarding the civil rights movement. Marx surveyed more than a thousand Black adults in the North and South in October 1964 and from his index of prejudice concluded that Black Americans were essentially moderate and rejected the extremism of certain Black nationalist movements. On the matter of anti-Semitism, Marx concluded that Blacks were no more prejudiced than whites and that, in fact, they were probably less anti-Semitic by most measures. Marx did find, however, that Blacks tended to have more "economically based anti-Semitism" than whites, a consequence, Marx believed, of frequent Black-Jewish economic interaction. Marx concluded that, "while African American anti-Semitism is deplorable, it certainly is more understandable than white anti-Semitism."[147]

Marx's study came under heavy criticism from other social scientists for relying solely on survey data and for letting his own personal bias toward the Black struggle for equality impinge on his methods of data collection.[148] Perhaps the most serious problem with the study was its limited inclusion of young Blacks and college-educated Blacks among those surveyed, which significantly reduced its power to predict how Black attitudes might evolve after 1964, the year the interviews were completed. Only 13 percent of Marx's respondents had some college education; only 22 percent were eighteen to twenty-nine years old. During the three years between the time the research was conducted and the book's publication, a number of significant events occurred that appear to have thrown the study's validity into serious doubt: the assassination of Malcolm X; the Watts riot; and the birth of Black Power, to name only a few. The increased alienation of Black Americans ages sixteen through twenty-five was captured in a study by *Fortune* magazine that found that nearly twice as many Blacks from that age group rejected integration as a primary objective compared to their elders.[149] Martin Duberman, a Princeton University historian, wrote in a 1968 review of the Marx study that the "question which then arises is whether a significant shift in Negro attitudes had taken place in the past year—that is, since Marx's book went to press."[150] By most indications, it had.

Nevertheless, many Jewish leaders and intellectuals used the Marx study to bolster their belief that Black anti-Semitism was not a major threat and that therefore the proper Jewish response would be to redouble efforts on behalf of Black Americans. Dore Schary, a leader of the Anti-Defamation League, condemned the Black extremism that he had witnessed in 1967 but cited the Marx study as evidence that Blacks were not inordinately prejudiced against Jews. Schary analyzed the results of the National Conference on New Politics in Chicago at which "the imperialist Zionist war" was condemned and at which the concept of racial separation was adopted as a goal, writing that the "Black demagogues" who ran the convention were "racist revolutionaries who hold nothing but contempt for the whole civil rights movement." In "utter dismay," Schary read SNCC's June/July newsletter, which contained attacks on Israel and Jews, and condemned SNCC for "parroting the vicious anti-Zionist and anti-Jewish diatribes of Arab and Soviet propagandists." Nevertheless, Schary paraphrased the Marx study on Black anti-Semitism. "To the degree that they [Blacks] distinguish between Jewish and non-Jewish whites, *they prefer Jews.*" Schary suggested that Jews should "get the message" the Black extremists were sending and recommit themselves to the alleviation of Black grievances.[151]

In a long pamphlet issued by the Reform movement's Union of American Hebrew Congregations in 1968, Rabbi Henry Cohen set out to define a "Jewish view of the Negro revolt." At its deepest religious core, Rabbi Cohen wrote, Judaism demanded that Jews pursue justice for all human beings, Jews and non-Jews alike, and this injunction had nothing to do with the response Jews got from those their efforts benefit. Cohen took a rather benign view of Black Power, arguing that only SNCC had taken the separatist element of Black Power very seriously and that most established Black leaders maintained their vision of "Black and white together." In order to validate this contention, Cohen used Gary Marx's study, claiming that "the overwhelming majority of American Negroes reject the varieties of Black Nationalism and accept the coalition and integration strategies of the older leadership." The Jewish response to Black anti-Semitism, according to Cohen, should be one of understanding and "sometimes asking ourselves how much we should give up for the sake of our neighbor."[152]

Cohen and Schary were by no means alone in their sentiments. In a speech to the World Jewish Congress in 1967, Chief Judge Gus J. Solomon of the United States District Court in Oregon reiterated Cohen's views, saying that although many of the Black extremists had become racist and anti-Semitic, he was convinced "that the conclusions of the Anti-Defamation League studies which showed less antagonism by African-Americans against Jews than against every other group of whites are accurate" and that Jews and others need to continue to extend help to the Black community.[153]

By superimposing the attitudes of older and less educated Blacks from the early 1960s onto the radicalized racial scene of the late 1960s, the Marx study seemed to complement a widespread effort among Jewish community relations professionals to hang on to the vestiges of the integrated civil rights movement. The urgent call of many Jewish leaders to remain involved in the Black struggle, combined with their call to understand Black Power, often made for an awkward mixture, with Jewish leaders espousing praise for Black Power and the virtues of Black self-help, while at the same time calling for greater Jewish involvement in Black affairs. This reflected a total disregard for the meaning and implications of Black Power and a commensurate rejection of the very idea of an autonomous Jewish community with independent purpose.

The case of Bertram Gold, the executive vice president of the American Jewish Committee, provides perhaps the most glaring example of a Jewish communal leader who stated his support for the Black Power objectives of self-help and group pride, only to recommend more Jewish commitment to the Black struggle, even to the extent of diverting communal resources from internal Jewish needs. In an address to the National Conference of Jewish Communal Service in 1968, Gold warned Jews not to build a mythology about Black militants and revealed his hopes that Jews would be able to carry on as allies of Blacks. "All Black militants are not alike," Gold wrote. "Not all Black militants reject alliance with whites. Not all Black militants are anti-Semitic. We have to devise strategies—and some of us are doing just that—for keeping lines of communication with these forces open." It was Gold's belief that Jewish communal agencies were too "inward" looking, and, surprisingly, that relations with other groups of Americans deserved a portion of Jewish communal resources equal to that reserved for Jewish education. The Jewish community system must enter what Gold believed was a new phase that "will recognize that the Jewish community system and the general community system are interdependent, and that along with the increasing attention we are giving to Jewish knowledge we must also give increasing attention to making our own tradition relevant to today's society." [154]

Obviously, in calling for an equal distribution of resources to both Jewish education and the race revolution, Gold revealed that he did not consider the problem of religious ignorance among Jews or the related problem of Jewish continuity in the United States to be particularly urgent. But Gold did not even perceive that his recommendations were antithetical to the objectives of Black Power. Despite declaring that Black Power desired temporary separation most of all, one of the most important objectives Gold outlined was for Jews to help Blacks create Black welfare federations and to extend themselves in every way possible where integration had a chance. For Gold, apparently, Black separation was acceptable, but only for rhetorical purposes, while Jewish separation and internal Jewish development was not a high priority at all. "The Jewish community," Gold concluded, "will not meet this challenge by leaving the larger struggle in a new isolation that would have us concentrate only on programs of narrowly defined Jewish concern." [155]

In playing down the bad in Black Power and emphasizing the positive, some Jewish leaders expressed the belief that Black Power would help create an atmosphere more conducive to true diversity and hence a United States in which American Jewish life could flourish in much greater freedom. But stating this required that these Jews ignore the paradox of Black

Power pluralism, which emphasized social divisions based on race and submerged the differences among white ethnic groups beneath the banner of "white skin privilege." Ismar Schorsch of the Jewish Theological Seminary believed that Black Power represented a real opportunity for American Jews and that dropping out of the Black struggle represented a betrayal of Jewish self-interest. Schorsch thought that ultimately Jews would gain from a "Negro victory" because it would enable Jews to overcome the psychological scars from which they had suffered as the price for emancipation. "The price we paid was the agreement not to identify ourselves publicly as Jews, to suppress every public display of Jewishness. . . . The victory of the Black revolution can only aid in strengthening our own identification with the Jewish community."[156] Albert Vorspan, director of the Commission on Social Action of Reform Judaism, also believed that Black Power would result in real benefits for Jews. "The drive for Black Power is, ideally, opening America to a new and true pluralism in which Jews will be one of the important beneficiary groups." For Vorspan, the problem with Judaism in America was not that it needed redefinition from within but that it was not concerned enough with crises and events outside of the Jewish community. The solution meant "an intoxication with shaping a better world."[157] Vorspan, like many of the others, advocated Black Power as good for Jewish autonomy, but he could not break from the liberal consensus that the first priority of Jews must be the affairs of the Black community.

All of which brings us to the work of Dr. Leonard Fein, a well-known scholar and a consultant to a number of national Jewish communal agencies, who emerged in the late 1960s as the foremost liberal spokesman on Black-Jewish relations. It is interesting to analyze Fein's position on the issue of Black Power because he has been a particularly creative and articulate proponent of Jewish continuity in the United States, and one who has convincingly argued that a Jewish preoccupation with anti-Semitism has been a primary obstacle to the development and sustenance of Jewish life and culture.[158] But Fein's approach to Black Power and Black anti-Semitism reveals that he himself was not free from reliance on Jewish victimization for his formulation of identity.

Fein saw Black Power as a reasonable response to the failure of integration, one that was fully within the historical patterns of American pluralism and a way by which the Black community could organize to gain its due, "not unlike the creation of the labor movement fifty years ago." Ignoring the historical examples of white Protestants and Jews, two of the most successful yet disunited and individualistic American ethnic groups, Fein energetically defended the integrity of the pluralistic assumptions behind Black Power.[159] Black Power, wrote Fein, is a recognition of what every other ethnic group in America knows: "The way to move ahead in this society is to organize, to move together as a group."[160] Nevertheless, he apparently did not take the objectives and principles of Black Power seriously and, consequently, recommended a path for whites that ran along lines antithetical to those principles: "The first is to do what we have never done before, to fulfill the promise of integration." Accordingly, Fein disregarded the Black Power preference for community control of school districts and suggested an "immediate metropolitanization of our school system, even if such a step were to involve some qualitative sacrifice in the educational excellence of white suburban schools."[161] Fein confessed that the messages of Black Power were confusing to him, but his own vision of Black Power, compatible with an effort at massive integration, seemed more a reflection of his preference for continuing a Black-Jewish alliance than an objective appraisal of Black demands.

Fein's position suffered from a serious inconsistency, in which the pluralist potential of Black Power was exalted but the Black Power insistence on the "whiteness" and similarity of all white ethnic groups was ignored. "If, therefore, it [Black Power] succeeds, we ourselves [Jews] will be among its unintended beneficiaries," Fein wrote.[162] But Black Power militants were not interested so much in cultural diversity and ethnic tolerance as they were in gaining power by using the political advantages accruing to the victims of white racism. Because of this limited view of American pluralism, anti-Semitism, if not inextricably linked to Black Power, may have been a necessary correlate because of the ambiguous status of Jews, at least in the Jewish psyche, vis-à-vis power and discrimination. Fein himself acknowledged this difficulty with Black Power, but instead of addressing it he set out to find a place for Jews in America's new pluralistic universe as something other than white, a position that would and did find much opposition within the ranks of Black Power. The word "Black," which the Black Power advocates preferred to "Negro," was unsettling for Fein because it implied an inaccurate Black-white racial dichotomy that Jews seemed to straddle. "The fact of the matter is," wrote Fein, "that Jews, however much we have accumulated the trappings of American success, are not white. We are not white symbolically, and we are not white literally. . . . We are too much an oppressed people, still, and too much a

rejected people, even in this country, to accept the designation 'white.' "
Fein admitted that Jews were not exactly "Black," but he believed they
possessed a special racial status that would serve as the key to a viable Jewish
future in the United States. The Jews must see to it that as a community
they do not act as whites, Fein wrote, "not only because we of all people
ought to know better, but because we shall cut ourselves off from our own
future if we do." [163]

Long one of the most thoughtful intellectuals on the Jewish scene, Fein
had been among the first to attest to the distraction that a preoccupation
with anti-Semitism has been for those trying to lead an affirmative Jewish
life. It was no surprise, then, that when it became almost impossible to
deny the significance of Black anti-Semitism, Fein did not attempt to dismiss it but, instead, refused to deal with it. As late as 1969, Fein argued
that Jews ought not to invest great attention in the matter of Black anti-
Semitism, "not because Black people need to be indulged, nor because we
need to be slapped in the face, but quite simply and quite plainly because
we have more serious matters to attend to." By the time of the major
Black-Jewish altercations of the late 1960s, Fein believed that an opportunity for a new Jewish awakening had been averted by "hysterical over-
reaction," which served to divert communal energies into defensive
patterns that were both familiar and unproductive. "It is . . . as if we need
anti-Semites, need to be confronted by others, lest we be forced to confront
ourselves." [164] In an interview with *Time* magazine for a major cover story
on the "crisis" between Blacks and Jews, Fein said that some Jews had
responded to Black anti-Semitism in a slightly paranoid manner and that
"Jews in a perverse kind of way need anti-Semites. Jews in this country
are in fairly serious trouble spiritually and ideologically, and it is very com-
forting to come once again to an old and familiar problem." [165]

But Fein did not consider that the identification of Jews with Blacks,
embodied in his own insistence that Jews were not white, derived from
the same dependency on anti-Semitism that Fein had identified as Jewish
paranoia. In his eloquent 1988 book, *Where Are We: The Inner Life of America's Jews,* Fein argued that Jews should not give up on the alliance with
Blacks, "for it has helped preserve our sense of ourselves as still, and in
spite of all the successes we've known, among the oppressed. . . . The alliance was born not only out of our empathy for Black misery, but also
out of our continuing need to see ourselves among the miserable—or, at
least, the still-threatened." [166] Apparently, Fein had not noticed that to view

oneself as "among the miserable" and the "still-threatened" requires the perception that anti-Semitism is still a primary operative force in American life.

Black Nationalism and Zionism: An Evaluation

Jewish leaders were conspicuous for the frequency with which they compared Black Power with Zionism, often without the slightest sensitivity to the differences between the two nationalist impulses in both theory and practice, or to their vastly different implications for Jewish life in the United States. Some Jewish leaders, in particular those associated with the Reconstructionist arm of Judaism, were of the belief that Black Power was the equivalent of Black Zionism, or even of Black Judaism, and they claimed to see virtually no difference between the two. Reconstructionist Jews were particularly enamored of this view because they were part of a movement that believed in the idea of continuously "reconstructed" *sancta* that function as phenomena in the ongoing life of a people.[167] Rabbi Allan Miller of the Society for the Advancement of Judaism in New York City, the "mother" synagogue of the Reconstructionist movement, believed that, through the Black Power movement, Black Americans were forming their own religion, a religion that was in its most fundamental presuppositions the equivalent of Judaism. "A Black religion is being born in the search of the Black man for an authentic identity. He cannot find it in American civilization alone. . . . If he succeeds in this struggle, America is safer for the Jew as well as for the Black man."[168] The Black Power urge to have independently controlled institutions was entirely understandable, Miller wrote, when seen as part of a genuine religious drive.

To substantiate his belief in the efficacy of this emerging Black religion, Miller equated the attempt to develop Swahili as an ethnic linguistic *sanctum* with the development of modern Hebrew vernacular by Zionists and the creation of "religious" holidays celebrating important dates in the Black Power movement with Jewish holidays. *"Uhuru"* or freedom, the anniversary of the Watts riot, was the Black Passover. *Kuzaliwa,* the birthday of Malcolm X, was for many Black public school students the equivalent of the Jewish New Year (*Rosh Hashana*) and the Day of Atonement (*Yom Kippur*) for Jewish students. The Black "bible," Miller argued, was emerging in which the works of men like Martin Luther King, Malcolm X, Eldridge Cleaver, and others that would be "canonized."[169] Ignoring the vast difficulties of Black repatriation, Miller even envisioned Black equivalents to the early Jewish settlers in Palestine in Africa. "There must even now be an Afro-American Henrietta Szold, conceiving a functionally equivalent Hadassah organization" in Africa, Miller wrote.[170] As for Black moderates who had been accused of not speaking out forcefully enough against extremists, Miller saw a parallel in the Zionist movement. Miller asked Jewish readers if they had forgotten the Stern Gang, the terrorist wing of the Jewish underground in Palestine. Neglecting to mention the cooperation Jewish authorities in Palestine gave to the British in tracking down Sternists, Miller asked, "Did any single member of the *Yishuv,* the Jewish community of Palestine under the mandate . . . ever betray a single one of those terrorists or publicly disown him?"[171]

Another writer for the *Reconstructionist,* Dov Peretz Elkins, could see no distinction between Black Power and Zionism. "Black Power is nothing more and nothing less than Negro Zionism," he wrote. Just as Zionism meant for Elkins Jewish group unity, the constructive use of Jewish economic and political power, and the giving of full expression to Jewish ethnic pride, Jews should support the efforts to foster a feeling among Blacks that "Black is beautiful." Apparently, Elkins saw no conflict between his hope for the development of Black Power and Black pride and his paternalistic feelings toward Blacks. "If we sincerely wish to integrate our society, we must do so even if it involves, on a temporary basis, a little extra help for the Negro than the white child or the white worker may receive."[172]

Other Jewish writers shared the sentiments of Elkins and Miller. Bertram Gold of the American Jewish Committee defined the meaning of the terms Black Power and Zionism as the "facilitation and empowerment" of both peoples "to be and become themselves." "As one reads the growing Black Power literature . . . one is reminded of Chaim Zhitlowsky's writings on Jewish Nationalism, Ahad Ha'am's emphasis on spiritual Zionism, the many articles on Jewish self-hate and the like."[173] Barbara Krasner, codirector of Wellsprings Ecumenical Renewal Associates in Philadelphia and a writer for Jewish publications, also believed that Zionism and Black Power were so similar that there were no significant distinctions to be made. "It is reasonably apparent," she wrote, "that the struggle for the Land of Israel . . . and the struggle for Black Power are one and the same, territory notwithstanding."[174]

In truth, the approach of most Jews, and especially American Jews, toward Zionism had always been far different from the Black American approach to Black nationalism, if for no other reason than the differences in the historical circumstances that gave birth to the two movements. When these differences are taken into account, it is possible to see that nationalist impulses find expression in a variety of ways, some of which make it possible for liberal values to survive and flourish and some of which facilitate the stifling and the suppression of liberal values.

It is true that the surface similarities between Black nationalism and Zionism make it difficult to distinguish between them. The three major expressions of modern Zionism consisted of the return to the historic homeland of the Jewish people, the land of Israel; "territorialism," which argued for the importance of a Jewish state anywhere; and the "autonomism" of such Zionists as Simon Dubnow, who thought that Jews should work to control their own lives in communities where they predominated.[175] All three of these nationalist forms were present in the Black nationalist movement, from Garvey's "Back to Africa" movement, to the Black Muslims who spoke of a separate "land of our own" in the United States, to Stokely Carmichael and Charles Hamilton, who argued for Black control of local Black institutions. But it is in the sphere of practical politics, rather than in theory, that Black nationalism and Zionism become clearly distinct from each other.

The magnitude of the Jewish diaspora made the quest for a Jewish state distinct in the process of its realization, and it has been perhaps the only successful modern nationalist movement based on the idea of return.[176] The focus on "return" and in-migration gave political Zionism a unique coloration. The goal of achieving emigration to Palestine at all costs, of "ingathering" the Jews from around the world, provided Zionism with an opportunity to escape, in part, the more common and immediate nationalist goal of political sovereignty, which is often accompanied by chauvinism and extremism.

The Zionist scholar Ben Halpern has explained that Zionism was unique among nationalisms because at most points in its history, political sovereignty was subordinated to other national goals.[177] It was true, of course, that there were Zionists who believed that political sovereignty in the land of Israel was the primary national aim. But political sovereignty had as a practical matter been relegated to a secondary concern for most of the existence of organized Zionism. This is a fact corroborated by the character of the debate that dominated the history of modern Zionism. At every turn, the debate revolved around the issue of migration and took place primarily between those Zionists who preferred to wait for Great Britain to secure Jewish emigration to Palestine and those who were working to achieve emigration by other methods. Even the Revisionist Zionists under Vladamir Jabotinsky, the one segment of the movement that openly favored an autonomous state as the end goal, did not view the sovereign Jewish state as a precondition for achieving national aims but believed that such a political entity would come sometime in the future as a crowning achievement. Jabotinsky's search for an alliance with an existing sovereign state as a prerequisite for evacuating Jews to Palestine is evidence of his willingness to discard sovereignty for more practical aims. "Thus, on occasion, the most extreme political Zionists could modify or mitigate their demands of sovereignty, or subordinate the exercise of sovereignty to other national aims which at the moment seemed more pressing," wrote Halpern.[178]

Eventually, Hitler's war against the Jews and the 1939 British White Paper prohibiting Jewish migration to Palestine resulted in the adoption of the "Biltmore" program of 1942, in which Zionists asked that an area called "Palestine" be established as a Jewish commonwealth. But up until the 1940s, a "Jewish state" was not Zionism's primary aim. While Theodore Herzl proclaimed the Jewish state a world necessity, he and his successors mentioned the state only infrequently for lack of a clear strategy for bringing it about. Most other Zionist leaders believed that at some time in the future Palestine would eventually become Jewish, not by war but through emigration. A survey of the Zionist press in the decade prior to the Biltmore conference indicated that the term "Jewish state" had almost disappeared from common usage.[179] "It took the advent of Nazism, the Holocaust and total Arab rejection of the national home to convert the Zionist movement to the belief in statehood," wrote the historian Walter Laqueur.[180] The most recent and comprehensive scholarly analysis of the connection between the Holocaust and the creation of the State of Israel demonstrates that the Holocaust revolutionized the Jewish political mind.[181] Even after 1942, when news of the Holocaust became known, the ideal of a more substantial and secure sovereignty rested on the achievement of the goal of mass migration, and Israel's formal sovereignty made this larger goal finally possible. Vladamir Jabotinsky and the Revisionists were virtually alone before 1930 in preaching the idea that a state was a normal form of existence for Jews.

That Zionism was infused with a goal that was distinct from the goal of political sovereignty became important for its subsequent development, because it permitted the state of Israel to engage in an unusually high degree of self-criticism, while at the same time enabling it to avoid being dominated by the extreme patriotic chauvinism associated with some Zionist sects.[182] The well-known Jewish critic Robert Alter has explained that Zionism's distinctiveness relative to other nationalisms derived from its objectivity toward the concept of sovereignty. At the heart of modern Zionism lay the goal of saving Jewish lives, Alter argued, and this allowed Zionism to be "ideologically reasonable," to escape the "self-hypnotizing fanaticism of many national movements" because it was not born of the rebellion of an indigenous people against foreign rulers. Zionism managed to avoid being dominated by its nationalistic messianic claims because it was linked to at least one practical moral purpose: "the unwavering obligation it preserves to provide a place of refuge for any Jews in the world who need refuge."[183] In short, historical exigencies made it possible for Zionists to be nationalistic while maintaining a "critical disengagement from the old potent Zionist myths."[184]

The development of Black nationalism was quite another story. In the first place, Black nationalism did not have a geographical focus. The link to the land of origin was not as firmly ensconced in Black American consciousness as it was for the East European Jew, who prayed daily for the return of his people to their land and the rebuilding of Jerusalem.[185] For Black Americans in the 1960s, the existence of numerous independent African nation-states must have dampened the impulse to create a state of their own, and the lack of a geographical focal point made the idea that Black Americans constituted a colonized people difficult to develop.[186] Black nationalists from Malcolm X to Stokely Carmichael to the Black Panthers to Julius Lester all fought with but ultimately failed to deal satisfactorily with the issue of land, leading one contemporary theorist to suggest that the Black ghetto is really only a "semi-colony."[187]

And so Black nationalism was destined to remain enclosed within the borders of the United States, and it was precisely this predicament that rendered it unique in its own right. The alternatives available within the United States for realizing the Black nationalist goal of self-determination were far different from those that faced the Zionists, and they led inevitably to an emphasis on Black political and cultural sovereignty in almost exactly opposite proportions to the Zionist emphasis on rescue and migration. "Black Power must be viewed as a projection of sovereignty, an embryonic sovereignty that Black people can focus on and through," commented the Black Panther Eldridge Cleaver. "The necessity upon Afro-Americans is to move, now . . . to demand that that sovereignty be recognized by other nations of the world."[188] The emphasis on sovereignty in Black nationalism was a necessity because the institution of slavery had precluded the continuation of "cultural narratives" that allow a group to develop values and standards not necessarily shared by the majority culture.[189] A number of scholars over the years have pointed out the existence of various "Africanisms" that carried over into the culture of Black Americans, as well as the existence of unique cultural traits growing out of the slave system itself.[190] A rich oral tradition (story telling) and a tradition of rhythm in dance and song are among the most prominent cultural traits that are said to have survived the midway passage.[191] But by 1750, more American slaves had been born in the United States than had been born in Africa, and by 1860 virtually all slaves had been born in the United States. While some second-, third-, and fourth-generation slaves undoubtedly carried various cultural imprimaturs from Africa, Black slaves in America lacked the freedom that could anchor a complete culture. Unlike the slaves in the Caribbean or South America, most slaves in the United States lived on family-owned plantations of between ten and twenty slaves where such staples of African culture as conjuring, witchcraft, and voodoo stood no chance of surviving.[192] The sheer diversity of the African tribes and cultures from which the slaves themselves came made the preservation of ancestral languages an impossibility. The majority of slaves eventually adopted both the language and the religion of their masters, though not without applying significant doses of African cultural residue to both realms.[193] That is to say, despite the long recorded history of slave rebellions, slaves in the United States, finding themselves outnumbered and outgunned, were left with no choice but to internalize the norms of the institution of slavery and to cooperate in their own subordination.[194] The adoption of Christianity by the overwhelming majority of slaves is only one indication of this cultural adaptation. As Laurence Thomas has written, "Given the character of slavery, it is thus most unlikely that the historical-cultural traditions of Africa would come to have a secure foothold among slaves in the United States."[195]

For better or worse, under slavery Blacks became an integral and permanent part of American life, and this fact has proven to be the greatest obstacle to the development of Black cultural and political autonomy. In large measure, the primary goal of Black nationalism, from the time of its inception in the middle of the nineteenth century to the present day, has been an attempt to gain autonomy, or "sovereignty," over the Black past and the Black present. As Stokely Carmichael and Charles Hamilton have written, "Our basic need is to reclaim our history and our identity. . . . We

shall have to struggle for the right to create our own terms through which
to define ourselves. . . . This is the first necessity of a free people."[196]

Herein lies the paradox for American Blacks. Having been systematically
excluded from enjoying the self-affirming aspects of American culture to
the fullest, they have also always carried out large and important roles in
that culture and have therefore experienced great difficulty in establishing
a set of countervailing cultural values separate and distinct from those of
the broader "white" culture. Having been alienated from the cultural nar-
rative of Africa and having been historically excluded from the rites and
rituals of the United States, Black Americans continue to see their only
alternative as to define themselves as both distinct *from* and yet necessarily
a part *of* the United States. Lacking the single most important trait of a
fully developed nationalism—namely, the realistic possibility of striving for
a separate state—Black nationalists are left only with the possibility of gaining entry into American life on their own terms. As the sociologist James
Blaut has written, "The demand for self-determination which is constantly
voiced in ghettos is a demand for enfranchisement and people's power, not
for independence."[197] This precarious psychological situation has made it
necessary to define Black American distinctiveness in opposition to the
white majority in the United States, based on their historic exclusion from
it. But the Black nationalism of the late 1960s came of age at a time when
the historic exclusion of Black Americans from the rest of society was being
substantially and consistently reduced, necessitating a more intense and strident call for Black cultural distinctiveness, the foundation for which was
the sanctification of white racism. In other words, the success of Black
Power was contingent upon the continued racialization of American life.

The 1964 Civil Rights Act and the 1965 Voting Rights Act stood as
the crowning achievements of the effort to provide greater equality for
Black Americans, but at the same time they made continued injustices more
intolerable and calls for communal autonomy more intense. Lacking both
an event as horrific as the Holocaust to trigger a permanent break with
America and an attachment to an ancestral homeland, Black Power advocates set as their primary goal the consolidation of political power
through racial unity in order to build and strengthen the Black community.
As one Black critic wrote, "The key fact remains . . . that radical Black
consciousness in the 1960s and 1970s was largely a discourse about inter-
secting with public power. . . . Even Pan-Africanists and cultural nationalists, whose ideologies supported quietistic withdrawal from American politics, consistently sought to align themselves with Black public officials . . .

and to mobilize around contesting the exercise of public authority in the Black community."[198] Because Blacks are such an integral part of American society, the fight of Black nationalists within the system, and the changes they sought, ended up changing the whole of American life. "Their fight within the system to be freed from it always requires taking the whole system with them to their destination," another Black critic has written.[199]

And change American life it did. Beginning in 1964, the ghetto riots were seen by the Black Power leadership not merely as an expression of need and deprivation but as an opportunity to link a stratum of Black leadership to a large mass following, something that had not been available to previous generations of Black elites. This situation resulted in the emergence of what one scholar has called the "paraintellectual" in the Black community—generally lower-class, self-made intellectuals skilled at verbal combat and possessed of a facility for confrontation that make them "cultural celebrities" in ghetto communities.[200] Eventually, every American city with a sizable Black population sported such a stratum of leaders. Guido St. Laurent of Boston, the founder and leader of the New England Grass Roots organization, and Eldridge Cleaver in San Francisco, a writer and leader of the Black Panther Party, were two paraintellectuals whose careers were typical of the cohort, both having spent time in jail for past criminal activities.

As the so-called "natural" leaders of their communities, the paraintellectuals came to control the terms upon which legitimacy in the urban Black community was defined, and it became exceedingly difficult for the established Black intelligentsia to ignore these terms. It was for this reason that Roy Innis of Brooklyn CORE said in the late 1960s that "a Black leader would be crazy to publicly repudiate Black anti-Semitism."[201] Of course, moderate Black leaders had spoken out against Black anti-Semitism on the national level frequently, but doing so became increasingly difficult for them, and almost impossible for Black leaders at the local level. Blackness in the United States in the 1960s was being transformed from a purely racial to a largely ideological category, in which militancy became the sole criterion by which legitimacy would be conferred upon Black leaders.[202] In this sense, Black nationalism was defined far more rigidly along the lines of ideological conformity than Zionism was.

While some in the established Black intelligentsia continued to concentrate on broadening and consolidating recent gains made possible by the moderate politics of the civil rights movement, large segments of the Black intelligentsia were forced to adopt or fabricate a lower-class-oriented Black militancy along the lines drawn by the paraintellectuals. Many in the established Black intelligentsia also found that the nationalist militancy of the paraintellectuals was a useful tool with which they were able to impress upon white establishment figures the need to open greater opportunities to Blacks. This dynamic worked in another direction as well. When white-controlled institutions began to concede new roles and benefits to the established Black intelligentsia, it helped to confer upon them legitimacy in the eyes of the urban Black lower classes.[203]

Another important aspect of this phenomenon was the relationship of the Black paraintellectuals to the 1960s cult of violence. The confluence of Black Power rhetoric and ideology with that of the New Left manifested itself in a number of ways, including the tendency to substitute rhetoric for political analysis and violent gestures for political action.[204] But where these tactics resulted in the dismal political failure of the New Left by the early 1970s, it had resounding success for the new Black intelligentsia, which looked upon antiwhite violence, both rhetorical and actual, as serving the twofold purpose of validating Black manhood and coercing concessions from white institutions. In a seemingly apt description of what took place during the New York City teachers' strike in 1968, one Black sociologist wrote, "In several cities, Black teachers, writers, and artists had joined forces with Black paraintellectuals to disseminate a veritable cult of violence."[205] Black Power's use of the "Mau-Mau," a phrase coined by the author Tom Wolfe to describe the technique of public extortion used by Black paraintellectuals, was particularly effective because it made demands of whites while at the same time insisting that white America could never repent for the evil it inflicted on Blacks.[206] As white Americans became increasingly conscious of past injustices against Blacks, and of their own relative affluence, they became eager to repent for America's racist past, and they were particularly receptive to what the progenitors of Black Power put forth as the most effective ways for doing so. This phenomenon was, in part, responsible for the adoption of the whole panoply of demands for race-based preferential treatment, including the redrawing of electoral districts to favor Black candidates, "open" and preferential university admissions, Black studies departments, government contract set-asides, community control of governmental institutions, and government and private foundation support for particular Black objectives. One may argue the relative merits of such policies for fulfilling the objectives of racial justice, but the role that Black Power played in getting them instituted seems all but undeniable.[207] Whatever they may ultimately mean for Black advancement, these changes have resulted in an official and legally acknowledged reracialization of American life, in which the important differences between groups come down to the color of their skin. This is as it always has been, except for the small window of opportunity that opened up somewhere during the years leading up to and through 1965 but that Black Power helped to quickly slam shut.

It is from the vantage point of these changes that a sober judgment must be rendered on the effectuation of Black Power in American life, and not from the standpoint of Zionism or any other nationalism. This seems to be the case particularly for liberal American Jews, whose attachment to such Enlightenment values as individualism, equal opportunity, personal freedom, and merit-based advance leaves them with much at stake in the success or failure of Black Power, as it has manifested itself in American life. Apparently, the reliance of some Jewish leaders and intellectuals on the Black American epic for their own identities prevented them from seeing the choices as clearly as they might have.

Ben Halpern and the Sober View of Black Nationalism

Of all Jewish thinkers in the postwar period, none seemed to wrestle as honestly, coherently, and realistically with Black Power as the scholar Ben Halpern. Halpern took the opportunity in his 1971 book, *Jews and Blacks,* to fully explicate his belief that the Black Power movement had, in fact, gone a long way toward developing an ideological consensus among Blacks and to explore the possibility that this may not have the positive effect on American pluralism that many liberal Jews expected it to.[208]

A lifelong Labor Zionist, Halpern firmly believed that American Jews, though they refused to recognize it, were still in exile, or *galut,* and that this condition put them on significantly less intimate terms with American culture than Black Americans. Even with the increasing ability of Jews to integrate on many different levels, Halpern believed that Jews remained unassimilable because, at bottom, the United States was a Christian society that held beliefs about group life that Jews simply could not hold. Blacks remained, of course, excluded because of the racist habits that had survived their emancipation, but the Jews were not of America, not integral to it, as Blacks were. As Halpern saw it, authentic Judaism did not provide principles for the social organization of America and was not essential to the American way of life. By contrast, the Civil War and Reconstruction fixed the pattern of American politics for generations, and the travail of the Black American belonged fully and tragically to American history. Therein lies the distinction Halpern made between the Jews as an "ideological" minority and the Blacks as a "social" minority; for Blacks, the primary source of their segregation was their social position, while for Jews it was the ancient culture they were identified with. But it was the strikingly divergent ways that both groups approached their group status that was most intriguing to him.

Halpern believed that Black Americans were developing something resembling a religious tradition, while American Jews were at the same time losing theirs. This role reversal was ironic, since Blacks based their own "quasi-revolution" largely on the myth of Jewish cohesiveness. In fact, Halpern wrote, the "Jew today is about as confused in his identity, as communally undisciplined, and, in his own way, as detached from historical roots as the American Negro." But while Halpern was under no illusions regarding the difficulty Blacks faced building their new ideological opposition to American society, he stood by his belief that American Jews faced a greater crisis than Black Americans and articulated his arguments in terms of the Jewish response to Black anti-Semitism.[209]

Halpern felt that there was only one adequate Jewish response to Black anti-Semitism: "immediate, unequivocal resistance." But Jews in their current position were not able to provide this response because their primary goal was assimilation. "Only liberated peoples, who do not want to integrate but only to coexist in equality, can achieve a reasonable, mutually agreeable, contractual relationship . . . with others." It was Jewish disorganization stemming from the desire to gain acceptance that prevented Blacks and Jews in America from enjoying a mutually respectful relationship. "For many purposes . . . [the Jews] are not a single community; and this is so precisely because of their unwillingness to place barriers in the way of their integration with American society."[210]

Halpern's assumption that anti-Semitism was more profound in the United States than racism derived from his view of America as a pluralistic society sharply divided along religious lines and probably led him to overestimate the continuing tension between Christianity and Judaism. While there can be no doubt that such tensions continue, it is not unreasonable to assume that the increasing secularization of American life has greatly weakened them. So while the pressures of being an ideological minority exist, they exist at a much lower level than they did before.[211]

But, on another level, Halpern's intimation that the United States is less hospitable to Jews than to Blacks takes on greater resonance than is at first obvious, and this has less to do with the existing level of anti-Semitism than with the extent to which the United States has been willing to accommodate the group aspirations of Black Americans. A highly intelligent debate in which Halpern engaged his younger Brandeis University colleague Jacob Cohen bears this out. In a bold and lucid critique of Halpern's book, Cohen expressed his belief that Black nationalism was here to stay and that Halpern should feel encouraged by this rather than be traumatized by its relatively "benign" anti-Semitism. Citing the establishment of what in effect are publicly funded parochial schools for Black students, the overwhelming acceptance of preferential quotas, government expenditures on "Black needs," foundation support for programs to develop "Black leaders" for the "Black community," the collaboration of "white universities" in the imposition of ideological tests on Black applicants, and the organization of Black political parties, Cohen argued that the term "Black" had been transformed from a biological to an ideological category, all with the approval of the wider American community. Cohen believed American Jews would greatly benefit from the success Blacks have had in stretching the pluralistic character of American life. If one were to compare what the Blacks had been doing with the Jewish minority rights movement of Eastern Europe eighty years prior, Cohen noted, "he might conclude that the Blacks are achieving what many, including Halpern, had thought impossible: quasi-official status as a legitimate minority; full acceptance of ideological/mythic dissidence."[212]

In response, Halpern elucidated the central point about what the Black revolution in America meant for Jews. The Black revolution, Halpern asserted, would not result in greater public recognition of all ideologically dissident groups because Blacks had a very deep and unique claim on the American conscience. Black demands were being tolerated because Blacks occupy a special position in the American social conscience and because the cry that Blacks make for greater group recognition is understood as a protest against social and economic discrimination. These demands would not be tolerated if they were put forth on the grounds that Blacks have a right to live permanently outside the consensus because of fundamentally different values, as any Jewish appeal of this nature would have to assert. If anything, Halpern felt that the Black revolution might result in the greater acceptance of public responsibility for the poor and disadvantaged, but he suggested that this would benefit certain other ethnic groups only to the extent that they were impoverished. Cohen's hopes for a Jewish group life that emulated the Black revolution were therefore inconceivable, since such a life would amount to a demand for the recognition of the same group rights that Blacks were beginning to obtain.

Though Halpern was a Labor Zionist deeply concerned about maintaining a Jewish communal consensus in the United States, he recognized not only that American Jews could never garner the same kind of public support Blacks received for their claim to permanent opposition but that a nation that would honor such a claim by Jews would have to honor all such claims. Jews might not, therefore, end up in as comfortable a situation as they currently enjoyed. Halpern was far happier with "consensus by tacit consent," and he felt better about being a Jew in a dominant Christian culture than he did about being one in a society with no consensus whatsoever. "What all this implies is that I confess to a certain fondness for the American way of life, in which I can only function as a member of a tolerated minority—and . . . as a citizen who observes voluntary self-denial in exercising his rights and duties as a participating American."[213] Demonstrating great prescience, Halpern argued that the creation of official categories of groups in the United States would not be as great an opportunity for Jewish group fulfillment as many liberal Jews seemed to believe it would, and he maintained a stubborn belief that it was better for American Jews to erect their own barriers to assimilation rather than have them erected by the state, as they had been for Blacks.

As it turns out, both Halpern and Cohen were good prognosticators. Even Cohen could not have predicted how far the Black revolution would stretch the bounds of group pluralism, a pluralism that now covers the public recognition of racial, nonwhite ethnic, gender, and, increasingly, sexual preference groups. But Halpern was right to assert that this would probably not benefit American Jews or strengthen the American Jewish group consensus. For public purposes Jews are "white," and "official" group pluralism is encouraged mainly for Blacks and other nonwhites. In this sense, Halpern's thesis that Jews are in some ways more estranged in the United States than Blacks takes on a sober and chilling resonance. History and circumstance have made the United States willing to accommodate publicly a Black ideological minority, just as history and circumstance have denied this to the Jews. For the most part, Jewish leaders and intellectuals have been unwilling to recognize and respond to the special burdens this implies.

5

The Jew as Middleman
Jewish Opposition to Black Power, 1967–1972

People preoccupied with their own identity are not wholly free.
—Robert Alter

There were, of course, American Jews who did not share with liberal and leftist Jews the penchant for sustaining a commitment to or a relationship with Black Americans. For the most part, those Jews who advocated a more conservative stance toward the Black revolution tended to be more religiously observant. By the late 1960s, events had made it so even the orthodox could no longer maintain their traditional silence on contemporary issues. "In the area of political life," wrote an orthodox journalist in 1967, "orthodox Jewry is now evolving into an ethnic pressure group, much the same in character as other ethnic groups." [1]

The debate over the urban crisis and Black Power among orthodox leaders and thinkers revolved largely around the issue of "relevance," or whether it was incumbent upon Jews to apply the precepts of Torah to present-day events. The question of "relevance" among orthodox thinkers had come as a response to the contention of liberal Jews and radical Jewish college students that the alienation of young people from Jewish life was a result of the failure of Jewish institutions to make themselves relevant to the issues of poverty, civil rights, and peace. Orthodox leaders had vehemently rejected an emphasis on relevance in prior decades, at least partly because it had been so strongly associated with Reform Judaism, which in its 1885 "Pittsburgh Platform" proclaimed Judaism's role to "participate in the great task of modern times, to solve, on the basis of justice and righteousness, the problems presented by the contrasts and evils of the present organization of society." [2] But by 1967, there were forces within orthodoxy that were propounding this view. Rabbi Maurice Lamm stated the view of the proponents, without himself endorsing it: "Among these activist forces, number one on the agenda of modern Jewry is relevancy. The most important concern today is relating Judaism to the world. Only as this is done will Judaism survive modern secularism. . . . Jews will not become or remain observant unless they see that Judaism is pertinent to their condition." Lamm himself cautioned that relevancy alone was never a measure of validity used by traditional Judaism.[3] But orthodox spokesmen who advocated more Jewish involvement generally held views of the Black revolution that, like those of Jewish liberals and leftists, were inspired by the memory of Jewish victimization. It is interesting that these spokesmen generally took a more cautious approach to the Black revolution, perhaps because of the geographic proximity of orthodox communities to the exploding Black ghettos. While Jewish leftists saw American Jews as surrogate oppressors whose true allies were Blacks, orthodox Jews were far more likely to view themselves as middlemen, caught in a storm of social change with allies on neither the right or the left, Black or white. Rabbi Jerry Hochbaum of Yeshiva University, for example, believed that orthodox communities should become involved in alleviating problems of Black poverty through social action and education because Jews would be harmed by the radicalism of both right and left. "Incipient revolution or Fascism?" wrote Hochbaum of the alternatives facing Jews. "So there must be Jewish involvement. No other position is socially expedient or morally acceptable."[4]

Orthodox Jews were by no means of one mind on the urban crisis. Leo Levi, a City University of New York physicist and an author on Jewish subjects, noted that there is no injunction for Jews to admonish non-Jews for immorality toward Blacks. "It is by living the Torah that we are to inspire the other nations," and Jews had long ago failed to live up to this mission, Levi insisted. By putting themselves beyond reproach, Jews would make a more lasting impression on the contemporary world than they would through a program of marching and protest.[5] Rabbi Yaakov Jacobs noted that the idea of relevancy was originally a Protestant idea stemming from "social gospel" thinkers of the late nineteenth century but that Protestants were already becoming disillusioned with those who would "substitute picket lines for prayer." It was Jacob's belief that the causes to which many wanted to make Judaism relevant might be worthy but that they were merely symptoms of deeper societal ills, namely, modern humanity's alienation from God. "The enemy is not discrimination or war," Jacobs wrote. "The enemy is the tidal wave of secularism and its twin brother, 'sciencism,' which have led us to believe that we can solve all human problems alone, while in fact we have compounded them."[6]

Most orthodox leaders agreed that Jews could best help themselves and others by leading pious Jewish lives but felt compelled to address the issue of the Black revolution because of their suspicion that nonorthodox Jewish leadership had gone far astray in their mission of defending Jewish interests. In doing so, orthodox leaders often revealed that they viewed Black anti-Semitism as part of a continuing historical saga in which Jews continued to be caught between oppressive rulers and an outraged populace, a line of reasoning not so very different from the left-wing Jews in the Jewish Liberation Movement. But in an interesting permutation of Jewish identity, the orthodox were inclined to see the Jews as standing alone in an alien culture, rather than as one oppressed group joined together in racial brotherhood with other oppressed groups. Rabbi Bernard Weinberger, a prominent leader of the Jewish community in Williamsburg, Brooklyn, believed that orthodox Jews, in contrast to nonorthodox Jews, had no illusions about the existence and prevalence of anti-Semitism, Black or white, and were therefore not shocked or dismayed when it manifested itself. "We do not need ADL studies to substantiate its existence," Weinberger wrote. It was the activist Jews in the civil rights movement, according to Weinberger, who threatened the survival of the Jewish community in the United States because they had failed to see that Jews had survived throughout the ages by not making themselves conspicuous: "That we have survived as Jews in such a hostile world is a miracle. . . . But, no small share of this miraculous survival is due to our awareness that we simply cannot afford to tell our neighbors how to govern their lives." Revealing his belief that Jews were still vulnerable outcasts, Weinberger held that what was permissible of others was not permissible for Jews and that this was as true in the United States as it had been in Nazi Germany. "The sad reality is that Jews simply cannot speak their mind, openly and honestly, without jeopardizing Jewish lives." Because orthodox Jews lived in proximity to Black neighborhoods, with their concomitant problems of rioting, burglaries, theft, and looting, Weinberger believed it was necessary for them to break their traditional silence and try to help solve some of the racial tensions that were threatening the stability that orthodox Jews depend on, but to do so by setting an example. What Jews could do by way of helping is to learn to live with Blacks rather than in fear of them and to offer them the example of the stable orthodox Jewish family. "Money, jobs, and equal opportunity alone cannot achieve this. The example provided by the orthodox Jewish community affords the Negro the inspiration which he instinctively feels compelled to emulate, and which is worth infinitely more than all our programs."[7]

Orthodox Jews might have remained silent on contemporary matters of race during the late 1960s had not the disparity in class and outlook between more assimilated middle-class Jews and the orthodox become so pronounced. During the late 1960s some Jewish critics came to suspect that American Jews were increasingly in the middle of an alliance between an uncaring white establishment and an agitated Black lower class and that, in fact, many in the "establishment" were liberal and assimilated Jews. For the first time since the 1920s, class differences among American Jews were showing signs of emerging as a class conflict. "Now," wrote a Jewish sociologist, "growing numbers of the non-upper Jews have begun to suspect that when it comes to the things that they are most concerned and anxious about, and that affect them most directly, the upper Jews could not care less, or are actually hostile, and contemptuous in the bargain."[8]

It was this class division between the predominantly working-class urban orthodox Jews and the more affluent, suburban liberal Jews that led to the rise of Rabbi Meier Kahane and the Jewish Defense League (JDL) in 1968. As an obscure rabbi at the Traditional Synagogue in Rochdale Village, Queens, and an editor at the politically conservative *Jewish Press,* Kahane had been able to accurately measure the pulse of less affluent urban Jews who were on the front lines of skyrocketing crime rates and Black anti-Semitism. Kahane's views reflected the anxieties of these Jews, many of whom began to feel that they were becoming extremely vulnerable to Black demands, the economic problems of the cities, and discontent over U.S. involvement in Vietnam. In response, Kahane formed the Jewish Defense League, ostensibly to "physically defend Jews . . . to go out among Jews and instill within them a feeling of Jewish pride, to defend the Jews from simply fading out."[9] In this sense, the JDL resembled a number of ethnic activist movements that emerged in the late 1960s and early 1970s, and it became an active presence in the various disputes between Blacks and Jews in New York City.[10] The JDL took a pro-union stance during the New York City teachers' strike, showed up with clubs and chains to prevent the unsolicited appearance of the Black militant James Forman at New York's Temple Emmanuel, picketed the Metropolitan Museum of Art to protest the Museum's catalogue to the exhibit "Harlem on My Mind," and publicly demanded that the left-wing radio station WBAI-FM dismiss the Black radical Julius Lester, who, on various occasions had invited anti-Semitic guests to speak on his show. In these actions, Kahane believed he was simply taking seriously what most establishment Jewish organizations did not: the growth of Black anti-Semitism. "It bothers me strongly that Jewish groups are so ready to see anti-Semitism under every white bed and will ignore blatant anti-Semitism on the part of Blacks," Kahane told the *New York Times* reporter Walter Goodman, "What kind of mind is it that refuses to see a danger because a person is Black?" It was Kahane's belief that increasingly extreme Black demands would be associated with Jews because of large-scale Jewish support for civil rights and that these demands would, paradoxically, have the effect of increasing white anti-Semitism. "Mr. Jew is blamed for Blacks—and in certain ways there is truth to it," Kahane explained. "An embittered white ethnic who sits and is out of work and is angry and worried . . . blames the Jew for the Black man. [The white ethnic thinks] 'If the Jews hadn't started this thing, there would be no Black problems.' "[11]

Despite Kahane's skillful exploitation of the feeling of many poorer Jews that they had been left in the lurch by establishment Jewish leaders, the increasingly extreme and confrontational tactics of the JDL eventually resulted in the movement's decline. Kahane and his followers interrupted concerts and performances, harassed and attacked Soviet diplomats, attacked members of Arab groups in the United States, invaded and occupied offices of Jewish organizations that disagreed with or denounced the JDL, and blew up the tourist office of a foreign government, an act that Kahane claimed to know nothing of but that he verbally supported. In July 1971, Kahane was arrested on a charge of conspiracy to violate federal gun and bomb regulations, for which he was given a five-year suspended sentence, fined five thousand dollars, and placed on five years' probation. Kahane and the JDL were effectively isolated by the larger Jewish community, which denied Kahane the right to speak at conferences, refused to engage him in public debate, and continuously and stridently denounced him and the organization he led.[12]

But perhaps most interesting was the opposition that Kahane and the JDL found within the orthodox community itself. The highly influential orthodox authority Rabbi Moshe Feinstein declared that the JDL's actions against governments and states were "contrary to the Torah." The Union of Orthodox Jewish Congregations of America unanimously voted to condemn Jewish extremists.[13] Following these denouncements, Kahane continued to experience a decline in fortunes and, in 1971, he and his family took up residence in Israel, from where he would continue to lead an almost fatally weakened JDL in the United States. Kahane's movement found its greatest support among Jews who could be considered "folk" orthodox, Jews only one or two generations removed from the immigrant world who by custom or upbringing remained ritually observant but who were not educated in the demanding and indoctrinating world of Jewish day schools. While Kahane's activities and political positions with regard to the State of Israel would later find support among a growing triumphalist orthodox right wing in the United States and Israel, the "folk" orthodox, among whom he found his earliest constituency, were a dying breed. Unable to sustain an adherence to Jewish observance among their young, and falling fast to the lures of secular education and suburban affluence, by the early 1970s it was obvious that this cohort, located primarily in the outer boroughs of New York and of other large cities, represented the final generation of American Jews with the recognizable imprimatur of earlier immigrant generations. Kahane's movement, despite its lack of appeal for the overwhelming majority of American Jews, touched the nerve of the last significant segment of working-class Jews, a segment of Jews increasingly absent from the concerns of the organized Jewish world and fading fast, along with the immigrant stamp on the American Jewish character.

Other Jewish Voices of Opposition

Aside from the orthodox, there were other, smaller yet quite vocal segments of the Jewish community that remained skeptical about Black Power and its meaning for American Jews. Essentially, these critics thought Black Power and the left were using their vast numbers to agitate and threaten the stability of American institutions important to American Jews and that the mostly white "Anglo-Saxon" establishment was showing a distinct willingness to sacrifice Jewish interests in order to appease the more dangerous Black agitators. This formulation was based on the belief that the Jews were vulnerable to oppression and not completely at ease in the United States, but, unlike the Jews on the New Left, these critics defined the problem as more a matter of power politics than one of an oppressive capitalist system. Like the Jewish leftists, these critics focused on anti-Semitism, but it was the present anti-Semitism on the left and in the Black community, rather than the anti-Semitism of the right, that concerned them, and they were thus willing to release themselves from what they now believed to be an anachronistic alliance with Black Power. That said, it should be pointed out that however more realistically and less sentimentally they were able to see new developments on the American political scene, these critics were, in effect, thrown back into the mire of Jewish history by the new anti-Semitism on the left. That is, Black anti-Semitism had the effect of enveloping these critics in the discourse surrounding the historic Jewish concern with safety and vulnerability, rather than with the challenge presented by freedom and assimilation.

Milton Himmelfarb was one such critic. Educated at the Jewish Theological Seminary, Himmelfarb was an astute observer of the Jewish scene, an accomplished sociologist, and perhaps the most gifted of the writers who subscribed to the "Jew as middleman" theme. Some months after the Six-Day War, Himmelfarb wrote that the Jews were changing in a way that suggested a profound disillusionment with the liberal outlook they had acquired as a result of the modern Enlightenment. "The French Revolution had equality for the Jews as a corollary. We were for the Revolution and its extension, and the right was against. Now the location of our enemies is not quite so simple. We have enemies on the right, but also on the left." [14] Writing of the infamous June-July newsletter of the Student Non-violent Coordinating Committee—"What's in a name"—and the editor's diatribe against the "Jew shops" in the Black ghettos, Himmelfarb responded with characteristic wit. "Say what you will about Marxism-Leninism-Maoism-Fidelism-Fanonism, what other mode of analysis would have been able to trace the causes of Negro oppression so unerringly to the real centers of economic and political power . . . Israel and the little Jew shops?" [15]

Himmelfarb was convinced that the Jews in America were becoming the middlemen between a white Protestant establishment and an increasingly agitated Black militancy. The establishment was most interested in maintaining order among urban Blacks, and in order to achieve its goal a certain number of Black elites would have to be mollified by being given a stake in the system. In the schools, what mattered was not so much the "ability to teach" but the ability to impose discipline, and Black Americans, the establishment felt, could perform that role better than Jews. Assuming the role of an imaginary WASP, Himmelfarb wrote that Jews would be hurt the most, but "fair is fair, and as between Blacks and Jews we have no reason to reproach ourselves when we give preference to the Blacks. . . . Blacks can cause trouble, real trouble, Jews only talk . . . the price must be paid, and this is both the easiest and the fairest." [16]

It is interesting that Himmelfarb suggested that Jews themselves were responsible, at least in part, for their interstitiality, because continuing Jew-ish support for such issues as open housing, free speech, and racial integra-tion had alienated them from other white ethnic groups, the only potential allies available. Allies of the Jews would not come from the right or the left, and they certainly would not come from the white ethnics, wrote Himmelfarb with tongue in cheek. "Why should Poles or Italians bestir themselves for the Jews? . . . In voting on money for the public schools, the Jews are for, they are against. The Jews go to college, they do not. They hunt, the Jews do not." [17]

A number of critics came to believe that, with the rise of Black Power, the idea that America was a unique place for Jews in the history of the diaspora had to be reconsidered. The turmoil of the late 1960s rankled the iconoclastic editor of the *Jewish Spectator,* Trude-Weiss Rosmarin, who ed-ited that magazine from 1938 until her death in 1989. An immigrant from Germany who had earned a doctorate in Semitics, archeology, and phi-losophy from the University of Berlin, Weiss-Rosmarin held a wide variety of original opinions on such issues as women in Jewish life, Zionism, and Jewish culture. One of the more controversial debates she entered into during her career involved the question of whether the Jews in the United States were in exile (*galut*) or whether America was different from the rest of the nations of the Jewish diaspora. In 1951, in response to an exchange between Jacob Blaustein, president of the American Jewish Committee and CEO of the American Oil Company, and Israeli President David Ben-Gurion, in which Blaustein affirmed that America was not *galut,* Weiss-Rosmarin asserted that "America is *galut* . . . because the American Jew must be a Jew, even when he does not want to be a Jew." [18] Eventually Weiss-Rosmarin came to reject the idea of America as *galut,* reasoning that "American Jews . . . are of America as all other Americans and resent . . . any intimation that they are not like all Americans." [19]

But with the advent of Black Power, Weiss-Rosmarin came to believe that Jews were getting caught in the crossfire between resentful Blacks and hostile WASPS. The events in the Black ghettos and Black Power, as well as the rumblings by some prominent literary WASPS that Jews had wide-spread control of the literary establishment, convinced her that "Jewish history also documents that whenever and wherever the outsiders became successful self-made insiders, popular resentment rose against them." [20] With her newly reinforced belief that Jew-hatred could not be fought or pre-vented even in the United States, Weiss-Rosmarin rejected the idea that America was different. "I have frequently expressed my belief that America is different. But this was before the urban crisis erupted in the conflagration of the fire this time," she wrote, concluding that all of the explosive ingredients that had triggered anti-Semitic outbreaks in the past were now present in the United States.[21]

Another influential spokesman for the idea that Jews had to reevaluate their position toward the race revolution was the rabbi and theologian Richard Rubenstein. Rubenstein is recognized today as one of the most imaginative Jewish theologians of the twentieth century for his "Death of God" thesis, formulated in his book *After Auschwitz* published in 1966.[22] Rubenstein argued for a radical new *midsrash,* a radical new myth, in the wake of the Holocaust because it was now no longer possible to speak of the caring, compassionate, personal God that Jews had historically conceived.[23] The harsh realism that Rubenstein brought to Jewish theology was also evident in his analysis of the American Jewish situation in the late 1960s, particularly with regard to race relations and the Black Power movement.

Rubenstein urged Jews to be more realistic politically and to stop relying on appeals to morality and moralism in dealing with both the white Christian and the Black communities. In 1963, Rubenstein had been one of nineteen rabbis to respond to Martin Luther King's request for support in his effort to fight racial segregation in Birmingham, Alabama.[24] But by 1965, Rubenstein felt that the eventual withdrawal of Jewish support from the Black revolution had become inevitable. The reasoning behind this change of mind was the gnawing feeling that Jews were once again being drawn into the historic pattern of showing sympathy for other people's national aspirations despite the anti-Semitism of the ensuing revolution. "I knew that every nationalist revolution in modern times had turned anti-Semitic. . . . It is unfortunately not true that victims seek justice. Very frequently, they seek victims of their own," Rubenstein wrote.[25]

Rubenstein clearly overstated the attachment of nationalist revolutions to anti-Semitism, and he need have looked no further than the American Revolution for evidence to the contrary. But with regard to anti-Semitism and the Black revolution, Rubenstein drew on the international connection between Black Power and anti-Zionism and insisted that it was incumbent upon the Jewish community to reexamine its fundamental political strategy. "The presuppositions of American Jewish liberalism worked well in the America of the thirties, forties, and fifties. . . . [But] the Jewish community can no longer remain true to its own fundamental aspirations . . . and, at the same time, support the Negro revolution."[26]

The Jewish Neoconservatives and the Common Culture

The rise of radical New Left and Black Power movements gave birth to a small but influential school of American political thought known broadly as neoconservatism. While this movement included such non-Jewish intellectuals as Daniel Patrick Moynihan, Robert Nisbet, Paul Seabury, Peter Berger, Samuel Huntington, and Michael Novak, a large portion of the movement's top figures were prominent Jewish intellectuals formerly of the radical New York Intellectual milieu. Irving Kristol, the editor of the neoconservative house organ *The Public Interest,* has been labeled the "father" of neoconservative thought and once metaphorically described a neoconservative as "a liberal who has been mugged by reality."[27] Other prominent Jewish neoconservatives have included Norman Podhoretz, Nathan Glazer, Gertrude Himmelfarb, Daniel Bell, Seymour Martin Lipset, Joseph Epstein, Earl Raab, Walter Laqueur, Aaron Wildavsky, Ronald Berman, Ben Wattenberg, Midge Decter, and Martin Diamond.

While American Jews have been mostly aligned with liberal politics, there have always been secular Jewish conservatives in the United States, some of whom became quite prominent in American intellectual life. Among these were the well-known anti-Communists Sidney Hook and Bertram Wolfe. At the University of Chicago, a whole school of conservative thought took root after World War II with the active participation of many prominent Jewish scholars, including Milton Friedman, the father of fiscal "monetarism," and Leo Strauss, the German émigré and founder of the University of Chicago school of social philosophy, which emphasized the "natural law" of civilized order and the rejection of socialist utopias. Jewish practitioners of the Chicago school included Hans Morgenthau, Mortimer Adler, and Hannah Arendt.[28] There was also a small cadre of secular Jewish conservatives who wrote for William F. Buckley's *National Review,* including Max Geltman, a journalist who wrote a number of articles on the Black revolution that were eventually published as a book. Geltman called for a "disengagement" of American Jews from the Black Power movement on the basis of the movement's open hostility toward Jews.[29]

But no particular group of conservative thinkers or conservative schools of thought had ever come close to carrying as sizable a Jewish imprint as the neoconservatives, a movement that attracted many recent arrivals from the precincts of the radical left. In the late 1960s, when a number of formerly left-wing intellectuals began to take on conservative colorations, it was no surprise that a large proportion of these intellectuals were of Jewish background, bringing with them specific Jewish preoccupations along the way.

Neoconservatism shared a great deal with traditional American conservatism on domestic and foreign issues, but it represented something new in that it was possibly the first programmatic system of thought in the United States that wholeheartedly accepted many important liberal principles. For neoconservatives, it went without saying that the inequality of racial minorities, women, and the poor was bad, that access to good public schools, higher education, and job opportunities should be expanded for all, that there was a definite need for a welfare state along the lines established by the New Deal and its immediate postwar expansion, and that the United States should consider its reputation for accepting and absorbing large numbers of new immigrants from all over the world a great virtue. No doubt the heavy Jewish and Catholic representation among the neoconservatives accounted for their concern with the "openness" of American life and the matter of equality in general, and this prompted one liberal writer to comment that neoconservatism was the first "serious American conservatism."[30]

But neoconservatism also represented something new in that it was in large measure a response to the rise of New Left radicalism in the late 1960s and, consequently, reflected an overarching concern with the stability of American political and social institutions. The primary concerns of the neoconservatives reflected their belief that a crisis of authority had occurred in the United States and in the West in general, that governing institutions had lost their legitimacy, and that the rise of a permanent "adversary culture" had come, by way of a soft "New Class" of liberal bureaucrats, to seriously threaten the social stability upon which the future of democracy depended. The idea of defending "liberal" civilization underlies the "newness" of the "neo" in the term neoconservative: it was a conservatism that did not, in its early stages, see itself as necessarily conservative in the traditional sense, but rather as a defender of postwar American liberalism against a destructive 1960s radicalism. It is instructive that the neoconservatives were not self-named; the name was coined by the democratic socialist Michael Harrington, who gave himself that label in order to distinguish himself from other Democratic party intellectuals after he had decided to drop his protest against electoral politics. To this day many neoconservatives continue to believe that it is a long-lost liberalism that they seek to recover, rather than a variant of conservatism.[31]

The stability of democratic institutions and the hostility of the radical left to the humanistic and rational traditions of the West was a major concern for a number of Jewish neoconservatives, most of whom were prompted into their ideological "apostasy" by the New Left and Black Power position on the 1967 Middle East war. Many of the Jewish neoconservatives experienced the same revival of Jewish pride after the Six-Day War that had affected most American Jews, and this change in mood was recorded famously in the pages of *Commentary* magazine by its editor, Norman Podhoretz.[32] Podhoretz explained that he had embarked on an extraordinary intellectual evolution that began in the early 1960s when he first started editing *Commentary,* with an effort "to revive the dormant spirit of radical social criticism within the American intellectual community." But by the end of the decade, Podhoretz wrote, "I found myself almost entirely out of sympathy with the political workings of the radical ethos," largely because of the "barbaric hostility to freedom of thought which by the late 1960s had become one of the hallmarks of this ethos."[33] But, as Podhoretz went on to state, in the case of his own disaffection, and that of the other Jewish writers around *Commentary,* "there was an element going beyond what is customarily considered political." For Podhoretz and his circle of writers, this other element seemed closely connected to their identities as Jews.

Podhoretz admitted that he was worried about the Jewish condition in America and that this anxiety was caused by two events—the Six-Day War and the New York City teachers' strike. Both of these events had served to break the taboo against the open expression of anti-Semitism that had prevailed in the United States since World War II. "[I]f the anti-Semitism of the right continues to live underground, the anti-Semitism of the left has moved in recent years out of the foul-smelling catacombs of the radical tradition and into the common light of day," Podhoretz wrote. Podhoretz was also convinced that the teachers' strike exposed in certain elements of the white power structure an "apparent readiness to purchase civil peace in the United States . . . at the direct expense of the Jews."[34]

Accordingly, when thinking about political and social issues, Podhoretz suggested that Jews should ask themselves the age-old question "Is it good for the Jews?" In a statement that reflected the cosmopolitan milieu from whence the Jewish neoconservatives came, Podhoretz admitted that only a short time earlier this question would have evoked a response of anger or embarrassment from American Jews like himself, who believed that it reflected a "mentality no broader than that of the tribe." But now it appeared that the "Golden Age" of American Jewry was over, and it was appropriate to ask such a question.

Between 1967 and 1972 Podhoretz fleshed out the program of Jewish neoconservatives with the help of a coterie of extremely talented writers, most of whom had embarked on an ideological evolution similar to the one he had taken. As with Podhoretz, these writers were deeply impacted by the anti-Semitism of the New Left and Black Power movements and by the stubborn refusal of Jewish leftists to denounce the ideological extremism of these movements. The feeling that the rise of New Left radicalism and Black Power and the acceptance of their premises by liberals had put American Jews in a precarious situation found articulate and strident expression through the writers at *Commentary*.

The neoconservative approach to Black Power and Black anti-Semitism was perhaps most fully fleshed out by the sociologist and Jewish communal leader Earl Raab. In a widely read article that appeared in *Commentary* in 1969, Raab attacked the irrelevance of studies that showed small amounts of Black anti-Semitism on the grounds that anti-Semitic political movements did not require large numbers of supporters in order to succeed. To demonstrate this point, Raab cited the political phenomenon of the Catholic priest Charles Coughlin in the 1930s. After a point the Coughlin movement became explicitly anti-Semitic, yet polls showed that only around 20 percent of Coughlin supporters said they would back a campaign against Jews.[35] While anti-Semitism might not have been a salient enough issue to attract supporters, it was also insufficient to inhibit support for a movement that had anti-Semitism as only one of its central platforms. It was for this reason that political anti-Semitism usually originates not in the grass roots but in the minds of elites who are capable of articulating an integrated ideology. Raab insisted that the anti-Semitism emerging from Black extremism was not the folk anti-Semitism that Black Americans shared with whites and that utilized the characterizations of Christian mythology but rather was political anti-Semitism, "the abstract and symbolic anti-Semitism which Jews instinctively find more chilling."[36] Accordingly, Raab insisted that, "as far as the 'vulnerability' of the population is concerned, the key is not the level of anti-Semitic beliefs, but the level of resistance to political anti-Semitism."[37] The relevant fact was that Black Power was developing an anti-Semitic ideology that many Blacks refused to reject because it met so many unexpressed needs in the Black community. While the majority of Black Americans might be horrified by expressions of anti-Semitism, Raab wrote, they were reluctant to oppose it on the community level "because it would seem to be an attack on the militant movement itself."[38]

The Jewish neoconservatives represented the first attempt within the American Jewish community to provide a programmatic alternative to the predominantly left-liberal tradition of Jewish politics in the United States. For perhaps the first time in the twentieth century, an identifiable group of well-placed and influential Jewish thinkers had exhibited a willingness to reorder the priorities of American Jews and to suggest in the strongest terms that Jewish well-being might not necessarily be tied to the political aspirations of Black Americans or to progressive social and political forces of any kind. But it was not the objective of the Jewish neoconservatives to deal in any programmatic depth with more substantive issues of Jewish culture. As intellectuals who had recently left the folds of American radicalism, the neoconservatives were necessarily of an insurgent psychology, concentrating specifically on ridding the Jewish community, and American political life at large, of what they considered to be dangerous new radical notions that had gained ascendancy in American intellectual and political life. The neoconservatives were therefore tied to the discourse of liberalism and all of its underlying preoccupations, including the ambivalence with which liberals approached their Jewish identities. Such liberal preoccupations included the idea that Jews were historically, and continued to be, potential victims and that the primary measure of Jewish welfare was the size of the buffer American Jews could put between the forces of anti-Semitism and themselves. Accordingly, Jewish neoconservatives saw the welfare of American Jews almost solely in political terms, in strengthening those forces they thought were less inclined toward anti-Semitism and weakening those they thought promoted it. But while this included a warmer approach toward Israel, in general, the neoconservative program was strictly political, more an attack against a liberalism "gone mad" than a prescription for an affirmative Jewish life.

It is not surprising, therefore, that the neoconservatives came under criticism from more religiously observant Jews for not focusing on religion or internal Jewish problems. Jacob Neusner, the renowned religious scholar, has claimed that *Commentary* magazine is "Jewish" but never "Judaic" and that anything "Jewish may find its place in the worldview of the neocons of Jewish origin, history, sociology, literature, politics—anything except religion."[39] It was Neusner's belief that, "when it comes to the rich and sanctifying Judaic religious life, with its sophisticated intellectual heritage of reflection and rigorous thought, these people stand at one with the left."[40] To their credit, and in striking contrast to the Jewish liberals and the Jews of the New Left, it was never the stated intention of the Jewish neoconservatives to be anything other than a loosely defined program of political and cultural criticism. The long liberal tradition of invoking Judaic injunctions to bolster political agendas, from the Reform rabbis of Germany, who pronounced that Judaism obligates its adherents to serve the Fatherland, to the Jews of the New Left, who argued that "true commitment to the Jewish tradition necessitates participation in revolutionary struggles," was not, on the whole, duplicated by the Jewish neocons. Podhoretz even wrote that "those of us who have been fighting the ideas of the radical left have been fighting precisely in the name of liberal values, not in the name of Judaism. It is shallow and vulgar, if not blasphemously presumptuous to think that Judaism gives its blessings or its warrant to a particular political position."[41]

Yet critics like Neusner are not wrong to point out the very secular nature of the neoconservative program. For Jewish neoconservatives like Earl Raab and the sociologist Nathan Glazer, the fight for Jewish security focused on the threat to America's political stability symbolized by the Black revolution and the mistaken commitment of intellectuals to antidemocratic thought. For the neocons, liberalism had come to mean something far different from what it had meant in the past, and its wayward trajectory was for them a more important development than any of the internal concerns of the Jewish community. In an article written in 1970, Raab declared that the question as to whether Jews could preserve their identity as Jews in an open society was now moot because the threat to an open society in the United States itself had superseded it. For Raab, "the most direct threat to the American Jewish community is not the seepage of assimilation but the growing inhospitality of the American political environment," an inhospitality attributed to the crisis of liberalism in which the United States was at the vanguard.[42]

Whereas left-liberal Jews attacked the Jewish middle class for its conformity and political complacence, the Jewish "new class" of upper middle-class intellectuals and students got it good from the neocons. Raab singled out the thousands of Jewish lawyers, businessmen, and housewives who he believed constituted the backbone of workaday ideological liberalism in communities across the land; he insisted that these people "should never be forgotten for the way in which they have heightened concern for human problems in the country" but that, in addition, "they should never be forgiven for the way they have tolerated and fostered a self-destructive liberal innocence while so engaged." Raab also detected the limitations of Black Power pluralism as it concerned American Jews. It was true that Jews continued to participate fully in big city government, usually as "advisers" or "social experts," but they were in these roles primarily as professionals whose departure from the Jewish community was "urban affairs" or the social sciences, Jews who identified with the rising urban minority groups, rather than as representatives of any particular segment of the Jewish community. "Indeed, the new liberal big-city coalition, in which the only ethnicity is Third World, bears with it a bias which is, if anything, anti-Israel and cool to the Jewish community." Jews who remained attached to the new liberalism were behaving in a "particularly pathological and self-destructive" way.[43]

One of the Jewish neocons most deeply influenced by the rise of Black Power was Nathan Glazer. Glazer's now famous early period of "mild" radicalism, when he encouraged young Jews to join progressive social movements and supported preferential treatment for Blacks, had by 1967 evolved into a self-described "mild" conservatism. The large-scale riots in Newark and Detroit had convinced Glazer that extremism had come to dominate the mood of the Black American, and, like Raab, he was skeptical about the meaning of this development for the stability of democratic institutions. "The line is difficult to draw between an aroused citizenry flooding council chambers to voice their grievances . . . and the threat that unless these grievances are immediately acted upon the city will be in ashes."[44]

Glazer was not sure what ignited the riots themselves, but he expressed the opinion that they were substantively different from earlier riots by urban Blacks because thirty years of what could reasonably be viewed as a "good deal of progress" had made no change in the mood or living conditions of the ghetto. Glazer argued that there were more Blacks in elected office, the civil service, the mass production industries, and white-collar and professional jobs; that there was better housing; and that the shame of Black disenfranchisement in the South was over—but that all this made little difference.

For Glazer, the prevalence of the belief that Black Americans were doing badly just as it became possible to demonstrate that there had been vast improvements in their condition constituted America's racial paradox, and the paradox had its roots in a fallacious idea about race and ethnic groups in America: that all white ethnic groups had been allowed to move rapidly into American society and achieve respectable levels of income, good conditions of living, and political power, while racially distinct groups had been held back from doing the same by racism. The truth, Glazer thought, was nothing like this. In the Northern cities, there were differences between Blacks and white immigrant groups, but the similarities and continuities were more important. White ethnic groups exhibited a wide range of experience, varying with time of arrival, skills at time of arrival, the character of the cities to which they came, and the degree of prejudice and discrimination they faced. Blacks, for example, had more "political power than Puerto Ricans in New York City, a somewhat higher income, a substantially higher proportion of professionals. . . . African-Americans probably have more college graduates than Polish Americans, more political muscle than Mexican Americans, more clout in the mass media than Italian Americans," Glazer wrote.[45] But even if one believed that Blacks were the worst off of all the distinctive ethnic groups, Glazer believed that it was possible to see that Blacks were part of a pattern that had seen some groups do better than others and all groups experience ups and downs within different time frames. "One can indeed contend that the Negro is the worst off of the major ethnic and racial groups in this country, but not that much worse off to explain by itself the special quality of despair and hysteria, and the tone of impending violence and doom that now dominates much African-American political discourse."[46]

The race paradox played a pivotal role in Glazer's ideological evolution. Like Earl Raab, Glazer saw unity in the forces on the New Left, the attack on the universities and public bureaucracies, the general movement away from humanism in the earlier radicalism, and the Black Power movement.[47] While the radicalization of Black Power may have been fed by frustration and deprivation at the grass-roots level, it was ideological at its core, aided and abetted, in Glazer's view, by the growing rage and hostility centered around radical students and encouraged by a wide range of intellectuals. Glazer indicted radical Jewish intellectuals for espousing the notion that those in the middle class were beneficiaries of white-skin privilege, that they acted in compliance with the racist order and, therefore, were not entitled to preserve their status, their property, or even their lives. If America "is believed to be inherently discriminatory and racist in its treatment of minority groups, the very success—economic, political, cultural—of the Jewish group becomes suspect: it becomes a success based on collaboration with the enemy." If Black anti-Semitism was primarily the work of the Black intelligentsia, then it was also "abetted and assisted and advised by a white, predominantly Jewish, intelligentsia." This led to a vituperative attack against radical Jewish writers and editors such as Andrew Kopkind, Robert and Barbara Silvers, Robert Scheer, Paul Jacobs, and Marvin Garson, whom Glazer accused of tolerating the Black use of antiwhite violence. After all, Glazer reasoned, if some WASP foundations and mayors saw anti-Semitism as an opportunity to divert Black rage, it was from the "experts," many of whom were Jewish, that they learned this. It was from these "disinterested experts" that they got the idea that judgment by universal criteria was discriminatory, that revolutionaries were closer to the grassroots needs of the people than were upholders of the "system," and that bureaucracies robbed people of their freedom—"And if Jews are doing these things, a serious job of education must be undertaken among them."[48]

In the early 1960s, Glazer considered the achievements of "gifted young Jews" to the arts, to radical politics, and to the labor movement the Jews' greatest gifts to the United States.[49] Less than ten years later, he questioned whether Jewish radicalism had ultimately been a good thing after all. "Anyone concerned for the future of Jews in America who sees what the intellectuals have accomplished will certainly think twice before applauding or rejoicing in the Jewish role in the transformation of the United States."[50] In the end, Glazer felt that the Jewish response to Black anti-Semitism depended on what Jews believed the character of American life to be. "If Jews really believe that America has not changed for the better and cannot change further, that democracy is a fraud, and that intelligence and political action within the scheme of the American political system can do nothing and have done nothing to improve the condition of minorities . . . [A]ll they can do is give the Blacks guns, and allow themselves to become the first victims."[51]

The vigorous frontal assault on Black Power and on Black anti-Semitism and those who appeared to countenance it clearly set the Jewish neoconservatives apart from the liberal Jewish establishment, which struggled to maintain an alliance with Blacks. Because of this, the neoconservatives and *Commentary* magazine occupied an influential but relatively isolated space in American Jewish life. The Jewish neocons broke cleanly with left-liberal Jews not only over the left's perception that the threat of Black anti-Semitism and Black Power were not particularly harmful but also over the liberal perception that Jews would inevitably benefit from Black Power because it was forcing the United States to accept a broader concept of cultural diversity. The Jewish neocons had no illusions about what a pluralism defined along the rigid lines of race would mean for white ethnic groups, and they held fast to the belief that American Jews were better off in a society that emphasized a strong common culture. Yet it was not the prospect of Jewish dissolution in a conglomeration of melted white ethnic groups that most concerned the neocons. What concerned them most was, rather, Black Power's espousal of involuntary ethnic association, the fear of which continued to characterize many of these writers from their days on the cosmopolitan left. Raab's and Glazer's conviction, for example, that the fundamental threat from Black Power derived from its threat to the "openness" and "freedom" of America betrayed their belief that the optimal life was not one in which individuals would be forced to submit to the demands and commitments of the groups to which they involuntarily belonged. In this, Glazer was exhibiting a remarkable ideological consistency. In the first edition of *Beyond the Melting Pot,* published in 1963, Glazer insisted not only that the various ethnic groups of New York City continued to be identifiable and important for social and political life but that they also no longer continued to exist as completely autonomous entities. "It is true that language and culture are very largely lost in the first and second generations," wrote Glazer and Moynihan of New York's ethnic groups, "and this makes the dream of 'cultural pluralism' . . . as unlikely as the melting pot."[52] It was this perceived prohibition against cultural separatism that made *Beyond the Melting Pot* so optimistic in tone. In the Northern model of group relations, which Glazer endorsed and used to describe New York City, there existed competition between groups and individuals, but it was muted and conducted through effectiveness of organization and achievement, rather than through violence. Most important, it was individual choice, rather than law or custom, that determined the extent to which any person participated in the life of an ethnic group and the pace at which one assimilated. Put another way, in the Northern model described by Glazer and Moynihan, ethnic groups acted as intermediate social structures, but individual choice was preserved.

This ideal represented the viewpoint of the Jewish neocons, and it was the belief in individualism, an attachment to the ambiguity of modern life, more than anything else that inspired the neocons to oppose Black Power and the accompanying resurgence of white ethnic assertiveness in the early 1970s. In fact, the movement for white ethnic assertiveness drew as much fire from the Jewish neocons as had the Black Power movement, and it is here again that the neoconservative preoccupation with the discourse of liberalism can be observed.

The movement among some white ethnics, including some leading Jewish spokesmen, for a resurgence of ethnicity and rigid group barriers began to take root in the late 1960s. While other objective conditions were responsible for the ethnic resurgence, it was clear that the Black Power search for Black identity helped to foster similar impulses in other ethnic groups.[53] Fashionable t-shirts and buttons proclaiming "Polish Power" and "Italian Power" inspired Andrew Greeley to write in 1971 that "the Blacks have legitimated definitively the idea of cultural pluralism. . . . If it is all right for Blacks, then it ought to be all right for everyone else."[54]

Some Jewish communal leaders and social scientists seemed to identify strongly with the new pluralism espoused by Greeley, Novak, and others. Murray Friedman, the Pennsylvania area director of the American Jewish Committee and a teacher at the University of Pennsylvania, collected and edited *Overcoming Middle-Class Rage,* a volume of essays and speeches on the subject, most of which originated in 1969 and 1970 when racial tensions were at a high.[55] The new pluralism may have been a response to Black Power, though not entirely in the reactionary way that some critics believed it was.[56] In effect, Black Power stripped white ethnicity of its myriad distinctions, and the advocates of the new pluralism, at least in part, were responding to this challenge. Yet the increasing assimilation and suburbanization of white ethnics during these years betrayed a tone of desperation in many white ethnic writers who seemed to insist that ethnicity had more meaning in the lives of white ethnics than the increasing convergence of cultural patterns suggested. Perhaps the last wall that separates ethnic groups, the intimate bond of marriage, crumbled rapidly for Jews almost as much as it had for other white ethnics. Between 1965 and 1975 the number of all Boston Jews opposed to intermarriage declined from 70 percent to 34 percent. By 1983 only 10 percent of non-Jewish Americans disapproved of marriage between Jews and Christians.[57] These numbers foretold of the landmark findings of the National Jewish Population Survey of 1990, which indicated that more than 50 percent of marriages involving Jews after 1985 consisted of marriage to a non-Jewish partner.[58] "At bottom," wrote one observer, "what all this obviously implies is the increasingly rapid development of cultural patterns that are common to all Americans regardless of religion." Warmly as many Americans embraced it, the ideal of cultural pluralism in the late 1960s and early 1970s was flawed in one crucial respect: it failed to allow for the fact that, in some of the most basic aspects of life, the melting pot, "far from being inoperative, was bubbling away more strongly than ever before."[59] Seen in this light, the "new pluralism" of the late 1960s and early 1970s was perhaps, more accurately, a last gasp attempt by consciously ethnic whites to avoid the psychic costs of assimilation by institutionalizing group differences. As the historian John Higham has noted, "loud assertions of pluralism almost invariably betray fears of assimilation."[60]

The response of some of the writers around *Commentary* magazine to the "new pluralism" revealed a great deal about the limitations of the new post-1967 Jewish consciousness among neoconservatives. In his controversial 1968 memoir *Making It,* Norman Podhoretz wrote about the "brutal bargain" Jews had been required to make in their figurative journey from the Jewish ghetto to the WASP gentile world of the Manhattan literary scene.[61] The brutality of the bargain consisted, of course, in the relinquishing of those cultural habits that the power brokers in Manhattan considered unbecoming. But despite Podhoretz's difficulty with the bargain, he would always remain enamored of the idea of an American "common culture" that was coextensive with WASP culture. When he became editor of *Commentary* in 1960, Podhoretz held to the idea of a higher culture in which all could share, insisting that "it was possible to be an avant-garde intellectual and at the same time to be interested in things Jewish."[62] Because of its emphasis on individualism, the WASP "common culture" was benign for American Jews, and the attack by the ethnic activists on the WASP foundation of American culture disturbed Podhoretz greatly. To denigrate the ideal of individual autonomy "and to imply moreover that the only choice we are offered is to remain in the ethnic community or to become facsimile WASPS," Podhoretz wrote in 1972, "is to falsify and impoverish our sense of what pluralism can mean in America." Podhoretz concluded that, "because just such a false and impoverishing view is implicit in the attitudes of certain ethnic enthusiasts, I find myself more bothered by their movement than—as an old believer in the value of cultural pluralism—I would ever have expected to be."[63]

Podhoretz's belief that the new ethnic particularists, first Black, then white, denied the existence of a common culture in America inspired him to publish two important articles in 1972 on the subject of the new pluralism. The articles were written by two scholars, Harold Isaacs and Robert Alter, both of whom had exhibited in their scholarship a commitment to the idea of ethnic particularism. These writers used the occasion of Murray Friedman's book *Overcoming Middle-Class Rage* and Michael Novak's *The Rise of the Unmeltable Ethnics* (1972) to express concern about the new pluralism, stemming from their perception that the new pluralists were advocating the idea that an individual's primary commitment was to his or her particular ethnic group.[64]

Isaacs, the author of a seminal work on the impact of the postcolonial age on Black American identity, felt that Friedman's refusal to assign "special virtue or culpability" to any one group amounted to a "dog-eat-dog" philosophy that opened the door for the legitimation of allegiance to such groups as the Ku Klux Klan.[65] Another concern for Isaacs was the various laws new pluralists were trying to get enacted that would institutionalize the recognition of ethnic group viewpoints. One of these bills—the Schweiker-Pucinski ethnic-studies bill, proposed to Congress in 1972—proposed federal funding of ethnic studies courses.[66] In response to Schweiker-Pucinski, Isaacs wrote, "[L]et anyone do what he can to instill whatever version of ethnic pride he wants in his fellows, but let him do it on his own time. . . . In the public domain, we have to live uncontrolled by any single view and open to all views."[67]

Robert Alter, a major Jewish literary critic, took pains to detail the very thin but important line between nationalism and ethnic chauvinism. In discussing Novak's *The Unmeltable Ethnics,* Alter claimed that Novak went way beyond the old ethnic politics of group self-interest to propose that ethnicity was the one "true and salubrious means to a viable sense of selfhood."[68] What concerned Alter most about Novak's book was the insistence that "people uncertain of their own identity are not wholly free," and he endorsed the flip side of Novak's ethnic coin: "People *preoccupied* with their own identity are not wholly free."[69] There may be a nucleus of truth, Alter conceded, to Novak's assertion that "when a person thinks, more than one generation's passions and images think in him," but it made Alter uneasy to present the individual as a "passive conduit" for the collective past and to place so much stress on the nonrational. Alter's fears were most aroused by Novak's claim that a Catholic writer could not relate to Jewish writers on the primary level. Claiming that there was an ability to transcend differences by people who really wanted to, and that the language of the common intellectual life allowed him to relate to Edmund Wilson more than to the thoughts of the Hasidic Satmar Rebbe, Alter wrote that he shared with the non-Jewish critic "an embracing realm of discourse with . . . an engagement in American culture and modern experience, and to that basic commonality of enterprise the differential element of Wilson's background is incidental." It was this aspect of modern culture for which we should all be grateful, Alter wrote, "for the fact that a person can at least in part free himself from subjugation (in some degree it is always that) to the community and the past in order to realize his selfhood according to his own needs."[70]

As the most distinct remnant of the New York Intellectual milieu, the Jewish neoconservatives took the transformative value of modern American life as their highest ideal, and they clearly preferred to live with the ambiguity of modern Jewish existence, rather than attempt to prescribe any specific program of Jewish commitment or responsibility. In this sense, neoconservatism was, in some very precise ways, a continuation of the postwar Jewish engagement with liberalism and the modern experience of emancipation. Central to this experience has been the negotiation of a tenuous balance between prejudice and freedom. In most instances, the focus on securing freedom by eliminating prejudice has denied to Jews the ability to face the growing dilemma of Jewish meaning in a free society and has redirected the attention of Jewish thinkers toward the world of external politics. As one historian has written, neoconservatism was part and parcel of the postwar shift in American Jewish life from "culture to causes." Whereas liberal and leftist Jews believed that serving the Jewish interest meant a commitment to progressive and radical politics, Podhoretz and the neoconservatives believed that the "American Jewish community would flourish best in a society in which conservative values and policies were ascendant."[71] The linkage between the two viewpoints involves the common definition of Jewish well-being. Both liberals and neoconservatives saw Jewish safety and vitality in a program of integration and the strengthening of the "common culture" held to be the highest American ideal. The difference between them was that liberals looked to Blacks, despite the advent of Black Power, as the primary catalyst for fulfilling the dream of a truly free society, while the neocons believed that Black Power had become the primary obstacle to achieving that cosmopolitan ideal. While the Jewish neoconservatives were more forthright in admitting the limitations of their program for Jewish culture, both movements were singularly committed to achieving political objectives consonant with Jewish safety and freedom, rather than with the search for Jewish meaning in modern America.

Conclusion

Blacks and Jews in American Popular Culture

"Yeah . . . I feel a part of me is black."

— Steven Spielberg

Arguing that it is in some ways more difficult to be a Jew in the United States than it is to be Black, as this book does, is in no way an attempt to minimize the very real impact of three hundred years of racial degradation or the continuing burden of contemporary racism. Nor is it to say that what American Jews as individuals, and sometimes as a group, have achieved under the freedom and opportunity they have enjoyed since the Second World War is in any way negligible. It is, rather, at its core, simply an attempt to demonstrate that Jewish life and culture have not been as easily adapted to American life as is commonly thought. In short, the tenets of American liberalism, around which so many Jews have organized their lives, have frequently diverged from the requisites of Jewish continuity, and this has been perhaps nowhere more evident than in the case of American race relations. This book shows not only that American cultural and political institutions have been more responsive to Black communal needs than to Jewish ones but that American Jewish leaders and intellectuals have been, at times, preoccupied with matters of race due primarily to their belief, stemming from a unique past, that freedom from external bigotry is all that is necessary for a minority group to flourish in this great land.

Perhaps the turmoil in the Jewish community over the issue of government-sponsored school voucher programs best dramatizes the extent to which the priorities of liberalism as it pertains to the Black community continue, in the 1990s, to dictate Jewish communal policy. Major American Jewish organizations have long opposed the idea of giving parents government subsidized vouchers to send their school-age children to the public or private school of their choice. Ostensibly, such opposition has been grounded in the liberal belief that vouchers pose a threat to the separation of church and state. The opposition of major Jewish groups such as the American Jewish Congress and the American Jewish Committee to voucher programs has remained steadfast, despite great enthusiasm from orthodox Jewish groups and substantial evidence that such programs strengthen Jewish education efforts, particularly religious day schools. The 1990 Jewish Population Study indicates that one of the most common characteristics among strongly identifying Jews is a day school education, which immerses youngsters in Jewish knowledge and a Jewish lifestyle.

Nevertheless, not only do most Jewish leaders remain opposed to school vouchers, but the motivation of those who are now beginning to break through the liberal line on this issue reveals that Jewish leadership has been much more responsive to the sensibilities of the Black community than to a clear-cut concern with Jewish education or issues of church and state. Mainstream Black organizations have long opposed voucher programs on the grounds that they would deplete inner-city public schools of students and resources. But now that some prominent Black leaders such as Queens Representative Floyd Flake and the Wisconsin state legislator Polly Williams have broken ranks on this issue, redefining vouchers as a way to Black empowerment, some Jewish spokespersons are calling for a "real, serious reassessment" of vouchers by the Jewish community. At a day-long conference on "School Vouchers and the Jewish Community" held in Washington, D.C., in May 1997, Jewish leaders made no effort to hide the fact that their shift on this issue has everything to do with Black education and almost nothing to do with Jewish education. During the conference, Barry Schrage, the president of the Combined Jewish Philanthropies of Greater Boston, said, "The issue of funding for Jewish day schools is less important than social justice." Larry Rubin, the executive director of the Jewish Council on Public Affairs (formerly the National Jewish Community Relations Advisory Council), said that, when pondering the efficacy of voucher programs, Jews must consider "the consequences of a failing educational system on the underclasses in an urban setting." As one Jewish sociologist has written about the position of Jewish leadership on the voucher issue, "When it comes to government aid that might possibly assist [Jewish] parochial schools, it seems that interests like Jewish continuity don't even make it on the radar screen."[1]

The problem for American Jews has not been their recognition that freedom from the burdens of bigotry is crucial to the success of minority groups or that the Black struggle in the United States to obtain this freedom has been perhaps the most worthy struggle of all, but rather their neglect of the other necessary ingredients for minority success: mainly, the maintenance of social and behavioral boundaries that separate the minority from the majority, boundaries that are now, as they always have been, for obvious reasons, far more difficult for Jews in the United States to draw than for Blacks. Moreover, Black culture, though born of exclusion, is largely American culture, whereas Jewish culture is largely, well, *Jewish* culture. Where Black Americans have historically needed only to respond to the weight of their history to affect American life and to stake their claim in it, Jews, it seems, have had to discard theirs before they could do the same. If Jewish life is going to continue among nonorthodox Jews in the United States, Jews will have to make concerted efforts to demarcate Jewish space from American space, a frequently difficult and unpleasant task.

In conclusion, perhaps a brief look at the wildly different, and commonly misunderstood, roles played by Black culture and Jewish culture in the popular arts of the United States will be instructive in bringing these points to light. In perhaps one of the most devastating cultural ironies, the Hollywood movie system, founded by Jews and commonly believed to be their greatest cultural gift to the United States, has proven to be the venue most strongly representative of Jewish assimilation. From the very beginning, Hollywood moguls like Louis B. Mayer, David O. Selznick, and Jack Warner were the ultimate Jewish assimilationists. "Hollywood Jews effaced their Judaism as a means of being accepted," writes the historian Neal Gabler. "There were a great many Jews [in Hollywood] who resented being branded outsiders, and they reacted against their Judaism aggressively."[2] With only a few notable exceptions, the Jewish image in Hollywood movies in recent decades has reflected the assimilationism of the Jewish moguls. In movies like *Radio Days* (1987), *The Adventures of Duddy Kravitz* (1974), *Avalon* (1990), *Goodbye, Columbus* (1969), *The Jazz Singer* (1927), *My Favorite Year* (1982), and *The Chosen* (1981), Jewish protagonists are shown fleeing from traditional Jewish fathers and Jewish cultural backwardness.[3] On the issue of intermarriage, a most recent concern, Hollywood carries on the tradition. In movies like *Dirty Dancing* (1987), *Marjorie Morningstar* (1955), *White Palace* (1990), *Heartburn* (1986), *When Harry Met Sally* (1989), *Chariots of Fire* (1981), *The Way We Were* (1973), and *Prince of Tides* (1991), as well as such recent television shows as *Sisters, Chicago Hope, Murder One, Mad About You, Cybill, Partners, Bless This House, The Single Guy, The Larry Sanders Show, Friends, Love and War, Seinfeld,* and *Murphy Brown,* more Jews and non-Jews are getting together than are members of any other ethnic group combination, a situation that leads one historian to comment that "Hollywood's happy ending is one that joins the Jew and non-Jew in matrimony, or at least love, triumphing over the narrowness of particularism."[4] Apparently, the Hollywood moguls achieved their goal. In the minds of most Americans, any differences that exist between Jews and gentiles are by no means substantial enough to keep them out of wedlock.

The history of Blacks in Hollywood, as elsewhere in American life, is of a far different order. From the beginning, Blacks have been excluded from the Hollywood movie system. Whenever Blacks did make it into a film, it was usually in the form of one or another degrading Black stereotype. In the 1940s and the decades after, Hollywood produced a number of liberal-minded "message" films about Blacks, usually directed by whites and featuring such stars as Sidney Poitier, Dorothy Dandridge, and Harry Belafonte. The 1970s saw the explosion of "Blaxploitation" films such as *Shaft* (1971) and *Superfly* (1972), which attracted the first crossover audiences. Today, however, the recognition and appreciation by movie-going audiences of Black culture as interesting and authentic has resulted in a virtual flood of Black movies and television shows. Apparently, the history of exclusion has, as in so many other instances, left a Black cultural legacy now regarded as distinctly Black, yet, paradoxically, somehow distinctly American, too. Unlike the Jewish moguls and later Jewish personalities in Hollywood, a slew of talented Black directors, actors, and actresses has emerged who are ready and willing to make affirmatively Black films, and Hollywood studios have flung open their doors and laid down big bucks for their efforts. Twenty-three-year-old John Singleton received ten million dollars for his first feature film, *Boyz in the Hood* (1991) from Columbia Pictures. Singleton's subsequent efforts like *Higher Education* (1994) and *Rosewood* (1997) and other Black films like Spike Lee's *Do the Right Thing* (1989), *Jungle Fever* (1991), and *Malcolm X* (1992), nineteen-year-old Matty Rich's *Straight Out of Brooklyn* (1991), Mario Van Peebles's *New Jack City* (1991), *Posse* (1993), and *Panther* (1995), and Julia Dash's *Daughters of the Dust* (1992) are by no means assimilationist films. According to one critic, they are "stridently confrontational in their depiction of a problem-riddled urban culture in conflict with a white mainstream."[5] Very rarely is the subject of racial intermarriage ever viewed positively in these Black films, as it is in films involving Jewish characters, and the idea of racial intermarriage has made little headway in television as well, as the demise of shows like *The Robert Guillaume Show, True Colors,* and *Murphy's Law* demonstrates.[6] The fact that large portions of the audience and an overwhelming number of writers and producers for these movies and shows are Black mitigates against the view that racial intermarriage has not worked in Hollywood simply because of white resistance to it. Here, what is often viewed by white liberals as a horrible racial injustice—limited choice in marriage partners—serves to strengthen Black cultural distinctiveness.

Compare also the two musical forms of jazz and the show music standard, two distinctly American art forms created almost exclusively by Blacks and Jews, respectively. As in the movie industry, Blacks had been excluded from the commercial development of jazz, in this case even despite having been its originators. As one historian recently wrote, "Almost without exception, popular-culture writing in the 1920s treated Negro primitivism as the raw material out of which whites fashioned jazz."[7] Some have seen the popularization of Black music as the consummate example of cultural theft. Amiri Baraka has written that "Jazz had rushed into the mainstream without so much as one Black face."[8] Later, there emerged a more accurate consensus among scholars that jazz was perhaps the most multicultural of artistic mediums, involving white, Southern folk, and Creole influences on an essentially Black urban idiom. However, the reracialization of American life since the 1960s has made race consciousness a powerful force in jazz. Just as the need to separate white from Black in popular culture once prevailed in music criticism, there is today a strong need to separate the Black from the white. Now, many critics talk about jazz as a singularly Black cultural idiom, and many record companies and concert halls give contracts almost exclusively to Black jazz musicians.[9]

And yet, perhaps appropriately, the association of jazz with Black culture is not paralleled by the association of the Broadway musical with Jewish culture, even though show music composition was dominated almost as completely in its origins by Jews as early jazz was by Blacks. Irving Berlin, Jerome Kern, Richard Rodgers, George Gershwin, Ira Gershwin, Dorothy Joseph, Herbert Fields, Lorenz Hart, Oscar Hammerstein II, Howard Dietz, and Arthur Schwartz were all of Jewish birth and by far the most important players in the creation of the Broadway standard. Perhaps Cole Porter, an Episcopalian, was the only major composer of popular standards not of Jewish birth, and even he confessed that his success was predicated upon his ability to write "Jewish tunes."[10] Here again, most of these Jews gained prominence after eschewing their Jewish backgrounds and making quintessentially "American" music. In fact, the show music made by Jewish composers combined the Viennese operetta and Black jazz to make what one critic called the "melting-pot music of the Jazz Age."[11] George Gershwin's music is more noticeably tied to the synagogue and its liturgical and cantorial melodies than the others, but even Gershwin, "the apotheosis of

American musical genius," adopted the tone of the Jewish ghetto to *Porgy and Bess,* the opera of another minority group.[12] "Although Gershwin was not shy about emphasizing the material/historical content of his Jewishness when it was convenient," writes one historian, "his career relied upon the ability to sell Jewishness as a flexible modality—and one particularly suited for absorbing African American music." Apparently, Gershwin had considered working on an opera derived from S. Ansky's Yiddish folktale *The Dybbuk,* but he found that the "material was too far from what he knew best, which most commentators agreed was African American music."[13] Gershwin's involvement with *Porgy and Bess* was, according to another scholar, a case of "beginning Jewish and ending up Black!"[14] That the role of Jews in American popular music is emblematic of the phenomenon in which the "American" in American Jew emerges as the "Jew" recedes is exemplified by the case of Irving Berlin, the most successful composer of popular American music and an immigrant Jew who wrote "White Christmas" and "Easter Parade" and who married the daughter of an anti-Semitic Catholic and raised his children as Protestants.[15] Only, it seems, in the frenzied effort to become American does the Jew have an impact on American culture.

Perhaps the most tragic part of all this is that no matter how great the effort, it is unlikely that Jews can ever have the impact on American culture that Blacks do. During the embryonic stages of American popular music in the early part of the twentieth century, it was not uncommon for music critics to interpret the "melting pot" music made by Jews like Berlin and Gershwin as "fake" and the ragtime or jazz music made by Black musicians like King Oliver and Jelly Roll Morton as "authentic."[16] However the critical debate among art historians turns out, popular opinion has issued its own verdict. One music critic recently compared jazz music with the popular standard. "The two traditions, born out of poverty and exclusion (and talent), would cross and interweave, but eventually the one shaped by men like Duke Ellington would take precedence over the one shaped by men like Berlin. All our currently predominant pop styles—rock, rap, rhythm-and-blues—derive from Black music; 'Jewish' music lives on only in the bits and pieces of the tradition that a few of the better pop artists have absorbed."[17] Here, as elsewhere in the United States, it was much easier for the Jew to assimilate, but the fact that Blacks could not, and the fact that nobody now is being asked to, has left Black Americans in a much stronger position today.

All of this is certainly not to say that Jewish life in the United States is without any redeeming value or hope. It is simply to say that corporate survival for Jews in the United States at the turn of the twenty-first century will be more difficult to justify and sustain than it ever was before and that previously held intellectual orientations may not be appropriate for this new kind of challenge. Whether there is a bright Jewish future in the United States may depend on the speed with which Jewish cultural, religious, and intellectual leaders absorb this unpleasant truth.

Notes

NOTES TO THE INTRODUCTION

1. The most comprehensive account of these changes is undoubtedly Murray Friedman, *What Went Wrong: The Creation and Collapse of the Black-Jewish Alliance* (New York: Free Press, 1995).

See also Jonathan Reider, *Canarsie: The Jews and Italians of Brooklyn Against Liberalism* (Cambridge, Mass.: Harvard University Press, 1985); Robert G. Weisbord and Richard Kazarian Jr., *Israel in the Black American Perspective* (Westport, Conn.: Greenwood Press, 1985), 121–140, 93–120; David Twersky, "Jesse Jackson's Candidacy: Assessment & Critique," *Congress Monthly* 55, no. 3 (July/August 1988): 3–6; Philip Gourevitch, "The Jeffries Affair," *Commentary* 93, no. 3 (March 1992).

2. Jonathan Kaufman, *Broken Alliance: The Turbulent Times Between Blacks and Jews in America* (New York: Scribner, 1988), 13–14.

3. Friedman, 15.

4. Robert G. Weisbord and Arthur Stein, *Bittersweet Encounter: African Americans and American Jews* (Westport, Conn.: Negro Universities Press, 1970), xxii, 218.

5. Vine DeLoria Jr., *Custer Died for Your Sins* (New York: Macmillan, 1969); Robert Blauner, *Racial Oppression in America* (New York: Harper and Row, 1972); Ronald Takaki, *From Different Shores: Perspectives on Race and Ethnicity in America* (New York: Oxford University Press, 1987); Michael Omi and Howard Winant, *Racial Formation in the United States from the 1960s to the 1990s,* 2d ed. (London: Routledge, 1994); Stephen Steinberg, *Turning Back: The Retreat from Racial Justice in American Thought and Politics* (Boston: Beacon Press, 1995).

6. Oscar Lewis, *La Vida: A Puerto Rican Family in the Culture of Poverty—San Juan and New York* (New York: Random House, 1965); Nathan Glazer and Daniel Patrick Moynihan, *Beyond the Melting Pot: The Negroes, Puerto Ricans, Jews, Italians, and Irish of New York City,* 2d ed. (Cambridge: Mass.: M.I.T. Press, 1963); Daniel Patrick Moynihan, "The Negro Family: The Case for National Action," in *The Moynihan Report and the Politics of Controversy,* ed. Lee Rainwater and William L. Yancey (Cambridge, Mass.: M.I.T. Press, 1967).

7. Stephen Steinberg, *The Ethnic Myth: Race, Ethnicity, and Class in America,* 2d ed. (Boston: Beacon Press, 1989), 103. Chapter 3 is devoted to demolishing the liberal view of Jewish mobility.

8. Stephen Steinberg, *The Academic Melting Pot: Catholics and Jews in American Higher Education* (New York: McGraw-Hill, 1974), 74.

9. Steinberg, *Turning Back,* 13.

Recent examples of the kind of work to which Steinberg stands in opposition include Lawrence Harrison, *Who Prospers: How Cultural Values Shape Economic and Political Success* (New York: Basic Books, 1992); Francis Fukayama, *Trust: The Social Virtues and the Creation of Prosperity* (New York: Free Press, 1995); Thomas Sowell, *Race and Culture: A World View* (New York: Basic Books, 1994).

10. Seymour Martin Lipset and Earl Raab, *Jews and the New American Scene* (Cambridge, Mass.: Harvard University Press, 1995), 1–8, 13; Milton Konvitz, *Judaism and the American Idea* (Ithaca, N.Y.: Cornell University Press, 1978); Ernest van den Haag, *The Jewish Mystique* (New York: Stein and Day, 1969).

11. Robert E. Park, *Race and Culture* (Glencoe, Ill.: Free Press, 1950), 354–355.

12. David Brion Davis, "The Other Zion: American Jews and the Meritocratic Experiment," *New Republic,* 12 April 1993, 29–36.

13. Milton Gordon, *Assimilation in American Life* (New York: Oxford University Press, 1964), 185. On the faster rise of Jews into the middle class, see Seymour Martin Lipset, "A Unique People in an Exceptional Country," in *American Pluralism and the Jewish Community* (New Brunswick, N.J.: Transaction Books, 1990), 3.

14. Stephen J. Whitfield, "The Bourgeois Humanism of American Jews," *Judaism* (1980): 155.

15. Karen Brodkin Sacks, "How Did Jews Become White Folks?" in *Race,* ed. Steven Gregory and Roger Sanjeck (New Brunswick, N.J.: Rutgers University Press, 1994), 84.

16. Ibid., 97.

17. For a good comparative analysis of immigrant mobility from an international perspective, see Thomas Sowell, *Migrations and Cultures: A Word View* (New York: Basic Books, 1996).

18. See Gerald Jaynes and Robin M. Williams Jr., eds., *A Common Destiny: Blacks and American Society* (Washington, D.C.: National Academy Press, 1989), 6–9; Abigail Thernstrom and Stephan Thernstrom, "The Prescience of Myrdal," *Public Interest,* (Fall 1997): 51.

19. Philip Kasinitz, *Caribbean New York: Black Immigrants and the Politics of Race* (Ithaca, N.Y.: Cornell University Press, 1992).

20. Lawrence Fuchs, "Introduction," *American Jewish Historical Quarterly* 66, no. 2 (December 1976): 187.

21. Beverly Allinsmith and Wesley Allinsmith, "Religious Affiliation and Political Economic Attitudes," *Public Opinion Quarterly* 12 (1948): 577–589.

22. Lipset and Raab, 148. This is a paraphrase of a statement widely attributed to the Jewish sociologist Milton Himmelfarb.

23. See Earl Raab, "Are American Jews Still Liberal," *Commentary* 101, no. 2

(February 1996): 43–45; Charles S. Liebman and Steven M. Cohen, "Jewish Liberalism Revisited," *Commentary* 102, no. 5 (November 1996): 51–53.

24. Steven Cohen, *1988 National Survey of American Jews* (New York: American Jewish Committee, 1988), 3; William B. Helmreich, "American Jews and the 1988 Presidential Elections," *Congress Monthly* 56 (January 1989); Peter Steinfels, "American Jews Stand Firmly on the Left," *New York Times*, 8 January 1988, E7; "Portrait of the Electorate," *New York Times*, 5 November 1992, table on 89.

25. Nathan Glazer, "The Anomalous Liberalism of American Jews," in *The Americanization of the Jews*, ed. Robert M. Seltzer and Norman J. Cohen (New York: New York University Press, 1995), 133.

26. Lawrence H. Fuchs, *The Political Behavior of American Jews* (Glencoe, Ill.: Free Press, 1956).

27. Werner Cohn, "The Sources of American Jewish Liberalism," in *The Jews: Social Patterns of an American Group*, ed. Marshall Sklare (Glencoe, Ill.: Free Press, 1958).

28. Charles S. Liebman, *The Ambivalent American Jew: Politics, Religion, and Family in American Jewish Life* (Philadelphia: Jewish Publication Society of America, 1973), 149–150.

29. Lipset and Raab, 162.

30. Histories of the Leo Frank case include Leonard Dinnerstein, *The Leo Frank Case* (New York: Columbia University Press, 1968); Albert S. Lindemann, *The Jew Accused: Three Anti-Semitic Affairs (Dreyfus, Beilis, Frank), 1894–1915* (New York: Cambridge University Press, 1991).

31. David Roediger, *Towards the Abolition of Whiteness: Essays on Race, Politics, and Working Class History* (London: Verso, 1994), 186–194.

32. Thaddeus Radzialowski, "The Competition for Jobs and Racial Stereotypes: Poles and Blacks in Chicago," *Polish-American Studies* 33 (Autumn 1976): 16–17; Paola Giordano, "Italian Immigration to the State of Louisiana," *Italian Americana* (Fall/Winter 1977): 172; Donna Misner Collins, *Ethnic Identification: The Greek Americans of Houston, Texas* (New York: 1991), 210–211; James W. Loewen, *The Mississippi Chinese: Between Black and White* (Cambridge, Mass.: Harvard University Press, 1971); "Irish Mornings and African Days on the Old Minstrel Stage: An Interview With Leni Sloan," *Callahan's Irish Quarterly* 2 (Spring 1982): 49–53.

33. Roediger, 189. See also Stanley Lieberson, *A Piece of the Pie: Blacks and White Immigrants Since 1880* (Berkeley: University of California Press, 1980).

34. Jeffrey Melnick, "Relatives and Ancestors: The Uncanny Relationship Among African Americans and Jews," (Ph.D. diss., Harvard University, 1994), 209.

35. Hasia Diner, *In the Almost Promised Land: Jews and Blacks 1915–1935* (Westport, Conn.: Greenwood Press, 1977), 164–191.

36. Harold Cruse, *The Crisis of the Negro Intellectual* (New York: Morrow, 1967), 364.

37. Ibid.

38. Andrew Hacker, "Jewish Racism, Black Anti-Semitism," in *Blacks and Jews: Alliances and Arguments,* ed. Paul Berman (New York: Delacorte Press, 1994), 162–163.

39. D. L. Lewis, "Parallels and Divergences: Assimilationist Strategies of Afro-American and Jewish Elites From 1910 to the Early 1930s," *Journal of American History* 71 (December 1984), 31.

40. Ibid., 85.

41. Diner, 89–117, 128–133.

On Jewish labor unions, see Roger Waldinger, *Still the Promised City? African-Americans and New Immigrants in Postindustrial New York* (Cambridge, Mass.: Harvard University Press, 1996), 144, 146.

42. David Brion Davis, "Jews in the Slave Trade," *Culturefront* 1, no. 2 (Fall 1992): 42–45; David Brion Davis, *Slavery and Human Progress* (New York: Oxford University Press, 1984), 83–101; Seymour Drescher, "The Role of Jews in the Transatlantic Slave Trade," *Immigrants and Minorities* 12, no. 2 (July 1993): 117; Bertram Korn, "Slave Trade," *Encyclopedia Judaica* 14: 1661–1663; Bertram Korn, "Jews and Negro Slavery in the Old South, 1789–1865," in *Jews in the South,* ed. Leonard Dinnerstein and Mary Dale Palsson (Baton Rouge: Louisiana State University Press, 1973); John Bracey and August Meier, "Towards a Research Agenda on Blacks and Jews in United States History," *Journal of American Ethnic History* 12, no. 3 (Spring 1993). Murray Friedman makes this point as well, 10.

43. Irving Howe, with assistance from Kenneth Libo, *World of Our Fathers* (New York: Touchstone/Simon and Schuster, 1976), 563; Michael Paul Rogin, *Blackface, White Noise: Jewish Immigrants in the Hollywood Melting Pot* (Berkeley: University of California Press, 1996).

44. James Weldon Johnson, *The Second Book of Negro Spirituals* (New York: Viking, 1969), 22; James Weldon Johnson, *Along This Way: The Autobiography of James Weldon Johnson* (New York: Penguin, 1990), 136; Albert Murray, *Stomping the Blues* (New York: Vintage, 1983), 205; Melnick, 686. See also Jeffrey Melnick, *A Right to Sing the Blues: African Americans, Jews, and Cultural Power* (Cambridge, Mass.: Harvard University Press, 1997).

45. Vernon J. Williams, *Rethinking Race: Frans Boas and His Contemporaries* (Lexington: University Press of Kentucky, 1996).

46. Taylor Branch, "Blacks and Jews: The Uncivil War," in *Bridges and Boundaries: African-Americans and American Jews,* ed. Jack Salzman, Adina Black, and Gretchen Sullivan Sorin (New York: George Braziller in association with the Jewish Museum, 1992).

A delegation of Black Americans investigating the matter found that there was no official racism involved in the case of Ben-Ami and his followers. See *Unpublished Report of the First Findings of the Delegation to Israel of BASIC and the A. Philip Randolph Educational Fund Regarding Human Rights as They Pertain to the Original Hebrew Israelite Nation* (17–28 January 1981), 3.

47. Kenneth Stampp, *The Peculiar Institution: Slavery in the Ante-Bellum South* (New York: Vintage Books, 1956), 30; Forrest G. Wood, *The Emergence of Faith: Christianity and Race in America from the Colonial Era to the Twentieth Century* (New York: Knopf, 1990).

48. Lawrence Levine, *Black Culture and Black Consciousness* (New York: Oxford University Press, 1978); Eugene Genovese, *Roll, Jordan, Roll* (New York: Pantheon Books, 1974); Sidney W. Mintz and Richard Price, *The Birth of African American Culture: An Anthropological Perspective* (Boston: Beacon Press, 1992).

49. For an impressive effort to show that a transnational Black identity has indeed taken root, see Paul Gilroy, *Black Atlantic: Modernity and Double Consciousness* (Cambridge, Mass.: Harvard University Press, 1993).

50. Albert Murray, *The Omni-Americans: New Perspectives on Black Experience and American Culture* (New York: Outerbridge and Dinstfrey, 1970), 22.

51. See Abraham J. Karp, "Ideology and Identity in Jewish Group Survival in America," *American Jewish Historical Quarterly* 65, no. 4 (June 1976): 311.

52. Norman Podhoretz uses this term in his autobiographical *Making It* (New York: Random House, 1967), 3.

53. Mark Schechner, "Jewish Writers," in *Harvard Guide to Contemporary American Writing,* ed. Daniel Hoffman (Cambridge, Mass.: Harvard University Press, Belknap Press, 1979), 193.

54. John Bodnar, *The Transplanted: A History of Immigrants in Urban America* (Bloomington: Indiana University Press, 1985), 1–54, 201.

55. Henry Feingold, "Introduction," *Zion in America: The Jewish Experience from Colonial Times to the Present* (New York: Hippocrene, 1974).

56. Liebman, p. 56; Jerold Auerbach, "Liberalism, Judaism, and American Jews: A Response," in *The Americanization of the Jews,* 144.

57. Diner, 238.

58. Auerbach, 147.

59. Jaynes and Williams, 13.

60. Ellis Cose, *The Rage of a Privileged Class* (New York: HarperCollins, 1993).

61. Ralph Ellison is most often identified as the standard bearer of the idea that Blacks have developed a culture beyond the reach of white racism. See his novel *Invisible Man* (New York: Random House, 1952) and his collection of essays, *Shadow and Act* (New York: Random House, 1964).

Contemporary efforts to combat Black essentialism include Henry Louis Gates Jr., *"Race," Writing, and Difference* (Chicago: University of Chicago Press, 1986); Manning Marable, *Beyond Black and White: Transforming African-American Politics* (London: Verso, 1995); Isaac Julien, "Black Is, Black Ain't: Notes on De-Essentializing Black Identities," in *Black Popular Culture,* ed. Gina Dent (Seattle: Bay Press, 1992), 255–263.

62. See Jack Wertheimer, *American Jews: A People Divided: Judaism in Contemporary America* (New York: Basic Books, 1993).

63. Henry Feingold, *A Time for Searching: Entering the Mainstream, 1920–1945* (Baltimore: Johns Hopkins University Press, 1992), 90–124.

64. For NJPS data summary, see Joshua O. Haberman, "The New Exodus Out of Judaism," *Moment* 17, no. 4 (August 1992): 34–35; Barry Kosmin, et al., *Highlights of the CJF National Jewish Population Survey* (New York: Council of Jewish Federations, 1991).

65. Wertheimer, xvii. On white ethnicity, see Richard D. Alba, *Ethnic Identity: The Transformation of White America* (New Haven: Yale University Press, 1990).

66. Quoted by Jonathan Sarna, "The Secret of Jewish Continuity," *Commentary* 98, no. 4 (October 1994): 55–58.

67. Wertheimer, xvii.

68. The recent establishment of the National Holocaust Museum on federal property in Washington, D.C., is a notable exception. See Edward T. Linenthal, *Preserving Memory: The Struggle to Create America's Holocaust Museum* (New York: Viking, 1995).

69. See, most recently, Joshua Muravchik, "Facing Up To Anti-Semitism," *Commentary* 100, no. 6 (December 1995): 26–30.

NOTES TO CHAPTER I

1. Gunnar Myrdal, *An American Dilemma* 1 (New York: Harper and Brothers, 1944), xli–lv.

2. Richard Polenberg, *One Nation Divisible: Class, Race, and Ethnicity in the United States since 1938* (New York: Viking, 1980), 53; Philip Gleason, "Americans All: World War Two and the Shaping of American Identity," *Review of Politics* 43, no. 4 (October 1981): 500–502.

3. From the inside cover of the magazine *Common Ground*. Cited by Gleason, 502.

4. Lucy Dawidowicz, *One Equal Terms: Jews in America 1881–1981* (New York: Holt, Rinehart and Winston, 1982), 129.

5. Charles Stember, ed., *Jews in the Mind of America* (New York: Basic Books, 1966), 31–236.

6. Dawidowicz, 131–132.

7. See Stember, especially "Recent History of Public Attitudes," 127–134; Edward Shapiro, *A Time for Healing: American Jewry since World War II* (Baltimore: Johns Hopkins University Press, 1992), 28–59.

8. Shapiro, 41.

9. See Thomas Pettigrew, "Parallel and Distinctive Changes in Anti-Semitic and Anti-Negro Attitudes," in Stember, p. 389.

10. Patricia Erens, *The Jew in American Cinema* (Bloomington: Indiana University Press, 1984), 170–173; Lester D. Friedman, *Hollywood's Images of the Jew* (New York: Frederick Ungar, 1982), 125; Shapiro, 18–19.

11. Gleason, 505.

12. Laura Hobson, *Gentleman's Agreement* (New York: Simon and Schuster, 1947).

13. "An Act of Affirmation," *Commentary* 1, no. 1 (November 1945).

14. Elliot E. Cohen, "Mr. Zanuck's 'Gentlemen's Agreement'," *Commentary* 5, no.1 (January 1948): 51.

15. Ibid.

16. Ibid., 56.

17. Diana Trilling, "America without Distinction," review of Laura Hobson's *Gentlemen's Agreement, Commentary* 3, no. 3 (March 1947): 290.

18. Leslie Fiedler, "The Breakthrough: The American Jewish Novelist and the Fictional Image of the Jew," *Midstream* 4, no. 1 (Winter 1958): 27.

19. See, for example, on the Irish, Andrew Greeley, *That Most Distressful Nation* (New York: Quadrangle, 1972), chap. 7. On the Italians, see Richard Gambino, *Blood of My Blood* (New York: Anchor, 1974), 315–316.

20. Will Herberg, *Protestant, Catholic, Jew: An Essay in American Religious Sociology* (Garden City, N.Y.: Doubleday, 1955).

21. Herberg, 20, 27, 30–31; Arthur A. Cohen, *The Natural and Supernatural Jew: A Historical and Theological Introduction* (New York: McGraw-Hill, 1964), 6–7; Robert Gordis, *The Root and the Branch: Judaism and the Free Society* (Chicago: University of Chicago Press, 1962), 66, 76, 158–171; William Toll, "Pluralism and Moral Force in the Black-Jewish Dialogue," *American Jewish History* 77, no. 1 (Spring 1987): 103–104.

22. Nathan Glazer, *American Judaism,* 2d ed. (Chicago: University of Chicago Press, 1957), 135–136.

23. Alexander Pekelis, "Full Equality in a Free Society," in *Law and Social Action: Selected Essays of Alexander H. Pekelis,* ed. Milton Konvitz (Ithaca, N.Y.: Cornell University Press, 1950), 223, 242.

24. Lenora Berson, *The Negroes and the Jews* (New York: Random House, 1971), 96.

25. Jack Greenberg, *Crusaders in the Courts: How a Dedicated Band of Lawyers Fought for the Civil Rights Revolution* (New York: Basic Books, 1994), 52–53.

26. Eli Ginzburg, *Agenda for American Jews* (New York: King's Crown Press, 1950), 1–90; Arthur Hertzberg, *The Jews in America: Four Centuries of an Uneasy Encounter* (New York: Simon and Schuster, 1989), 331.

27. Murray Friedman, "Civil Rights," in *Jewish-American History and Culture: An Encyclopedia,* ed. Jack Fischel and Sanford Pinsker (New York: Garland, 1992), 89.

28. Naomi Cohen, *Not Free to Desist: The American Jewish Committee 1906–1966* (Philadelphia: Jewish Publication Society, 1972), 386.

29. Quoted in Esther Levine, "Southern Jews Views on Segregation," *Jewish Life* 10, no. 10 (August 1956): 35.

30. Berson, 97.

31. Neil A. Wynn, "The Impact of the Second World War on the American Negro," *Journal of Contemporary History* 6, no. 2 (1971): 45–46.

32. John Bracey, August Meier, and Elliott Rudwick, "Introduction," *Black Nationalism in America* (New York: Bobbs-Merrill, Inc., 1970), xlv; John Henrik Clarke, "Introduction," in Amy Jacques Garvey, *Garvey and Garveyism* (New York: Octagon, 1978).

33. Toll, 96.

34. Friedman, 90.

35. Stephen Whitfield, "Jews and Other Southerners," in *Voices of Jacob, Hands of Esau: Jews in American Life and Thought,* ed. Stephen Whitfield (Hamden, Conn.: Archon, 1984), 224.

36. Howard Sachar, *A History of the Jews in America* (New York: Vintage, 1992), 23; Leonard Dinnerstein, *Anti-Semitism in America* (New York: Oxford University Press, 1994), 5.

37. Richard Hofstadter, *The Age of Reform: From Bryan to F.D.R.* (New York: Vintage, 1955), 77–81; Daniel Bell, "The Grass Roots of American Jew Hatred," *Jewish Frontier* 6 (October 1948): 374–378; Oscar Handlin, "American Views of the Jew at the Opening of the Twentieth Century," *Publications of the American Jewish Historical Society,* no. 40 (June 1951), 323–344.

38. Hofstadter, 81.

39. Leonard Dinnerstein, "A Neglected Aspect of Southern Jewish History," in *Uneasy at Home: Anti-Semitism and the American Experience* (New York: Columbia University Press, 1987), 83–99.

40. Bertram Wallace Korn, "Jews and Negro Slavery in the Old South, 1789–1865," *Publications of the American Jewish Historical Society* 50 (March 1961). Reprinted in *Jews in the South,* ed. Leonard Dinnerstein and Mary Dale Palsson (Baton Rouge: Louisiana State University Press, 1973), 123.

41. Ibid., 132.

42. Albert Vorspan, "The Dilemma of the Southern Jew," *Reconstructionist* 24, no. 18 (January 9, 1959): 6.

43. A. R. Suritz, "A Southerner Looks at Jews in the South," *National Jewish Monthly* 72, no. 9 (June 1958): 4.

44. John Dollard, *Caste and Class in a Southern Town* (New York: Doubleday, 1937), 128.

45. Ibid., 129.

46. Kenneth Clark, "A Positive Transition," *Anti-Defamation League Bulletin* (December 12, 1957), 5.

47. Ibid.

48. Will Maslow, "My Brother's Keeper . . . ," *World Jewry* 1, no. 2 (April 1958): 5; Cohen, 392–393.

49. Benjamin Ringer, "Jews and the Desegregation Crisis," Stember, 202.

50. Alfred Hero, "Southern Jews, Race Relations, and Foreign Policy," *Jewish*

Social Studies 27, no. 4 (October 1965). Reprinted in Dinnerstein and Palsson, 222.

51. Joshua A. Fishman, "Southern City," *Midstream* 7 (Summer 1961). Reprinted in Dinnerstein and Palsson, 323.

52. Hero, 216–217.

53. Theodore Lowi, "Southern Jews: The Two Communities," *Jewish Social Studies* 6 (June 1964): 112.

54. Cited by Albert Vorspan, "The South, Segregation, and the Jew," *Jewish Frontier* 23, no. 10 (November 1956): 19.

55. Lawrence H. Fuchs, *The Political Behavior of American Jews* (Glencoe, Ill.: Free Press, 1956), 108.

56. Quoted in Allen Krause, "Rabbis and Negro Rights in the South: 1954–1967," *American Jewish Archives* 21 (April 1969). Reprinted in Dinnerstein and Palsson, 362.

57. T. W. Adorno et al., *The Authoritarian Personality* (New York: Harper and Brothers, 1950); Charles Y. Glock and Rodney Stark, *Christian Beliefs and Anti-Semitism* (New York: Harper and Row, 1966); Gary T. Marx, *Protest and Prejudice: A Study of Belief in the Black Community* (New York: Harper and Row, 1967); Harold F. Quinley and Charles Y. Glock, *Anti-Semitism in America* (New York: Free Press, 1979).

58. See Leonard Dinnerstein, "American Jewish Organizational Efforts to Combat Antisemitism in the United States since 1945," in *Antisemitism in the Contemporary World,* ed. Michael Curtis (Boulder: Westview Press, 1986), 305; Friedman, "Civil Rights," 89.

59. Shapiro, 32–34; Eli Evans, *The Provincials: A Personal History of Jews in the South* (New York: Atheneum, 1973), 211–226; Lucy Dawidowicz, "Can Anti-Semitism Be Measured," *Commentary* 50, no. 1 (July 1970).

60. Shad Polier, "Law and Social Action," *Congress Weekly* 17, no. 31 (November 27, 1950): 2.

61. David Danzig, "Challenging Issues in a Changing South," (address to Southwest Regional Conference, Houston, Texas, March 22, 1959), Southern States Folder, American Jewish Committee, Blaustein Library, 12.

62. John Higham, "Anti-Semitism in the Gilded Age: A Reinterpretation," *Mississippi Valley Historical Review* 43 (March 1957): 572.

63. Louis Galambo, *The Public Image of Big Business in America: 1880–1940* (Baltimore: Johns Hopkins University Press, 1975), 63–64; John Higham, "Social Discrimination against Jews in America 1830–1930," *American Jewish Historical Quarterly* 47 (September 1957): 30–31; Whitfield, 19.

64. James Wax, "The Attitude of the Jews in the South Toward Integration," *Central Conference of American Rabbis Journal,* no. 26 (June 1959).

65. Whitfield, 220.

66. Evans, appendices A and B.

67. Harry Golden, "Jew and Gentile in the New South," *Commentary* 20, no. 5 (November 1955): 403, 405.

68. Korn, 132.

69. I. J. Benjamin, *Three Years in America* (Philadelphia: 1956), 76, in Korn, 133.

70. Winthrop Jordan, *White over Black: American Attitudes toward the Negro: 1550–1812* (Chapel Hill: University of North Carolina Press, 1968), 34; Winthrop Jordan, *The White Man's Burden* (New York: Oxford University Press, 1974), 106, 197.

71. Norman Cohn, "The Myth of the Jewish World Conspiracy," *Commentary* 41, no. 5 (June 1966): 40.

72. Quoted in Evans, 212.

73. Ibid., 224.

74. Stember, 224–225.

75. Reported by Pettigrew, 389.

76. Isaac Toubin, "Recklessness or Responsibility," *Southern Israelite,* 27 February 1959, 14.

77. Ibid., 14.

78. Charles Glicksberg, "The Negro and the Jew," *Chicago Jewish Forum* 5, no. 4 (Summer 1947): 229.

79. Louis Ruchames, "Parallels of Jewish and Negro History," *Negro History Bulletin* (December 1955): 63.

80. Sanford Goldner, *The Jewish People and the Fight for Negro Rights* (Los Angeles: Committee for Negro Jewish Relations, 1953), 38.

81. Carl Alpert, "A Jewish Problem in the South," *Reconstructionist* 12, no. 3 (March 22, 1946): 11.

82. Levine, 35.

83. Ibid., 23.

84. David Halberstam, "The White Citizen's Councils," *Commentary* 22, no. 4 (October 1956): 293–294, 301.

85. Ibid.

86. Arnold Foster, "The South: New Field for an Old Game," *Anti-Defamation League Bulletin* 15, no. 8 (October 1958): 1–2.

87. Levine, 35.

88. Toubin, 14.

89. Vorspan, "The Dilemma of the Southern Jew," 7, 8.

90. Ibid., 9.

91. American Jewish Committee, "The Nationwide Poll of March, 1959" (New York: American Jewish Committee, 1959), 47–50; Oscar Cohen, "Public Opinion and Anti-Jewish Prejudice in the South" (CMS of the Anti-Defamation League, New York, 1959), in Hero, 240–243.

92. William Malev, "The Jew of the South in the Conflict on Segregation," *Conservative Judaism* 13, no. 1 (Fall 1958): 44; Nathan Perlmutter, "Bombing in Miami," *Commentary* 25, no. 6 (June 1958).

93. "Anti-Semitism in the South," *Richmond News Leader*, 7 July 1958, Editorial Page.

94. Murray Friedman, "One Episode in Southern Jewry's Response to Desegregation: An Historical Memoir," *American Jewish Archives* 33, no. 1 (April 1981): 178; Murray Friedman, "Virginia Jewry in the School Crisis: Anti-Semitism and Desegregation," *Commentary* 27, no. 1 (January 1959). Reprinted in Dinnerstein and Palsson, 349–350.

95. Friedman, "One Episode," 181.

96. Levine, 21.

97. Ibid.

98. Fishman, 323.

99. Ibid., 35.

100. Cohen, 387.

101. Danzig, 13.

102. Cohen, 395–396.

103. Golden, 404–405; Lowi, 106–107, 112.

104. Lowi, 115.

105. Morton J. Gaba, "Segregation and a Southern Jewish Community," *Jewish Frontier* 21, no. 10 (October 1954): 15.

106. Gerald Wolpe, "The Southern Jew and 'The Problem'," *Reconstructionist* 22, no. 16 (December 14, 1956): 29.

107. Perry E. Nussbaum, "Pulpit in Mississippi, Anyone?: The Southern Rabbi Faces the Problem of Desegregation," *Central Conference of American Rabbis Journal*, no. 14 (June 1956): 2–3.

108. Perry E. Nussbaum, "And Then There Was One—in the Capital City of Mississippi," *Central Conference of American Rabbis Journal* 11, no. 3 (October 1963): 16–17, 19.

109. William Malev, "The Jew of the South in the Conflict on Segregation," *Conservative Judaism* 13, no. 1 (Fall 1958): 40, 50.

110. Krause, 379.

111. Jacob M. Rothschild, "The Rabbi Will Serve No Good Purpose in Leading Crusades," *Central Conference of American Rabbis Journal* 14 (June 1956): 6.

112. Marvin Braiterman, "Mississippi Marrano," *Midstream* (September 1964): 32.

113. Alpert, "A Jewish Problem," 11.

114. Joel C. Dobin, "Portrait of a Southern Community," *Congress Weekly* 25, no. 9 (April 28, 1958): 8.

115. Albert Vorspan, "The Negro Victory and the Jewish Failure," *American Judaism* 13, no. 1 (Fall 1963): 50.

116. Ibid., 52.

117. Andre Ungar, "To Birmingham, and Back," *Conservative Judaism* 18, no. 1 (Fall 1963): 11.

118. Harry Golden, "The Vertical Negro Plan," *Only in America* (Cleveland: World, 1958), 121–122.

119. Ibid., 123.

120. Ibid.

121. Evans, 317.

122. Golden, "Unease in Dixie: Caught in the Middle," *Midstream* 11, no. 4 (Autumn 1956): 38.

123. Ibid., 40.

124. Toll, 96.

NOTES TO CHAPTER 2

1. Samuel Lubell, *White and Black: Test of a Nation* (New York: Harper and Row, 1964), 121.

2. Charles Silberman, *Crisis in Black and White* (New York: Random House, 1964), 7–8.

3. Milton Gordon, *Assimilation in American Life: The Role of Race, Religion, and National Origins* (New York: Oxford University Press, 1964), 67.

4. Gordon, 67; Edward Shapiro, *A Time for Healing: American Jewry since World War II* (Baltimore: Johns Hopkins University Press, 1992), 200.

5. Oscar Handlin, *Fire-Bell in the Night: The Crisis in Civil Rights* (Boston: Little, Brown, 1964), 55.

6. Ibid.

7. Arnold R. Hirsch, "Massive Resistance in the Urban North: Trumbull Park, Chicago, 1953–1966"; Thomas J. Sugrue, "Crabgrass-Roots Politics: Race, Rights, and the Reaction against Liberalism in the Urban North, 1940–1964"; Gary Gerstle, "Race and the Myth of Liberal Consensus," *Journal of American History* 82, no. 2 (September 1995): 522–579.

8. Kenneth Jackson, *Crabgrass Frontier: The Suburbanization of the United States* (New York: Oxford University Press, 1985).

9. Lubell, 121; Oscar Handlin, *The Newcomers: Negroes and Puerto Ricans in a Changing Metropolis* (Cambridge, Mass.: Harvard University Press, 1959), 61–64.

10. Handlin, *Firebell in the Night*, 56.

11. Harold Isaacs, "Integration and the Negro Mood," *Commentary* 6, no. 34 (December 1962): 489.

12. "The Negro Revolution," *Dissent* 10, no. 3 (Summer 1963): 205.

13. Charles B. Turner Jr., "The Black Man's Burden: The White Liberal," *Dissent* 10, no. 3 (Summer 1963): 7.

14. August Meier, "New Currents in the Civil Rights Movement," *New Politics* 2, no.3 (Summer 1963): 7.

15. Nathan Glazer, "Negroes and Jews: The New Challenge to Pluralism," *Commentary* (December 1964): 29–35.

16. Lucy Dawidowicz and Leon J. Goldstein, "Why Jews Vote for Liberal

Candidates," *Jewish Digest* 9, no. 11 (August 1964): 41; Murray Friedman, *What Went Wrong: The Creation and Collapse of the Black-Jewish Alliance* (New York: Free Press, 1995), 179–181; Milton Himmelfarb, "How We Are," *Commentary* 39, no. 1 (January 1965): 69.

17. Glazer, "Negroes and Jews," 32–33.

18. Howard Palley, "The Civil Rights Movement: Liberalism and Populism," *Jewish Frontier* 32, no. 4 (May 1965): 8.

19. Quoted in Deborah Dash Moore, "At Home in America," in *The American Jewish Experience,* ed. Jonathan Sarna (New York: Holmes and Meier, 1986), 265.

20. Edward Shapiro, *A Time for Healing: American Jewry Since World War II* (Baltimore: Johns Hopkins University Press, 1992), 200.

21. Kaplan is quoted in Jack Wertheimer, *A People Divided: Judaism in Contemporary America* (New York: Basic Books, 1994), 14.

22. Leonard Fein, *Where Are We?: The Inner Life of America's Jews* (New York: Harper and Row, 1988), 168.

23. Shapiro, 200.

24. Jonathan Woocher, *Sacred Survival: The Civil Religion of American Jews* (Bloomington, Ind.: Indiana University Press, 1986), vii.

25. Ibid.

26. Ibid., 20.

27. Howard Sachar, *A History of the Jews in America* (New York: Vintage, 1992), 409–410.

28. Moore, 260. This is a synopsis of her full-length volume *At Home In America: Second-Generation New York Jews* (New York: Columbia University Press, 1981).

29. Sachar, 408.

30. Nathan Glazer, *American Judaism* (Chicago: University of Chicago Press, 1957), 132.

31. Nathan Glazer and Daniel Patrick Moynihan, *Beyond the Melting Pot: The Negroes, Puerto Ricans, Jews, Italians, and Irish of New York City,* 2d ed. (Cambridge: M.I.T. Press, 1970), 162.

32. Alan Wood, "I Sell My House," *Commentary* 26, no. 5 (November 1958): 386.

33. C. Eric Lincoln, *Negro and Jew: Encounter in America,* ed. Shlomo Katz (New York: Macmillan, 1967), 90–91; Jack Nusan Porter, "John Henry and Mr. Goldberg: The Relationship between Blacks and Jews," *Journal of Ethnic Studies* 7, no. 3 (Fall 1979): 73–86.

34. James Baldwin, "The Harlem Ghetto," *Notes of a Native Son* (Boston: Beacon Press, 1955), 67.

35. Louis E. Lomax, *The Negro Revolt* (New York: Harper and Row, 1962), 184.

36. Ibid., 185–186.

37. Herbert Hill, "The ILGWU Today—The Decay of a Labor Union," *New*

Politics 1, no. 4 (Spring 1962): 6; Gus Tyler's response "The Truth About the ILGWU," *New Politics* 2, no. 1 (Fall 1962): 16–17; Tom Brooks, "Negro Militants, Jewish Liberals, and the Unions," *Commentary* 32, no. 3 (September 1961); Herbert Hill, "Labor Unions and the Negro," *Commentary* 28, no. 6 (December 1959); Harry Fleischman, "Is Labor Color Blind?" *Progressive* 23, no. 11 (November 1959).

38. See Roger Waldinger, *Still the Promised City? African-Americans and New Immigrants in Postindustrial New York* (Cambridge, Mass.: Harvard University Press, 1996), 107–108.

39. Ibid., 44, 46.

40. Lucy Dawidowicz, "The Jewishness of the Jewish Labor Movement in the United States," in Sarna, 158–166; Glazer and Moynihan, pp. 144–145.

41. C. Bezalel Sherman, "In the American Jewish Community—Negro-Jewish Relations," *Jewish Frontier* (July 1964): 17.

42. Abraham Duker, "On Negro-Jewish Relations—A Contribution to a Discussion," *Jewish Social Studies* 27, no. 1 (January 1965): 22.

43. Joachim Prinz, "Address at the March on Washington, Lincoln Memorial," *Congress Bi-Weekly* 30, no. 13 (October 1963); Joachim Prinz, "Negro March for Freedom Has Lessons for Jews," *Congress Bi-Weekly* 6, no. 5: 7.

44. Friedman, 191.

45. Abraham Joshua Heschel, "Religion and Race," *The Insecurity of Freedom* (New York: Farrar, Straus, and Giroux, 1966), 92,93.

46. Ibid., 97.

47. Silberman, *Crisis in Black and White,* 123, 42.

48. Charles Silberman, "A Jewish View of the Racial Crisis," *Conservative Judaism* 19, no. 4 (Summer 1965): 1–2.

49. Ibid., 2.

50. Ibid., 9.

51. Ibid., 4.

52. Ibid., 5.

53. Arnold Jacob Wolf, "The Negro Revolution and Jewish Theology," *Conservative Judaism* 13, no. 4 (Fall 1964): 479.

54. Ibid., 479.

55. Ibid., 483.

56. Henry Cohen, "How Big Is the 'Jewish Backlash'?" *National Jewish Monthly* 79 (January 1965): 6.

57. B. Z. Sobel and May L. Sobel, "Negroes and Jews: American Minority Groups In Conflict," *Judaism* 15 (Winter 1966). Reprinted in *The Ghetto and Beyond: Essays On Jewish Life in America,* ed. Peter I. Rose (New York: Random House, 1969), 403.

58. Ibid., 404.

59. Ibid., 406.

60. Silberman, "A Jewish View of the Racial Crisis," 7.

61. Albert Chernin, "Implications for Jewish Community Relations," *Journal of Jewish Communal Service* 41, no. 4 (Summer 1965): 347.

62. Quoted in Lenora Berson, *The Negroes and the Jews* (New York: Random House, 1971), 124.

63. Marvin Schick, "The Orthodox Jew and The Negro Revolution," *Jewish Observer* (December 1964): 17.

64. "Jewish Young Freedom Fighters and the Role of the Jewish Community: An Evaluation," *Jewish Currents* 19 (July/August 1965): 8.

65. Ibid., 10.

66. Ibid., 13.

67. Friedman, 188, 189.

68. Newfield quoted in Berson, 126. See Jack Newfield, *Prophetic Minority* (New York: New American Library, 1966).

69. C. Eric Lincoln, *The Black Muslim in America* (Grand Rapids, Mich.: William B. Eerdmans, 1994), 71–75; Essien Udosen Essien-Udom, *Black Nationalism: A Search for an Identity in America* (Chicago: University of Chicago, 1962), 126–142.

70. Jeremiah X quoted in Horace Mann Bond, "Negro Attitudes toward Jews," *Jewish Social Studies* 27, no. 1 (January 1965): 8.

71. Lawrence B. Goodheart, "The Ambivalent Anti-Semitism of Malcolm X," *Patterns of Prejudice* 28, no. 1 (January 1994): 10.

72. Milton Himmelfarb, "Blacks, Jews, and Muzhiks," *Commentary* 42, no. 4 (October 1966); reprinted in Rose, 417.

73. Peter Goldman, *The Death and Life of Malcolm X* (New York: Harper and Row, 1974), 16. See also Alan Shelton, "Malcolm X and the Jews," *Midstream* 42, no. 4 (May 1996): 20–23.

74. Leonard Dinnerstein, *Anti-Semitism in America* (New York: Oxford University Press, 1994), 210.

75. "Racism Is Racism," *Congress Bi-Weekly* 33, no. 4 (February 21, 1966).

76. Gary T. Marx, *Protest and Prejudice: A Study of Belief in the Black Community* (New York: Harper and Row, 1967), 167. Surveys for this study were conducted during and before 1964.

77. Paul Jacobs, "Negro-Jewish Relations in America: A Symposium," *Midstream* 12, no. 10 (December 1966): 3.

78. Bayard Rustin, "Negro and Jewish Relationships: Three Addresses Delivered at the American Jewish Congress Convention," *Congress Bi-Weekly* (May 23, 1966).

79. Charles E. Silberman, "Negro and Jewish Relationships: Three Addresses Delivered at the American Jewish Congress Convention," *Congress Bi-Weekly* (May 23, 1966), 8.

80. Ibid., 8.

81. Arthur Lelyveld, "Negro and Jewish Relationships: Three Addresses Deliv-

ered to the American Jewish Congress Convention," *Congress Bi-Weekly* (May 23, 1966), 10.

82. Albert Vorspan, "Black Power," *American Judaism* 16, no. 1 (Fall 1966): 19.

83. Kurt Flascher, "New Developments in Negro Jewish Relations," *Jewish Currents* (May 1963): 17.

84. Morris Schappes, "New Developments in Negro Jewish Relations," *Jewish Currents* (May 1963): 18.

85. "Appraising the Convention," *Congress Bi-Weekly* 31, no. 8 (May 11, 1964): 17.

86. Ibid., 17.

87. David Caplovitz, *The Poor Pay More* (New York: Free Press of Glencoe, 1963). Caplovitz's findings are excerpted in Caplovitz, "The Merchant and the Low-Income Consumer," *Jewish Social Studies* 17, no. 1 (January 1965): 45–52.

88. David Caplovitz, "The Merchant and the Low-Income Consumer," 52.

89. Dick Gregory, *Nigger: An Autobiography* (New York: Dutton, 1964), 49; Friedman, 215.

90. Harold M. Schulweis, "The Voice of Esau," *Reconstructionist* (10 December 1965): 12.

91. "The Negroes and the Jews," *Reconstructionist* 37, no. 1 (October 14, 1966): 4.

92. See Marc Lee Raphael, "Jewish Responses to the Integration of a Suburb: Cleveland Heights, Ohio,: 1960–1980," *American Jewish Archives* 44, no. 2 (Fall 1992): 541–561.

93. See particularly Stephen Steinberg, *Turning Back: The Retreat from Racial Justice in American Thought and Policy* (Boston: Beacon Press, 1995), 1–18; Bob Blauner, *Racial Oppression in America* (New York: Harper and Row, 1972); Ronald Takaki, *From Different Shores: Perspectives on Race and Ethnicity in America* (New York: Oxford University Press, 1987).

94. Norman L. Friedman, "The Problem of the 'Runaway Jewish Intellectuals': Social Definition and Sociological Perspective," *Jewish Social Studies* 31 (1969): 3–19; Milton Konvitz, "The Jewish Intellectual, The University and the Jewish Community," in *The Jewish Intellectual, the University and the Jewish Community* (Washington, D.C.: B'nai B'rith Hillel Foundations, 1964).

95. Milton Goldberg, "A Qualification of the Marginal Man Theory," *American Sociological Review* 6 (February 1941): 52–58; Arnold Green, "A Re-examination of the Marginal Man Concept," *Social Forces* 26 (December 1947): 167–171.

96. Allan Mazur, "The Accuracy of Classic Types of Ethnic Personalities," *Jewish Social Studies* (1971): 190.

97. David Hollinger, "Ethnic Diversity, Cosmopolitanism and the Emergence of the American Liberal Intelligentsia," *American Quarterly* (May 1975): 133–151.

98. See Richard Pells, *The Liberal Mind in a Conservative Age: American Intellectuals in the 1940s and 1950s* (New York: Harper and Row, 1985), 130–148.

99. Glazer and Moynihan, vii. The authors explain that Glazer was responsible for the chapters dealing with all but the Irish group in New York, and I therefore ascribe to him the views contained in those chapters.

100. Ibid.

101. Ibid., xxiii–xxiv.

102. Ibid., xiii. See also Glazer's comments in "Liberalism and the Negro: A Round-Table Discussion," *Commentary* 37, no. 3 (March 1964): 28–29.

103. Irving Kristol, "The Negro of Today Is Like the Immigrant of Yesterday," *New York Times Magazine,* 1 September 1966. Reprinted in *Nation of Nations: The Ethnic Experience and the Racial Crisis,* ed. Peter I. Rose (New York: Random House, 1972), 205–206.

104. Marcus Ravage, *The Young Men's Hebrew Associations* (New York: 1948); Robert Morris and Michael Freund, *Trends and Issues in Jewish Social Service in the United States, 1899–1952* (Philadelphia: Jewish Publication Society, 1966); Sachar, 156–158.

105. John Slawson, "Mutual Aid and the Negro," *Commentary* 41, no. 4 (April 1966): 45; E. Franklin Frazier, *Black Bourgeoisie* (New York: Free Press, 1957): 1–146.

106. Harold Cruse, *Rebellion and Revolution* (New York: Apollo, 1968), 201; Tom Milstein, "A Perspective on the Panthers," *Commentary* 50, no. 3 (September 1970): 37.

107. Allen J. Matusow, *The Unravelling of America: A History of Liberalism in the 1960s* (New York: Harper and Row, 1984), 352–355; Clayborne Carson, *In Struggle: SNCC and the Black Awakening of the 1960s* (Cambridge, Mass.: Harvard University Press, 1981), 260–269.

108. Charles V. Hamilton, "An Advocate of Black Power Defines It," in *The Rhetoric of Black Power,* ed. Robert Scott and Wayne Brocksiede (New York: Harper and Row, 1969); John T. McCartney, *Black Power Ideologies: An Essay in African-American Political Thought* (Philadelphia: Temple University Press, 1992), 111–132.

109. Irving Kristol, "A Few Kind Words for Uncle Tom," *Harper's Magazine* 230, no. 1377 (February 1965): 97.

110. Ibid., 99.

111. Howard Brotz, *The Black Jews of Harlem: Negro Nationalism and the Dilemmas of Negro Leadership* (New York: Schocken, 1964).

112. Howard Brotz, "The Jewish Community and the Contemporary Race Crisis," *Jewish Social Studies* 27, no. 1 (January 1965): 15.

113. Ibid., 16.

114. Brotz, *The Black Jews of Harlem,* 119. The one-dimensional view of Du Bois as a "protest" leader does not do justice to his life and influence. See David Levering Lewis, *W. E. B. Du Bois: The Biography of a Race, 1868–1919* (New York: Henry Holt, 1993).

115. Ibid., 126.

116. Ibid., 11–12.

117. Nathan Glazer "Negro Independence," a review of Brotz, *The Black Jews of Harlem, Commentary* 38, no. 4 (October 1964): 77.

118. Ibid., 78.

119. Brotz, "The Jewish Community and the Contemporary Race Crisis," 12.

120. Milton Himmelfarb, "Catacombs and Khazars," *Commentary* 37, no. 5 (May 1964): 74.

121. Steven S. Schwarzchild, "Negro Nationalism and Black Jews," *Midstream* 10, no. 4 (December 1964): 107–108.

122. Glazer and Moynihan, 180.

123. Ibid., 179.

124. See Nathan Glazer, "Address Made to Plenary Session of the National Community Relations Advisory Council," June 1961, adapted as "Intergroup Relations in the Exploding Metropolis: The Jewish Stake in a Sound Community," *Jewish Digest* 9, no. 2 (November 1963): 33–40.

125. Glazer, "Intergroup Relations in the Exploding Metropolis," 36.

126. Nathan Glazer, "Effects of Emerging Urban-Suburban and Anti-Segregation Developments on Jewish Communal Service," *Journal of Jewish Communal Service* 41, no. 1 (Fall 1964): 150.

127. Ibid.

128. See Steinberg, 1–18; Takaki, 10–89; Blauner.

129. Glazer later wrote that in the early 1960s he had considered himself a "mild radical." See "On Being Deradicalized," *Commentary* 50, no. 4 (October 1970): 74–80.

130. Nathan Glazer, "Is 'Integration' Possible in the New York Schools?" *Commentary* 30, no. 3 (September 1960): 192. Also see Glazer and Moynihan, 44–50.

131. Ibid.

132. See Nathan Glazer, *Affirmative Discrimination: Ethnic Inequality and Public Policy* (New York: Basic Books, 1975).

133. Nathan Glazer, "Integration in the United States," *Jewish Frontier,* 32, no. 3 (April 1965): 13.

134. See Glazer, "On Being Deradicalized," 74–80.

135. See sections on Glazer in chapter 5.

136. Sherman, 17.

137. Lloyd Gartner, "The Racial Revolution and Jewish Communal Policy," *Conservative Judaism* 20, no. 3 (Spring 1966): 49.

138. William Avrunin, "The Human Values in the Central City—Implications for Jewish Communal Service," *Journal of Jewish Communal Service* (Fall 1963): 69.

139. Walter Lurie, "Implications for Jewish Community Organization," *Journal of Jewish Communal Services* 41, no. 5 (Summer 1965): 356; "Changing Race Relations and Jewish Communal Service: Implications" (symposium), *Journal of Jewish Communal Service* 41, no. 4 (Summer 1965): 334–364; Alan Handel, "Where Are

We Going in Jewish Communal Relations?" *Journal of Jewish Communal Service* 43 (Winter 1966); Bernard Warach, "The Comprehensive Community Center," *Journal of Jewish Communal Service* 42, no. 2 (Winter 1965); William Kahn, "Confrontation in a Jewish Center between a Resolution on Equal Opportunity and Practical Reality," *Journal of Jewish Communal Service* 42, no. 2 (Winter 1965).

140. Seymour Cohen, "Negroes and Jews," *Jewish Spectator* 27, no. 9 (November 1962): 11.

141. Dan Dodson, "Human Values in the Inner City: Implications for Jewish Communal Services," *Journal of Jewish Communal Service* (Fall 1963): 58–66.

142. Manheim Shapiro, "Probing the Prejudices of American Jews," *Jewish Digest* 10, no. 2 (November 1964): 3.

143. Ibid., 5.

144. Arthur Hertzberg, "Changing Relations in Jewish Communal Service," *Journal of Jewish Communal Service* 41, no. 4 (Summer 1965): 324.

145. Ibid., 327.

146. Ibid.

147. Ibid., 333.

148. See symposium "Changing Race Relations and Jewish Communal Service: Implications," 334–364.

149. Chernin, 349.

150. Mark A. Raider, "Labor Zionism and the Ethos of American Zionism: 1919–48," *Jewish Frontier* 61 (January 1994): 11.

151. Raider, 14.

152. Daniel Mann, "The Test of Relevance," *Jewish Frontier* 33 (July/August 1966): 16–17.

153. Ibid., 18.

154. C. Bezalel Sherman, *Labor Zionism in America* (New York: Labor Zionist Organization of America Poale Zion, 1957); Herbert Parzen, "The Passing of Jewish Secularism in the United States," *Judaism* 8, no. 3 (Summer 1959); Ben Halpern, "The Jewish Consensus," *Jewish Frontier* 29, no. 9 (September 1962): 9–13; Parzen, 201.

155. Marie Syrkin, "Can Minorities Oppose 'De Facto' Segregation?" *Jewish Frontier* 31, no. 8 (September 1964).

156. Ibid., 8.

157. See Marie Syrkin, *Your School, Your Children* (New York: L. B. Fischer, 1944). Found in Carole Kessner, "Marie Syrkin: An Exemplary Life," *The "Other" New York Intellectuals* (New York: New York University Press, 1994), 60.

158. Syrkin, "Can Minorities Oppose De Facto Segregation," 10.

159. "De Facto Segregation: A Discussion—A Reply," *Jewish Frontier* 31, no. 10 (November 1964): 11.

160. "De Facto Segregation: A Discussion," *Jewish Frontier* 31, no. 10 (November 1964).

161. Ibid.

162. Ben Halpern, "Minorities and Minorities," *Jewish Frontier* 31, no. 10 (November 1964): 5.

163. Ibid.

164. "De Facto Segregation: A Discussion—A Reply," 11.

NOTES TO CHAPTER 3

1. Michael Berube, "Public Academy," *The New Yorker*, 9 January 1995, 73–80; Robert S. Boynton, "The New Intellectuals," *Atlantic*, March 1995, 53–70; Norman Podhoretz, *Making It* (New York: Random House, 1967), 109.

2. The best work on the New York Intellectuals includes Alexander Bloom, *Prodigal Sons: The New York Intellectuals and Their World* (New York: Oxford University Press, 1986); Terry Cooney, *The Rise of the New York Intellectuals: Partisan Review and Its Circle* (Madison: University of Wisconsin Press, 1986); Neil Jumonville, *Critical Crossings: The Intellectuals in Postwar America* (Berkeley: University of California Press, 1991).

3. S. A. Longstaff, "The New York Family," *Queens Quarterly* (Winter 1976).

4. See Ruth Wisse, "The New York (Jewish) Intellectuals," *Commentary* 84 (November 1987); Robert L. Fishman, "The Mind of the Metropolis: New York and Its Intellectuals," *Journal of Urban History* 16, no. 1 (November 1989): 78–90; "The New York Intellectuals: A Symposium," *American Jewish History* (Spring 1991): 321–395.

5. Russell Jacoby, *The Last Intellectuals: American Culture in the Age of Academe* (New York: Basic Books, 1987); see also Jacob Weisberg, "Norman Podhoretz Was Here," *New York*, 30 January 1995, 54–59.

6. Boynton, 53.

7. See Leon Wieseltier, "All or Nothing at All," *New Republic*, 6 March 1995, 31–36.

8. Boynton, 60.

9. Berube, 75.

10. Boynton, 60.

11. Irving Howe, "The New York Intellectuals," in *Decline of the New* (New York: Harcourt, Brace and World, 1970), 211.

12. Podhoretz, 110.

13. Daniel Bell, "Reflections on Jewish Identity," *Commentary* 31, no. 6 (June 1961): 476.

14. Isaac Rosenfeld, *Passage from Home* (New York: Dial, 1946).

15. Ibid. 272.

16. Irving Howe, "Of Fathers and Sons: Review of Passage from Home," *Commentary* 2, no. 2 (April 1946): 190–191.

17. Bloom, 51.

18. Ibid., 51.

19. "Under Forty: A Symposium on American Literature and the Younger Generation of Jews," *Contemporary Jewish Record* (February 1994).

20. Ibid., 16.

21. Ibid., 34.

22. Ibid., 10; Norman Podhoretz, "Introduction: Jewishness and the Younger Intellectuals," *Commentary* 31, no. 4 (April 1961): 307.

23. "Under Forty," 14, 35; Wisse, 34; Terry Cooney, "New York Intellectuals and the Question of Jewish Identity," *American Jewish History* (Spring 1991); 347.

24. See Daniel Bell, *End of Ideology* (New York: Free Press, 1960).

25. Irving Howe, *A Margin of Hope* (New York: Harcourt, Brace and World, 1982), 251.

26. Alfred Kazin, *New York Jew* (New York: Knopf, 1978), 30, 34.

27. Howe, *A Margin of Hope,* 251.

28. Ibid., 253.

29. Hannah Arendt, *Eichmann in Jerusalem* (New York: 1963).

30. Hannah Arendt, *The Origins of Totalitarianism* (New York: Harcourt, Brace, 1951).

31. Norman Podhoretz, "Hannah Arendt on Eichmann," *Commentary* 36, no. 3 (September 1963): 201–208.

32. Norman Podhoretz, *Breaking Ranks: A Political Memoir* (New York: Harper and Row, 1979), 161–163.

33. Irving Howe, "The Range of the New York Intellectual," in *Creators and Disturbers: Reminiscences by Jewish Intellectuals of New York,* ed. Bernard Rosenberg and Ernest Goldstein (New York: Columbia University Press, 1982), 285–286.

34. Alfred Kazin, *Walker in the City* (New York: Harcourt, Brace, 1951); Lionel Trilling, "Wordsworth and the Rabbis," *The Opposing Self: Nine Essays in Criticism* (New York: Viking, 1955).

35. Howe, *A Margin of Hope,* 259.

36. Podhoretz, "Introduction," 308.

37. Melville Herskovitz, *The Myth of the Negro Past* (New York: Harper Brothers, 1941); E. Franklin Frazier, *The Negro Family in the United States* (Chicago: Chicago University Press, 1939); Lawrence Levine, *Black Culture and Black Consciousness* (New York: Oxford University Press, 1977), 80; John Blassingame, *The Slave Community* (New York: Oxford University Press, 1972), 145; Sidney W. Mintz and Richard Price, *The Birth of African American Culture* (Boston: Beacon Press, 1992).

38. Lewis A. Erenberg, "Things to Come: Swing Bands, Bebop, and the Rise of a Postwar Jazz Scene," in *Recasting America: Culture and Politics in the Age of Cold War,* ed. Lary May (Chicago: University of Chicago Press, 1989), 223.

39. DiNesh D'Souza, *The End of Racism* (New York: Free Press, 1995), 99–100.

40. Erenberg, 237.

41. LeRoi Jones, *Blues People: Negro Music in White America* (New York: Morrow, 1967), 181.

42. See Carl Van Vechten, *Keep A-Inchin Along: Selected Writings of Carl Van Vechten about Black Art and Letters,* ed. Bruce Kellner (Westport, Conn.: Greenwood Press, 1979); Milton Mezzrow and Bernard Wolfe, *Really the Blues* (New York: Random House, 1946), pp. 206–233.

43. See John Tytell, *Naked Angels: The Lives and Literature of the Beat Generation* (New York: McGraw-Hill, 1976).

44. Norman Mailer, "The White Negro," *Dissent* (Summer 1957). Reprinted in *The White Negro* (San Francisco: City Lights Books, 1970), 2.

45. Morris Dickstein, *Gates of Eden: American Culture in the Sixties* (New York: Basic Books, 1976), 53.

46. Norman Mailer, "Norman Mailer Replies," *Dissent* 5, no. 1 (Winter 1958): 75.

47. George Steiner, "Naked But Not Dead," *Encounter* 17, no. 6 (December 1961): 69; Norman Podhoretz, "Norman Mailer: The Embattled Vision," *Partisan Review* (Summer 1959): 384–385; Diana Trilling, "The Radical Moralism of Norman Mailer," *Encounter* 19, no. 5 (November 1962; reprinted in *Norman Mailer: A Collection of Critical Essays,* ed. Leo Braudy [Englewood Cliffs, N.J.: Prentice-Hall, 1972], 58).

48. Ned Polsky, "Reflections on Hipsterism," *Dissent* 5, no. 2 (Winter 1958): 80.

49. Ibid; Jean Malaquais, "Reflections on Hipsterism," *Dissent* 5, no. 2 (Winter 1958): 73.

50. Peter Manso, *Mailer: His Life and Times* (New York: Simon and Schuster, 1985).

51. James Baldwin, "The Black Boy Looks at the White Boy," *Esquire* 55, no. 5 (May 1961): 102–106. Reprinted in Braudy, 69.

52. Ibid.

53. Manso, 254.

54. Murray Friedman, *What Went Wrong: The Creation and Collapse of the Black-Jewish Alliance* (New York: Free Press, 1995), 271–272.

55. Norman Podhoretz, "The Know-Nothing Bohemians," in *Doings and Undoings: The Fifties and After in American Literature* (New York: Noonday Press, 1964), 151.

56. Nat Hentoff, *The New Equality* (New York: Viking, 1964), 67–68.

57. Ibid.

58. Herbert Gutman, *The Black Family in Slavery and Freedom* (New York: Pantheon, 1976); Jesse Bernard, *Marriage and Family among Negroes* (Englewood Cliffs, N.J.: Prentice-Hall, 1966); Elliott Liebow, *Tally's Corner* (Boston: Little Brown, 1967); Baldwin, 74.

59. Seymour Krim, "Ask for a White Cadillac," *Exodus* (1959). Reprinted in *Views of a Nearsighted Cannoneer* (New York: Dutton, 1968), 88–89.

60. Ibid., 100.

61. Ibid., 90–91.

62. Ibid., 101.

63. Ibid., 97–98.

64. Ibid., 103.

65. Podhoretz, "The Know-Nothing Bohemians," 147.

66. Cooney, 358.

67. David Hollinger, "Ethnic Diversity, Cosmopolitanism, and the Emergence of the American Liberal Intelligentsia," *American Quarterly* (May 1975): 135.

68. Harold Rosenberg, "Jewish Identity in a Free Society," *Commentary* (May 1950): 509.

69. Ibid., 510.

70. See particularly Werner Sollors, *Beyond Ethnicity: Consent and Descent in American Culture* (New York: Oxford University Press, 1986), 244.

71. David A. Hollinger, "A Response to Essays," *American Jewish History* (Spring 1991): 379; Leslie Fiedler, "The Breakthrough: The American Jewish Novelist and the Fictional Image of the Jew," *Midstream* 4, no. 1 (Winter 1958): 23.

72. See "Introduction," *A Treasury of Yiddish Stories,* ed. Irving Howe and Eliezer Greenberg (New York: Schocken, 1955).

73. Howe, *A Margin of Hope,* 263, 269.

74. Norman Podhoretz, "Jewish Culture and the Intellectuals," in *Doings and Undoings,* 124.

75. Norman Podhoretz, "The Intellectual and Jewish Fate," *Midstream* 3, no. 1 (Winter 1957).

76. Quoted by Roger Kimball, "Clement Greenberg: An Appreciation," *Commentary* 98, no. 3 (September 1994): 51; Paul R. Gorman, *Left Intellectuals and Popular Culture in Twentieth-Century America* (Chapel Hill: University of North Carolina Press, 1996), 137–157.

77. Podhoretz, "Introduction," 2–3.

78. Irving Howe, *Politics and the Novel* (New York: Horizon, 1957), 15; Lionel Trilling, *Beyond Culture* (New York: Harcourt Brace Jovanovich, 1979), iii–iv; Howe, *A Margin of Hope,* 154.

79. Mel Watkins, "The Black Revolution in Books," *New York Times Book Review,* 10 August 1969, 8.

80. Larry Neal, "The Black Arts Movement," in *The Norton Anthology of African-American Literature,* ed. Henry Louis Gates Jr. and Nellie Y. McKay (New York: Norton, 1997), 1960.

81. See Norman Cantor, *Twentieth-Century Culture: From Modernism to Deconstruction* (New York: Peter Lang, 1988), 249–260, 345–402; Daniel Bell, "The Cul-

ture Wars: American Intellectual Life: 1965–1992," *Wilson Quarterly*, Part 3 (Summer 1992).

82. Richard Gilman, "White Standards and Black Writing," in *The Confusion of Realms* (New York: Random House, 1969), 9; LeRoi Jones, "Jazz and Revolutionary Nationalism," *Jazz* (November 1966): 38.

83. See Hilton Kramer, "Saul Bellow, Our Contemporary," *Commentary* 97, no. 6 (June 1994): 37–41.

84. Nathan Glazer, "The Fire This Time," *New Republic*, 20 December 1985, 41.

85. Ibid., 42.

86. James Baldwin, "Everybody's Protest Novel," *Partisan Review* (June 1949), 23; James Baldwin, "Many Thousands Gone," *Partisan Review* (November-December 1951). Both reprinted in James Baldwin, *Notes of a Native Son* (Boston: Beacon Press, 1955), 13–45.

87. Baldwin, "Many Thousands Gone," 41.

88. James Baldwin, *The Fire Next Time* (New York: Dial, 1963).

89. Ibid., 108.

90. Podhoretz, *Making It*, 309.

91. Bernard Avishai, "Breaking Faith: *Commentary* and the Jews," *Dissent* (Spring 1981): 237.

92. Found in Michael Wyschogrod, "My *Commentary* Problem—And Ours," *Judaism* 17, no. 2 (Spring 1968): 148–161.

93. Norman Podhoretz, "My Negro Problem—And Ours," *Commentary* 25, no. 2 (February 1963).

94. Podhoretz, *Making It*, 340.

95. Podhoretz, "My Negro Problem," 97.

96. Ibid.

97. Ibid., 99.

98. Podhoretz, *Breaking Ranks*, pp. 123–124.

99. Podhoretz, "My Negro Problem," p. 99.

100. See Ralph Ellison, "No Apologies," *Harper's Magazine*, July 1967.

101. Podhoretz, "My Negro Problem," 101.

102. Norman Podhoretz, "The Issue," *Commentary* (March 1960). Found in Wyschogrod, 148–161.

103. Podhoretz, "My Negro Problem," 101.

104. See Daniel Aaron, "The 'Inky' Curse: Miscegenation in the White American Literary Imagination," *Social Science Information* 22 (1983); Toni Morrison, *Playing in the Dark: Whiteness and the Literary Imagination* (Cambridge, Mass.: Harvard University Press, 1982).

105. Barry Rubin, *Assimilation and Its Discontents* (New York: Random House, 1995), 126.

106. Leslie Fiedler, *Love and Death in the American Novel* (New York: Criterion, 1960), 197.

107. Leslie Fiedler, "Come Back to the Raft Ag'In, Huck Honey!" *Partisan Review* (June 1948). Reprinted in *An End to Innocence* (Boston: Beacon Press, 1955), 145.

108. Ibid.

109. Ibid., 151.

110. Leslie Fiedler, "The Jig Is Up," in *Waiting for the End* (New York: Stein and Day, 1964), 122.

111. Leslie Fiedler, "Indian or Injun?" in *Waiting for the End,* 107.

112. Ibid., 116.

113. Fiedler, "The Jig Is Up," 133.

114. *Negro and Jew: Encounter in America,* ed. Shlomo Katz (New York: Macmillan, 1967), 31.

115. Ibid., 40.

116. Ibid.

117. Irving Howe, "Black Boys and Native Sons," *Dissent* (Autumn 1963). Reprinted in *Decline of the New,* 168.

118. Ibid., 168.

119. Ibid., 174.

120. Ibid.

121. Ibid., 175.

122. Ibid., 177.

123. Ibid.

124. Ralph Ellison, *Invisible Man* (New York: Random House, 1952); Ralph Ellison, "Brave Words for a Startling Occasion," in *Shadow and Act* (New York: Random House, 1964), 104–105.

125. Howe, "Black Boys and Native Sons," 180, 181.

126. Ralph Ellison, *The New Leader* (December 9, 1964, and February 3, 1964). Reprinted as "The World and the Jug," 107–143.

127. Ellison, "The World and the Jug," 112.

128. Ibid., 118.

129. See Henry Louis Gates Jr., *Loose Canons: Notes on the Culture Wars* (New York: Oxford University Press, 1992); Henry Louis Gates Jr., *"Race," Writing, and Difference* (Chicago: University of Chicago Press, 1986); Isaac Julien, "Black Is, Black Ain't: Notes on De-Essentializing Black Identities," in *Black Popular Culture,* ed. Gina Dent (Seattle: Bay Press, 1992), 255–263.

130. Ellison, "The World and the Jug," 136–137, 126.

131. Daniel Aaron, "The Hyphenate Writer and American Letters," *Smith Alumnae Quarterly* 55, no. 4 (July 1964): 215, 217.

132. Ellison, "The World and the Jug," 126–127.

133. Cynthia Ozick, "Literary Blacks and Jews," *Midstream* (1972). Reprinted in Blacks and Jews: *Alliances and Arguments,* ed. Paul Berman (New York: Delacorte, 1994), 53.

134. Howe, *A Margin of Hope,* 275–276.

135. Leon Wieseltier, "Remembering Irving Howe," *New York Times Book Review,* 23 May 1993.

136. Howe, *A Margin of Hope,* 269.

137. Irving Howe, "The Limits of Ethnicity," *New Republic,* 25 June 1977, 18.

138. Ozick, "Afterword," in Berman, 74.

139. Howe, "Afterward—Black Boys and Native Sons," 189.

140. Eugene Goodheart, "The Abandoned Legacy," *American Jewish History* (Spring 1991): 368.

141. Norman Podhoretz, "The Rise and Fall of the American Jewish Novelist," in *Jewish Life in America: Historical Perspectives,* ed. Gladys Rosen (New York: KTAV, 1978), 145.

142. Robert Alter, "The Jew Who Didn't Get Away: On the Possibility of an American Jewish Culture," in *The American Jewish Experience,* ed. Jonathan Sarna (New York: Holmes and Meier, 1986), 269–283.

143. Ralph Ellison, "A Very Stern Disciple," *Harpers,* March 1967, 78.

144. Carole S. Kessner, "Introduction," *The "Other" New York Jewish Intellectuals* (New York: New York University Press, 1994).

145. Ibid., 10.

146. Ibid., 2.

147. Cynthia Ozick, "American: Toward Yavneh," *Judaism* (Summer 1970): p. 275.

148. On the decline of the Yiddish press and theater see Henry Feingold, *A Time for Searching: Entering the Mainstream* (Baltimore: Johns Hopkins University Press, 1992), 32, 68, 70–71, 75. A recent study found that only 16 percent of Jews in the New York metropolitan area can read a Hebrew newspaper, while only 15 percent could read a Yiddish newspaper. See *The 1991 New York Jewish Population Study* (New York: United Jewish Appeal-Federation of Jewish Philanthropies of New York), xvi.

149. Lauren B. Strauss, "Staying Afloat in the Melting Pot: Constructing an American Jewish Identity in the *Menorah Journal* of the 1920s," *American Jewish History* 84, no. 4 (December 1996): 315–332.

150. See Mel Scult, "Americanism and Judaism in Mordecai Kaplan," in *The Americanization of the Jews,* ed. Robert Seltzer and Norman J. Cohen (New York: New York University Press, 1995), 339–354; David G. Dalin, "Will Herberg's Path from Marxism to Judaism: A Case Study in the Transformation of Jewish Belief," in Seltzer and Cohen, 119–132.

151. Henry Feingold, "As Diverse as Postemancipation Judaism," *Midstream* 51, no. 4 (May 1995): 38.

152. Edward S. Shapiro, "Jewishness and the New York Intellectuals," *Judaism* (Fall 1989): 292.

153. Irving Howe, *World of Our Fathers* (New York: Harcourt Brace Jovanovich, 1976), 586; Norman Podhoretz, "The Rise and Fall of the American Jewish Novelist," 141–150; Leslie Fiedler, "Growing Up Post-Jewish," in Fiedler, *Fiedler on the Roof: Essays on Literature and Jewish Identity* (Boston: David R. Godine, 1991), 117–122.

154. Howe, *A Margin of Hope,* 341.

155. Podhoretz, "The Rise and Fall of the American Jewish Novelist," 145.

156. Henry Louis Gates Jr., "Bad Influence—Makes Me Wanna Holler," *New Yorker* 70, no. 3 (7 March 1994): 94–98.

157. Ruth Wisse, "Jewish Writers on the New Diaspora," in *The Americanization of the Jews,* 74.

158. Avishai, 237.

NOTES TO CHAPTER 4

1. Bayard Rustin, "From Protest to Politics," *Commentary* (February 1965): 25–27.

2. Jerald E. Podair, " 'White' Values, 'Black' Values: The Ocean Hill-Brownsville Controversy and New York City Culture, 1965–1975," *Radical History Review* (Spring 1994): 57.

3. Nathan Caplan, "The New Ghetto Man: A Review of Recent Empirical Studies," *Journal of Social Issues* 26 (Winter 1970): 59–73; Allen J. Matusow, *The Unraveling of America: A History of Liberalism in the 1960s* (New York: Harper and Row, 1984), 362.

4. Matusow, 360–362.

5. Ibid., 362.

6. *Report of the National Advisory Commission on Civil Disorders* (1968). Reprinted in *To Redeem a Nation: A History and Anthology of the Civil Rights Movement,* ed. Thomas R. West and James R. Mooney (St. James, N.Y.: Brandywine Press, 1993), 177.

7. Found in Henry Cohen, *Justice, Justice: A Jewish View of the Negro Revolt* (New York: Union of American Hebrew Congregations, 1968), 76.

8. Malcolm X as told to Alex Haley, *The Autobiography of Malcolm X* (New York: Ballantine, 1964), 283.

9. John Henrik Clarke, *Malcolm X: The Man and His Times* (New York: Macmillan, 1969), 306.

10. Quoted in Matusow, 365.

11. Robert Blauner, "Internal Colonialism and Ghetto Revolt," *Social Problems* 16 (Spring 1969): 393–408; Nathan Glazer, "Blacks and Ethnic Groups: The Difference and the Political Difference It Makes," *Ethnic Dilemmas: 1964–1982* (Cambridge, Mass.: Harvard University Press, 1983), 70–93; James M. Blaut, "The

Ghetto as an Internal Neocolony," *Antipode* 6, no. 1 (1974); Douglas Massey and Nancy A. Denton, *American Apartheid: Segregation and the Making of the Underclass* (Cambridge, Mass.: Harvard University Press, 1993), 67, 85–87.

12. Harold Cruse, *Rebellion and Revolution* (New York: Apollo, 1968), 75–76.

13. John H. Bracey, August Meier, and Elliott Rudwick, eds., *Black Nationalism in America* (Indianapolis: Bobbs-Merrill, 1970), xlviii.

14. Stokely Carmichael and Charles Hamilton, *Black Power: The Politics of Liberation in America* (New York: Random House, 1967), 80.

15. Robert Weisbord and Arthur Stein, *Bittersweet Encounter: The Afro-American and the American Jew* (Westport, Conn.: Negro Universities Press, 1970), 103.

16. Jerome Bakst, "Negro Radicalism Turns Anti-Semitic: SNCC's *Volte Face*," *Wiener Library Bulletin* 22, no. 1 (Winter 1967): 21.

17. Ibid.

18. Clayborne Carson, *In Struggle: SNCC and the Black Awakening of the 1960s* (Cambridge, Mass.: Harvard University Press, 1981), 268–269, 340.

19. Charles V. Hamilton, "An Advocate of Black Power Defines It," in *The Rhetoric of Black Power*, ed. Robert Scott and Wayne Brocksiede (New York: Harper and Row, 1969); John T. McCartney, *Black Power Ideologies: An Essay in African-American Political Thought* (Philadelphia: Temple University Press, 1992), 111–132; Bracey, Meier, and Rudwick, lvi.

20. Harold Cruse, *The Crisis of the Negro Intellectual* (New York: Morrow, 1967), 344.

21. Ibid., 441.

22. Ibid., 8.

23. Moses Rischin, "The Jewish Labor Movement in America: A Social Interpretation," *Labor History* 4 (1963); Deborah Dash Moore, "From *Kehillah* to Federation: The Communal Functions of Federated Philanthropy in New York City, 1917–1933," *American Jewish History* (December 1978); Shelley Tennenbaum, "Immigrants and Capital: Jewish Loan Societies in the U.S. 1880–1945," *American Jewish History* 76 (September 1986): 67–77; Henry Feingold, *A Time for Searching: Entering the Mainstream 1920–1945* (Baltimore: Johns Hopkins University Press, 1992), 142–143.

24. Howard Sachar, *A History of the Jews in America* (New York: Vintage Books, 1992), 341, 145, 647; Beth Wenger, *New York Jews and the Depression: Uncertain Promise* (New Haven: Yale University Press, 1996), 15; Henry Feingold, "From Equality to Liberty: The Changing Political Culture of American Jews," in *The Americanization of the Jews*, ed. Robert M. Seltzer and Norman J. Cohen (New York: New York University Press, 1995), 104.

25. On the ethnic niche-making in municipal civil service jobs, see Roger Waldinger, *Still the Promised City? African-Americans and New Immigrants in Postindustrial New York* (Cambridge, Mass.: Harvard University Press, 1996), 215–273.

26. See Karen Brodkin Sacks, "How Did Jews Become White Folks?" in *Race,*

ed. Steven Gregory and Roger Sanjeck (New Brunswick, N.J.: Rutgers University Press, 1994), 84.

27. Thomas Sowell, *Ethnic America: A History* (New York: Basic Books, 1981), 88–89; Leonard Dinnerstein, "Education and the Advancement of American Jews," in *American Education and the European Immigrant, 1840–1940,* ed. Bernard J. Weiss (Urbana, Ill.: University of Illinois Press, 1982), pp. 44–60.

28. Nathan Glazer, "Social Characteristics of American Jews, 1654–1954," *American Jewish Yearbook* (Philadelphia: Jewish Publication Society, 1955): 20–24.

29. Podair, 44.

30. For a good discussion of Jewish representation in government employment, see Benjamin Ginsburg, *The Fatal Embrace: Jews and the State* (Chicago: University of Chicago Press, 1993), 97–145.

31. Naomi Levine with Richard Cohen, *Ocean Hill-Brownsville: A Case History of Schools in Crisis* (New York: Popular Library, 1969), 9.

32. Tom Brooks, "The Tragedy of Ocean Hill," *Dissent* 16, no. 1 (January 2, 1969): 3.

33. Gary T. Marx, *Protest and Prejudice: A Study of Belief in the Black Community* (New York: Harper and Row, 1967).

34. Brooks, 3.

35. This quote comes from an article by Fred Ferretti that appeared in the *Columbia Journal Review* in the fall of 1969. Apparently Ferretti obtained a transcript of the December 26, 1968, "Julius Lester Program" on station WBAI-FM, on which Leslie Campbell read the full poem allegedly written by a "young sister" named Thea Behran. Ferretti does not acknowledge anyone as the poet. For full text of the poem see Jonathan Kaufman, *Broken Alliance: The Turbulent Times between Blacks and Jews in America* (New York: Scribner's, 1988), 159–160, which reprinted it in its entirety, citing Ferretti's article.

36. Jerald E. Podair, "The Failure to 'See': Jews, Blacks, and the Ocean Hill-Brownsville Controversy, 1968" (Philadelphia: Center for American Jewish History, Temple University, 1992), 186, 194.

37. Diane Ravitch, *The Great School Wars: New York City, 1805–1973: A History of the Public Schools as Battlefield of Social Change* (New York: Basic Books, 1974), 370.

38. "Black Anti-Semitism and Its Mindless Sponsors," *Congress Bi-Weekly* 36, no. 2 (January 27, 1969): 2.

39. Ibid.

40. Thomas Hoving, *Making the Mummies Dance* (New York: Simon and Schuster, 1993), 179.

41. *Afro-American Teacher's Forum* (November-December 1967): 2.

42. Weisbord and Stein, 155; "Blackwash at NYU," *Jewish Frontier* 35 (September 1968): 6; Lois Waldman, "What Price Peace at NYU?" *Congress Bi-Weekly* 35, no. 10 (September 16, 1968): 3–5.

43. Ibid., 157.

44. Ernest Dunbar, "The Black Studies Thing," *New York Times Magazine*, 6 April 1969, 68; Armstead Robinson, Craig C. Foster, Donald H. Ogilvie, eds., *Black Studies in the University: A Symposium* (New Haven: Yale University Press, 1969).

45. Melissa Faye Green, *The Temple Bombing* (New York: Addison-Wesley, 1996), 177.

46. Lenora Berson, *The Negroes and the Jews* (New York: Random House, 1971), 313–314.

47. Stephen Steinberg, "How Jewish Quotas Began," *Commentary* (September 1971); Marcia Graham Synnott, *The Half-Opened Door: Discrimination and Admissions at Harvard, Yale, and Princeton 1900–1970* (Westport, Conn.: 1979).

48. Irving Howe, *World of Our Fathers* (New York: Harcourt, Brace, Jovanovich, 1976), 282; James Traub, *City on a Hill: Testing the American Dream at City College* (Reading: Addison-Wesley, 1994), 34, 37.

49. Lloyd Gartner, "Five Demands at City College," *Midstream* 15, no. 8 (October 1969): 16–17.

50. Howard L. Adelson, "City University: A Jewish Tragedy," *American Zionist* 67, no. 1 (September 1971): 17; Marnin Feinstein, "The Campus Upheaval at City College," *Reconstructionist* 35, no. 8 (July 25, 1969): 14–26.

51. See Nicholas Lemann, "Taking Affirmative Action Apart," *New York Times Magazine*, 11 June 1995, 36–66.

There is a vast literature on affirmative action, its history, and its effects. See the case *against* by Terry Eastland, *Ending Affirmative Action: The Case for a Colorblind Justice* (New York: Basic Books, 1996) and the case *for* by Stephen Steinberg, *Turning Back: The Retreat from Racial Justice in American Thought and Politics* (Boston: Beacon Press, 1995), 164–178.

52. Lemann, 43.

53. Nathan Glazer, "On Jewish Forebodings," *Commentary* (August 1985): 32–36; Paul L. Goodman, "A Jewish Look at 'Affirmative Action,' " *Jewish Frontier* (October 1972): 27–30.

54. See discussion on "Affirmative Action and Jewish Women," in Susan Weidman Schneider, *Jewish and Female: Choices and Changes in Our Lives Today* (New York: Simon and Schuster, 1984), 492–503; Morris B. Abram and Howard I. Friedman, "Affirmative Action," *Commentary* 100, no. 3 (September 1995): 2.

55. Michael Lind, *The Next American Nation: The New Nationalism and the Fourth American Revolution* (New York: Free Press, 1995), 129.

56. On the evolution of Jewish whiteness, see Karen Brodkin Sacks, "How Did Jews Become White Folks?" 84; Matthew Frye Jacobson, *Becoming Caucasian: Vicissitudes of Whiteness in American Political Culture* (Cambridge, Mass.: Harvard University Press, 1998); Michael Paul Rogin, *Blackface, White Noise: Jewish Immigrants in the Hollywood Melting Pot* (Berkeley: University of California Press, 1996).

57. Shelby Steele, *The Content of Our Character* (New York: St. Martin's, 1990), 149–165.

58. Cruse, *The Crisis of the Negro Intellectual,* 364.

59. Ibid., 158.

60. Wilson Record, *The Negro and the Communist Party* (Chapel Hill: University of North Carolina Press, 1951); William A. Nolan, *Communism Versus the Negro* (Chicago: Regnery, 1951); Nathan Glazer, *The Social Basis of American Communism* (New York: Harcourt, Brace and World, 1961), 170.

61. Nathan Glazer, "The Jewish Role in Student Activism," *Remembering the Answers: Essays on the American Student Revolt* (New York: Basic Books, 1970), 229–230.

62. Ibid., 56.

63. Glazer, *The Social Basis of American Communism,* pp. 150–156.

64. Cruse, *The Crisis of the Negro Intellectual,* 168–169.

65. Ibid., 480.

66. Ibid., 483.

67. James Baldwin, "Negroes Are Anti-Semitic Because They're Anti-White," *New York Times Magazine* (1967). Reprinted in *Black Anti-Semitism and Jewish Racism,* ed. Nat Hentoff (New York: Schocken, 1970), 6, 9.

68. C. Eric Lincoln, *The Black Muslims in America* (Grand Rapids, Mich.: William B. Eerdmans, 1994), 13.

69. Baldwin, 9.

70. Found in Nathan Glazer, "America's Race Paradox," *Encounter* (October 1968). Reprinted in *Nation of Nations: The Ethnic Experience and the Racial Crisis,* ed. Peter I. Rose (New York: Random House, 1972), 171.

71. James Baldwin, "A Question of Commitment," *New York Times Book Review,* 2 June 1968, 2.

72. Eddie Ellis, "Semitism in the Black Ghetto," *Liberator* (February 1966); James Baldwin, "Anti-Semitism and Black Power," *Freedomways* (First Quarter 1967). Reprinted by American Jewish Committee (New York: American Jewish Committee, Blaustein Library).

73. James Baldwin, "An Open Letter to My Sister, Miss Angela Davis," *New York Review of Books,* 7 January 1971, 15; Shlomo Katz, "An Open Letter to James Baldwin," *Midstream* 17, no. 4 (April 1971): 3–5; James Baldwin and Shlomo Katz, "Of Angela Davis and 'the Jewish Housewife Headed for Dachau': An Exchange," *Midstream* 17, no. 6 (June/July 1971): 3–10.

74. Julius Lester, "A Response," in Hentoff, 232, 234.

75. Leonard Fein, *Where Are We?: The Inner Life of America's Jews* (New York: Harper and Row, 1988), 256.

76. Seymour Martin Lipset and Everett Carll Ladd Jr., "Jewish Academics in the United States: Their Achievements, Culture and Politics," *American Jewish Year Book* (Philadelphia: American Jewish Committee-Jewish Publication Society of

America, 1971), 90; Charles Silberman, *A Certain People: American Jews and Their Lives Today* (New York: Summit, 1985), 99–100.

77. Edward Shapiro, *A Time for Healing: American Jewry since World War II* (Baltimore: Johns Hopkins University Press, 1992), 100–101.

78. See Charles Kadushin, *The American Intellectual Elite* (Boston: Little, Brown, 1974), 23–31.

79. Silberman, 82–95. On past discrimination, see Richard L. Zweigenhaft and G. William Domhoff, *Jews in the Protestant Establishment* (New York: Praeger, 1982), esp. chap. 2.

80. Silberman, 94–98. See Jerrold Auerbach, "From Rags to Robes: The Legal Profession, Social Mobility and the American Jewish Experience," *American Jewish Historical Quarterly* 66, no. 4 (December 1976).

81. Milton Himmelfarb, "Would You Vote for a Jew for President?" (New York: American Jewish Committee, n.d.). Found in Silberman, 103.

82. Robert Gordis, "American Jewry: Fourth Century," in *Jewish Life in America,* ed. Theodore Friedman and Robert Gordis (New York: 1955), 14.

83. Lloyd Gartner, "The Midpassage of American Jewry," in *The American Jewish Experience,* ed. Jonathan Sarna (New York: Holmes and Meier, 1986), 231.

84. Leon Wieseltier is quoted in Judith Miller, *One, by One, by One: Facing the Holocaust* (New York: Simon and Schuster, 1990), 231–232.

85. Morris N. Kertzer, *Today's American Jew* (New York: McGraw-Hill, 1967), 295. Found in Shapiro, 207.

86. Walter Laqueur, "Israel, The Arabs, and World Opinion," *Commentary* 44, no. 2 (August 1967): 50.

87. Arthur Hertzberg, "Israel and American Jewry," *Commentary* 44, no. 2 (August 1967): 69, 70.

88. Shapiro, 207–208.

89. Michael Kazin, "Some Notes on SDS," *American Scholar* (Autumn 1969): 650.

90. See Students for a Democratic Society, *The Port Huron Statement,* mimeographed (1962), 7; Edward Walter, *The Rise and Fall of Leftist Radicalism in America* (Westport, Conn.: Praeger, 1992), 102.

91. For the difference between the old left and the New, see Maurice Isserman, *If I Had a Hammer: The Death of the Old Left and the Birth of the New Left* (New York: Basic, 1987); Todd Gitlin, *The Sixties: Years of Hope—Days of Rage* (New York: Bantam, 1987), 81–194.

92. Walter, 111–112.

93. Nathan Glazer, "The New Left and the Jews," *Jewish Journal of Sociology* 11, no. 2 (December 1969): 130; Richard Israel, "The Hillel Conference of Jewish Students," *Judaism* 18, no. 4 (Fall 1969): 468.

For example, see *Confrontation: The Student Rebellion and the Universities,* ed. Daniel Bell and Irving Kristol (New York: Basic Books, 1969); Nathan Glazer,

Remembering the Answers: Essays on the American Student Movement (New York: Basic Books, 1970).

94. Kaufman, 210.

95. Quoted in Arthur Liebman, *Jews and the Left* (New York: Wiley, 1979), 510, 574.

96. Arthur Hertzberg, *The French Enlightenment and the Jews* (New York: Columbia University Press, 1968), 360.

97. Robert Wistrich, "Rosa Luxemburg, Leo Jogiches and the Jewish Labour Movement, 1893–1903," in Ada Rapoport-Albert and Steven Zipperstein, *Jewish History: Essays in Honor of Chimen Abramsky* (London: Halban, 1989), 542.

98. J. L. Talmon, "Jews and Revolution," *Maariv*, 21 September 1969. Found in Seymour Martin Lipset, "The Socialism of Fools," in *The New Left and the Jews*, ed. Mordecai S. Chertoff (New York: Pitman, 1971), 105–107.

99. Lipset, "The Socialism of Fools," 107.

100. "Is SNCC Racist or Radical?" *Jewish Currents* 20, no. 7 (July–August 1966): 3; "James Baldwin and Anti-Semitism," *Jewish Currents* 21, no. 6 (June 1967): 3; "Civil Liberties for Black Panthers," *Jewish Currents* 24, no. 2 (February 1970): 3, 9; Morris Schappes, "Black Power and the Jews," *Jewish Currents* (January 1967): 16.

101. This quote comes from then director of the American Jewish Committee's Trends Analyses Division Milton Ellerin's report on the Black Panthers, published by the American Jewish Committee, *The Black Panther Party—The Anti-Semitic and Anti-Israel Component* (New York: American Jewish Committee, 1970), 3, in which he quotes this song parody, which appeared in the June 1967 issue of the Panther newsletter *Black Power*.

102. Noam Chomsky, "Israel and the New Left," in Lipset, *The New Left and the Jews*, 199.

103. Nat Hentoff, "Introduction," *Black Anti-Semitism and Jewish Racism*, xvii.

104. Robert Alter, "Israel and the Intellectuals," *Commentary* 44, no. 4 (October 1967): 49.

105. I. F. Stone, "Holy War," *New York Review of Books*, 3 August 1967, 11, 12.

106. I. F. Stone, "The Mason-Dixon Line Moves to New York," in *Polemics and Prophecies: 1967–1970* (Boston: Little Brown, 1970), 108.

107. Liebman, chap. 2, and 541.

108. See Ken Kenniston, "The Sources of Student Dissent," *Journal of Social Issues* (June 1967): 108–136; Richard Flacks, "Who Protests: A Study of Student Activists," in *Protest: Student Activism in America*, ed. Julian Foster and Durwood Long (New York: Morrow, 1970); Glazer, "The New Left and the Jews," 127–128.

109. Liebman, 536.

110. Glazer, "The New Left and the Jews," 127–129.

111. Jack Nusan Porter and Peter Dreier, "Introduction," *Jewish Radicalism: A Selected Anthology* (New York: Grove, 1973), xxxiii; Walter Laqueur, "Revolutionism and the Jews: 1 New York and Jerusalem," *Commentary* 51, no. 2 (February 1971): 41.

112. Liebman, 577; Bill Novak, "The Failure of Jewish Radicalism," in *Jewish Radicalism*, 305–307.

113. Michael J. Rosenberg, "Israel without Apology," *The New Jews*, ed. James A. Sleeper and Alan L. Mintz (New York: Vintage, 1971), 82, 86.

114. J. J. Goldberg, "Is Zionism Compatible with Radicalism," *Activist* (Spring 1970). Reprinted in *Jewish Radicalism*, xxxi.

115. Jack Nusan Porter, "Jewish Student Activism," *Jewish Currents* 24, no. 5 (May 1970): 32.

116. Robert Alter, "Revolutionism and the Jews: 2. Appropriating the Religious Tradition," *Commentary* 51, no. 2 (February 1971): 48.

117. The Freedom Seder (Holt, Rinehart and Winston, 1970), 56.

118. Alter, "Revolutionism and the Jews: 2," 50.

119. Arthur I. Waskow, "Judaism and Revolution Today," *Judaism* 20, no. 4 (Fall 1971). Reprinted in *Jewish Radicalism*, 25.

120. Ibid., 13.

121. Joel Harris, "The Conference of the World Union of Jewish Students," *Judaism* 18, no. 4 (Fall 1969): 471.

122. Aviva Cantor Zuckoff, "The Oppression of America's Jews," in *Jewish Radicalism*, 30.

123. M. Jay Rosenberg, "To Uncle Tom and Other Such Jews," *Reconstructionist* 35, no. 11 (October 31, 1969): 28.

124. Waskow, 21, 24.

125. Michael Lerner, "Jewish New Leftism at Berkeley," *Judaism* 18, no. 4 (Fall 1969): 475–476.

126. Joel Ziff, "Black Man and Jew," *Response* (Winter 1968): 24.

127. Arthur Waskow, *The Bush Is Burning! Radical Judaism Faces the Pharaohs of the Modern Superstate* (New York: Macmillan, 1971), 7–20.

128. Susannah Heschel, "Introduction," *On Being a Jewish Feminist: A Reader* (New York: Schocken, 1983), xv.

129. *The Jewish Woman: New Perspectives*, ed. Elizabeth Koltun (New York: Schocken, 1976).

130. Charlotte Baum, Paula Hyman, and Sonya Michel, eds., *The Jewish Woman in America* (New York: Dial, 1976); Anita Lebeson, *Recall to Life: The Jewish Woman in America* (New York: Yoseloff, 1970).

131. Elly Bulkin, "Extensions," in *Yours in Struggle: Three Feminist Perspectives on Anti-Semitism and Racism*, ed. Elly Bulkin, Minnie Bruce Pratt, and Barbara Smith (New York: Long Haul, 1984), 98.

132. Bulkin, 97.

133. Jenny Bourne, "Homelands of the Mind: Jewish Feminism and Identity Politics," *Race & Class* 29, no. 1 (Summer Bourne): 4–9.

134. Letty Cotton Pogrebin, *Deborah, Golda and Me: Being Female and Jewish in America* (New York: Crown, 1991), 213.

135. Elly Bulkin, "Separations," in Bulkin, Pratt, and Smith, 112.

136. Evelyn Torton Beck, "Why Is This Book Different from All Other Books?" *Nice Jewish Girls: A Lesbian Anthology* (Watertown, Mass.: Persephone Press, 1982; republished and redistributed by Crossing Press, 1984), xxii.

137. "Briefs," *The National Jewish Monthly* 84, no. 2 (October 1969): pp 7, 18–19.

138. "American Jewry Divided on Strategy," *Reconstructionist* 34, no. 14 (November 22, 1968): 1.

139. Quoted in Murray Zuckoff, "Jewish Priorities in the Urban Crisis," *Israel Horizons* (April 1969): 19.

140. Ibid., 20.

141. Harry Halpern, "Confrontation and Anti-Semitism," *United Synagogue Review* (January 1969): 6.

142. Murray Friedman, *What Went Wrong: The Creation and Collapse of the Black-Jewish Alliance* (New York: Free Press, 1995), 271.

143. Weisbord and Stein, 197.

144. Ibid.

145. Harry Fleischman, "Negroes and Jews: Brotherhood or Bias?" *Pioneer Woman* (March 1967): 4.

146. Gary T. Marx, *Protest and Prejudice: A Study of Belief in the Black Community* (New York: Harper and Row, 1967).

147. Ibid., 139, 167.

148. See Lucy Dawidowicz, "Can Anti-Semitism Be Measured?" *Commentary* 50, no. 1 (July 1970); Martin Duberman, "Baby, You Better Believe," *New York Times Book Review,* 21 January 1968).

149. Roger Beardwood, "The New Negro Mood," *Fortune* (January 1968): 146.

150. Duberman, 3.

151. Dore Schary, *ADL Bulletin* 24, no. 8 (October 1967): 1, 8.

152. Cohen, 4, 31, 123.

153. Gus J. Solomon, "The Jewish Role in the American Civil Rights Movement" (Address at the World Jewish Congress, London, 1967), 24, 26–27.

154. Bertram Gold, "Jews and the Urban Crisis" (Address at the National Conference of Jewish Communal Service, Detroit, Michigan, June 10, 1968), 13, 19.

155. Ibid., 24.

156. Ismar Schorsch, "Reflections on a Jewish Dilemma," (speech to American Federations of Jews From Central Europe Conference on Anti-Semitism), Negro-Jewish Relations Folder, American Jewish Committee, Blaustein Library, 51, 52.

157. Albert Vorspan, "Blacks and Jews," in Hentoff, 220, 226.

158. See "Leonard Fein: Reflections on Jewish Commitment and Education—1968," in *Great Jewish Speeches throughout History,* ed. Steve Israel and Seth Forman (Northvale, N.J.: Jason Aronson, 1994), 211.

159. On this point see John Higham, *Send These to Me: Jews and Other Immigrants in Urban America* (New York: Atheneum, 1975), 242.

160. Leonard Fein, "The Summer of Our Discontent: Notes on the State of the Urban Crisis," *Congress Bi-Weekly* 34, no. 16 (December 4, 1967): 9.

161. Ibid., 10.

162. Leonard Fein, "Israel's Crisis: Its Effects on the American Jewish Community and Its Implications for Jewish Communal Service," *Journal of Jewish Communal Service* 45, no. 1 (Fall 1968): 14, 15.

163. Ibid.

164. Ibid.

165. "The Black and the Jew: A Falling Out of Allies," *Time,* 31 January 1969, 55–59.

166. Fein, *Where Are We?*, 255.

167. See Mordecai Kaplan, *Judaism as a Civilization: Toward a Reconstruction of American Jewish Life* (Philadelphia: Jewish Publication Society of America, 1981), 319.

168. Allan W. Miller, "Black Anti-Semitism/Jewish Racism," in Hentoff, 111.

169. Ibid., 112.

170. Allan W. Miller, "Post-Passover Thoughts on Jews and Afro-Americans," *Reconstructionist,* 2 May 1969, 13.

171. Miller, in Hentoff, 104.
On the response of Jews to Jewish terrorism see Walter Laqueur, *A History of Zionism* (New York: Holt, Rinehart, and Winston, 1972), 557; Melvin I. Urofsky, *We Are One! American Jewry and Israel* (Garden City, N.Y.: Anchor Press, 1978), p. 149.

172. Dov Peretz Elkins, "Negro-Jewish Relations after the Kerner Report," *Reconstructionist* 34, no. 7 (May 17, 1968): 22.

173. Gold, 4.

174. Barbara Krasner, "A History of Suffering," *Dimensions in American Judaism* 11, no. 4 (Summer 1968): 21.

175. Marc Saperstein, "Nationalism and the Dilemma of the American Jewish Liberal," *Dimensions in American Judaism* 3 (Spring 1969): 29; Arthur Hertzberg, *The Zionist Idea* (New York: Atheneum, 1959), 247–270.

176. Gideon Shimoni, *The Zionist Ideology* (Waltham, Mass.: Brandeis University Press, 1995), 6.

177. Ben Halpern, *The Idea of the Jewish State* (Cambridge, Mass.: Harvard University Press, 1961), 20.

178. Ibid., 33.

179. Urofsky, 7.

180. Laqueur, *A History of Zionism,* 595.

181. Monty Noam Penkower, *The Holocaust and Israel Reborn: From Catastrophe to Sovereignty* (Urbana: University of Illinois Press, 1994).

182. Robert Alter, "Zionism for the 70s," *Commentary* 49, n. 2 (February 1970).

183. Ibid., 51.

184. Robert Alter, "The Unique and the Universal," *Commentary* (May 1970): 14.

185. Abraham J. Karp, "Ideology and Identity in Jewish Group Survival in America," *American Jewish Historical Quarterly* 65, no. 4 (June 1976): 311.

186. Theodore Draper, *The Rediscovery of Black Nationalism* (New York: Basic Books, 1970), 121.

187. Ibid., 86–147; James Blaut, *The National Question* (London: Zeb Books, 1987), 165.

188. Draper, 115.

189. Laurence Mordekai Thomas, *Vessels of Evil: American Slavery and the Holocaust* (Philadelphia: Temple University Press, 1993), 156.

190. See, most importantly, Melville Herskovitz, *The Myth of the Negro Past* (Boston: Beacon Press, 1941); Sterling Stuckey, *Slave Culture: Nationalist Theory and the Foundations of Black America* (New York: Oxford University Press, 1987); John Blassingame, *The Slave Community* (New York: Oxford University Press, 1972), "Enslavement, Acculturation and African Survivals."

191. See Albert Murray, *The Omni-Americans: New Perspectives on Black Experience and American Culture* (New York: Outerbridge and Dienstfrey, 1970), 17–18; Mary Frances Berry and John Blassingame, *Long Memory* (New York: Oxford University Press, 1982).

192. Stanley Elkins, *Slavery: A Problem in American Institutional and Intellectual Life* (Chicago: University of Chicago, 1956).

193. E. Franklin Frazier, *The Negro Family in the United States* (Chicago: University of Chicago Press, 1966), 6–7; Lawrence Levine, *Black Culture and Black Consciousness* (New York: Oxford University Press, 1977), 80; Blassingame, 145.

194. See Herbert Aptheker, *American Negro Slave Revolts* (New York: International Publishers, 1963).

195. L. M. Thomas, 156.

196. Carmichael and Hamilton, 34, 35.

197. Blaut, *The National Question,* 165.

198. Adolph Reed Jr., "The Allure of Malcolm X and the Changing Character of Black Politics," in *Malcolm X: In Our Own Image,* ed. Joe Wood (New York: St. Martin's, 1992), 210.

199. Cornel West quoted in Michael Lerner and Cornel West, *Blacks and Jews: Let the Healing Begin* (New York: Grosset/Putnam, 1995), 163.

200. Martin Kilson, "Black Power: Anatomy of a Paradox," *Harvard Journal of*

Negro Affairs 2, no. 1 (1968): 32; Martin Kilson, "The New Black Intellectuals," *Dissent* 16, no. 4 (July/August 1969): 304–316.

201. Quoted in Abe Duker, "Jews and Blacks: The Growing Crisis," *Jewish Horizon* (March/April 1969): 11.

202. Henry Louis Gates Jr., "Black Demagogues and Pseudo-Scholars," *New York Times,* 20 July 1992. Quoted in Joshua Muravchik, "Facing Up to Black Anti-Semitism," *Commentary* 100, no. 6 (December 1995): 29.

203. Kilson, "The New Black Intellectuals," 307.

204. Christopher Lasch, "The Trouble with Black Power," *New York Review of Books,* 29 February 1968, 7.

205. Kilson, "The New Black Intellectuals," 308.

206. Tom Wolfe, *Radical Chic & Mau-Mauing the Flak Catchers* (New York: Farrar, Straus, and Giroux, 1970), 97–153.

207. See Shelby Steele, "White Guilt," *American Scholar* (Autumn 1990): 502.

208. Ben Halpern, *Jews and Blacks: The Classic American Minorities* (New York: Herder and Herder, 1971), pp. 106–107, 65; Ben Halpern, *The American Jew: A Zionist Analysis* (New York: Theodore Herzl Foundation, 1956), 41; Ben Halpern, "The Emancipated and the Liberated," *Jewish Frontier* 3, no. 2 (March 1964): 10.

209. Ibid., 75.

210. Ibid., 141, 185, 186.

211. See Irving Howe's review of Halpern, "Groups in Conflict," *Commentary* (October 1971): 11.

212. Jacob Cohen, "Jews and Blacks: A Response to Ben Halpern," *Jewish Frontier* 38, no. 8 (September 1971): 19.

213. Ben Halpern, "A Program for American Jews," *Jewish Frontier* (November 1971): 15.

NOTES TO CHAPTER 5

1. Marvin Schick, "The New Style of American Orthodox Jewry," *Jewish Life* 34, no. 3 (1967): 29–36.

2. Michael Meyer, *Response to Modernity: A History of the Reform Movement in Judaism* (New York: Oxford University Press, 1988), 388.

3. Maurice Lamm, "Escalating the Wars of the Lord," *Tradition* (Spring/Summer 1967): 10.

4. Jerry Hochbaum, "The Orthodox Community and the Urban Crisis," *Tradition* 10, no. 3 (Spring 1969): 48, 44–45.

5. Leo Levi, "Torah and Relevance," *Jewish Observer* (September 1967): 15.

6. Yaakov Jacobs, "To Picket or to Pray?" *Jewish Observer* 5, no. 2 (April 1968): 6.

7. Bernard Weinberger, "The Negro and the (Orthodox) Jew," *Jewish Observer* 5, no. 4 (September 1968): 12, 14.

8. Milton Himmelfarb, "Jewish Class Conflict?" *Commentary* (January 1970). Reprinted in *Overcoming Middle-Class Rage,* ed. Murray Friedman (Philadelphia: Westminster, 1971), 212–213.

9. Walter Goodman, "I'd Love to See the J.D.L. Fold Up But—" *New York Times Magazine,* 21 November 1971, 33.

10. Janet L. Dolgin, *Jewish Identity and the JDL* (Princeton: Princeton University Press, 1977), I.

11. Gerald S. Strober, *American Jews: Community in Crisis* (Garden City, N.Y.: Doubleday, 1974), 153.

12. Haskell L. Lazere, "Haganah U.S.A.," *Dimensions* 4, no.3 (Spring 1970): 7–12; Stanley C. Diamond, "The Jewish Defense League: With Friends Like These . . . ," *Congress Bi-Weekly* 37, no. 7 (May 22, 1970): 6–8.

13. Strober, 64–65.

14. Milton Himmelfarb, "In the Light of Israel's Victory," *Commentary* (October 1967): 54–55.

15. Ibid., 55.

16. Milton Himmelfarb, "Is American Jewry in Crisis?" *Commentary* 47, no. 3 (March 1969): 37–38.

17. Ibid., 37.

18. Quoted in Debra Dash Moore, "Trude Weiss-Rosmarin and the *Jewish Spectator,*" in The "Other" *New York Jewish Intellectuals,* ed. Carole S. Kessner (New York: New York University Press, 1994), 114–115.

19. Ibid., 116–117.

20. For discussions of WASP accusations against Jewish critics, see Alvin Rosenfeld, "What to Do about Literary Anti-Semitism," *Midstream* (December 1978); Richard Kostelanetz, "Militant Minorities," *Hudson Review* (Autumn 1965).

21. Trude Weiss-Rosmarin, "The Editor's Pages," *Jewish Spectator* 34, no. 1 (January 1969): 5.

22. Richard Rubenstein, *After Auschwitz: Radical Theology and Contemporary Judaism* (New York: Macmillan, 1966).

23. See Neil Gillman, *Sacred Fragments: Recovering Theology for the Modern Jew* (Philadelphia: Jewish Publication Society, 1990), 203.

24. See Richard Rubenstein, "Why 19 Conservative Rabbis Went to Birmingham," *National Jewish Monthly* (July/August 1963).

25. Richard Rubenstein, "Jews, Negroes and the New Politics," *Reconstructionist* 33 (November 17, 1967): 15.

26. Ibid; Richard Rubenstein, "The Politics of Powerlessness," *Reconstructionist* (May 17, 1968): 12.

27. See *The Neoconservative Imagination: Essays in Honor of Irving Kristol,* ed. Christopher DeMuth and William Kristol (Washington: AEI Press, 1995), 176.

28. See Hannah Arendt, *The Origins of Totalitarianism* (New York: Harcourt, Brace, 1951).

29. Max Geltman, *The Confrontation: Black Power, Anti-Semitism, and the Myth of Integration* (Englewood Cliffs, N.J.: Prentice-Hall, 1970).

30. Peter Steinfels, *The Neoconservatives: The Men Who Are Changing America's Politics* (New York: Simon and Schuster, 1979), 50–53.

31. See Daniel Bell, "American Intellectual Life, 1965–1992," *Wilson Quarterly* (Summer 1992): 85; William F. Buckley, *In Search of Anti-Semitism* (New York: Continuum, 1992).

32. For detailed descriptions of this evolution, see William Novak, "*Commentary* and the Jewish Community: The Record Since 1960," *Response* 7, no. 3 (Fall 1973): 49–66; Joseph Epstein, "The New Conservatives: Intellectuals in Retreat," in *The New Conservatives*, ed. Lewis A. Coser and Irving Howe (New York: Quadrangle, 1973), 9–28.

33. Norman Podhoretz, "Laws, Kings, and Cures," *Commentary* 50, no. 4 (October 1970): 30.

34. Norman Podhoretz, "Is It Good for the Jews," *Commentary* (February 1972): 8; Norman Podhoretz, "A Certain Anxiety," *Commentary* 52, no. 2 (August 1971): 8.

35. See Alan Brinkley, *Voices of Protest: Huey Long, Father Coughlin, and the Great Depression* (New York: Knopf, 1982), 269–283.

36. See Leonard Dinnerstein, "Origins of Black Anti-Semitism," *American Jewish Archives* 38, no. 2 (November 1986): 114; Earl Raab, "The Black Revolution and the Jewish Question," *Commentary* 47, no. 1 (January 1969): 29.

37. Raab, 26.

38. Ibid., 30.

39. Jacob Neusner, "Why Are Jewish Neo-Cons Atheists?" in *Conservative, American, and Jewish: I Wouldn't Have It Any Other Way* (Lafayette: Huntington House, 1993), 194.

40. Ibid.

41. Robert Alter, "Zionism for the 70s," *Commentary* 49, no. 2 (February 1970): 56; Steven Plaut, "Jewish Liberal PC and Ethical Posturing," *Midstream* 42, no. 6 (August/September 1996): 20–21; Podhoretz, "A Certain Anxiety," 10.

42. Earl Raab, "The Deadly Innocenses of American Jews," *Commentary* 50, no. 6 (December 1970): 32.

43. Ibid., 35, 39.

44. Nathan Glazer, "The Ghetto Crisis," *Encounter* 29, no. 5 (November 11, 1967): 16.

45. Nathan Glazer, "Blacks and Ethnic Groups: The Difference and the Political Difference It Makes," in *Key Issues in the Afro-American Experience*, vol. 2, ed. Nathan I. Huggins et al. (New York: Harcourt, Brace, Jovanovich, 1971). Reprinted in Nathan Glazer, *Ethnic Dilemmas: 1964–1982* (Cambridge, Mass.: Harvard University Press, 1983), 90.

46. Nathan Glazer, "America's Race Paradox," *Encounter* (October 1968). Re-

printed in *Nation of Nations: The Ethnic Experience and the Racial Crisis,* ed. Peter I. Rose (New York: Random House, 1972), 171.

47. Nathan Glazer, "On Being Deradicalized," *Commentary* 50, no. 4 (October 1970): 76.

48. Nathan Glazer, "Blacks, Jews and the Intellectuals," *Commentary* 47, no. 4 (April 1969): 35, 36.

49. Nathan Glazer and Daniel Patrick Moynihan, *Beyond the Melting Pot: The Negroes, Puerto Ricans, Jews, Italians, and Irish of New York City,* 2d ed. (Cambridge, Mass.: M.I.T. Press, 1963), 180.

50. Nathan Glazer, "Revolutionism and the Jews," *Commentary* 51, no. 2 (February 1971): 58.

51. Glazer, "Blacks, Jews, and the Intellectuals," 38.

52. Glazer and Moynihan, 13.

53. For example, Vine DeLoria, "The Red and the Black," in Rose, 309–321.

54. Andrew Greeley, "The Rediscovery of Diversity," *Antioch Review* (Fall 1971): 360; Michael Novak, *The Rise of the Unmeltable Ethnics: Politics and Culture in the Seventies* (New York: Macmillan, 1972).

55. Friedman, *Overcoming Middle-Class Rage.*

56. See Stephen Steinberg, *The Ethnic Myth: Race, Ethnicity, and Class in America* (New York: Atheneum, 1981).

57. Robert C. Christopher, *Crashing the Gates: The De-Wasping of America's Power Elite* (New York: Simon and Schuster, 1989), 54.

58. Barry Kosmin et al., *Highlights of the Council of Jewish Federations 1990 National Jewish Population Survey* (New York: Council of Jewish Federations, 1991).

59. Christopher, 51, 54.

60. Quoted by Howard Sachar, *A History of the Jews in America* (New York: Vintage, 1992), 863.

61. Norman Podhoretz, *Making It* (New York: Random House, 1967), 3.

62. Quoted in Novak, "*Commentary* and the Jewish Community," 51.

63. Norman Podhoretz, "The Idea of a Common Culture," *Commentary* (June 1972): 4–5.

64. See Harold R. Isaacs, "The New Pluralists," *Commentary* (March 1972); Robert Alter, "A Fever of Ethnicity," *Commentary* (June 1972): 70; "Letters from Readers," *Commentary* 54, no. 4 (October 1972): 10–24; "Letters from Readers," *Commentary* (June 1972): 8–15.

65. Harold Isaacs, *The New World of Negro Americans* (New York: Harper-Collins, 1964).

66. Congress enacted the Ethnic Heritage Studies Program Act in 1972.

67. Harold R. Isaacs, "Ethnics and Pluralists," *Commentary* (June 1972): 13–14.

68. Alter, "A Fever of Ethnicity," 69.

69. Ibid., 70.

70. Ibid., 71.

71. Edward Shapiro, *A Time for Healing: American Jewry since World War II* (Baltimore: Johns Hopkins University Press, 1992), 228.

NOTES TO THE CONCLUSION

1. Marshall Breger, editorial, *Moment* (August 1997): 28; Ira Stoll, "Social Justice Swaying Liberals on Question of School Vouchers," *Forward*, 5 May 1997, 1; "Blacks, Jews Ink Alliance on Vouchers," *Forward*, 1 August 1997, 1.

2. Neal Gabler, *An Empire of Their Own: How the Jewish Invented Hollywood* (New York: Crown, 1988), 168.

3. Stephen Whitfield, "Movies in America as Paradigms of Accommodation," *The Americanization of the Jews*, ed. Robert M. Seltzer and Norman J. Cohen (New York: New York University Press, 1995), 82.

4. Alina Sivorinovsky, "Images of Modern Jews on Television," *Midstream* 41, no. 9 (December 1995): 39; Whitfield, 83.

5. Karen Grigsby Bates, "They've Gotta Have Us," *New York Times Magazine*, 14 July 1991, 15–16.

6. Sivorinovsky, 40.

7. Michael Paul Rogin, *Black Face, White Noise: Jewish Immigrants in the Hollywood Melting Pot* (Berkeley: University of California Press, 1996), 113.

8. LeRoi Jones [Amiri Baraka], *Blues People: Negro Music in White America* (New York: Morrow, 1963), 99.

9. See Terry Teachout, "The Color of Jazz," *Commentary* 100, no. 3 (September 1995): 50–53.

10. Jesse Green, "The Song Is Ended," *New York Times Magazine*, 2 June 1996, 51.

11. Rogin, 113.

12. Howard Sachar, *A History of the Jews in America* (New York: Vintage Books, 1992), 367–371.

13. Jeffrey Melnick, "Relatives and Ancestors: The Uncanny Relationship of African Americans and Jews" (Ph.D. diss., Harvard University, 1994), 471, 353.

14. Ronald Sanders, "Jewish Composers and American Popular Song," *Next Year in Jerusalem: Portraits of the Jew in the Twentieth Century*, ed. Douglass Villiers (New York: Viking, 1976), 199.

15. Barry Rubin, *Assimilation and Its Discontents* (New York: Times Books, 1995), 80.

16. Sanders, 197–219.

17. Green, 51.

Index

Aaron, Daniel, 125–26
Abram, Morris, 147
Academic Melting Pot, The, 5
Adler, Mortimer, 202
Adler, Rachel, 169
Affirmative action, 6, 18, 188; Nathan
 Glazer's view of, 87–88; link to Black
 anti-Semitism, 148–58
AFL-CIO, 31
Afro-American Teacher's Association, 144
Afro-American Teacher's Forum, 146
After Auschwitz, 201
Agee, James, 100
Agenda for American Jews, 30
Agus, Arlene, 169
Ali, Muhammad, 140
Ali, Noble Drew, 70
Alpert, Carl, 42, 50
Alter, Robert, 184, 193, 213–15
Amalgamated Clothing Workers, 63
American Civil Liberties Union, 31
American Dilemma, An, 42
American Jewish Committee, 29, 31, 33,
 38, 45–47, 61, 172, 173, 175, 181, 212,
 216
American Jewish Congress, 29, 38, 41, 44,
 45–47, 59, 61, 65, 72, 74, 172, 216
Americans for Democratic Action, 59
"Angel Levine," 129
Another Country, 122
Ansky, S., 221
Anti-Defamation League (of B'nai B'rith),
 29, 31, 42, 44, 45–47, 49, 69, 144, 172,
 174, 175
Anti-Semitism: Black, 1–2, 70–77, 139–48;
 Black, and link to Jewish whiteness, 148–
 58; decline of, 25–28, 156–58; in the
 South, 34–54; Jewish response to, 74–77,
 163–80, 171–80, 190, 195
Aptheker, Herbert, 152

Arendt, Hannah, 103–4, 166, 202
Armstrong, Louis, 105
Aronowitz, Stanley, 165
Aronson, Arnold, 59
Assimilation: Jewish, 18–20, 32, 156–58,
 212; white, 19, 212–13
Assimilation in American Life, 7
Avrunin, William, 89

Baldwin, James, 62, 76, 100, 107–8, 112,
 114–15, 154–55, 163; and Irving Howe,
 122–24; and Norman Podhoretz, 116–17
Baraka, Amiri, 105, 113, 220. *See also*
 Jones, LeRoi
Bar-Kochba, 82
Barrett, William, 100
Beat movement, 104–10
Beck, Evelyn Torton, 170
Behran, Thea, 251n. 35
Belafonte, Harry, 219
Bell, Daniel, 101, 202
Bellow, Saul, 102, 129
Ben-Gurion, David, 92, 200
Benjamin, I. J., 39
Berger, Peter, 202
Berlin, Irving, 14, 220–21
Berman, Ronald, 202
Berryman, John, 100
Berube, Martin, 99
Beyond the Melting Pot, 4, 79, 85, 87, 211
Big Man, 121
Bilbo, Theodore, 25
Bittersweet Encounter, 2
Black Arts movement, 112–13, 125, 127
Black Boy, 114
"Black Boys and Native Sons," 122–27
Black culture, 16–17; the "bad nigger,"
 105–7; hipsterism, 105–10
Black Face, White Noise, 14
Black hipster, the, 105–10

About the Author

Seth Forman received his doctorate in American history at the State University of New York at Stony Brook in 1996. He is the coeditor of the 1994 volume *Great Jewish Speeches throughout History* (Northvale, N.J.: Jason Aronson) and the author of articles that have appeared in the *American Scholar, Midstream,* and *American Jewish History.* Dr. Forman works as a Senior Planner for the Long Island Regional Planning Board and lives in Nesconsett, New York, with his wife and daughter.